W9-BVJ-598

FOX'S BOOK OF MARTYRS

A HISTORY OF THE LIVES, SUFFER-
INGS AND TRIUMPHANT DEATHS
OF THE EARLY CHRISTIAN AND
THE PROTESTANT MARTYRS

Edited by

WILLIAM BYRON FORBUSH, D.D.

1080 96

THE JOHN C. WINSTON COMPANY

PHILADELPHIA   CHICAGO

Copyright, 1926
The John C. Winston Company

PRINTED IN THE U. S. A.

272
F79

FOX'S BOOK OF MARTYRS

"When one recollects that until the appearance of the Pilgrim's Progress the common people had almost no other reading matter except the Bible and Fox's Book of Martyrs, we can understand the deep impression that this book produced; and how it served to mold the national character. Those who could read for themselves learned the full details of all the atrocities performed on the Protestant reformers; the illiterate could see the rude illustrations of the various instruments of torture, the rack, the gridiron, the boiling oil, and then the holy ones breathing out their souls amid the flames. Take a people just awakening to a new intellectual and religious life; let several generations of them, from childhood to old age, pore over such a book, and its stories become traditions as individual and almost as potent as songs and customs on a nation's life." DOUGLAS CAMPBELL, *The Puritan in Holland, England, and America.*

"If we divest the book of its accidental character of feud between churches, it yet stands, in the first years of Elizabeth's reign, a monument that marks the growing strength of a desire for spiritual freedom, defiance of those forms that seek to stifle conscience and fetter thought." HENRY MORLEY, *English Writers.*

"After the Bible itself, no book so profoundly influenced early Protestant sentiment as the Book of Martyrs. Even in our own time it is still a living force. It is more than a record of persecution. It is an arsenal of controversy, a storehouse of romance, as well as a source of edification." JAMES MILLER DODDS, *English Prose.*

6672

CONTENTS

CONTENTS

CONTENTS

CONTENTS

SKETCH OF THE AUTHOR

John Fox (or Foxe) was born at Boston, in Lincolnshire, in 1517, where his parents are stated to have lived in respectable circumstances. He was deprived of his father at an early age; and notwithstanding his mother soon married again, he still remained under the parental roof. From an early display of talents and inclination to learning, his friends were induced to send him to Oxford, in order to cultivate and bring them to maturity.

During his residence at this place, he was distinguished for the excellence and acuteness of his intellect, which was improved by the emulation of his fellow collegians, united to an indefatigable zeal and industry on his part. These qualities soon gained him the admiration of all; and as a reward for his exertions and amiable conduct, he was chosen fellow of Magdalen College; which was accounted a great honor in the university, and seldom bestowed unless in cases of great distinction. It appears that the first display of his genius was in poetry; and that he composed some Latin comedies, which are still extant. But he soon directed his thoughts to a more serious subject, the study of the sacred Scriptures: to divinity, indeed, he applied himself with more fervency than circumspection, and discovered his partiality to the Reformation, which had then commenced, before he was known to its supporters, or to those who protected them; a circumstance which proved to him the source of his first troubles.

He is said to have often affirmed that the first matter which occasioned his search into the popish doctrine was that he saw divers things, most repugnant in their nature to one another, forced upon men at the same time; upon this foundation his resolution and intended obedience to that Church were somewhat shaken, and by degrees a dislike to the rest took place.

His first care was to look into both the ancient and modern history of the Church; to ascertain its beginning and progress; to consider the causes of all those controversies which in the meantime had sprung up, and diligently to weigh their effects, solidity, infirmities, etc.

Before he had attained his thirtieth year, he had studied the Greek and Latin fathers, and other learned authors, the transactions of the Councils, and decrees of the consistories, and had acquired a very competent skill in the Hebrew language. In these occupations he frequently spent a considerable part, or even the whole of the night; and in order to unbend his mind after such incessant study, he would resort to a grove near the college, a place much frequented by the students in the evening, on account of its sequestered gloominess In these solitary walks he was often heard to ejaculate heavy sobs and sighs, and with tears to pour forth his prayers to God. These nightly retirements, in the sequel, gave rise to the first suspicion of his alienation from the Church of Rome. Being pressed for an explanation of this alteration in his conduct, he scorned to call in fiction to his excuse; he stated his opinions; and was, by the sentence of the college *convicted, condemned as a heretic, and expelled.*

His friends, upon the report of this circumstance, were highly offended, when he was thus forsaken by his own friends, a refuge offered itself in the house of Sir Thomas Lucy, of Warwickshire, by whom he was sent for to instruct his children. The house is within easy walk of Stratford-on-Avon, and it was this estate which, a few years later, was the scene of Shakespeare's traditional boyish poaching expedition. Fox died when Shakespeare was three years old.

In the Lucy house Fox afterward married. But the fear of the popish inquisitors hastened his departure thence; as they were not contented to pursue public offences, but began also to dive into the secrets of private families. He now began to consider what was best to be done to free himself from further inconvenience, and resolved either to go to his wife's father or to his father-in-law.

His wife's father was a citizen of Coventry, whose heart was not alienated from him, and he was more likely to be well entreated, for his daughter's sake. He resolved first to go to him; and, in the meanwhile, by letters, to try whether his father-in-law would receive him or not. This he accordingly did, and he received for answer, "that it seemed to him a hard condition to take one into his house whom he knew to be guilty and condemned for a capital offence; neither was he ignorant what hazard he should undergo in so doing; he would, however, show himself a kinsman, and neglect his own danger. If he would alter his mind, he might come, on condition to stay as long as he himself desired; but if he could not be persuaded to that, he must content himself with a shorter stay, and not bring him and his mother into danger."

No condition was to be refused; besides, he was secretly advised by his mother to come, and not to fear his father-in-law's severity; "for that, perchance, it was needful to write as he did, but when occasion should be offered, he would make recompense for his words with his actions." In fact he was better received by both of them than he had hoped for.

By these means he kept himself concealed for some time, and afterwards made a journey to London, in the latter part of the reign of

Henry VIII. Here, being unknown, he was in much distress, and was even reduced to the danger of being starved to death, had not Providence interfered in his favor in the following manner:

One day as Mr. Fox was sitting in St. Paul's Church, exhausted with long fasting, a stranger took a seat by his side, and courteously saluted him, thrust a sum of money into his hand, and bade him cheer up his spirits; at the same time informing him, that in a few days new prospects would present themselves for his future subsistence. Who this stranger was, he could never learn; but at the end of three days he received an invitation from the Duchess of Richmond to undertake the tuition of the children of the Earl of Surry who, together with his father, the Duke of Norfolk, was imprisoned in the Tower, by the jealousy and ingratitude of the king. The children thus confided to his care were, Thomas, who succeeded to the dukedom; Henry, afterwards Earl of Northampton; and Jane who became Countess of Westmoreland. In the performance of his duties, he fully satisfied the expectations of the duchess, their aunt.

These halcyon days continued during the latter part of the reign of Henry VIII and the five years of the reign of Edward VI until Mary came to the crown, who, soon after her accession, gave all power into the hands of the papists.

At this time Mr. Fox, who was still under the protection of his noble pupil, the duke, began to excite the envy and hatred of many, particularly Dr. Gardiner, then Bishop of Winchester, who in the sequel became his most violent enemy.

Mr. Fox, aware of this, and seeing the dreadful persecutions then commencing, began to think of quitting the kingdom. As soon as the duke knew his intention, he endeavored to persuade him to remain; and his arguments were so powerful, and given with so much sincerity, that he gave up the thought of abandoning his asylum for the present.

At that time the Bishop of Winchester was very intimate with the duke (by the patronage of whose family he had risen to the dignity he then enjoyed,) and frequently waited on him to present his service when he several times requested that he might see his old tutor. At first the duke denied his request, at one time alleging his absence, at another, indisposition. At length it happened that Mr. Fox, not knowing the bishop was in the house, entered the room where the duke and he were in discourse; and seeing the bishop, withdrew. Gardiner asked who that was; the duke answered that he was "his physician, who was somewhat uncourtly, as being new come from the university." "I like his countenance and aspect very well," replied the bishop, "and when occasion offers, I will send for him." The duke understood that speech as the messenger of some approaching danger; and now himself thought it high time for Mr. Fox to

quit the city, and even the country. He accordingly caused everything necessary for his flight to be provided in silence, by sending
one of his servants to Ipswich to hire a bark, and prepare all the requisites for his departure. He also fixed on the house of one of his
servants, who was a farmer, where he might lodge until the wind became favorable; and everything being in readiness, Mr. Fox took
leave of his noble patron, and with his wife, who was pregnant at the
time, secretly departed for the ship.

The vessel was scarcely under sail, when a most violent storm came
on, which lasted all day and night, and the next day drove them
back to the port from which they had departed. During the time
that the vessel had been at sea, an officer, despatched by the bishop
of Winchester, had broken open the house of the farmer with a
warrant to apprehend Mr. Fox wherever he might be found, and
bring him back to the city. On hearing this news he hired a horse,
under the pretence of leaving the town immediately; but secretly returned the same night, and agreed with the captain of the vessel
to sail for any place as soon as the wind should shift, only desiring
him to proceed, and not to doubt that God would prosper his undertaking. The mariner suffered himself to be persuaded, and within
two days landed his passengers in safety at Nieuport.

After spending a few days in that place, Mr. Fox set out for
Basle, where he found a number of English refugees, who had
quitted their country to avoid the cruelty of the persecutors, with
these he associated, and began to write his "History of the Acts and
Monuments of the Church," which was first published in Latin at
Basle in 1554, and in English in 1563.

In the meantime the reformed religion began again to flourish in
England, and the popish faction much to decline, by the death of
Queen Mary; which induced the greater number of the Protestant
exiles to return to their native country.

Among others, on the accession of Elizabeth to the throne, Mr.
Fox returned to England; where, on his arrival, he found a faithful and active friend in his late pupil, the Duke of Norfolk, until
death deprived him of his benefactor: after which event, Mr. Fox
inherited a pension bequeathed to him by the duke, and ratified by
his son, the Earl of Suffolk.

Nor did the good man's successes stop here. On being recommended to the queen by her secretary of state, the great Cecil, her
majesty granted him the prebendary of Shipton, in the cathedral
of Salisbury, which was in a manner forced upon him; for it was
with difficulty that he could be persuaded to accept it.

On his resettlement in England, he employed himself in revising
and enlarging his admirable Martyrology. With prodigious pains
and constant study he completed that celebrated work in eleven
years. For the sake of greater correctness, he wrote every line of

this vast book with his own hand, and transcribed all the records and papers himself. But, in consequence of such excessive toil, leaving no part of his time free from study, nor affording himself either the repose or recreation which nature required, his health was so reduced, and his person became so emaciated and altered, that such of his friends and relations as only conversed with him occasionally, could scarcely recognize his person. Yet, though he grew daily more exhausted, he proceeded in his studies as briskly as ever, nor would he be persuaded to diminish his accustomed labors. The papists, foreseeing how detrimental his history of their errors and cruelties would prove to their cause, had recourse to every artifice to lessen the reputation of his work; but their malice was of signal service, both to Mr. Fox himself, and to the Church of God at large, as it eventually made his book more intrinsically valuable, by inducing him to weigh, with the most scrupulous attention, the certainty of the facts which he recorded, and the validity of the authorities from which he drew his information.

But while he was thus indefatigably employed in promoting the cause of truth, he did not neglect the other duties of his station; he was charitable, humane, and attentive to the wants, both spiritual and temporal, of his neighbors. With the view of being more extensively useful, although he had no desire to cultivate the acquaintance of the rich and great on his own account, he did not decline the friendship of those in a higher rank who proffered it, and never failed to employ his influence with them in behalf of the poor and needy. In consequence of his well-known probity and charity, he was frequently presented with sums of money by persons possessed of wealth, which he accepted and distributed among those who were distressed. He would also occasionally attend the table of his friends, not so much for the sake of pleasure, as from civility, and to convince them that his absence was not occasioned by a fear of being exposed to the temptations of the appetite. In short his character as a man and as a Christian was without reproach.

Although the recent recollection of the persecutions under Bloody Mary gave bitterness to his pen, it is singular to note that he was personally the most conciliatory of men, and that while he heartily disowned the Roman Church in which he was born, he was one of the first to attempt the concord of the Protestant brethren. In fact, he was a veritable apostle of toleration.

When the plague or pestilence broke out in England, in 1563, and many forsook their duties, Fox remained at his post, assisting the friendless and acting as the almsgiver of the rich. It was said of him that he could never refuse help to any one who asked it in the name of Christ. Tolerant and large-hearted he exerted his influence with Queen Elizabeth to confirm her intention to no longer keep up the cruel practice of putting to death those of opposing religious convictions. The queen held him in respect and referred to him as "Our Father Foxe."

Mr. Fox had joy in the fruits of his work while he was yet alive. It passed through four large editions before his decease, and it was ordered by the bishops to be placed in every cathedral church in England, where it was often found chained, as the Bible was in those days, to a lectern for the access of the people.

At length, having long served both the Church and the world by his ministry, by his pen, and by the unsullied luster of a benevolent, useful, and holy life, he meekly resigned his soul to Christ, on the eighteenth of April, 1587, being then in the seventieth year of his age. He was interred in the chancel of St. Giles', Cripplegate; of which parish he had been, in the beginning of Elizabeth's reign, for some time vicar.

BOOK OF MARTYRS

CHAPTER I

History of Christian Martyrs to the First General Persecutions Under Nero

CHRIST our Savior, in the Gospel of St. Matthew, hearing the confession of Simon Peter, who, first of all other, openly acknowledged Him to be the Son of God, and perceiving the secret hand of His Father therein, called him (alluding to his name) a rock, upon which rock He would build His Church so strong that the gates of hell should not prevail against it. In which words three things are to be noted: First, that Christ will have a Church in this world. Secondly, that the same Church should mightily be impugned, not only by the world, but also by the uttermost strength and powers of all hell. And, thirdly, that the same Church, notwithstanding the uttermost of the devil and all his malice, should continue.

Which prophecy of Christ we see wonderfully to be verified, insomuch that the whole course of the Church to this day may seem nothing else but a verifying of the said prophecy. First, that Christ hath set up a Church, needeth no declaration. Secondly, what force of princes, kings, monarchs, governors, and rulers of this world, with their subjects, publicly and privately, with all their strength and cunning, have bent themselves against this Church! And, thirdly, how the said Church, all this notwithstanding, hath yet endured and holden its own! What storms and tempests it hath overpast, wondrous it is to behold: for the more evident declaration whereof, I have addressed this present history, to the end, first, that the wonderful works of God in His Church might appear to His glory; also that, the continuance and proceedings of the Church, from time to time, being set forth, more knowledge and experience may redound thereby, to the profit of the reader and edification of Christian faith.

As it is not our business to enlarge upon our Savior's history, either before or after His crucifixion, we shall only find it necessary to remind our readers of the discomfiture of the Jews by His subsequent resurrection. Although one apostle had betrayed Him; although another had denied Him, under the solemn sanction of an

1

oath; and although the rest had forsaken Him, unless we may except "the disciple who was known unto the high-priest"; the history of His resurrection gave a new direction to all their hearts, and, after the mission of the Holy Spirit, imparted new confidence to their minds. The powers with which they were endued emboldened them to proclaim His name, to the confusion of the Jewish rulers, and the astonishment of Gentile proselytes.

I. St. Stephen

St. Stephen suffered the next in order. His death was occasioned by the faithful manner in which he preached the Gospel to the betrayers and murderers of Christ. To such a degree of madness were they excited, that they cast him out of the city and stoned him to death. The time when he suffered is generally supposed to have been at the passover which succeeded to that of our Lord's crucifixion, and to the era of his ascension, in the following spring.

Upon this a great persecution was raised against all who professed their belief in Christ as the Messiah, or as a prophet. We are immediately told by St. Luke, that "there was a great persecution against the church which was at Jerusalem;" and that "they were all scattered abroad throughout the regions of Judæa and Samaria, except the apostles."

About two thousand Christians, with Nicanor, one of the seven deacons, suffered martyrdom during the "persecution that arose about Stephen."

II. James the Great

The next martyr we meet with, according to St. Luke, in the History of the Apostles' Acts, was James the son of Zebedee, the elder brother of John, and a relative of our Lord; for his mother Salome was cousin-german to the Virgin Mary. It was not until ten years after the death of Stephen that the second martyrdom took place; for no sooner had Herod Agrippa been appointed governor of Judea, than, with a view to ingratiate himself with them, he raised a sharp persecution against the Christians, and determined to make an effectual blow, by striking at their leaders. The account given us by an eminent primitive writer, Clemens Alexandrinus, ought not to be overlooked; that, as James was led to the place of martyrdom, his accuser was brought to repent of his conduct by the apostle's extraordinary courage and undauntedness, and fell down at his feet to request his pardon, professing himself a Christian, and resolving that James should not receive the crown of martyrdom alone. Hence they were both beheaded at the same time. Thus did the first apostolic martyr cheerfully and resolutely receive that cup, which he had told our Savior he was ready to drink. Timon and Parmenas suffered martyrdom about the same time; the one at Philippi, and the other in Macedonia. These events took place A. D. 44.

III. Philip

Was born at Bethsaida, in Galilee and was first called by the name of "disciple." He labored diligently in Upper Asia, and suffered martyrdom at Heliopolis, in Phrygia. He was scourged, thrown into prison, and afterwards crucified, A. D. 54.

IV. Matthew

Whose occupation was that of a toll-gatherer, was born at Nazareth. He wrote his gospel in Hebrew, which was afterwards translated into Greek by James the Less. The scene of his labors was Parthia, and Ethiopia, in which latter country he suffered martyrdom, being slain with a halberd in the city of Nadabah, A. D. 60.

V. James the Less

Is supposed by some to have been the brother of our Lord, by a former wife of Joseph. This is very doubtful, and accords too much with the Catholic superstition, that Mary never had any other children except our Savior. He was elected to the oversight of the churches of Jerusalem; and was the author of the Epistle ascribed to James in the sacred canon. At the age of ninety-four he was beat and stoned by the Jews; and finally had his brains dashed out with a fuller's club.

VI. Matthias

Of whom less is known than of most of the other disciples, was elected to fill the vacant place of Judas. He was stoned at Jerusalem and then beheaded.

VII. Andrew

Was the brother of Peter. He preached the gospel to many Asiatic nations; but on his arrival at Edessa he was taken and crucified on a cross, the two ends of which were fixed transversely in the ground. Hence the derivation of the term, St. Andrew's Cross.

VIII. St. Mark

Was born of Jewish parents of the tribe of Levi. He is supposed to have been converted to Christianity by Peter, whom he served as an amanuensis, and under whose inspection he wrote his Gospel in the Greek language. Mark was dragged to pieces by the people of Alexandria, at the great solemnity of Serapis their idol, ending his life under their merciless hands.

IX. Peter Furant

Among many other saints, the blessed apostle Peter was condemned to death, and crucified, as some do write, at Rome; albeit some others, and not without cause, do doubt thereof. Hegesippus saith that Nero sought matter against Peter to put him to death; which, when the people perceived, they entreated Peter with much ado that he would fly the city. Peter, through their importunity at length persuaded, prepared himself to avoid. But, coming to the gate, he saw the Lord Christ come to meet him, to whom he, worshipping, said, "Lord, whither dost Thou go?" To whom He answered and said, "I am come again to be crucified." By this, Peter, perceiving his suffering to be understood, returned into the city. Jerome saith that he was crucified, his head being down and his feet upward, himself so requiring, because he was (he said) unworthy to be crucified after the same form and manner as the Lord was.

X. Paul

Paul, the apostle, who before was called Saul, after his great travail and unspeakable labors in promoting the Gospel of Christ, suffered also in this first persecution under Nero. Abdias, declareth that under his execution Nero sent two of his esquires, Ferega and Parthemius, to bring him word of his death. They, coming to Paul instructing the people, desired him to pray for them, that they might believe; who told them that shortly after they should believe and be baptised at His sepulcher. This done, the soldiers came and led him out of the city to the place of execution, where he, after his prayers made, gave his neck to the sword.

XI. Jude

The brother of James, was commonly called Thaddeus. He was crucified at Edessa, A. D. 72.

XII. Bartholomew

Preached in several countries, and having translated the Gospel of Matthew into the language of India, he propagated it in that country. He was at length cruelly beaten and then crucified by the impatient idolaters.

XIII. Thomas

Called Didymus, preached the Gospel in Parthia and India, where exciting the rage of the pagan priests, he was martyred by being thrust through with a spear.

XIV. Luke

The evangelist, was the author of the Gospel which goes under his name. He travelled with Paul through various countries, and is supposed to have been hanged on an olive tree, by the idolatrous priests of Greece.

XV. Simon

Surnamed Zelotes, preached the Gospel in Mauritania, Africa, and even in Britain, in which latter country he was crucified, A. D. 74.

XVI. John

The "beloved disciple," was brother to James the Great. The churches of Smyrna, Pergamos, Sardis, Philadelphia, Laodicea, and Thyatira, were founded by him. From Ephesus he was ordered to be sent to Rome, where it is affirmed he was cast into a cauldron of boiling oil. He escaped by miracle, without injury. Domitian afterwards banished him to the Isle of Patmos, where he wrote the Book of Revelation. Nerva, the successor of Domitian, recalled him. He was the only apostle who escaped a violent death.

XVII. Barnabas

Was of Cyprus, but of Jewish descent, his death is supposed to have taken place about A. D. 73.

And yet, notwithstanding all these continual persecutions and horrible punishments, the Church daily increased, deeply rooted in the doctrine of the apostles and of men apostolical, and watered plenteously with the blood of saints.

CHAPTER II

The Ten Primitive Persecutions

The First Persecution, Under Nero, A. D. 67

THE first persecution of the Church took place in the year 67, under Nero, the sixth emperor of Rome. This monarch reigned for the space of five years, with tolerable credit to himself, but then gave way to the greatest extravagancy of temper, and to the most atrocious barbarities. Among other diabolical whims, he ordered that the city of Rome should be set on fire, which order was executed by his officers, guards, and servants. While the imperial city was in flames, he went up to the tower of Macænas, played upon his harp, sung the song of the burning of Troy, and openly declared that 'he wished the ruin of all things before his death.' Besides the noble pile, called the Circus, many other palaces and houses were consumed; several thousands perished in the flames, were smothered in the smoke, or buried beneath the ruins.

This dreadful conflagration continued nine days; when Nero, finding that his conduct was greatly blamed, and a severe odium cast upon him, determined to lay the whole upon the Christians, at once to excuse himself, and have an opportunity of glutting his sight with new cruelties. This was the occasion of the first persecution; and the barbarities exercised on the Christians were such as even excited the commiseration of the Romans themselves. Nero even refined upon cruelty, and contrived all manner of punishments for the Christians that the most infernal imagination could design. In particular, he had some sewed up in skins of wild beasts, and then worried by dogs until they expired; and others dressed in shirts made stiff with wax, fixed to axletrees, and set on fire in his gardens, in order to illuminate them. This persecution was general throughout the whole Roman Empire; but it rather increased than diminished the spirit of Christianity. In the course of it, St. Paul and St. Peter were martyred.

To their names may be added, Erastus, chamberlain of Corinth; Aristarchus, the Macedonian, and Trophimus, an Ephesian, converted by St. Paul, and fellow-laborer with him, Joseph, commonly called Barsabas, and Ananias, bishop of Damascus; each of the Seventy.

The Second Persecution, Under Domitian, A. D. 81

The emperor Domitian, who was naturally inclined to cruelty, first slew his brother, and then raised the second persecution against the Christians. In his rage he put to death some of the Roman senators, some through malice; and others to confiscate their estates. He then commanded all the lineage of David to be put to death.

Among the numerous martyrs that suffered during this persecution was Simeon, bishop of Jerusalem, who was crucified; and St. John, who was boiled in oil, and afterward banished to Patmos. Flavia, the daughter of a Roman senator, was likewise banished to Pontus; and a law was made, "That no Christian, once brought before the tribunal, should be exempted from punishment without renouncing his religion."

A variety of fabricated tales were, during this reign, composed in order to injure the Christians. Such was the infatuation of the pagans, that, if famine, pestilence, or earthquakes afflicted any of the Roman provinces, it was laid upon the Christians. These persecutions among the Christians increased the number of informers and many, for the sake of gain, swore away the lives of the innocent.

Another hardship was, that, when any Christians were brought before the magistrates, a test oath was proposed, when, if they refused to take it, death was pronounced against them; and if they confessed themselves Christians, the sentence was the same.

The following were the most remarkable among the numerous martyrs who suffered during this persecution.

Dionysius, the Areopagite, was an Athenian by birth, and educated in all the useful and ornamental literature of Greece. He then travelled to Egypt to study astronomy, and made very particular observations on the great and supernatural eclipse, which happened at the time of our Savior's crucifixion.

The sanctity of his conversation and the purity of his manners recommended him so strongly to the Christians in general, that he was appointed bishop of Athens.

Nicodemus, a benevolent Christian of some distinction, suffered at Rome during the rage of Domitian's persecution.

Protasius and Gervasius were martyred at Milan.

Timothy was the celebrated disciple of St. Paul, and bishop of Ephesus, where he zealously governed the Church until A. D. 97. At this period, as the pagans were about to celebrate a feast called Catagogion, Timothy, meeting the procession, severely reproved them for their ridiculous idolatry, which so exasperated the people that they fell upon him with their clubs, and beat him in so dreadful a manner that he expired of the bruises two days after.

The Third Persecution, Under Trajan, A. D. 108

In the third persecution Pliny the Second, a man learned and famous, seeing the lamentable slaughter of Christians, and moved therewith to pity, wrote to Trajan, certifying him that there were many thousands of them daily put to death, of which none did any thing contrary to the Roman laws worthy persecution. "The whole account they gave of their crime or error (whichever it is to be called) amounted only to this—viz. that they were accustomed on a stated day to meet before daylight, and to repeat together a set form of prayer to Christ as a God, and to bind themselves by an obligation—not indeed to commit wickedness; but, on the contrary—never to commit theft, robbery, or adultery, never to falsify their word, never to defraud any man: after which it was their custom to separate, and reassemble to partake in common of a harmless meal."

In this persecution suffered the blessed martyr, Ignatius, who is held in famous reverence among very many. This Ignatius was appointed to the bishopric of Antioch next after Peter in succession. Some do say, that he, being sent from Syria to Rome, because he professed Christ, was given to the wild beasts to be devoured. It is also said of him, that when he passed through Asia, being under the most strict custody of his keepers, he strengthened and confirmed the churches through all the cities as he went, both with his exhortations and preaching of the Word of God. Accordingly, having come to Smyrna, he wrote to the Church at Rome, exhorting them not to use means for his deliverance from martyrdom, lest they should deprive him of that which he most longed and hoped for. "Now I begin to be a disciple. I care for nothing, of visible or invisible things, so that I may but win Christ. Let fire and the cross, let the companies of wild beasts, let breaking of bones and tearing of limbs, let the grinding of the whole body, and all the malice of the devil, come upon me; be it so, only may I win Christ Jesus!" And even when he was sentenced to be thrown to the beasts, such was the burning desire that he had to suffer, that he spake, what time he heard the lions roaring, saying: "I am the wheat of Christ: I am going to be ground with the teeth of wild beasts, that I may be found pure bread."

Trajan being succeeded by Adrian, the latter continued this third persecution with as much severity as his predecessor. About this time Alexander, bishop of Rome, with his two deacons, were martyred; as were Quirinus and Hernes, with their families; Zenon, a Roman nobleman, and about ten thousand other Christians.

In Mount Ararat many were crucified, crowned with thorns, and spears run into their sides, in imitation of Christ's passion. Eustachius, a brave and successful Roman commander, was by the emperor ordered to join in an idolatrous sacrifice to celebrate some of his own victories; but his faith (being a Christian in his heart) was so much greater than his vanity, that he nobly refused it. Enraged at the denial, the ungrateful emperor forgot the service of this skilful commander, and ordered him and his whole family to be martyred.

At the martyrdom of Faustines and Jovita, brothers and citizens of Brescia, their torments were so many, and their patience so great, that Calocerius, a pagan, beholding them, was struck with admiration, and exclaimed in a kind of ecstasy, "Great is the God of the Christians!" for which he was apprehended, and suffered a similar fate.

Many other similar cruelties and rigors were exercised against the Christians, until Quadratus, bishop of Athens, made a learned apology in their favor before the emperor, who happened to be there and Aristides, a philosopher of the same city, wrote an elegant epistle, which caused Adrian to relax in his severities, and relent in their favor.

Adrian dying A. D. 138, was succeeded by Antoninus Pius, one of the most amiable monarchs that ever reigned, and who stayed the persecutions against the Christians.

The Fourth Persecution, Under Marcus Aurelius Antoninus, A. D. 162

Marcus Aurelius, followed about the year of our Lord 161, a man of nature more stern and severe; and, although in study of philosophy and in civil government no less commendable, yet, toward the Christians sharp and fierce; by whom was moved the fourth persecution.

The cruelties used in this persecution were such that many of the spectators shuddered with horror at the sight, and were astonished at the intrepidity of the sufferers. Some of the martyrs were obliged to pass, with their already wounded feet, over thorns, nails, sharp shells, etc. upon their points, others were scourged until their sinews and veins lay bare, and after suffering the most excruciating tortures that could be devised, they were destroyed by the most terrible deaths.

Germanicus, a young man, but a true Christian, being delivered to the wild beasts on account of his faith, behaved with such astonishing courage that several pagans became converts to a faith which inspired such fortitude.

Polycarp, the venerable bishop of Smyrna, hearing that persons were seeking for him, escaped, but was discovered by a child. After feasting the guards who apprehended him, he desired an hour in prayer, which being allowed, he prayed with such fervency, that his guards repented that they had been instrumental in taking him. He was, however, carried before the proconsul, condemned, and burnt in the market place.

The proconsul then urged him, saying, "Swear, and I will release thee;—reproach Christ."

Polycarp answered, "Eighty and six years have I served him, and he never once wronged me; how then shall I blaspheme my King, Who hath saved me?" At the stake, to which he was only tied, but not nailed as usual, as he assured them he should stand immovable, the flames, on their kindling the fagots, encircled his body, like an arch, without touching him; and the executioner, on seeing this, was ordered to pierce him with a sword, when so great a quantity of blood flowed out as extinguished the fire. But his body, at the instigation of the enemies of the Gospel, especially Jews, was ordered to be consumed in the pile, and the request of his friends, who wished to give it Christian burial, rejected. They nevertheless collected his bones and as much of his remains as possible, and caused them to be decently interred.

Metrodorus, a minister, who preached boldly, and Pionius, who made some excellent apologies for the Christian faith, were likewise burnt. Carpus and Papilus, two worthy Christians, and Agathonica, a pious woman, suffered martyrdom at Pergamopolis, in Asia.

Felicitatis, an illustrious Roman lady, of a considerable family, and the most shining virtues, was a devout Christian. She had seven sons, whom she had educated with the most exemplary piety.

Januarius, the eldest, was scourged, and pressed to death with weights; Felix and Philip, the two next had their brains dashed out with clubs; Silvanus, the fourth, was murdered by being thrown from a precipice; and the three younger sons, Alexander, Vitalis, and Martial, were beheaded. The mother was beheaded with the same sword as the three latter.

Justin, the celebrated philosopher, fell a martyr in this persecution. He was a native of Neapolis, in Samaria, and was born A. D. 103. Justin was a great lover of truth, and a universal scholar; he investigated the Stoic and Peripatetic philosophy, and attempted the Pythagorean; but the behavior of one of its professors disgusting him, he applied himself to the Platonic, in which he took great delight. About the year 133, when he was thirty years of age, he became a convert to Christianity, and then, for the first time, perceived the real nature of truth.

He wrote an elegant epistle to the Gentiles, and employed his talents in convincing the Jews of the truth of the Christian rites; spending a great deal of time in travelling, until he took up his abode in Rome, and fixed his habitation upon the Viminal mount.

He kept a public school, taught many who afterward became great men, and wrote a treatise to confuse heresies of all kinds. As the pagans began to treat the Christians with great severity, Justin wrote his first apology in their favor. This piece displays great learning and genius, and occasioned the emperor to publish an edict in favor of the Christians.

Soon after, he entered into frequent contests with Crescens, a person of a vicious life and conversation, but a celebrated cynic philosopher; and his arguments appeared so powerful, yet disgusting to the cynic, that he resolved on, and in the sequel accomplished, his destruction.

The second apology of Justin, upon certain severities, gave Crescens the cynic an opportunity of prejudicing the emperor against the writer of it; upon which Justin, and six of his companions, were apprehended. Being commanded to sacrifice to the pagan idols, they refused, and were condemned to be scourged, and then beheaded; which sentence was executed with all imaginable severity.

Several were beheaded for refusing to sacrifice to the image of Jupiter; in particular Concordus, a deacon of the city of Spolito.

Some of the restless northern nations having risen in arms against Rome, the emperor marched to encounter them. He was, however, drawn into an ambuscade, and dreaded the loss of his whole army. Enveloped with mountains, surrounded by enemies, and perishing with thirst, the pagan deities were invoked in vain; when the men belonging to the militine, or thundering legion, who were all Christians, were commanded to call upon their God for succor. A miraculous deliverance immediately ensued; a prodigious quantity of rain fell, which, being caught by the men, and filling their dykes, afforded a sudden and astonishing relief. It appears that the storm which miraculously flashed in the face of the enemy so intimidated them, that part deserted to the Roman army; the rest were defeated, and the revolted provinces entirely recovered.

This affair occasioned the persecution to subside for some time, at least in those parts immediately under the inspection of the emperor; but we find that it soon after raged in France, particularly at Lyons, where the tortures to which many of the Christians were put, almost exceed the powers of description.

The principal of these martyrs were Vetius Agathus, a young man; Blandina, a Christian lady, of a weak constitution; Sanctus, a deacon of Vienna; red hot plates of brass were placed upon the tenderest parts of his body; Biblias, a weak woman, once an apostate. Attalus, of Pergamus; and Pothinus, the venerable bishop of Lyons, who was ninety years of age. Blandina, on the day when she and the three other champions were first brought into the amphitheater, she was suspended on a piece of wood fixed in the ground, and exposed as food for the wild beasts; at which time, by her earnest prayers, she encouraged others. But none of the wild beasts would touch her, so that she was remanded to prison. When she was again produced for the third and last time, she was accompanied by Ponticus, a youth of fifteen, and the constancy of their faith so enraged the multitude that neither the sex of the one nor the youth of the other were respected, being exposed to all manner of punishments and tortures. Being strengthened by Blandina, he persevered unto death; and she, after enduring all the torments heretofore mentioned, was at length slain with the sword.

When the Christians, upon these occasions, received martyrdom, they were ornamented, and crowned with garlands of flowers; for which they, in heaven, received eternal crowns of glory.

It has been said that the lives of the early Christians consisted of "persecution above ground and prayer below ground." Their lives are expressed by the Coliseum and the catacombs. Beneath Rome are the excavations which we call the catacombs, which were at once temples and tombs. The early Church of Rome might well be called the Church of the Catacombs. There are some sixty catacombs near Rome, in which some six hundred miles of galleries have been traced, and these are not all. These galleries are about eight feet high and from three to five feet wide, containing on either side several rows of long, low, horizontal recesses, one above another like berths in a ship. In these the dead bodies were placed and the front closed, either by a single marble slab or several great tiles laid in mortar. On these slabs or tiles, epitaphs or symbols are graved or painted. Both pagans and Christians buried their dead in these catacombs. When the Christian graves have been opened, the skeletons tell their own terrible tale. Heads are found severed from the body, ribs and shoulder blades are broken, bones are often calcined from fire. But despite the awful story of persecution that we may read here, the inscriptions breathe forth peace and joy and triumph. Here are a few:

"Here lies Marcia, put to rest in a dream of peace."

"Lawrence to his sweetest son, borne away of angels."

"Victorious in peace and in Christ."

"Being called away, he went in peace."

Remember when reading these inscriptions the story the skeletons tell of persecution, of torture, and of fire.

But the full force of these epitaphs is seen when we contrast them with the pagan epitaphs, such as:

"Live for the present hour, since we are sure of nothing else."

"I lift my hands against the gods who took me away at the age of twenty though I had done no harm."

"Once I was not. Now I am not. I know nothing about it, and it is no concern of mine."

"Traveler, curse me not as you pass, for I am in darkness and cannot answer."

The most frequent Christian symbols on the walls of the catacombs, are, the good shepherd with the lamb on his shoulder, a ship under full sail, harps, anchors, crowns, vines, and above all the fish.

The Fifth Persecution, Commencing with Severus, A. D. 192

Severus, having been recovered from a severe fit of sickness by a Christian, became a great favorer of the Christians in general; but the prejudice and fury of the ignorant multitude prevailing, obsolete laws were put in execution against the Christians. The progress of Christianity alarmed the pagans, and they revived the stale calumny of placing accidental misfortunes to the account of its professors, A. D. 192.

But, though persecuting malice raged, yet the Gospel shone with resplendent brightness; and, firm as an impregnable rock, withstood the attacks of its boisterous enemies with success. Tertullian, who lived in this age, informs us that if the Christians had collectively withdrawn themselves from the Roman territories, the empire would have been greatly depopulated.

Victor, bishop of Rome, suffered martyrdom in the first year of the third century, A. D. 201. Leonidus, the father of the celebrated Origen, was beheaded for being a Christian. Many of Origen's hearers likewise suffered martyrdom; particularly two brothers, named Plutarchus and Serenus; another Serenus, Heron, and Heraclides, were beheaded. Rhais had boiled pitch poured upon her head, and was then burnt, as was Marcella her mother. Potainiena, the sister of Rhais, was executed in the same manner as Rhais had been; but Basilides, an officer belonging to the army, and ordered to attend her execution, became her convert.

Basilides being, as an officer, required to take a certain oath, refused, saying, that he could not swear by the Roman idols, as he was a Christian. Struck with surprise, the people could not, at first, believe what they heard; but he had no sooner confirmed the same, than he was dragged before the judge, committed to prison, and speedily afterward beheaded.

Irenæus, bishop of Lyons, was born in Greece, and received both a polite and a Christian education. It is generally supposed that the account of the persecutions at Lyons was written by himself. He succeeded the martyr Pothinus as bishop of Lyons, and ruled his diocese with great propriety; he was a zealous opposer of heresies in general, and, about A. D. 187, he wrote a celebrated tract against heresy. Victor, the bishop of Rome, wanting to impose the keeping of Easter there, in preference to other places, it occasioned some disorders among the Christians. In particular, Irenæus wrote him a synodical epistle, in the name of the Gallic churches. This zeal, in favor of Christianity, pointed him out as an object of resentment to the emperor; and in A. D. 202, he was beheaded.

The persecutions now extending to Africa, many were martyred in that quarter of the globe; the most particular of whom we shall mention.

Perpetua, a married lady, of about twenty-two years. Those who suffered with her were, Felicitas, a married lady, big with child at the time of her being apprehended, and Revocatus, catechumen of Carthage, and a slave. The names of the other prisoners, destined to suffer upon this occasion, were Saturninus, Secundulus, and Satur. On the day appointed for their execution, they were led to the amphitheater. Satur, Saturninus, and Revocatus were ordered to run the gauntlet between the hunters, or such as had the care of the wild beasts. The hunters being drawn up in two ranks, they ran between, and were severely lashed as they passed. Felicitas and Perpetua were stripped, in order to be thrown to a mad bull, which made his first attack upon Perpetua, and stunned her; he then darted at Felicitas, and gored her dreadfully; but not killing them, the executioner did that office with a sword. Revocatus and Satur were destroyed by wild beasts; Saturninus was beheaded; and Secundulus died in prison. These executions were in the year 205, on the eighth day of March.

Speratus and twelve others were likewise beheaded; as was Andocles in France. Asclepiades, bishop of Antioch, suffered many tortures, but his life was spared.

Cecilia, a young lady of good family in Rome, was married to a gentleman named Valerian. She converted her husband and brother, who were beheaded; and the maximus, or officer, who led them to execution, becoming their convert, suffered the same fate. The lady was placed naked in a scalding bath, and having continued there a considerable time, her head was struck off with a sword, A. D. 222.

Calistus, bishop of Rome, was martyred, A. D. 224; but the manner of his death is not recorded; and Urban, bishop of Rome, met the same fate A. D. 232.

The Sixth Persecution, Under Maximus, A. D. 235

A. D. 235, was in the time of Maximinus. In Cappadocia, the president, Seremianus, did all he could to exterminate the Christians from that province.

The principal persons who perished under this reign were Pontianus, bishop of Rome; Anteros, a Grecian, his successor, who gave offence to the government by collecting the acts of the martyrs, Pammachius and Quiritus, Roman senators, with all their families, and many other Christians; Simplicius, senator; Calepodius, a Christian minister, thrown into the Tyber; Martina, a noble and beautiful virgin; and Hippolitus, a Christian prelate, tied to a wild horse, and dragged until he expired.

During this persecution, raised by Maximinus, numberless Christians were slain without trial, and buried indiscriminately in heaps, sometimes fifty or sixty being cast into a pit together, without the least decency.

The tyrant Maximinus dying, A. D. 238, was succeeded by Gordian, during whose reign, and that of his successor Philip, the Church was free from persecution for the space of more than ten years; but in A. D. 249, a violent persecution broke out in Alexandria, at the instigation of a pagan priest, without the knowledge of the emperor.

The Seventh Persecution, Under Decius A. D. 249

This was occasioned partly by the hatred he bore to his predecessor Philip, who was deemed a Christian and was partly by his jealousy concerning the amazing increase of Christianity; for the heathen temples began to be forsaken, and the Christian churches thronged.

These reasons stimulated Decius to attempt the very extirpation of the name of Christian; and it was unfortunate for the Gospel, that many errors had, about this time, crept into the Church: the Christians were at variance with each other; self-interest divided those whom social love ought to have united; and the virulence of pride occasioned a variety of factions.

The heathens in general were ambitious to enforce the imperial decrees upon this occasion, and looked upon the murder of a Christian as a merit to themselves. The martyrs, upon this occasion, were innumerable; but the principal we shall give some account of.

Fabian, the bishop of Rome, was the first person of eminence who felt the severity of this persecution. The deceased emperor, Philip, had, on account of his integrity, committed his treasure to the care of this good man. But Decius, not finding as much as his avarice made him expect, determined to wreak his vengeance on the good prelate. He was accordingly seized; and on January 20, A. D. 250, he suffered decapitation.

Julian, a native of Cilicia, as we are informed by St. Chrysostom, was seized upon for being a Christian. He was put into a leather bag, together with a number of serpents and scorpions, and in that condition thrown into the sea.

Peter, a young man, amiable for the superior qualities of his body and mind, was beheaded for refusing to sacrifice to Venus. He said, "I am astonished you should sacrifice to an infamous woman, whose debaucheries even your own historians record, and whose life consisted of such actions as your laws would punish. No, I shall offer the true God the acceptable sacrifice of praises and prayers." Optimus, the proconsul of Asia, on hearing this, ordered the prisoner to be stretched upon a wheel, by which all his bones were broken, and then he was sent to be beheaded.

Nichomachus, being brought before the proconsul as a Christian, was ordered to sacrifice to the pagan idols. Nichomachus replied, "I cannot pay that respect to devils, which is only due to the Almighty." This speech so much enraged the proconsul that Nichomachus was put to the rack. After enduring the torments for a time, he recanted; but scarcely had he given this proof of his frailty, than he fell into the greatest agonies, dropped down on the ground, and expired immediately.

Denisa, a young woman of only sixteen years of age, who beheld this terrible judgment, suddenly exclaimed, "O unhappy wretch, why would you buy a moment's ease at the expense of a miserable eternity!" Optimus, hearing this, called to her, and Denisa avowing herself to be a Christian, she was beheaded, by his order, soon after.

Andrew and Paul, two companions of Nichomachus the martyr, A. D. 251, suffered martyrdom by stoning, and expired, calling on their blessed Redeemer.

Alexander and Epimachus, of Alexandria, were apprehended for being Christians: and, confessing the accusation, were beat with staves, torn with hooks, and at length burnt in the fire; and we are informed, in a fragment preserved by Eusebius, that four female martyrs suffered on the same day, and at the same place, but not in the same manner; for these were beheaded.

Lucian and Marcian, two wicked pagans, though skilful magicians, becoming converts to Christianity, to make amends for their former errors, lived the lives of hermits, and subsisted upon bread and water only. After some time spent in this manner, they became zealous preachers, and made many converts. The persecution, however, raging at this time, they were seized upon, and carried before Sabinus, the governor of Bithynia. On being asked by what authority they took upon themselves to preach, Lucian answered, 'That the laws of charity and humanity obliged all men to endeavor the conversion of their neighbors, and to do everything in their power to rescue them from the snares of the devil.'

Lucian having answered in this manner, Marcian said, "Their

conversion was by the same grace which was given to St. Paul, who, from a zealous persecutor of the Church, became a preacher of the Gospel."

The proconsul, finding that he could not prevail with them to renounce their faith, condemned them to be burnt alive, which sentence was soon after executed.

Trypho and Respicius, two eminent men, were seized as Christians, and imprisoned at Nice. Their feet were pierced with nails; they were dragged through the streets, scourged, torn with iron hooks, scorched with lighted torches, and at length beheaded, February 1, A. D. 251.

Agatha, a Sicilian lady, was not more remarkable for her personal and acquired endowments, than her piety: her beauty was such, that Quintian, governor of Sicily, became enamored of her, and made many attempts upon her chastity without success. In order to gratify his passions with the greater conveniency, he put the virtuous lady into the hands of Aphrodica, a very infamous and licentious woman. This wretch tried every artifice to win her to the desired prostitution; but found all her efforts were vain; for her chastity was impregnable, and she well knew that virtue alone could procure true happiness. Aphrodica acquainted Quintian with the inefficacy of her endeavors, who, enraged to be foiled in his designs, changed his lust into resentment. On her confessing that she was a Christian, he determined to gratify his revenge, as he could not his passion. Pursuant to his orders, she was scourged, burnt with red-hot irons, and torn with sharp hooks. Having borne these torments with admirable fortitude, she was next laid naked upon live coals, intermingled with glass, and then being carried back to prison, she there expired on February 5, 251.

Cyril, bishop of Gortyna, was seized by order of Lucius, the governor of that place, who, nevertheless, exhorted him to obey the imperial mandate, perform the sacrifices, and save his venerable person from destruction; for he was now eighty-four years of age. The good prelate replied that as he had long taught others to save their souls, he should only think now of his own salvation. The worthy prelate heard his fiery sentence without emotion, walked cheerfully to the place of execution, and underwent his martyrdom with great fortitude.

The persecution raged in no place more than the Island of Crete; for the governor, being exceedingly active in executing the imperial decrees, that place streamed with pious blood.

Babylas, a Christian of a liberal education, became bishop of Antioch, A. D. 237, on the demise of Zebinus. He acted with inimitable zeal, and governed the Church with admirable prudence during the most tempestuous times.

The first misfortune that happened to Antioch during his mission, was the siege of it by Sapor, king of Persia; who, having overrun all Syria, took and plundered this city among others, and used the Christian inhabitants with greater severity than the rest, but was soon totally defeated by Gordian.

After Gordian's death, in the reign of Decius, that emperor came to Antioch, where, having a desire to visit an assembly of Christians, Babylas opposed him, and absolutely refused to let him come in. The emperor dissembled his anger at that time; but soon sending for the bishop, he sharply reproved him for his insolence, and then ordered him to sacrifice to the pagan deities as an expiation for his offence. This being refused, he was committed to prison, loaded with chains, treated with great severities, and then beheaded, together with three young men who had been his pupils. A. D. 251.

Alexander, bishop of Jerusalem, about this time was cast into prison on account of his religion, where he died through the severity of his confinement.

Julianus, an old man, lame with the gout, and Cronion, another Christian, were bound on the backs of camels, severely scourged, and then thrown into a fire and consumed. Also forty virgins, at Antioch, after being imprisoned, and scourged, were burnt.

In the year of our Lord 251, the emperor Decius having erected a pagan temple at Ephesus, he commanded all who were in that city to sacrifice to the idols. This order was nobly refused by seven of his own soldiers, viz. Maximianus, Martianus, Joannes, Malchus, Dionysius, Seraion, and Constantinus. The emperor wishing to win these soldiers to renounce their faith by his entreaties and lenity, gave them a considerable respite until he returned from an expedition. During the emperor's absence, they escaped, and hid themselves in a cavern; which the emperor being informed of at his return, the mouth of the cave was closed up, and they all perished with hunger.

Theodora, a beautiful young lady of Antioch, on refusing to sacrifice to the Roman idols, was condemned to the stews, that her virtue might be sacrificed to the brutality of lust. Didymus, a Christian, disguised himself in the habit of a Roman soldier, went to the house, informed Theodora who he was, and advised her to make her escape in his clothes. This being effected, and a man found in the brothel instead of a beautiful lady, Didymus was taken before the president, to whom confessing the truth, and owning that he was a Christian the sentence of death was immediately pronounced against him. Theodora, hearing that her deliverer was likely to suffer, came to the judge, threw herself at his feet, and begged that the sentence might fall on her as the guilty person; but, deaf to the cries of the innocent, and insensible to the calls of justice, the inflexible judge condemned both; when they were executed accordingly, being first beheaded, and their bodies afterward burnt.

Secundianus, having been accused as a Christian, was conveyed to prison by some soldiers. On the way, Verianus and Marcellinus said, "Where are you carrying the innocent?" This interrogatory occasioned them to be seized, and all three, after having been tortured, were hanged and decapitated.

Origen, the celebrated presbyter and catechist of Alexandria, at the age of sixty-four, was seized, thrown into a loathsome prison, laden with fetters, his feet placed in the stocks, and his legs extended to the utmost for several successive days. He was threatened with fire, and tormented by every lingering means the most infernal imaginations could suggest. During this cruel temporizing, the emperor Decius died, and Gallus, who succeeded him, engaging in a war with the Goths, the Christians met with a respite. In this interim, Origen obtained his enlargement, and, retiring to Tyre, he there remained until his death, which happened when he was in the sixty-ninth year of his age.

Gallus, the emperor, having concluded his wars, a plague broke out in the empire: sacrifices to the pagan deities were ordered by the emperor, and persecutions spread from the interior to the extreme parts of the empire, and many fell martyrs to the impetuosity of the rabble, as well as the prejudice of the magistrates. Among these were Cornelius, the Christian bishop of Rome, and Lucius, his successor, in 253.

Most of the errors which crept into the Church at this time arose from placing human reason in competition with revelation; but the fallacy of such arguments being proved by the most able divines, the opinions they had created vanished away like the stars before the sun.

The Eighth Persecution, Under Valerian, A. D. 257

Began under Valerian, in the month of April, 257, and continued for three years and six months. The martyrs that fell in this persecution were innumerable, and their tortures and deaths as various and painful. The most eminent martyrs were the following, though neither rank, sex, nor age were regarded.

Rufina and Secunda were two beautiful and accomplished ladies, daughters of Asterius, a gentleman of eminence in Rome. Rufina, the elder, was designed in marriage for Armentarius, a young nobleman; Secunda, the younger, for Verinus, a person of rank and opulence. The suitors, at the time of the persecution's commencing, were both Christians; but when danger appeared, to save their fortunes, they renounced their faith. They took great pains to persuade the ladies to do the same, but, disappointed in their purpose, the lovers were base enough to inform against the ladies, who, being apprehended as Christians, were brought before Junius Donatus, governor of Rome, where, A. D. 257, they sealed their martyrdom with their blood.

Stephen, bishop of Rome, was beheaded in the same year, and about that time Saturninus, the pious orthodox bishop of Toulouse, refusing to sacrifice to idols, was treated with all the barbarous indignities imaginable, and fastened by the feet to the tail of a bull. Upon a signal given, the enraged animal was driven down the steps of the temple, by which the worthy martyr's brains were dashed out.

Sextus succeeded Stephen as bishop of Rome. He is supposed to have been a Greek by birth or by extraction, and had for some time served in the capacity of a deacon under Stephen. His great fidelity, singular wisdom, and uncommon courage distinguished him upon many occasions; and the happy conclusion of a controversy with some heretics is generally ascribed to his piety and prudence. In the year 258, Marcianus, who had the management of the Roman government, procured an order from the emperor Valerian, to put to death all the Christian clergy in Rome, and hence the bishop with six of his deacons, suffered martyrdom in 258.

Let us draw near to the fire of martyred Lawrence, that our cold hearts may be warmed thereby. The merciless tyrant, understanding him to be not only a minister of the sacraments, but a distributor also of the Church riches, promised to himself a double prey, by the apprehension of one soul. First, with the rake of avarice to scrape to himself the treasure of poor Christians; then with the fiery fork of tyranny, so to toss and turmoil them, that they should wax weary of their profession. With furious face and cruel countenance, the greedy wolf demanded where this Lawrence had bestowed the substance of the Church: who, craving three days' respite, promised to declare where the treasure might be had. In the meantime, he caused a good number of poor Christians to be congregated. So, when the day of his answer was come, the persecutor strictly charged him to stand to his promise. Then valiant Lawrence, stretching out his arms over the poor, said: "These are the precious treasure of the Church; these are the treasure indeed, in whom the faith of Christ reigneth, in whom Jesus Christ hath His mansion-place. What more precious jewels can Christ have, than those in whom He hath promised to dwell? For so it is written, 'I was an hungered, and ye gave me meat: I was thirsty, and ye gave me drink: I was a stranger, and ye took me in.' And again, 'Inasmuch as ye have done it unto one of the least of these my brethren, ye have done it unto me.' What greater riches can Christ our Master possess, than the poor people in whom He loveth to be seen?"

O, what tongue is able to express the fury and madness of the tyrant's heart! Now he stamped, he stared, he ramped, he fared as one out of his wits: his eyes like fire glowed, his mouth like a boar

3

foamed, his teeth like a hellhound grinned. Now, not a reasonable man, but a roaring lion, he might be called.

"Kindle the fire (he cried)—of wood make no spare. Hath this villain deluded the emperor? Away with him, away with him: whip him with scourges, jerk him with rods, buffet him with fists, brain him with clubs. Jesteth the traitor with the emperor? Pinch him with fiery tongs, gird him with burning plates, bring out the strongest chains, and the fire-forks, and the grated bed of iron: on the fire with it; bind the rebel hand and foot; and when the bed is fire-hot, on with him: roast him, broil him, toss him, turn him: on pain of our high displeasure do every man his office, O ye tormentors."

The word was no sooner spoken, but all was done. After many cruel handlings, this meek lamb was laid, I will not say on his fiery bed of iron, but on his soft bed of down. So mightily God wrought with his martyr Lawrence, so miraculously God tempered His element the fire; that it became not a bed of consuming pain, but a pallet of nourishing rest.

In Africa the persecution raged with peculiar violence; many thousands received the crown of martyrdom, among whom the following were the most distinguished characters:

Cyprian, bishop of Carthage, an eminent prelate, and a pious ornament of the Church. The brightness of his genius was tempered by the solidity of his judgment; and with all the accomplishments of the gentleman, he blended the virtues of a Christian. His doctrines were orthodox and pure; his language easy and elegant; and his manners graceful and winning: in fine, he was both the pious and polite preacher. In his youth he was educated in the principles of Gentilism, and having a considerable fortune, he lived in the very extravagance of splendor, and all the dignity of pomp.

About the year 246, Cœcilius, a Christian minister of Carthage, became the happy instrument of Cyprian's conversion: on which account, and for the great love that he always afterward bore for the author of his conversion, he was termed Cœcilius Cyprian. Previous to his baptism, he studied the Scriptures with care and being struck with the beauties of the truths they contained, he determined to practise the virtues therein recommended. Subsequent to his baptism, he sold his estate, distributed the money among the poor, dressed himself in plain attire, and commenced a life of austerity. He was soon after made a presbyter; and, being greatly admired for his virtues and works, on the death of Donatus, in A. D. 248, he was almost unanimously elected bishop of Carthage.

Cyprian's care not only extended over Carthage, but to Numidia and Mauritania. In all his transactions he took great care to ask the advice of his clergy, knowing that unanimity alone could be of service to the Church, this being one of his maxims, "That the bishop was in the church, and the church in the bishop; so that unity can only be preserved by a close connexion between the pastor and his flock."

In A. D. 250, Cyprian was publicly proscribed by the emperor Decius, under the appellation of Cœcilius Cyprian, bishop of the Christians; and the universal cry of the pagans was, "Cyprian to the lions, Cyprian to the beasts." The bishop, however, withdrew from the rage of the populace, and his effects were immediately confiscated. During his retirement, he wrote thirty pious and elegant letters to his flock; but several schisms that then crept into the Church, gave him great uneasiness. The rigor of the persecution abating, he returned to Carthage, and did everything in his power to expunge erroneous opinions. A terrible plague breaking out in Carthage, it was as usual, laid to the charge of the Christians; and the magistrates began to persecute accordingly, which occasioned an epistle from them to Cyprian, in answer to which he vindicates the cause of Christianity. A. D. 257, Cyprian was brought before the proconsul Aspasius Paturnus, who exiled him to a little city on the Lybian sea. On the death of this proconsul, he returned to Carthage, but was soon after seized, and carried before the new governor, who condemned him to be beheaded; which sentence was executed on the fourteenth of September, A. D. 258.

The disciples of Cyprian, martyred in this persecution, were Lucius, Flavian, Victoricus, Remus, Montanus, Julian, Primelus, and Donatian.

At Utica, a most terrible tragedy was exhibited: three hundred Christians were, by the orders of the proconsul, placed round a burning limekiln. A pan of coals and incense being prepared, they were commanded either to sacrifice to Jupiter, or to be thrown into the kiln. Unanimously refusing, they bravely jumped into the pit, and were immediately suffocated.

Fructuosus, bishop of Tarragon, in Spain, and his two deacons, Augurius and Eulogius, were burnt for being Christians.

Alexander, Malchus, and Priscus, three Christians of Palestine, with a woman of the same place, voluntarily accused themselves of being Christians; on which account they were sentenced to be devoured by tigers, which sentence was executed accordingly.

Maxima, Donatilla, and Secunda, three virgins of Tuburga, had gall and vinegar given them to drink, were then severely scourged, tormented on a gibbet, rubbed with lime, scorched on a gridiron, worried by wild beasts, and at length beheaded.

It is here proper to take notice of the singular but miserable fate of the emperor Valerian, who had so long and so terribly persecuted the Christians. This tyrant, by a stratagem, was taken prisoner by Sapor, emperor of Persia, who carried him into his own country, and there treated him with the most unexampled indignity, making him kneel down as the meanest slave, and treading upon him as a footstool when he mounted his horse. After having kept him for the space of seven years in this abject state of slavery, he caused his eyes to be put out, though he was then eighty-three years of age. This not satiating his desire of revenge, he soon after ordered his body to be flayed alive, and rubbed with salt, under which torments he expired; and thus fell one of the most tyrannical emperors of Rome, and one of the greatest persecutors of the Christians.

A. D. 260, Gallienus, the son of Valerian, succeeded him, and during his reign (a few martyrs excepted) the Church enjoyed peace for some years.

The Ninth Persecution Under Aurelian, A. D. 274

The principal sufferers were: Felix, bishop of Rome. This prelate was advanced to the Roman see in 274. He was the first martyr to Aurelian's petulancy, being beheaded on the twenty-second of December, in the same year.

Agapetus, a young gentleman, who sold his estate, and gave the money to the poor, was seized as a Christian, tortured, and then beheaded at Præneste, a city within a day's journey of Rome.

These are the only martyrs left upon record during this reign, as it was soon put to a stop by the emperor's being murdered by his own domestics, at Byzantium.

Aurelian was succeeded by Tacitus, who was followed by Probus, as the latter was by Carus: this emperor being killed by a thunder storm, his sons, Carnious and Numerian, succeeded him, and during all these reigns the Church had peace.

Diocletian mounted the imperial throne, A. D. 284; at first he showed great favor to the Christians. In the year 286, he associated Maximian with him in the empire; and some Christians were put to death before any general persecution broke out. Among these were Felician and Primus, two brothers.

Marcus and Marcellianus were twins, natives of Rome, and of noble descent. Their parents were heathens, but the tutors, to whom the education of the children was intrusted, brought them up as Christians. Their constancy at length subdued those who wished them to become pagans, and their parents and whole family became converts to a faith they had before reprobated. They were martyred by being tied to posts, and having their feet pierced with nails. After remaining in this situation for a day and a night, their sufferings were put to an end to by thrusting lances through their bodies.

Zoe, the wife of the jailer, who had the care of the before-mentioned martyrs, was also converted by them, and hung upon a tree, with a fire of straw lighted under her. When her body was taken down, it was thrown into a river, with a large stone tied to it, in order to sink it.

In the year of Christ 286, a most remarkable affair occurred; a legion of soldiers, consisting of six thousand six hundred and sixty-six men, contained none but Christians. This legion was called the Theban Legion, because the men had been raised in Thebias: they were quartered in the east until the emperor Maximian ordered them to march to Gaul, to assist him against the rebels of Burgundy. They passed the Alps into Gaul, under the command of Mauritius, Candidus, and Exupernis, their worthy commanders, and at length joined the emperor. Maximian, about this time, ordered a general sacrifice, at which the whole army was to assist; and likewise he commanded that they should take the oath of allegiance and swear, at the same time, to assist in the extirpation of Christianity in Gaul. Alarmed at these orders, each individual of the Theban Legion absolutely refused either to sacrifice or take the oaths prescribed. This so greatly enraged Maximian, that he ordered the legion to be decimated, that is, every tenth man to be selected from the rest, and put to the sword. This bloody order having been put in execution, those who remained alive were still inflexible, when a second decimation took place, and every tenth man of those living was put to death. This second severity made no more impression than the first had done; the soldiers preserved their fortitude and their principles, but by the advice of their officers they drew up a loyal remonstrance to the emperor. This, it might have been presumed, would have softened the emperor, but it had a contrary effect: for, enraged at their perseverance and unanimity, he commanded that the whole legion should be put to death, which was accordingly executed by the other troops, who cut them to pieces with their swords, September 22, 286.

Alban, from whom St. Alban's, in Hertfordshire, received its name, was the first British martyr. Great Britain had received the Gospel of Christ from Lucius, the first Christian king, but did not suffer from the rage of persecution for many years after. He was originally a pagan, but converted by a Christian ecclesiastic, named Amphibalus, whom he sheltered on account of his religion. The enemies of Amphibalus, having intelligence of the place where he was secreted, came to the house of Alban; in order to facilitate his escape, when the soldiers came, he offered himself up as the person they were seeking for. The deceit being detected, the governor ordered him to be scourged, and then he was sentenced to be beheaded, June 22, A. D. 287.

The venerable Bede assures us, that, upon this occasion, the executioner suddenly became a convert to Christianity, and entreated permission to die for Alban, or with him. Obtaining the latter request, they were beheaded by a soldier, who voluntarily undertook the task of executioner. This happened on the twenty-second of June, A. D. 287, at Verulam, now St. Alban's, in Hertfordshire, where a magnificent church was erected to his memory about the time of Constantine the Great. The edifice, being destroyed in the Saxon wars, was rebuilt by Offa, king of Mercia, and a monastery erected adjoining to it, some remains of which are still visible, and the church is a noble Gothic structure.

Faith, a Christian female, of Acquitain, in France, was ordered to be broiled upon a gridiron, and then beheaded; A. D. 287.

o Quintin was a Christian, and a native of Rome, but determined to attempt the propagation of the Gosepl in Gaul, with one Lucian, they preached together in Amiens; after which Lucian went to Beaumaris, where he was martyred. Quintin remained in Picardy, and was very zealous in his ministry. Being seized upon as a Christian, he was stretched with pullies until his joints were dislocated; his body was then torn with wire scourges, and boiling oil and pitch poured on his naked flesh; lighted torches were applied to his sides and armpits; and after he had been thus tortured, he was remanded back to prison, and died of the barbarities he had suffered, October 31, A. D. 287. His body was sunk in the Somme.

The Tenth Persecution, Under Diocletian, A. D. 303

Under the Roman emperors, commonly called the Era of the Martyrs, was occasioned partly by the increasing number and luxury of the Christians, and the hatred of Galerius, the adopted son of Diocletian, who, being stimulated by his mother, a bigoted pagan, never ceased persuading the emperor to enter upon the persecution, until he had accomplished his purpose.

The fatal day fixed upon to commence the bloody work, was the twenty-third of February, A. D. 303, that being the day in which the Terminalia were celebrated, and on which, as the cruel pagans boasted, they hoped to put a termination to Christianity. On the appointed day, the persecution began in Nicomedia, on the morning of which the prefect of that city repaired, with a great number of officers and assistants, to the church of the Christians, where, having forced open the doors, they seized upon all the sacred books, and committed them to the flames.

The whole of this transaction was in the presence of Diocletian and Galerius, who, not contented with burning the books, had the church levelled with the ground. This was followed by a severe edict, commanding the destruction of all other Christian churches and books; and an order soon succeeded, to render Christians of all denomination outlaws.

The publication of this edict occasioned an immediate martyrdom, for a bold Christian not only tore it down from the place to which it was affixed, but execrated the name of the emperor for his injustice. A provocation like this was sufficient to call down pagan vengeance upon his head; he was accordingly seized, severely tortured, and then burned alive.

All the Christians were apprehended and imprisoned; and Galerius privately ordered the imperial palace to be set on fire, that the Christians might be charged as the incendiaries, and a plausible pretence given for carrying on the persecution with the greater severities. A general sacrifice was commenced, which occasioned various martyrdoms. No distinction was made of age or sex; the name of Christian was so obnoxious to the pagans that all indiscriminately fell sacrifices to their opinions. Many houses were set on fire, and whole Christian families perished in the flames; and others had stones fastened about their necks, and being tied together were driven into the sea. The persecution became general in all the Roman provinces, but more particularly in the east; and as it lasted ten years, it is impossible to ascertain the numbers martyred, or to enumerate the various modes of martyrdom.

Racks, scourges, swords, daggers, crosses, poison, and famine, were made use of in various parts to dispatch the Christians; and invention was exhausted to devise tortures against such as had no crime, but thinking differently from the votaries of superstition.

A city of Phrygia, consisting entirely of Christians, was burnt, and all the inhabitants perished in the flames.

Tired with slaughter, at length, several governors of provinces represented to the imperial court, the impropriety of such conduct. Hence many were respited from execution, but, though they were not put to death, as much as possible was done to render their lives miserable, many of them having their ears cut off, their noses slit, their right eyes put out, their limbs rendered useless by dreadful dislocations, and their flesh seared in conspicuous places with red-hot irons.

It is necessary now to particularize the most conspicuous persons who laid down their lives in martyrdom in this bloody persecution.

Sebastian, a celebrated martyr, was born at Narbonne, in Gaul, instructed in the principles of Christianity at Milan, and afterward became an officer of the emperor's guard at Rome. He remained a true Christian in the midst of idolatry; unallured by the splendors of a court, untainted by evil examples, and uncontaminated by the hopes of preferment. Refusing to be a pagan, the emperor ordered him to be taken to a field near the city, termed the Campus Martius, and there to be shot to death with arrows; which sentence was executed accordingly. Some pious Christians coming to the place of execution, in order to give his body burial, perceived signs of life in him, and immediately moving him to a place of security, they, in a short time effected his recovery, and prepared him for a second martyrdom; for, as soon as he was able to go out, he placed himself intentionally in the emperor's way as he was going to the temple, and reprehended him for his various cruelties and unreasonable prejudices against Christianity. As soon as Diocletian had overcome his surprise, he ordered Sebastian to be seized, and carried to a place near the palace, and beaten to death; and, that the Christians should not either use means again to recover or bury his body, he ordered that it should be thrown into the common sewer. Nevertheless, a Christian lady, named Lucina, found means to remove it from the sewer, and bury it in the catacombs, or repositories of the dead.

The Christians, about this time, upon mature consideration, thought it unlawful to bear arms under a heathen emperor. Maximilian, the son of Fabius Victor, was the first beheaded under this regulation.

Vitus, a Sicilian of considerable family, was brought up a Christian; when his virtues increased with his years, his constancy supported him under all afflictions, and his faith was superior to the most dangerous perils. His father, Hylas, who was a pagan, finding that he had been instructed in the principles of Christianity by the nurse who brought him up, used all his endeavors to bring him back to paganism, and at length sacrificed his son to the idols, June 14, A. D. 303.

Victor was a Christian of a good family at Marseilles, in France; he spent a great part of the night in visiting the afflicted, and confirming the weak; which pious work he could not, consistently with his own safety, perform in the daytime; and his fortune he spent in relieving the distresses of poor Christians. He was at length, however, seized by the emperor Maximian's decree, who ordered him to be bound, and dragged through the streets. During the execution of this order, he was treated with all manner of cruelties and indignities by the enraged populace. Remaining still inflexible, his courage was deemed obstinacy. Being by order stretched upon the rack, he turned his eyes toward heaven, and prayed to God to endue him with patience, after which he underwent the tortures with most admirable fortitude. After the executioners were tired with inflicting torments on him, he was conveyed to a dungeon. In his confinement, he converted his jailers, named Alexander, Felician, and Longinus. This affair coming to the ears of the emperor, he ordered them immediately to be put to death, and the jailers were accordingly beheaded. Victor was then again put to the rack, unmercifully beaten with batoons, and again sent to prison. Being a third time examined concerning his religion, he persevered in his principles; a small altar was then brought, and he was commanded to offer incense upon it immediately. Fired with indignation at the request, he boldly stepped forward, and with his foot overthrew both altar and idol. This so enraged the emperor Maximian, who was present, that he ordered the foot with which he had kicked the altar to be immediately cut off; and Victor was thrown into a mill, and crushed to pieces with the stones, A. D. 303.

Maximus, governor of Cilicia, being at Tarsus, three Christians were brought before him; their names were Tarachus, an aged man, Probus, and Andronicus. After repeated tortures and exhortations to recant, they, at length, were ordered for execution.

Being brought to the amphitheater, several beasts were let loose upon them; but none of the animals, though hungry, would touch them. The keeper then brought out a large bear, that had that very day destroyed three men; but this voracious creature and a fierce lioness both refused to touch the prisoners. Finding the design of destroying them by the means of wild beasts ineffectual, Maximus ordered them to be slain by the sword, on October 11, A. D. 303.

Romanus, a native of Palestine, was deacon of the church of Cæsarea at the time of the commencement of Diocletian's persecution. Being condemned for his faith at Antioch, he was scourged, put to the rack, his body torn with hooks, his flesh cut with knives, his face scarified, his teeth beaten from their sockets, and his hair plucked up by the roots. Soon after he was ordered to be strangled, November 17, A. D. 303.

Susanna, the niece of Caius, bishop of Rome, was pressed by the emperor Diocletian to marry a noble pagan, who was nearly related to him. Refusing the honor intended her, she was beheaded by the emperor's order.

Dorotheus, the high chamberlain of the household to Diocletian, was a Christian, and took great pains to make converts. In his religious labors, he was joined by Gorgonius, another Christian, and one belonging to the palace. They were first tortured and then strangled.

Peter, a eunuch belonging to the emperor, was a Christian of singular modesty and humility. He was laid on a gridiron, and broiled over a slow fire until he expired.

Cyprian, known by the title of the magician, to distinguish him from Cyprian, bishop of Carthage, was a native of Antioch. He received a liberal education in his youth, and particularly applied himself to astrology; after which he traveled for improvement through Greece, Egypt, India, etc. In the course of time he became acquainted with Justina, a young lady of Antioch, whose birth, beauty, and accomplishments, rendered her the admiration of all who knew her. A pagan gentleman applied to Cyprian, to promote his suit with the beautiful Justina; this he undertook, but soon himself became converted, burnt his books of astrology and magic, received baptism, and felt animated with a powerful spirit of grace. The conversion of Cyprian had a great effect on the pagan gentleman who paid his addresses to Justina, and he in a short time embraced Christianity. During the persecutions of Diocletian, Cyprian and Justina were seized upon as Christians, the former was torn with pincers, and the latter chastised; and, after suffering other torments, both were beheaded.

Eulalia, a Spanish lady of a Christian family, was remarkable in her youth for sweetness of temper, and solidity of understanding seldom found in the capriciousness of juvenile years. Being apprehended as a Christian, the magistrate attempted by the mildest means, to bring her over to paganism, but she ridiculed the pagan deities with such asperity, that the judge, incensed at her behavior, ordered her to be tortured. Her sides were accordingly torn by hooks, and her breasts burnt in the most shocking manner, until she expired by the violence of the flames, December, A. D. 303.

In the year 304, when the persecution reached Spain, Dacian, the governor of Terragona, ordered Valerius the bishop, and Vincent the deacon, to be seized, loaded with irons, and imprisoned. The prisoners being firm in their resolution, Valerius was banished, and Vincent was racked, his limbs dislocated, his flesh torn with hooks, and he was laid on a gridiron, which had not only a fire placed under it, but spikes at the top, which ran into his flesh. These torments neither destroying him, nor changing his resolutions, he was remanded to prison, and confined in a small, loathsome, dark dungeon, strewed with sharp flints, and pieces of broken glass, where he died, January 22, 304. His body was thrown into the river.

The persecution of Diocletian began particularly to rage in A. D. 304, when many Christians were put to cruel tortures and the most painful and ignominious deaths; the most eminent and particular of whom we shall enumerate.

Saturninus, a priest of Albitina, a town of Africa, after being tortured, was remanded to prison, and there starved to death. His four children, after being variously tormented, shared the same fate with their father.

Dativas, a noble Roman senator; Thelico, a pious Christian; Victoria, a young lady of considerable family and fortune, with some others of less consideration, all auditors of Saturninus, were tortured in a similar manner, and perished by the same means.

Agrape, Chionia, and Irene, three sisters, were seized upon at Thessalonica, when Diocletian's persecution reached Greece. They were burnt, and received the crown of martyrdom in the flames, March 25, A. D. 304. The governor, finding that he could make no impression on Irene, ordered her to be exposed naked in the streets, which shameful order having been executed, a fire was kindled near the city wall, amidst whose flames her spirit ascended beyond the reach of man's cruelty.

Agatho, a man of a pious turn of mind, with Cassice, Phillippa, and Eutychia, were martyred about the same time; but the particulars have not been transmitted to us.

Marcellinus, bishop of Rome, who succeeded Caius in that see, having strongly opposed paying divine honors to Diocletian, suffered martyrdom, by a variety of tortures, in the year 324, comforting his soul until he expired with the prospect of those glorious rewards it would receive by the tortures suffered in the body.

Victorius, Carpophorus, Severus, and Severianus, were brothers, and all four employed in places of great trust and honor in the city of Rome. Having exclaimed against the worship of idols, they were apprehended, and scourged, with the plumbetæ, or scourges, to the ends of which were fastened leaden balls. This punishment was exercised with such excess of cruelty that the pious brothers fell martyrs to its severity.

Timothy, a deacon of Mauritania, and Maura his wife, had not been united together by the bands of wedlock above three weeks, when they were separated from each other by the persecution. Timothy, being apprehended as a Christian, was carried before Arrianus, the governor of Thebais, who, knowing that he had the keeping of the Holy Scriptures, commanded him to deliver them up to be burnt; to which he answered, "Had I children, I would sooner deliver them up to be sacrificed, than part with the Word of God." The governor being much incensed at this reply, ordered his eyes to be put out, with red-hot irons, saying "The books shall at least be useless to you, for you shall not see to read them." His patience under the operation was so great that the governor grew more exasperated; he, therefore, in order, if possible, to overcome his fortitude, ordered him to be hung up by the feet, with a weight tied about his neck, and a gag in his mouth. In this state, Maura his wife, tenderly urged him for her sake to recant; but, when the gag was taken out of his mouth, instead of consenting to his wife's entreaties, he greatly blamed her mistaken love, and declared his resolution of dying for the faith. The consequence was, that Maura resolved to imitate his courage and fidelity and either to accompany or follow him to glory. The governor, after trying in vain to alter her resolution, ordered her to be tortured, which was executed with great severity. After this, Timothy and Maura were crucified near each other, A. D. 304.

Sabinus, bishop of Assisium, refusing to sacrifice to Jupiter, and pushing the idol from him, had his hand cut off by the order of the governor of Tuscany. While in prison, he converted the governor and his family, all of whom suffered martyrdom for the faith. Soon after their execution, Sabinus himself was scourged to death, December, A. D. 304.

Tired with the farce of state and public business, the emperor Diocletian resigned the imperial diadem, and was succeeded by Constantius and Galerius; the former a prince of the most mild and humane disposition and the latter equally remarkable for his cruelty and tyranny. These divided the empire into two equal governments, Galerius ruling in the east, and Constantius in the west; and the people in the two governments felt the effects of the dispositions of the two emperors; for those in the west were governed in the mildest manner, but such as resided in the east felt all the miseries of oppression and lengthened tortures.

Among the many martyred by the order of Galerius, we shall enumerate the most eminent.

Amphianus was a gentleman of eminence in Lucia, and a scholar of Eusebius; Julitta, a Lycaonian of royal descent, but more celebrated for her virtues than noble blood. While on the rack, her child was killed before her face. Julitta, of Cappadocia, was a lady of distinguished capacity, great virtue, and uncommon courage. To complete the execution, Julitta had boiling pitch poured on her feet, her sides torn with hooks, and received the conclusion of her martyrdom, by being beheaded, April 16, A. D. 305.

Hermolaus, a venerable and pious Christian, of a great age, and an intimate acquaintance of Panteleon's, suffered martyrdom for the faith on the same day, and in the same manner as Panteleon.

Eustratius, secretary to the governor of Armina, was thrown into a fiery furnace for exhorting some Christians who had been apprehended, to persevere in their faith.

Nicander and Marcian, two eminent Roman military officers, were apprehended on account of their faith. As they were both men of great abilities in their profession, the utmost means were used to induce them to renounce Christianity; but these endeavors being found ineffectual, they were beheaded.

In the kingdom of Naples, several martyrdoms took place, in particular, Januaries, bishop of Beneventum; Sosius, deacon of Misene; Proculus, another deacon; Eutyches and Acutius, two laymen; Festus, a deacon; and Desiderius, a reader; all, on account of being Christians, were condemned by the governor of Campania to be devoured by the wild beasts. The savage animals, however, would not touch them, and so they were beheaded.

Quirinus, bishop of Siscia, being carried before Matenius, the governor, was ordered to sacrifice to the pagan deities, agreeably to the edicts of various Roman emperors. The governor, perceiving his constancy, sent him to jail, and ordered him to be heavily ironed; flattering himself, that the hardships of a jail, some occasional tortures and the weight of chains, might overcome his resolution. Being decided in his principles, he was sent to Amantius, the principal governor of Pannonia, now Hungary, who loaded him with chains, and carried him through the principal towns of the Danube, exposing him to ridicule wherever he went. Arriving at length at Sabaria, and finding that Quirinus would not renounce his faith, he ordered him to be cast into a river, with a stone fastened about his neck.

This sentence being put into execution, Quirinus floated about for some time, and, exhorting the people in the most pious terms, concluded his admonitions with this prayer: "It is no new thing, O all-powerful Jesus, for Thee to stop the course of rivers, or to cause a man to walk upon the water, as Thou didst Thy servant Peter; the people have already seen the proof of Thy power in me; grant me now to lay down my life for Thy sake, O my God." On pronouncing the last words he immediately sank, and died, June 4, A. D. 308. His body was afterwards taken up, and buried by some pious Christians.

Pamphilus, a native of Phœnicia, of a considerable family, was a man of such extensive learning that he was called a second Origen. He was received into the body of the clergy at Cæsarea, where he established a public library and spent his time in the practice of every Christian virtue. He copied the greatest part of the works of Origen with his own hand, and, assisted by Eusebius, gave a correct copy of the Old Testament, which had suffered greatly by the ignorance or negligence of former transcribers. In the year 307, he was apprehended, and suffered torture and martyrdom.

Marcellus, bishop of Rome, being banished on account of his faith, fell a martyr to the miseries he suffered in exile, January 16, A. D. 310.

Peter, the sixteenth bishop of Alexandria, was martyred November 25, A. D. 311, by order of Maximus Cæsar, who reigned in the east.

Agnes, a virgin of only thirteen years of age, was beheaded for being a Christian; as was Serene, the empress of Diocletian. Valentine, a priest, suffered the same fate at Rome; and Erasmus, a bishop, was martyred in Campania.

Soon after this the persecution abated in the middle parts of the empire, as well as in the west; and Providence at length began to manifest vengeance on the persecutors. Maximian endeavored to corrupt his daughter Fausta to murder Constantine her husband; which she discovered, and Constantine forced him to choose his own death, when he preferred the ignominious death of hanging after being an emperor near twenty years.

Constantine was the good and virtuous child of a good and virtuous father, born in Britain. His mother was named Helena, daughter of King Coilus. He was a most bountiful and gracious prince, having a desire to nourish learning and good arts, and did oftentimes use to read, write, and study himself. He had marvellous good success and prosperous achieving of all things he took in hand, which then was (and truly) supposed to proceed of this, for that he was so great a favorer of the Christian faith. Which faith when he had once embraced, he did ever after most devoutly and religiously reverence.

Thus Constantine, sufficiently appointed with strength of men but especially with strength of God, entered his journey coming towards Italy, which was about the last year of the persecution, A. D. 313. Maxentius, understanding of the coming of Constantine, and trusting more to his devilish art of magic than to the good will of his subjects, which he little deserved, durst not show himself out of the city, nor encounter him in the open field, but with privy garrisons laid wait for him by the way in sundry straits, as he should come; with whom Constantine had divers skirmishes, and by the power of the Lord did ever vanquish them and put them to flight.

Notwithstanding, Constantine yet was in no great comfort, but in great care and dread in his mind (approaching now near unto Rome) for the magical charms and sorceries of Maxentius, wherewith he had vanquished before Severus, sent by Galerius against him. Wherefore, being in great doubt and perplexity in himself, and revolving many things in his mind, what help he might have against the operations of his charming, Constantine, in his journey drawing toward the city, and casting up his eyes many times to heaven, in the south part, about the going down of the sun, saw a great brightness in heaven, appearing in the similitude of a cross, giving this inscription, *In hoc vince,* that is, "In this overcome."

Eusebius Pamphilus doth witness that he had heard the said Constantine himself oftentimes report, and also to swear this to be true and certain, which he did see with his own eyes in heaven, and also his soldiers about him. At the sight whereof when he was greatly astonished, and consulting with his men upon the meaning thereof, behold, in the night season in his sleep, Christ appeared to him with the sign of the same cross which he had seen before, bidding him to make the figuration thereof, and to carry it in his wars before him, and so should he have the victory.

Constantine so established the peace of the Church that for the space of a thousand years we read of no set persecution against the Christians, unto the time of John Wickliffe.

So happy, so glorious was this victory of Constantine, surnamed the Great! For the joy and gladness whereof, the citizens who had sent for him before, with exceeding triumph brought him into the city of Rome, where he was most honorably received, and celebrated the space of seven days together; having, moreover, in the market place, his image set up, holding in his right hand the sign of the cross, with this inscription: "With this wholesome sign, the true token of fortitude, I have rescued and delivered our city from the yoke of the tyrant."

We shall conclude our account of the tenth and last general persecution with the death of St. George, the titular saint and patron of England. St. George was born in Cappadocia, of Christian parents; and giving proofs of his courage, was promoted in the army of the emperor Diocletian. During the persecution, St. George threw up

his command, went boldly to the senate house, and avowed his being
a Christian, taking occasion at the same time to remonstrate against
paganism, and point out the absurdity of worshipping idols.   This
freedom so greatly provoked the senate that St. George was ordered
to be tortured, and by the emperor's orders was dragged through the
streets, and beheaded the next day.

The legend of the dragon, which is associated with this martyr, is
usually illustrated by representing St. George seated upon a charging
horse and transfixing the monster with his spear.   This fiery dragon
symbolizes the devil, who was vanquished by St. George's steadfast
faith in Christ, which remained unshaken in spite of torture and
death.

CHAPTER III

Persecutions of the Christians in Persia

THE Gospel having spread itself into Persia, the pagan priests,
who worshipped the sun, were greatly alarmed, and dreaded the loss
of that influence they had hitherto maintained over the people's minds
and properties.   Hence they thought it expedient to complain to the
emperor that the Christians were enemies to the state, and held a
treasonable correspondence with the Romans, the great enemies of
Persia.

The emperor Sapores, being naturally averse to Christianity, easily
believed what was said against the Christians, and gave orders to persecute them in all parts of his empire.   On account of this mandate,
many eminent persons in the church and state fell martyrs to the
ignorance and ferocity of the pagans.

Constantine the Great being informed of the persecutions in Persia,
wrote a long letter to the Persian monarch, in which he recounts the
vengeance that had fallen on persecutors, and the great success that
had attended those who had refrained from persecuting the Christians.

Speaking of his victories over rival emperors of his own time, he
said, "I subdued these solely by faith in Christ; for which God
was my helper, who gave me victory in battle, and made me triumph
over my enemies.   He hath likewise so enlarged to me the bounds
of the Roman Empire, that it extends from the Western Ocean
almost to the uttermost parts of the East: for this domain I neither
offered sacrifices to the ancient deities, nor made use of charm or
divination; but only offered up prayers to the Almighty God, and
followed the cross of Christ.   Rejoiced should I be if the throne of
Persia found glory also, by embracing the Christians: that so you
with me, and they with you, may enjoy all happiness."

In consequence of this appeal, the persecution ended for the time, but it was renewed in later years when another king succeeded to the throne of Persia.

Persecutions Under the Arian Heretics

The author of the Arian heresy was Arius, a native of Lybia, and a priest of Alexandria, who, in A. D. 318, began to publish his errors. He was condemned by a council of Lybian and Egyptian bishops, and that sentence was confirmed by the Council of Nice, A. D. 325. After the death of Constantine the Great, the Arians found means to ingratiate themselves into the favor of the emperor Constantinus, his son and successor in the east; and hence a persecution was raised against the orthodox bishops and clergy. The celebrated Athanasius, and other bishops, were banished, and their sees filled with Arians.

In Egypt and Lybia, thirty bishops were martyred, and many other Christians cruelly tormented; and, A. D. 386, George, the Arian bishop of Alexandria, under the authority of the emperor, began a persecution in that city and its environs, and carried it on with the most infernal severity. He was assisted in his diabolical malice by Catophonius, governor of Egypt; Sebastian, general of the Egyptian forces; Faustinus, the treasurer; and Heraclius, a Roman officer.

The persecutions now raged in such a manner that the clergy were driven from Alexandria, their churches were shut, and the severities practiced by the Arian heretics were as great as those that had been practiced by the pagan idolaters. If a man, accused of being a Christian, made his escape, then his whole family were massacred, and his effects confiscated.

Persecution Under Julian the Apostate

This emperor was the son of Julius Constantius, and the nephew of Constantine the Great. He studied the rudiments of grammar under the inspection of Mardonius, a eunuch, and a heathen of Constantinople. His father sent him some time after to Nicomedia, to be instructed in the Christian religion, by the bishop of Eusebius, his kinsman, but his principles were corrupted by the pernicious doctrines of Ecebolius the rhetorician, and Maximus the magician.

Constantius, dying in the year 361, Julian succeeded him, and had no sooner attained the imperial dignity than he renounced Christianity and embraced paganism, which had for some years fallen into great disrepute. Though he restored the idolatrous worship, he made no public edicts against Christianity. He recalled all banished pagans, allowed the free exercise of religion to every sect, but deprived all Christians of offices at court, in the magistracy, or in the army. He was chaste, temperate, vigilant, laborious, and pious; yet he prohibited any Christian from keeping a school or public seminary of learning, and deprived all the Christian clergy of the privileges granted them by Constantine the Great.

Bishop Basil made himself first famous by his opposition to Arianism, which brought upon him the vengeance of the Arian bishop of Constantinople; he equally opposed paganism. The emperor's agents in vain tampered with Basil by means of promises, threats, and racks, he was firm in the faith, and remained in prison to undergo some other sufferings, when the emperor came accidentally to Ancyra. Julian determined to examine Basil himself, when that holy man being brought before him, the emperor did every thing in his power to dissuade him from persevering in the faith. Basil not only continued as firm as ever, but, with a prophetic spirit foretold the death of the emperor, and that he should be tormented in the other life. Enraged at what he heard, Julian commanded that the body of Basil should be torn every day in seven different parts, until his skin and flesh were entirely mangled. This inhuman sentence was executed with rigor, and the martyr expired under its severities, on June 28, A. D. 362.

Donatus, bishop of Arezzo, and Hilarinus, a hermit, suffered about the same time; also Gordian, a Roman magistrate. Artemius, commander in chief of the Roman forces in Egypt, being a Christian, was deprived of his commission, then of his estate, and lastly of his head.

The persecution raged dreadfully about the latter end of the year 363; but, as many of the particulars have not been handed down to us, it is necessary to remark in general, that in Palestine many were burnt alive, others were dragged by their feet through the streets naked until they expired; some were scalded to death, many stoned, and great numbers had their brains beaten out with clubs. In Alexandria, innumerable were the martyrs who suffered by the sword, burning, crucifixion and stoning. In Arethusa, several were ripped open, and corn being put into their bellies, swine were brought to feed therein, which, in devouring the grain, likewise devoured the entrails of the martyrs, and, in Thrace, Emilianus was burnt at a stake; and Domitius murdered in a cave, whither he had fled for refuge.

The emperor, Julian the apostate, died of a wound which he received in his Persian expedition, A. D. 363, and even while expiring, uttered the most horrid blasphemies. He was succeeded by Jovian, who restored peace to the Church.

After the decease of Jovian, Valentinian succeeded to the empire, and associated to himself Valens, who had the command in the east, and was an Arian and of an unrelenting and persecuting disposition.

Persecution of the Christians by the Goths and Vandals.

Many Scythian Goths having embraced Christianity about the time

4

of Constantine the Great, the light of the Gospel spread itself considerably in Scythia, though the two kings who ruled that country, and the majority of the people continued pagans. Fritegern, king of the West Goths, was an ally to the Romans, but Athanarich, king of the East Goths, was at war with them. The Christians, in the dominions of the former, lived unmolested, but the latter, having been defeated by the Romans, wreaked his vengeance on his Christian subjects, commencing his pagan injunctions in the year 370.

In religion the Goths were Arians, and called themselves Christians; therefore they destroyed all the statues and temples of the heathen gods, but did no harm to the orthodox Christian churches. Alaric had all the qualities of a great general. To the wild bravery of the Gothic barbarian he added the courage and skill of the Roman soldier. He led his forces across the Alps into Italy, and although driven back for the time, returned afterward with an irresistible force.

The Last Roman "Triumph"

After this fortunate victory over the Goths a "triumph," as it was called, was celebrated at Rome. For hundreds of years successful generals had been awarded this great honor on their return from a victorious campaign. Upon such occasions the city was given up for days to the marching of troops laden with spoils, and who dragged after them prisoners of war, among whom were often captive kings and conquered generals. This was to be the last Roman triumph, for it celebrated the last Roman victory. Although it had been won by Stilicho, the general, it was the boy emperor, Honorius, who took the credit, entering Rome in the car of victory, and driving to the Capitol amid the shouts of the populace. Afterward, as was customary on such occasions, there were bloody combats in the Colosseum, where gladiators, armed with swords and spears, fought as furiously as if they were on the field of battle.

The first part of the bloody entertainment was finished; the bodies of the dead were dragged off with hooks, and the reddened sand covered with a fresh, clean layer. After this had been done the gates in the wall of the arena were thrown open, and a number of tall, well-formed men in the prime of youth and strength came forward. Some carried swords, others three-pronged spears and nets. They marched once around the walls, and stopping before the emperor, held up their weapons at arm's length, and with one voice sounded out their greeting, *Ave, Cæsar, morituri te salutant!* "Hail, Cæsar, those about to die salute thee!"

The combats now began again; the gladiators with nets tried to entangle those with swords, and when they succeeded mercilessly stabbed their antagonists to death with the three-pronged spear. When a gladiator had wounded his adversary, and had him lying helpless at his feet, he looked up at the eager faces of the spectators, and cried out, *Hoc habet!* "He has it!" and awaited the pleasure of the audience to kill or spare.

If the spectators held out their hands toward him, with thumbs upward, the defeated man was taken away, to recover if possible from his wounds. But if the fatal signal of "thumbs down" was given, the conquered was to be slain; and if he showed any reluctance to present his neck for the death blow, there was a scornful shout from the galleries, *Recipe ferrum!* "Receive the steel!" Privileged persons among the audience would even descend into the arena, to better witness the death agonies of some unusually brave victim, before his corpse was dragged out at the death gate.

The show went on; many had been slain, and the people, madly excited by the desperate bravery of those who continued to fight, shouted their applause. But suddenly there was an interruption. A rudely clad, robed figure appeared for a moment among the audience, and then boldly leaped down into the arena. He was seen to be a man of rough but imposing presence, bareheaded and with sun-browned face. Without hesitating an instant he advanced upon two gladiators engaged in a life-and-death struggle, and laying his hand upon one of them sternly reproved him for shedding innocent blood, and then, turning toward the thousands of angry faces ranged around him, called upon them in a solemn, deep-toned voice which resounded through the deep inclosure. These were his words: "Do not requite God's mercy in turning away the swords of your enemies by murdering each other!"

Angry shouts and cries at once drowned his voice: "This is no place for preaching!—the old customs of Rome must be observed! —On, gladiators!" Thrusting aside the stranger, the gladiators would have again attacked each other, but the man stood between, holding them apart, and trying in vain to be heard. "Sedition! sedition! down with him!" was then the cry; and the gladiators, enraged at the interference of an outsider with their chosen vocation, at once stabbed him to death. Stones, or whatever missiles came to hand, also rained down upon him from the furious people, and thus he perished, in the midst of the arena.

His dress showed him to be one of the hermits who vowed themselves to a holy life of prayer and self-denial, and who were reverenced by even the thoughtless and combat-loving Romans. The few who knew him told how he had come from the wilds of Asia on a pilgrimage, to visit the churches and keep his Christmas at Rome; they knew he was a holy man, and that his name was Telemachus— no more. His spirit had been stirred by the sight of thousands flocking to see men slaughter one another, and in his simple-hearted zeal he had tried to convince them of the cruelty and wickedness of their conduct. He had died, but not in vain. His work was accomplished at the moment he was struck down, for the shock of such a death before their eyes turned the hearts of the people: they saw the hideous aspects of the favorite vice to which they had blindly surrendered themselves; and from the day Telemachus fell dead in the Colosseum, no other fight of gladiators was ever held there.

Persecutions from About the Middle of the Fifth, to the Conclusion of the Seventh Century

Proterius was made a priest by Cyril, bishop of Alexandria, who was well acquainted with his virtues, before he appointed him to preach. On the death of Cyril, the see of Alexandria was filled by Discorus, an inveterate enemy to the memory and family of his predecessor. Being condemned by the council of Chalcedon for having embraced the errors of Eutyches, he was deposed, and Proterius chosen to fill the vacant see, who was approved of by the emperor. This occasioned a dangerous insurrection, for the city of Alexandria was divided into two factions; the one to espouse the cause of the old, and the other of the new prelate. In one of the commotions, the Eutychians determined to wreak their vengeance on Proterius, who fled to the church for sanctuary: but on Good Friday, A. D. 457, a large body of them rushed into the church, and barbarously murdered the prelate; after which they dragged the body through the streets, insulted it, cut it to pieces, burnt it, and scattered the ashes in the air.

Hermenigildus, a Gothic prince, was the eldest son of Leovigildus, a king of the Goths, in Spain. This prince, who was originally an Arian, became a convert to the orthodox faith, by means of his wife Ingonda. When the king heard that his son had changed his religious sentiments, he stripped him of the command at Seville, where he was governor, and threatened to put him to death unless he renounced the faith he had newly embraced. The prince, in order to prevent the execution of his father's menaces, began to put himself into a posture of defence; and many of the orthodox persuasion in Spain declared for him. The king, exasperated at this act of rebellion, began to punish all the orthodox Christians who could be seized by his troops, and thus a very severe persecution commenced: he likewise marched against his son at the head of a very powerful army. The prince took refuge in Seville, from which he fled, and was at length besieged and taken at Asieta. Loaded with chains, he was sent to Seville, and at the feast of Easter refusing to receive the Eucharist from an Arian bishop, the enraged king ordered his guards to cut the prince to pieces, which they punctually performed, April 13, A. D. 586.

Martin, bishop of Rome, was born at Todi, in Italy. He was naturally inclined to virtue, and his parents bestowed on him an admirable education. He opposed the heretics called Monothelites, who were patronized by the emperor Heraclius. Martin was condemned at Constantinople, where he was exposed in the most public places to the ridicule of the people, divested of all episcopal marks of distinction, and treated with the greatest scorn and severity. After lying some months in prison, Martin was sent to an island at some distance, and there cut to pieces, A. D. 655.

John, bishop of Bergamo, in Lombardy, was a learned man, and a good Christian. He did his utmost endeavors to clear the Church from the errors of Arianism, and joining in this holy work with John, bishop of Milan, he was very successful against the heretics, on which account he was assassinated on July 11, A. D. 683.

Killien was born in Ireland, and received from his parents a pious and Christian education. He obtained the Roman pontiff's license to preach to the pagans in Franconia, in Germany. At Wurtzburg he converted Gozbert, the governor, whose example was followed by the greater part of the people in two years after. Persuading Gozbert that his marriage with his brother's widow was sinful, the latter had him beheaded, A. D. 689.

Persecutions from the Early Part of the Eighth, to Near the Conclusion of the Tenth Century

Boniface, archbishop of Mentz, and father of the German church, was an Englishman, and is, in ecclesiastical history, looked upon as one of the brightest ornaments of this nation. Originally his name was Winfred, or Winfrith, and he was born at Kirton, in Devonshire, then part of the West-Saxon kingdom. When he was only about six years of age, he began to discover a propensity to reflection, and seemed solicitous to gain information on religious subjects. Wolfrad, the abbot, finding that he possessed a bright genius, as well as a strong inclination to study, had him removed to Nutscelle, a seminary of learning in the diocese of Winchester, where he would have a much greater opportunity of attaining improvements than at Exeter.

After due study, the abbot seeing him qualified for the priesthood, obliged him to receive that holy order when he was about thirty years old. From which time he began to preach and labor for the salvation of his fellow creatures; he was released to attend a synod of bishops in the kingdom of West-Saxons. He afterwards, in 719, went to Rome, where Gregory II who then sat in Peter's chair, received him with great friendship, and finding him full of all virtues that compose the character of an apostolic missionary, dismissed him without commission at large to preach the Gospel to the pagans wherever he found them. Passing through Lombardy and Bavaria, he came to Thuringia, which country had before received the light of the Gospel, he next visited Utrecht, and then proceeded to Saxony, where he converted some thousands to Christianity.

During the ministry of this meek prelate, Pepin was declared king of France. It was that prince's ambition to be crowned by the most holy prelate he could find, and Boniface was pitched on to perform that ceremony, which he did at Soissons, in 752. The next year, his great age and many infirmities lay so heavy on him, that, with the consent of the new king, and the bishops of his diocese, he consecrated Lullus, his countryman, and faithful disciple, and placed him in the see of Mentz. When he had thus eased himself of his charge, he recommended the church of Mentz to the care of the new bishop in very strong terms, desired he would finish the church at Fuld, and see him buried in it, for his end was near. Having left these orders, he took boat to the Rhine, and went to Friesland, where he converted and baptized several thousands of barbarous natives, demolished the temples, and raised churches on the ruins of those superstitious structures. A day being appointed for confirming a great number of new converts, he ordered them to assemble in a new open plain, near the river Bourde. Thither he repaired the day before; and, pitching a tent, determined to remain on the spot all night, in order to be ready early in the morning. Some pagans, who were his inveterate enemies, having intelligence of this, poured down upon him and the companions of his mission in the night, and killed him and fifty-two of his companions and attendants on June 5, A. D. 755. Thus fell the great father of the Germanic Church, the honor of England, and the glory of the age in which he lived.

Forty-two persons of Armorian in Upper Phrygia, were martyred in the year 845, by the Saracens, the circumstances of which transactions are as follows:

In the reign of Theophilus, the Saracens ravaged many parts of the eastern empire, gained several considerable advantages over the Christians, took the city of Armorian, and numbers suffered martyrdom.

Flora and Mary, two ladies of distinction, suffered martyrdom at the same time.

Perfectus was born at Corduba, in Spain, and brought up in the Christian faith. Having a quick genius, he made himself master of all the useful and polite literature of that age; and at the same time was not more celebrated for his abilities than admired for his piety. At length he took priest's orders, and performed the duties of his office with great assiduity and punctuality. Publicly declaring Mahomet an impostor, he was sentenced to be beheaded, and was accordingly executed, A. D. 850; after which his body was honorably interred by the Christians.

Adalbert, bishop of Prague, a Bohemian by birth, after being involved in many troubles, began to direct his thoughts to the conversion of the infidels, to which end he repaired to Dantzic, where he converted and baptized many, which so enraged the pagan priests, that they fell upon him, and despatched him with darts, on April 23, A. D. 997.

Persecutions in the Eleventh Century

Alphage, archbishop of Canterbury, was descended from a considerable family in Gloucestershire, and received an education suitable to his illustrious birth. His parents were worthy Christians, and Alphage seemed to inherit their virtues.

The see of Winchester being vacant by the death of Ethelwold, Dunstan, archbishop of Canterbury, as primate of all England, consecrated Alphage to the vacant bishopric, to the general satisfaction of all concerned in the diocese.

Dunstan had an extraordinary veneration for Alphage, and, when at the point of death, made it his ardent request to God that he might succeed him in the see of Canterbury; which accordingly happened, though not until about eighteen years after Dunstan's death in 1006.

After Alphage had governed the see of Canterbury about four years, with great reputation to himself, and benefit to his people, the Danes made an incursion into England, and laid siege to Canterbury. When the design of attacking this city was known, many of the principal people made a flight from it, and would have persuaded Alphage to follow their example. But he, like a good pastor, would not listen to such a proposal. While he was employed in assisting and encouraging the people, Canterbury was taken by storm; the enemy poured into the town, and destroyed all that came in their way by fire and sword. He had the courage to address the enemy, and offer himself to their swords, as more worthy of their rage than the people: he begged they might be saved, and that they would discharge their whole fury upon him. They accordingly seized him, tied his hands, insulted and abused him in a rude and barbarous manner, and obliged him to remain on the spot until his church was burnt, and the monks massacred. They then decimated all the inhabitants, both ecclesiastics and laymen, leaving only every tenth person alive; so that they put 7236 persons to death, and left only four monks and 800 laymen alive, after which they confined the archbishop in a dungeon, where they kept him close prisoner for several months.

During his confinement they proposed to him to redeem his liberty with the sum of £3000, and to persuade the king to purchase their departure out of the kingdom, with a further sum of £10,000. As Alphage's circumstances would not allow him to satisfy the exorbitant demand, they bound him, and put him to severe torments, to oblige him to discover the treasure of the church; upon which they assured him of his life and liberty, but the prelate piously persisted in refusing to give the pagans any account of it. They remanded him to prison again, confined him six days longer, and then, taking him prisoner with them to Greenwich, brought him to trial there. He still remained inflexible with respect to the church treasure; but exhorted them to forsake their idolatry, and embrace Christianity. This so greatly incensed the Danes, that the soldiers dragged him out of the camp and beat him unmercifully. One of the soldiers, who had been converted by him, knowing that his pains would be lingering, as his death was determined on, actuated by a kind of barbarous compassion, cut off his head, and thus put the finishing stroke to his martyrdom, April 19, A. D. 1012. This transaction happened on the very spot where the church at Greenwich, which is dedicated to him, now stands. After his death his body was thrown into the Thames, but being found the next day, it was buried in the cathedral of St. Paul's by the bishops of London and Lincoln; from whence it was, in 1023, removed to Canterbury by Ethelmoth, the archbishop of that province.

Gerard, a Venetian, devoted himself to the service of God from his tender years: entered into a religious house for some time, and then determined to visit the Holy Land. Going into Hungary, he became acquainted with Stephen, the king of that country, who made him bishop of Chonad.

Ouvo and Peter, successors of Stephen, being deposed, Andrew, son of Ladislaus, cousin-german to Stephen, had then a tender of the crown made him upon condition that he would employ his authority in extirpating the Christian religion out of Hungary. The ambitious prince came into the proposal, but Gerard being informed of his impious bargain, thought it his duty to remonstrate against the enormity of Andrew's crime, and persuade him to withdraw his promise. In this view he undertook to go to that prince, attended by three prelates, full of like zeal for religion. The new king was at Alba Regalis, but, as the four bishops were going to cross the Danube, they were stopped by a party of soldiers posted there. They bore an attack of a shower of stones patiently, when the soldiers beat them unmercifully, and at length despatched them with lances. Their martyrdoms happened in the year 1045.

Stanislaus, bishop of Cracow, was descended from an illustrious Polish family. The piety of his parents was equal to their opulence, and the latter they rendered subservient to all the purposes of charity and benevolence. Stanislaus remained for some time undetermined whether he should embrace a monastic life, or engage among the secular clergy. He was at length persuaded to the latter by Lambert Zula, bishop of Cracow, who gave him holy orders, and made him a canon of his cathedral. Lambert died on November 25, 1071, when all concerned in the choice of a successor declared for Stanislaus, and he succeeded to the prelacy.

Bolislaus, the second king of Poland, had, by nature, many good qualities, but giving away to his passions, he ran into many enormities, and at length had the appellation of Cruel bestowed upon him. Stanislaus alone had the courage to tell him of his faults, when, taking a private opportunity, he freely displayed to him the enormities of his crimes. The king, greatly exasperated at his repeated freedoms, at length determined, at any rate, to get the better of a prelate who was so extremely faithful. Hearing one day that the bishop was by himself, in the chapel of St. Michael, at a small distance from the town, he despatched some soldiers to murder him. The soldiers readily undertook the bloody task; but, when they came into the presence of Stanislaus, the venerable aspect of the prelate struck them with such awe that they could not perform what they had promised. On their return, the king, finding that they had not obeyed his orders, stormed at them violently, snatched a dagger from one of them, and ran furiously to the chapel, where, finding Stanislaus at the altar, he plunged the weapon into his heart. The prelate immediately expired on May 8, A. D. 1079.

CHAPTER IV

Papal Persecutions

Thus far our history of persecution has been confined principally to the pagan world. We come now to a period when persecution, under the guise of Christianity, committed more enormities than ever disgraced the annals of paganism. Disregarding the maxims and the spirit of the Gospel, the papal Church, arming herself with the power of the sword, vexed the Church of God and wasted it for several centuries, a period most appropriately termed in history, the "dark ages." The kings of the earth, gave their power to the "Beast," and submitted to be trodden on by the miserable vermin that often filled the papal chair, as in the case of Henry, emperor of Germany. The storm of papal persecution first burst upon the Waldenses in France.

Persecution of the Waldenses in France

Popery having brought various innovations into the Church, and overspread the Christian world with darkness and superstition, some few, who plainly perceived the pernicious tendency of such errors, determined to show the light of the Gospel in its real purity, and to disperse those clouds which artful priests had raised about it, in order to blind the people, and obscure its real brightness.

The principal among these was Berengarius, who, about the year 1000, boldly preached Gospel truths, according to their primitive purity. Many, from conviction, assented to his doctrine, and were, on that account, called Berengarians. To Berengarius succeeded

Peter Bruis, who preached at Toulouse, under the protection of an earl, named Hildephonsus; and the whole tenets of the reformers, with the reasons of their separation from the Church of Rome, were published in a book written by Bruis, under the title of ANTICHRIST.

By the year of Christ 1140, the number of the reformed was very great, and the probability of its increasing alarmed the pope, who wrote to several princes to banish them from their dominions, and employed many learned men to write against their doctrines.

In A. D. 1147, because of Henry of Toulouse, deemed their most eminent preacher, they were called Henericians; and as they would not admit of any proofs relative to religion, but what could be deduced from the Scriptures themselves, the popish party gave them the name of apostolics. At length, Peter Waldo, or Valdo, a native of Lyons, eminent for his piety and learning, became a strenuous opposer of popery; and from him the reformed, at that time, received the appellation of Waldenses or Waldoys.

Pope Alexander III being informed by the bishop of Lyons of these transactions, excommunicated Waldo and his adherents, and commanded the bishop to exterminate them, if possible, from the face of the earth; hence began the papal persecutions against the Waldenses.

The proceedings of Waldo and the reformed, occasioned the first rise of the inquisitors; for Pope Innocent III authorized certain monks as inquisitors, to inquire for, and deliver over, the reformed to the secular power. The process was short, as an accusation was deemed adequate to guilt, and a candid trial was never granted to the accused.

The pope, finding that these cruel means had not the intended effect, sent several learned monks to preach among the Waldenses, and to endeavor to argue them out of their opinions. Among these monks was one Dominic, who appeared extremely zealous in the cause of popery. This Dominic instituted an order, which, from him, was called the order of Dominican friars; and the members of this order have ever since been the principal inquisitors in the various inquisitions in the world. The power of the inquisitors was unlimited; they proceeded against whom they pleased, without any consideration of age, sex, or rank. Let the accusers be ever so infamous, the accusation was deemed valid; and even anonymous informations, sent by letter, were thought sufficient evidence. To be rich was a crime equal to heresy; therefore many who had money were accused of heresy, or of being favorers of heretics, that they might be obliged to pay for their opinions. The dearest friends or nearest kindred could not, without danger, serve any one who was imprisoned on account of religion. To convey to those who were confined, a little straw, or give them a cup of water, was called favoring of the heretics, and they were prosecuted accordingly. No lawyer dared to plead for his own brother, and their malice even extended beyond the grave; hence the bones of many were dug up and burnt, as examples to the living. If a man on his deathbed was accused of being a follower of Waldo, his estates were confiscated, and the heir to them defrauded of his inheritance; and some were sent to the Holy Land, while the Dominicans took possession of their houses and properties, and, when the owners returned, would often pretend not to know them. These persecutions were continued for several centuries under different popes and other great dignitaries of the Catholic Church.

Persecutions of the Albigenses

The Albigenses were a people of the reformed religion, who inhabited the country of Albi. They were condemned on the score of religion in the Council of Lateran, by order of Pope Alexander III. Nevertheless, they increased so prodigiously, that many cities were inhabited by persons only of their persuasion, and several eminent noblemen embraced their doctrines. Among the latter were Raymond, earl of Toulouse, Raymond, earl of Foix, the earl of Beziers, etc.

A friar, named Peter, having been murdered in the dominions of the earl of Toulouse, the pope made the murder a pretense to persecute that nobleman and his subjects. To effect this, he sent persons throughout all Europe, in order to raise forces to act coercively against the Albigenses, and promised paradise to all that would come to this war, which he termed a Holy War, and bear arms for forty days. The same indulgences were likewise held out to all who entered themselves for the purpose as to such as engaged in crusades to the Holy Land. The brave earl defended Toulouse and other places with the most heroic bravery and various success against the pope's legates and Simon, earl of Montfort, a bigoted Catholic nobleman. Unable to subdue the earl of Toulouse openly, the king of France, and the queen mother, and three archbishops raised another formidable army, and had the art to persuade the earl of Toulouse to come to a conference, when he was treacherously seized upon, made a prisoner, forced to appear barefooted and bareheaded before his enemies, and compelled to subscribe an abject recantation. This was followed by a severe persecution against the Albigenses; and express orders that the laity should not be permitted to read the sacred Scriptures. In the year 1620 also, the persecution against the Albigenses was very severe. In 1648 a heavy persecution raged throughout Lithuania and Poland. The cruelty of the Cossacks was so excessive that the Tartars themselves were ashamed of their barbarities. Among others who suffered was the Rev. Adrian Chalinski, who was roasted alive by a slow fire, and whose sufferings and mode of death may depict the horrors which the professors of Christianity have endured from the enemies of the Redeemer.

The reformation of papistical error very early was projected in France; for in the third century a learned man, named Almericus, and six of his disciples, were ordered to be burnt at Paris for asserting that God was no otherwise present in the sacramental bread than in any other bread; that it was idolatry to build altars or shrines to saints and that it was ridiculous to offer incense to them.

The martyrdom of Almericus and his pupils did not, however, prevent many from acknowledging the justness of his notions, and seeing the purity of the reformed religion, so that the faith of Christ continually increased, and in time not only spread itself over many parts of France, but diffused the light of the Gospel over various other countries.

In the year 1524, at a town in France, called Melden, one John Clark set up a bill on the church door, wherein he called the pope Antichrist. For this offence he was repeatedly whipped, and then branded on the forehead. Going afterward to Mentz, in Lorraine, he demolished some images, for which he had his right hand and nose cut off, and his arms and breast torn with pincers. He sustained these cruelties with amazing fortitude, and was even sufficiently cool to sing the One hundredth and fifteenth Psalm, which expressly forbids idolatry; after which he was thrown into the fire, and burnt to ashes.

Many persons of the reformed persuasion were, about this time, beaten, racked, scourged, and burnt to death, in several parts of France, but more particularly at Paris, Malda, and Limosin.

A native of Malda was burnt by a slow fire, for saying that Mass was a plain denial of the death and passion of Christ. At Limosin, John de Cadurco, a clergyman of the reformed religion, was apprehended and ordered to be burnt.

Francis Bribard, secretary to cardinal de Pellay, for speaking in favor of the reformed, had his tongue cut out, and was then burnt, A. D. 1545. James Cobard, a schoolmaster in the city of St. Michael, was burnt, A. D. 1545, for saying 'That Mass was useless and absurd'; and about the same time, fourteen men were burnt at Malda, their wives being compelled to stand by and behold the execution.

A. D. 1546, Peter Chapot brought a number of Bibles in the French tongue to France, and publicly sold them there; for which he was brought to trial, sentenced, and executed a few days afterward. Soon after, a cripple of Meaux, a schoolmaster of Fera, named Stephen Poliot, and a man named John English, were burnt for the faith.

Monsieur Blondel, a rich jeweler, was, in A. D. 1548, apprehended at Lyons, and sent to Paris; there he was burnt for the faith by order of the court, A. D. 1549. Herbert, a youth of nineteen years of age, was committed to the flames at Dijon; as was also Florent Venote in the same year.

In the year 1554, two men of the reformed religion, with the son and daughter of one of them, were apprehended and committed to the castle of Niverne. On examination, they confessed their faith, and were ordered to execution; being smeared with grease, brimstone, and gunpowder, they cried, "Salt on, salt on this sinful and rotten flesh." Their tongues were then cut out, and they were afterward committed to the flames, which soon consumed them, by means of the combustible matter with which they were besmeared.

The Bartholomew Massacre at Paris, etc.

On the twenty second day of August, 1572, commenced this diabolical act of sanguinary brutality. It was intended to destroy at one stroke the root of the Protestant tree, which had only before partially suffered in its branches. The king of France had artfully proposed a marriage, between his sister and the prince of Navarre, the captain and prince of the Protestants. This imprudent marriage was publicly celebrated at Paris, August 18, by the cardinal of Bourbon, upon a high stage erected for the purpose. They dined in great pomp with the bishop, and supped with the king at Paris. Four days after this, the prince (Coligny), as he was coming from the Council, was shot in both arms; he then said to Maure, his deceased mother's minister, "O my brother, I do now perceive that I am indeed beloved of my God, since for His most holy sake I am wounded." Although the Vidam advised him to fly, yet he abode in Paris, and was soon after slain by Bemjus; who afterward declared he never saw a man meet death more valiantly than the admiral.

The soldiers were appointed at a certain signal to burst out instantly to the slaughter in all parts of the city. When they had killed the admiral, they threw him out at a window into the street, where his head was cut off, and sent to the pope. The savage papists, still raging against him, cut off his arms and private members, and, after dragging him three days through the streets, hung him by the heels without the city. After him they slew many great and honorable persons who were Protestants; as Count Rochfoucault, Telinius, the admiral's son-in-law, Antonius, Clarimontus, marquis of Ravely, Lewes Bussius, Bandineus, Pluvialius, Burneius, etc., and falling upon the common people, they continued the slaughter for many days; in the three first they slew of all ranks and conditions to the number of ten thousand. The bodies were thrown into the rivers, and blood ran through the streets with a strong current, and the river appeared presently like a stream of blood. So furious was their hellish rage, that they slew all papists whom they suspected to be not very staunch to their diabolical religion. From Paris the destruction spread to all quarters of the realm.

At Orleans, a thousand were slain of men, women, and children, and six thousand at Rouen.

At Meldith, two hundred were put into prison, and later brought out by units, and cruelly murdered.

At Lyons, eight hundred were massacred. Here children hanging about their parents, and parents affectionately embracing their children, were pleasant food for the swords and bloodthirsty minds of those who call themselves the Catholic Church. Here three hundred were slain in the bishop's house; and the impious monks would suffer none to be buried.

At Augustobona, on the people hearing of the massacre at Paris, they shut their gates that no Protestants might escape, and searching diligently for every individual of the reformed Church, imprisoned and then barbarously murdered them. The same cruelty they practiced at Avaricum, at Troys, at Toulouse, Rouen and many other places, running from city to city, towns, and villages, through the kingdom.

As a corroboration of this horrid carnage, the following interesting narrative, written by a sensible and learned Roman Catholic, appears in this place, with peculiar propriety.

"The nuptials (says he) of the young king of Navarre with the French king's sister, was solemnized with pomp; and all the endearments, all the assurances of friendship, all the oaths sacred among men, were profusely lavished by Catharine, the queen-mother, and by the king; during which, the rest of the court thought of nothing but festivities, plays, and masquerades. At last, at twelve o'clock at night, on the eve of St. Bartholomew, the signal was given. Immediately all the houses of the Protestants were forced open at once. Admiral Coligny, alarmed by the uproar jumped out of bed, when a company of assassins rushed in his chamber. They were headed by one Besme, who had been bred up as a domestic in the family of the Guises. This wretch thrust his sword into the admiral's breast, and also cut him in the face. Besme was a German, and being afterwards taken by the Protestants, the Rochellers would have brought him, in order to hang and quarter him; but he was killed by one Bretanville. Henry, the young duke of Guise, who afterwards framed the Catholic league, and was murdered at Blois, standing at the door until the horrid butchery should be completed, called aloud, 'Besme! is it done?' Immediately after this, the ruffians threw the body out of the window, and Coligny expired at Guise's feet.

"Count de Teligny also fell a sacrifice. He had married, about ten months before, Coligny's daughter. His countenance was so engaging, that the ruffians, when they advanced in order to kill him, were struck with compassion; but others, more barbarous, rushing forward, murdered him.

"In the meantime, all the friends of Coligny were assassinated throughout Paris; men, women, and children were promiscuously slaughtered and every street was strewed with expiring bodies. Some priests, holding up a crucifix in one hand, and a dagger in the other, ran to the chiefs of the murderers, and strongly exhorted them to spare neither relations nor friends.

"Tavannes, marshal of France, an ignorant, superstitious soldier, who joined the fury of religion to the rage of party, rode on horseback through the streets of Paris, crying to his men, 'Let blood! let blood! bleeding is as wholesome in August as in May.' In the memories of the life of this enthusiastic, written by his son, we are told that the father, being on his deathbed, and making a general confession of his actions, the priest said to him, with surprise, 'What! no mention of St. Bartholomew's massacre?' to which Tavannes replied, 'I consider it as a meritorious action, that will wash away all my sins.' Such horrid sentiments can a false spirit of religion inspire!

"The king's palace was one of the chief scenes of the butchery; the king of Navarre had his lodgings in the Louvre, and all his domestics were Protestants. Many of these were killed in bed with their wives; others, running away naked, were pursued by the soldiers through the several rooms of the palace, even to the king's antichamber. The young wife of Henry of Navarre, awaked by the dreadful uproar, being afraid for her consort, and for her own life, seized with horror, and half dead, flew from her bed, in order to throw herself at the feet of the king her brother. But scarce had she opened her chamber door, when some of her Protestant domestics rushed in for refuge. The soldiers immediately followed, pursued them in sight of the princess, and killed one who crept under her bed. Two others, being wounded with halberds, fell at the queen's feet, so that she was covered with blood.

"Count de la Rochefoucault, a young nobleman, greatly in the king's favor for his comely air, his politeness, and a certain peculiar happiness in the turn of his conversation, had spent the evening until eleven o'clock with the monarch, in pleasant familiarity; and had given a loose, with the utmost mirth, to the sallies of his imagination. The monarch felt some remorse, and being touched with a kind of compassion, bid him, two or three times, not to go home, but lie in the Louvre. The count said he must go to his wife; upon which the king pressed him no farther, but said, 'Let him go! I see God has decreed his death.' And in two hours after he was murdered.

"Very few of the Protestants escaped the fury of their enthusiastic persecutors. Among these was young La Force (afterwards the famous Marshal de la Force) a child about ten years of age, whose deliverance was exceedingly remarkable. His father, his elder brother, and he himself were seized together by the Duke of Anjou's soldiers. These murderers flew at all three, and struck them at random, when they all fell, and lay one upon another. The youngest did not receive a single blow, but appearing as if he was dead, escaped the next day; and his life, thus wonderfully preserved, lasted four score and five years.

"Many of the wretched victims fled to the water side, and some swam over the Seine to the suburbs of St. Germaine. The king saw them from his window, which looked upon the river, and fired upon them with a carbine that had been loaded for that purpose by one of his pages; while the queen-mother, undisturbed and serene in the midst of slaughter, looking down from a balcony, encouraged the murderers and laughed at the dying groans of the slaughtered. This barbarous queen was fired with a restless ambition, and she perpetually shifted her party in order to satiate it.

"Some days after this horrid transaction, the French court endeavored to palliate it by forms of law. They pretended to justify the massacre by a calumny, and accused the admiral of a conspiracy, which no one believed. The parliament was commended to proceed against the memory of Coligny; and his dead body was hanged in chains on Montfaucon gallows. The king himself went to view this shocking spectacle. So one of his courtiers advised him to retire, and complaining of the stench of the corpse, he replied, 'A dead enemy smells well.' The massacres on St. Bartholomew's day are painted in the royal saloon of the Vatican at Rome, with the following inscription: *Pontifex, Coligny necem probat, i. e.,* 'The pope approves of Coligny's death.'

"The young king of Navarre was spared through policy, rather than from the pity of the queen-mother, she keeping him prisoner until the king's death, in order that he might be as a security and pledge for the submission of such Protestants as might effect their escape.

"This horrid butchery was not confined merely to the city of Paris. The like orders were issued from court to the governors of all the provinces in France; so that, in a week's time, about one hundred thousand Protestants were cut to pieces in different parts of the kingdom! Two or three governors only refused to obey the king's orders. One of these, named Montmorrin, governor of Auvergne, wrote the king the following letter, which deserves to be transmitted to the latest posterity.

"Sire: I have received an order, under your majesty's seal, to put to death all the Protestants in my province. I have too much respect for your majesty, not to believe the letter a forgery; but if (which God forbid) the order should be genuine, I have too much respect for your majesty to obey it."

At Rome the horrid joy was so great, that they appointed a day of high festival, and a jubilee, with great indulgence to all who kept it and showed every expression of gladness they could devise! and the man who first carried the news received 1000 crowns of the cardinal of Lorraine for his ungodly message. The king also commanded the day to be kept with every demonstration of joy, concluding now that the whole race of Huguenots was extinct.

Many who gave great sums of money for their ransom were immediately after slain; and several towns, which were under the king's promise of protection and safety, were cut off as soon as they delivered themselves up, on those promises, to his generals or captains.

At Bordeaux, at the instigation of a villainous monk, who used to urge the papists to slaughter in his sermons, two hundred and sixty-four were cruelly murdered; some of them senators. Another of the same pious fraternity produced a similar slaughter at Agendicum, in Maine, where the populace at the holy inquisitors' satanical suggestion, ran upon the Protestants, slew them, plundered their houses, and pulled down their church.

The duke of Guise, entering into Blois, suffered his soldiers to fly upon the spoil, and slay or drown all the Protestants they could find. In this they spared neither age nor sex; defiling the women, and then murdering them; from whence he went to Mere, and committed the same outrages for many days together. Here they found a minister named Cassebonius, and threw him into the river.

At Anjou, they slew Albiacus, a minister; and many women were defiled and murdered there; among whom were two sisters, abused before their father, whom the assassins bound to a wall to see them, and then slew them and him.

The president of Turin, after giving a large sum for his life, was cruelly beaten with clubs, stripped of his clothes, and hung feet upwards, with his head and breast in the river: before he was dead, they opened his belly, plucked out his entrails, and threw them into the river; and then carried his heart about the city upon a spear.

At Barre great cruelty was used, even to young children, whom they cut open, pulled out their entrails, which through very rage they gnawed with their teeth. Those who had fled to the castle, when they yielded, were almost hanged. Thus they did at the city of Matiscon; counting it sport to cut off their arms and legs and afterward kill them; and for the entertainment of their visitors, they often threw the Protestants from a high bridge into the river, saying, "Did you ever see men leap so well?"

At Penna, after promising them safety, three hundred were inhumanly butchered; and five and forty at Albia, on the Lord's Day. At Nonne, though it yielded on conditions of safeguard, the most horrid spectacles were exhibited. Persons of both sexes and conditions were indiscriminately murdered; the streets ringing with doleful cries, and flowing with blood; and the houses flaming with fire, which the abandoned soldiers had thrown in. One woman, being dragged from her hiding place with her husband, was first abused by the brutal soldiers, and then with a sword which they commanded her to draw, they forced it while in her hands into the bowels of her husband.

At Samarobridge, they murdered above one hundred Protestants, after promising them peace; and at Antisidor, one hundred were killed, and cast part into a jakes, and part into a river. One hundred put into a prison at Orleans, were destroyed by the furious multitude.

The Protestants at Rochelle, who were such as had miraculously escaped the rage of hell, and fled there, seeing how ill they fared who submitted to those holy devils, stood for their lives; and some other cities, encouraged thereby, did the like. Against Rochelle, the king sent almost the whole power of France, which besieged it seven months; though by their assaults, they did very little execution on the inhabitants, yet by famine, they destroyed eighteen thousand out of two and twenty. The dead, being too numerous for the living to bury, became food for vermin and carnivorous birds. Many took their coffins into the church yard, laid down in them, and breathed their last. Their diet had long been what the minds of those in plenty shudder at; even human flesh, entrails, dung, and the most loathsome things, became at last the only food of those champions for that truth and liberty, of which the world was not worthy. At every attack, the besiegers met with such an intrepid reception, that they left one hundred and thirty-two captains, with a proportionate number of men, dead in the field. The siege at last was broken up at the request of the duke of Anjou, the king's brother, who was proclaimed king of Poland, and the king, being wearied out, easily complied, whereupon honorable conditions were granted them.

It is a remarkable interference of Providence, that, in all this dreadful massacre, not more than two ministers of the Gospel were involved in it.

The tragical sufferings of the Protestants are too numerous to detail; but the treatment of Philip de Deux will give an idea of the rest. After the miscreants had slain this martyr in his bed, they went to his wife, who was then attended by the midwife, expecting every moment to be delivered. The midwife entreated them to stay the murder, at least till the child, which was the twentieth, should be born. Notwithstanding this, they thrust a dagger up to the hilt into the poor woman. Anxious to be delivered, she ran into a corn loft; but hither they pursued her, stabbed her in the belly, and then threw her into the street. By the fall, the child came from the dying mother, and being caught up by one of the Catholic ruffians, he stabbed the infant, and then threw it into the river.

From the Revocation of the Edict of Nantes, to the French Revolution, in 1789

The persecutions occasioned by the revocation of the edict of Nantes took place under Louis XIV. This edict was made by Henry the Great of France in 1598, and secured to the Protestants an equal right in every respect, whether civil or religious, with the other subjects of the realm. All those privileges Louis the XIV confirmed to the Protestants by another statute, called the edict of Nismes, and kept them inviolably to the end of his reign.

On the accession of Louis XIV the kingdom was almost ruined by civil wars. At this critical juncture, the Protestants, heedless of our Lord's admonition. "They that take the sword shall perish with the sword," took such an active part in favor of the king, that he was constrained to acknowledge himself indebted to their arms for his establishment on the throne. Instead of cherishing and rewarding tnat party who had fought for him, he reasoned that the same power which had protected could overturn him, and, listening to the popish machinations, he began to issue out proscriptions and restrictions, indicative of his final determination. Rochelle was presently fettered with an incredible number of denunciations. Montauban and Millau were sacked by soldiers. Popish commissioners were appointed to preside over the affairs of the Protestants, and there was no appeal from their ordinance, except to the king's council. This struck at the root of their civil and religious exercises, and prevented them, being Protestants, from suing a Catholic in any court of law. This was followed by another injunction, to make an inquiry in all parishes into whatever the Protestants had said or done for twenty years past. This filled the prisons with innocent victims, and condemned others to the galleys or banishment.

Protestants were expelled from all offices, trades, privileges, and employs; thereby depriving them of the means of getting their bread: and they proceeded to such excess in this brutality, that they would not suffer even the midwives to officiate, but compelled their women to submit themselves in that crisis of nature to their enemies, the brutal Catholics. Their children were taken from them to be educated by the Catholics, and at seven years of age, made to embrace popery. The reformed were prohibited from relieving their own sick or poor, from all private worship, and divine service was to be performed in the presence of a popish priest. To prevent the unfortunate victims from leaving the kingdom, all the passages on the frontiers were strictly guarded; yet, by the good hand of God, about 150,000 escaped their vigilance, and emigrated to different countries to relate the dismal narrative.

All that has been related hitherto were only infringements on their established charter, the edict of Nantes. At length the diabolical revocation of that edict passed on the eighteenth of October, 1685, and was registered the twenty-second, contrary to all form of law. Instantly the dragoons were quartered upon the Protestants throughout the realm, and filled all France with the like news, that the king would no longer suffer any Huguenots in his kingdom, and therefore they must resolve to change their religion. Hereupon the intendants in every parish (which were popish governors and spies set over the Protestants) assembled the reformed inhabitants, and told them they must, without delay, turn Catholics, either freely or by force. The Protestants replied, that they 'were ready to sacrifice their lives and estates to the king, but their consciences being God's they could not so dispose of them.'

Instantly the troops seized the gates and avenues of the cities, and placing guards in all the passages, entered with sword in hand, crying, "Die, or be Catholics!" In short, they practiced every wickedness and horror they could devise to force them to change their religion.

They hanged both men and women by their hair or their feet, and smoked them with hay until they were nearly dead; and if they still refused to sign a recantation, they hung them up again and repeated their barbarities, until, wearied out with torments without death, they forced many to yield to them.

Others, they plucked off all the hair of their heads and beards with pincers. Others they threw on great fires, and pulled them out again, repeating it until they extorted a promise to recant.

Some they stripped naked, and after offering them the most infamous insults, they stuck them with pins from head to foot, and lanced them with penknives; and sometimes with red-hot pincers they dragged them by the nose until they promised to turn. Sometimes they tied fathers and husbands, while they ravished their wives and daughters before their eyes. Multitudes they imprisoned in the most noisome dungeons, where they practised all sorts of torments in secret. Their wives and children they shut up in monasteries.

Such as endeavored to escape by flight were pursued in the woods, and hunted in the fields, and shot at like wild beasts; nor did any condition or quality screen them from the ferocity of these infernal dragoons: even the members of parliament and military officers, though on actual service, were ordered to quit their posts, and repair directly to their houses to suffer the like storm. Such as complained to the king were sent to the Bastile, where they drank the same cup. The bishops and the intendants marched at the head of the dragoons, with a troop of missionaries, monks, and other ecclesiastics to animate the soldiers to an execution so agreeable to their Holy Church, and so glorious to their demon god and their tyrant king.

In forming the edict to repeal the edict of Nantes, the council were divided; some would have all the ministers detained and forced into popery as well as the laity: others were for banishing them, because their presence would strengthen the Protestants in perseverance: and if they were forced to turn, they would ever be secret and powerful enemies in the bosom of the Church, by their great knowledge and experience in controversial matters. This reason prevailing, they were sentenced to banishment, and only fifteen days allowed them to depart the kingdom.

On the same day that the edict for revoking the Protestants' charter was published, they demolished their churches and banished their ministers, whom they allowed but twenty-four hours to leave Paris. The papists would not suffer them to dispose of their effects, and threw every obstacle in their way to delay their escape until the limited time was expired which subjected them to condemnation for life to the galleys. The guards were doubled at the seaports, and the prisons were filled with the victims, who endured torments and wants at which human nature must shudder.

The sufferings of the ministers and others, who were sent to the galleys, seemed to exceed all. Chained to the oar, they were exposed to the open air night and day, at all seasons, and in all weathers; and when through weakness of body they fainted under the oar, instead of a cordial to revive them, or viands to refresh them, they received only the lashes of a scourge, or the blows of a cane or rope's end. For the want of sufficient clothing and necessary cleanliness, they were most grievously tormented with vermin, and cruelly pinched with the cold, which removed by night the executioners who beat and tormented them by day. Instead of a bed, they were allowed sick or well, only a hard board, eighteen inches broad, to sleep on, without any covering but their wretched apparel; which was a shirt of the coarsest canvas, a little jerkin of red serge, slit on each side up to the armholes, with open sleeves that reached not to the elbow; and once in three years they had a coarse frock, and a little cap to cover their heads, which were always kept close shaved as a mark of their infamy. The allowance of provision was as narrow as the sentiments of those who condemned them to such miseries, and their treatment when sick is too shocking to relate; doomed to die upon the boards of a dark hold, covered with vermin, and without the least convenience for the calls of nature. Nor was it among the least of the horrors they endured, that, as ministers of Christ, and honest men, they were chained side by side to felons and the most execrable villains, whose blasphemous tongues were never idle. If they refused to hear Mass, they were sentenced to the bastinado, of which dreadful punishment the following is a description. Preparatory to it, the chains are taken off, and the victims delivered into the hands of the Turks that preside at the oars, who strip them quite naked, and stretching them upon a great gun, they are held so that they cannot stir; during which there reigns an awful silence throughout the galley. The Turk who is appointed the executioner, and who thinks the sacrifice acceptable to his prophet Mahomet, most cruelly beats the wretched victim with a rough cudgel, or knotty rope's end, until the skin is flayed off his bones, and he is near the point of expiring; then they apply a most tormenting mixture of vinegar and salt, and consign him to that most intolerable hospital where thousands under their cruelties have expired.

Martyrdom of John Calas

We pass over many other individual martyrdoms to insert that of John Calas, which took place as recently as 1761, and is an indubitable proof of the bigotry of popery, and shows that neither experience nor improvement can root out the inveterate prejudices of the Roman Catholics, or render them less cruel or inexorable to Protestants.

John Calas was a merchant of the city of Toulouse, where he had been settled, and lived in good repute, and had married an English woman of French extraction. Calas and his wife were Protestants, and had five sons, whom they educated in the same religion; but Lewis, one of the sons, became a Roman Catholic, having been converted by a maidservant, who had lived in the family about thirty years. The father, however, did not express any resentment or ill-will upon the occasion, but kept the maid in the family and settled an annuity upon the son. In October, 1761, the family consisted of John Calas and his wife, one woman servant, Mark Antony Calas, the eldest son, and Peter Calas, the second son. Mark Antony was bred to the law, but could not be admitted to practice, on account of his being a Protestant; hence he grew melancholy, read all the books he could procure relative to suicide, and seemed determined to destroy himself. To this may be added that he led a dissipated life, was greatly addicted to gaming, and did all which could constitute the character of a libertine; on which account his father frequently reprehended him and sometimes in terms of severity, which considerably added to the gloom that seemed to oppress him.

On the thirteenth of October, 1761, Mr. Gober la Vaisse, a young gentleman about 19 years of age, the son of La Vaisse, a celebrated advocate of Toulouse, about five o'clock in the evening, was met by John Calas, the father, and the eldest son Mark Antony, who was his friend. Calas, the father, invited him to supper, and the family and their guest sat down in a room up one pair of stairs; the whole company, consisting of Calas the father, and his wife, Antony and Peter Calas, the sons, and La Vaisse the guest, no other person being in the house, except the maidservant who has been already mentioned.

It was now about seven o'clock. The supper was not long; but before it was over, Antony left the table, and went into the kitchen, which was on the same floor, as he was accustomed to do. The maid asked him if he was cold? He answered, "Quite the contrary, I burn"; and then left her. In the meantime his friend and family left the room they had supped in, and went into a bed-chamber; the father and La Vaisse sat down together on a sofa; the younger son Peter in an elbow chair; and the mother in another chair; and, without making any inquiry after Antony, continued in conversation together until between nine and ten o'clock, when La Vaisse took his leave, and Peter, who had fallen asleep, was awakened to attend him with a light.

On the ground floor of Calas's house was a shop and a warehouse, the latter of which was divided from the shop by a pair of folding doors. When Peter Calas and La Vaisse came downstairs into the shop, they were extremely shocked to see Antony hanging in his shirt, from a bar which he had laid across the top of the two folding doors, having half opened them for that purpose. On discovery of this horrid spectacle, they shrieked out, which brought down Calas the father, the mother being seized with such terror as kept her trembling in the passage above. When the maid discovered what had happened, she continued below, either because she feared to carry an account of it to her mistress, or because she busied herself in doing some good office to her master, who was embracing the body of his son, and bathing it in his tears. The mother, therefore, being thus left alone, went down and mixed in the scene that has been already described, with such emotions as it must naturally produce. In the meantime Peter had been sent for La Moire, a surgeon in the neighborhood. La Moire was not at home, but his apprentice, Mr. Grosle, came instantly. Upon examination, he found the body quite dead; and by this time a papistical crowd of people were gathered about the house, and, having by some means heard that Antony Calas was suddenly dead, and that the surgeon who had examined the body, declared that he had been strangled, they took it into their heads he had been murdered; and as the family was Protestant, they presently supposed that the young man was about to change his religion, and had been put to death for that reason.

The poor father, overwhelmed with grief for the loss of his child, was advised by his friends to send for the officers of justice to prevent his being torn to pieces by the Catholic multitude, who supposed he had murdered his son. This was accordingly done and David, the chief magistrate, or capitol, took the father, Peter the son, the mother, La Vaisse, and the maid, all into custody, and set a guard over them. He sent for M. de la Tour, a physician, and MM. la Marque and Per-ronet, surgeons, who examined the body for marks of violence, but found none except the mark of the ligature on the neck; they found also the hair of the deceased done up in the usual manner, perfectly smooth, and without the least disorder: his clothes were also regularly folded up, and laid upon the counter, nor was his shirt either torn or unbuttoned.

Notwithstanding these innocent appearances, the capitol thought proper to agree with the opinion of the mob, and took it into his head that old Calas had sent for La Vaisse, telling him that he had a son to be hanged; that La Vaisse had come to perform the office of executioner: and that he had received assistance from the father and brother.

As no proof of the supposed fact could be procured, the capitol had recourse to a monitory, or general information, in which the crime was taken for granted, and persons were required to give such testimony against it as they were able. This recites that La Vaisse was commissioned by the Protestants to be their executioner in ordinary, when any of their children were to be hanged for changing their religion: it recites also, that, when the Protestants thus hang their children, they compel them to kneel, and one of the interrogatories was, whether any person had seen Antony Calas kneel before his father when he strangled him: it recites likewise, that Antony died a Roman Catholic, and requires evidence of his catholicism.

But before this monitory was published, the mob had got a notion that Antony Calas was the next day to have entered into the fraternity of the White Penitents. The capitol therefore caused his body to be buried in the middle of St. Stephen's Church. A few days after the interment of the deceased, the White Penitents performed a solemn service for him in their chapel; the church was hung with white, and a tomb was raised in the middle of it, on the top of which was placed a human skeleton, holding in one hand a paper, on which was written, "Abjuration of heresy," and in the other a palm, the emblem of martyrdom. The next day the Franciscans performed a service of the same kind for him.

The capitol continued the persecution with unrelenting severity, and, without the least proof coming in, thought fit to condemn the unhappy father, mother, brother, friend, and servant, to the torture, and put them all into irons on the eighteenth of November.

From these dreadful proceedings the sufferers appealed to the parliament, which immediately took cognizance of the affair, and annulled the sentence of the capitol as irregular, but they continued the prosecution, and, upon the hangman deposing it was impossible Antony should hang himself as was pretended, the majority of the parliament were of the opinion, that the prisoners were guilty, and therefore ordered them to be tried by the criminal court of Toulouse. One voted him innocent, but after long debates the majority was for the torture and wheel, and probably condemned the father by way of experiment, whether he was guilty or not, hoping he would, in the agony, confess the crime, and accuse the other prisoners, whose fate, therefore, they suspended.

Poor Calas, however, an old man of sixty-eight, was condemned to this dreadful punishment alone. He suffered the torture with great constancy, and was led to execution in a frame of mind which excited the admiration of all that saw him, and particularly of the two Dominicans (Father Bourges and Father Coldagues) who attended him in his last moments, and declared that they thought him not only innocent of the crime laid to his charge, but also an exemplary instance of true Christian patience, fortitude. and charity. When he saw the executioner prepared to give him the last stroke, he made a fresh declaration to Father Bourges, but while the words were still in his mouth, the capitol, the author of this catastrophe, who came upon the scaffold merely to gratify his desire of being a witness of his punishment and death, ran up to him, and bawled out, "Wretch, there are the fagots which are to reduce your body to ashes! speak the truth." M. Calas made no reply, but turned his head a little aside; and that moment the executioner did his office.

The popular outcry against this family was so violent in Languedoc, that every body expected to see the children of Calas broke upon the wheel, and the mother burnt alive.

Young Donat Calas was advised to fly into Switzerland: he went, and found a gentleman who, at first, could only pity and relieve him, without daring to judge of the rigor exercised against the father, mother, and brothers. Soon after, one of the brothers, who was only banished, likewise threw himself into the arms of the same person, who, for more than a month, took every possible precaution to be assured of the innocence of the family. Once convinced, he thought himself obliged, in conscience, to employ his friends, his purse, his pen, and his credit, to repair the fatal mistake of the seven judges of Toulouse, and to have the proceedings revised by the king's council. This revision lasted three years, and it is well known what honor Messrs. de Grosne and Bacquancourt acquired by investigating this memorable cause. Fifty masters of the Court of Requests unanimously declared the whole family of Calas innocent, and recommended them to the benevolent justice of his majesty. The Duke de Choiseul, who never let slip an opportunity of signalizing the greatness of his character, not only assisted this unfortunate family with money, but obtained for them a gratuity of 36,000 livres from the king.

On the ninth of March, 1765, the arret was signed which justified the family of Calas, and changed their fate. The ninth of March, 1762, was the very day on which the innocent and virtuous father of that family had been executed. All Paris ran in crowds to see them come out of prison, and clapped their hands for joy, while the tears streamed from their eyes.

This dreadful example of bigotry employed the pen of Voltaire in deprecation of the horrors of superstition; and though an infidel himself, his essay on toleration does honor to his pen, and has been a blessed means of abating the rigor of persecution in most European states. Gospel purity will equally shun superstition and cruelty, as the mildness of Christ's tenets teaches only to comfort in this world, and to procure salvation in the next. To persecute for being of a different opinion is as absurd as to persecute for having a different countenance: if we honor God, keep sacred the pure doctrines of Christ, put a full confidence in the promises contained in the Holy Scriptures, and obey the political laws of the state in which we reside, we have an undoubted right to protection instead of persecution, and to serve heaven as our consciences, regulated by the Gospel rules, may direct.

CHAPTER V

An Account of the Inquisition

WHEN the reformed religion began to diffuse the Gospel light throughout Europe, Pope Innocent III entertained great fear for the Romish Church. He accordingly instituted a number of inquisitors, or persons who were to make inquiry after, apprehend, and punish, heretics, as the reformed were called by the papists.

At the head of these inquisitors was one Dominic, who had been canonized by the pope, in order to render his authority the more respectable. Dominic, and the other inquisitors, spread themselves into various Roman Catholic countries, and treated the Protestants with the utmost severity. In process of time, the pope, not finding these roving inquisitors so useful as he had imagined, resolved upon the establishment of fixed and regular courts of Inquisition. After the order for these regular courts, the first office of Inquisition was established in the city of Toulouse, and Dominic became the first regular inquisitor, as he had before been the first roving inquisitor.

Courts of Inquisition were now erected in several countries; but the Spanish Inquisition became the most powerful, and the most dreaded of any. Even the kings of Spain themselves, though arbitrary in all other respects, were taught to dread the power of the lords of the Inquisition; and the horrid cruelties they exercised compelled multitudes, who differed in opinion from the Roman Catholics, carefully to conceal their sentiments.

The most zealous of all the popish monks, and those who most implicitly obeyed the Church of Rome, were the Dominicans and Franciscans: these, therefore, the pope thought proper to invest with an exclusive right of presiding over the different courts of Inquisition, and gave them the most unlimited powers, as judges delegated by him, and immediately representing his person: they were permitted to excommunicate, or sentence to death whom they thought proper, upon the most slight information of heresy. They were allowed to publish crusades against all whom they deemed heretics, and enter into leagues with sovereign princes, to join their crusades with their forces.

In 1244, their power was further increased by the emperor Frederic II, who declared himself the protector and friend of all the inquisitors, and published the cruel edicts, viz., 1. That all heretics who continued obstinate, should be burnt. 2. That all heretics who repented, should be imprisoned for life.

This zeal in the emperor, for the inquisitors of the Roman Catholic persuasion, arose from a report which had been propagated throughout Europe, that he intended to renounce Christianity, and turn Mahometan; the emperor therefore, attempted, by the height of bigotry, to contradict the report, and to show his attachment to popery by cruelty.

The officers of the Inquisition are three inquisitors, or judges, a fiscal proctor, two secretaries, a magistrate, a messenger, a receiver, a jailer, an agent of confiscated possessions; several assessors, counsellors, executioners, physicians, surgeons, doorkeepers, familiars, and visitors, who are sworn to secrecy.

The principal accusation against those who are subject to this tribunal is heresy, which comprises all that is spoken, or written, against any of the articles of the creed, or the traditions of the Roman Church. The inquisition likewise takes cognizance of such as are accused of being magicians, and of such who read the Bible in the common language, the Talmud of the Jews, or the Alcoran of the Mahometans.

Upon all occasions the inquisitors carry on their processes with the utmost severity, and punish those who offend them with the most unparalleled cruelty. A Protestant has seldom any mercy shown him, and a Jew, who turns Christian, is far from being secure.

A defence in the Inquisition is of little use to the prisoner, for a suspicion only is deemed sufficient cause of condemnation, and the greater his wealth the greater his danger. The principal part of the inquisitors' cruelties is owing to their rapacity: they destroy the life to possess the property; and, under the pretence of zeal, plunder each obnoxious individual.

A prisoner in the Inquisition is never allowed to see the face of his accuser, or of the witnesses against him, but every method is taken by threats and tortures, to oblige him to accuse himself, and by that means corroborate their evidence. If the jurisdiction of the Inquisition is not fully allowed, vengeance is denounced against such as call it in question for if any of its officers are opposed, those who oppose them are almost certain to be sufferers for the temerity; the maxim of the Inquisition being to strike terror, and awe those who are the objects of its power into obedience. High birth, distinguished rank, great dignity, or eminent employments, are no protection from its severities; and the lowest officers of the Inquisition can make the highest characters tremble.

When the person impeached is condemned, he is either severely whipped, violently tortured, sent to the galleys, or sentenced to death;

and in either case the effects are confiscated. After judgment, a procession is performed to the place of execution, which ceremony is called an *auto da fé,* or act of faith.

The following is an account of an *auto da fé,* performed at Madrid in the year 1682.

The officers of the Inquisition, preceded by trumpets, kettledrums, and their banner, marched on the thirtieth of May, in cavalcade, to the palace of the great square, where they declared by proclamation, that, on the thirtieth of June, the sentence of the prisoners would be put in execution.

Of these prisoners, twenty men and women, with one renegade Mahometan, were ordered to be burned; fifty Jews and Jewesses, having never before been imprisoned, and repenting of their crimes, were sentenced to a long confinement, and to wear a yellow cap. The whole court of Spain was present on this occasion. The grand inquisitor's chair was placed in a sort of tribunal far above that of the king.

Among those who were to suffer, was a young Jewess of exquisite beauty, and but seventeen years of age. Being on the same side of the scaffold where the queen was seated, she addressed her, in hopes of obtaining a pardon, in the following pathetic speech: "Great queen, will not your royal presence be of some service to me in my miserable condition? Have regard to my youth; and, oh! consider, that I am about to die for professing a religion imbibed from my earliest infancy!" Her majesty seemed greatly to pity her distress, but turned away her eyes, as she did not dare to speak a word in behalf of a person who had been declared a heretic.

Now Mass began, in the midst of which the priest came from the altar, placed himself near the scaffold, and seated himself in a chair prepared for that purpose.

The chief inquisitor then descended from the amphitheater, dressed in his cope, and having a miter on his head. After having bowed to the altar, he advanced towards the king's balcony, and went up to it, attended by some of his officers, carrying a cross and the Gospels, with a book containing the oath by which the kings of Spain oblige themselves to protect the Catholic faith, to extirpate heretics, and to support with all their power and force the prosecutions and decrees of the Inquisition: a like oath was administered to the counsellors and whole assembly. The Mass was begun about twelve at noon, and did not end until nine in the evening, being protracted by a proclamation of the sentences of the several criminals, which were already separately rehearsed aloud one after the other.

After this followed the burnings of the twenty-one men and women, whose intrepidity in suffering that horrid death was truly astonishing. The king's near situation to the criminals rendered their dying groans very audible to him; he could not, however, be absent from this dreadful scene, as it is esteemed a religious one; and his coronation oath obliged him to give a sanction by his presence to all the acts of the tribunal.

What we have already said may be applied to inquisitions in general, as well as to that of Spain in particular. The Inquisition belonging to Portugal is exactly upon a similar plan to that of Spain, having been instituted much about the same time, and put under the same regulations. The inquisitors allow the torture to be used only three times, but during those times it is so severely inflicted, that the prisoner either dies under it, or continues always after a cripple, and suffers the severest pains upon every change of weather. We shall give an ample description of the severe torments occasioned by the torture, from the account of one who suffered it the three respective times, but happily survived the cruelties he underwent.

At the first time of torturing, six executioners entered, stripped him naked to his drawers, and laid him upon his back on a kind of stand, elevated a few feet from the floor. The operation commenced by putting an iron collar round his neck, and a ring to each foot, which fastened him to the stand. His limbs being thus stretched out, they wound two ropes round each thigh; which ropes being passed under the scaffold, through holes made for that purpose, were all drawn tight at the same instant of time, by four of the men, on a given signal.

It is easy to conceive that the pains which immediately succeeded were intolerable; the ropes, which were of a small size, cut through the prisoner's flesh to the bone, making the blood to gush out at eight different places thus bound at a time. As the prisoner persisted in not making any confession of what the inquisitors required, the ropes were drawn in this manner four times successively.

The manner of inflicting the second torture was as follows: they forced his arms backwards so that the palms of his hands were turned outward behind him; when, by means of a rope that fastened them together at the wrists, and which was turned by an engine, they drew them by degrees nearer each other, in such a manner that the back of each hand touched, and stood exactly parallel to each other. In consequence of this violent contortion, both his shoulders became dislocated, and a considerable quantity of blood issued from his mouth. This torture was repeated thrice; after which he was again taken to the dungeon, and the surgeon set the dislocated bones.

Two months after the second torture, the prisoner being a little recovered, was again ordered to the torture room, and there, for the last time, made to undergo another kind of punishment, which was inflicted twice without any intermission. The executioners fastened a thick iron chain round his body, which crossing at the breast, terminated at the wrists. They then placed him with his back against a thick board, at each extremity whereof was a pulley, through which there ran a rope that caught the end of the chain at his wrists. The executioner then, stretching the end of his rope by means of a roller, placed at a distance behind him, pressed or bruised his stomach in proportion as the ends of the chains were drawn tighter. They tortured him in this manner to such a degree, that his wrists, as well as his shoulders, were quite dislocated. They were, however, soon set by the surgeons; but the barbarians, not yet satisfied with this species of cruelty, made him immediately undergo the like torture a second time, which he sustained (though, if possible, attended with keener pains,) with equal constancy and resolution. After this, he was again remanded to the dungeon, attended by the surgeon to dress his bruises and adjust the part dislocated, and here he continued until their *auto da fé,* or jail delivery, when he was discharged, crippled and diseased for life.

An Account of the Cruel Handling and Burning of Nicholas Burton, an English Merchant, in Spain

The fifth day of November, about the year of our Lord 1560, Mr. Nicholas Burton, citizen sometime of London, and merchant, dwelling in the parish of Little St. Bartholomew, peaceably and quietly, following his traffic in the trade of merchandise, and being in the city of Cadiz, in the party of Andalusia, in Spain, there came into his lodging a Judas, or, as they term them, a familiar of the fathers of Inquisition; who asking for the said Nicholas Burton, feigned that he had a letter to deliver into his own hands; by which means he spake with him immediately. And having no letter to deliver to him, then the said promoter, or familiar, at the motion of the devil his master, whose messenger he was, invented another lie, and said he would take lading for London in such ships as the said Nicholas Burton had freighted to lade, if he would let any; which was partly to know where he loaded his goods, that they might attach them, and chiefly to protract the time until the sergeant of the Inquisition might come and apprehend the body of the said Nicholas Burton; which they did incontinently.

He then well perceiving that they were not able to burden or charge him that he had written, spoken, or done any thing there in that country against the ecclesiastical or temporal laws of the same realm, boldly asked them what they had to lay to his charge that they did so arrest him, and bade them to declare the cause, and he would answer them. Notwithstanding they answered nothing, but commanded him with threatening words to hold his peace, and not speak one word to them.

And so they carried him to the filthy common prison of the town of Cadiz where he remained in irons fourteen days amongst thieves.

All which time he so instructed the poor prisoners in the Word of God, according to the good talent which God had given him in that behalf, and also in the Spanish tongue to utter the same, that in that short space he had well reclaimed several of those superstitious and ignorant Spaniards to embrace the Word of God, and to reject their popish traditions.

Which being known unto the officers of the Inquisition, they conveyed him laden with irons from thence to a city called Seville, into a more cruel and straiter prison called Triana, where the said fathers of the Inquisition proceeded against him secretly according to their accustomable cruel tyranny, that never after he could be suffered to write or speak to any of his nation: so that to this day it is unknown who was his accuser.

Afterward, the twentieth of December, they brought the said Nicholas Burton, with a great number of other prisoners, for professing the true Christian religion, into the city of Seville, to a place where the said inquisitors sat in judgment which they called *auto,* with a canvas coat, whereupon in divers parts was painted the figure of a huge devil, tormenting a soul in a flame of fire, and on his head a copping tank of the same work.

His tongue was forced out of his mouth with a cloven stick fastened upon it, that he should not utter his conscience and faith to the people, and so he was set with another Englishman of Southampton, and divers other condemned men for religion, as well Frenchmen as Spaniards, upon a scaffold over against the said Inquisition, where their sentences and judgments were read and pronounced against them.

And immediately after the said sentences given, they were carried from there to the place of execution without the city, where they most cruelly burned them, for whose constant faith, God is praised.

This Nicholas Burton by the way, and in the flames of fire, had so cheerful a countenance, embracing death with all patience and gladness, that the tormentors and enemies which stood by, said, that the devil had his soul before he came to the fire; and therefore they said his senses of feeling were past him.

It happened that after the arrest of Nicholas Burton aforesaid, immediately all the goods and merchandise which he brought with him into Spain by the way of traffic, were (according to their common usage) seized, and taken into the sequester; among which they also rolled up much that appertained to another English merchant, wherewith he was credited as factor. Whereof as soon as news was brought to the merchant as well of the imprisonment of his factor, as of the arrest made upon his goods, he sent his attorney into Spain, with authority from him to make claim to his goods, and to demand them; whose name was John Fronton, citizen of Bristol.

When his attorney was landed at Seville, and had shown all his letters and writings to the holy house, requiring them that such goods might be delivered into his possession, answer was made to him that he must sue by bill, and retain an advocate (but all was doubtless to delay him,) and they forsooth of courtesy assigned him one to frame his supplication for him, and other such bills of petition, as he had to exhibit into their holy court, demanding for each bill eight reals, albeit they stood him in no more stead than if he had put up none at all. And for the space of three or four months this fellow missed not twice a day attending every morning and afternoon at the inquisitors' palace, suing unto them upon his knees for his despatch, but especially to the bishop of Tarracon, who was at that very time chief of the Inquisition at Seville, that he of his absolute authority would command restitution to be made thereof; but the booty was so good and great that it was very hard to come by it again.

At length, after he had spent four whole months in suits and requests, and also to no purpose, he received this answer from them, that he must show better evidence, and bring more sufficient certificates out of England for proof of this matter, than those which he had already presented to the court. Whereupon the party forthwith posted to London, and with all speed returned to Seville again with more ample and large letters testimonial, and certificates, according to their requests, and exhibited them to the court.

Notwithstanding, the inquisitors still shifted him off, excusing themselves by lack of leisure, and for that they were occupied in more weighty affairs, and with such answers put him off, four months after.

At last, when the party had well nigh spent all his money, and therefore sued the more earnestly for his despatch, they referred the matter wholly to the bishop, of whom, when he repaired unto him, he made answer, 'That for himself, he knew what he had to do, howbeit he was but one man, and the determination appertained to the other commissioners as well as unto him;' and thus by posting and passing it from one to another, the party could obtain no end of his suit. Yet for his importunity's sake, they were resolved to despatch him: it was on this sort: one of the inquisitors, called Gasco, a man very well experienced in these practices, willed the party to resort unto him after dinner.

The fellow being glad to hear this news, and supposing that his goods should be restored unto him, and that he was called in for that purpose to talk with the other that was in prison to confer with him about their accounts, rather through a little misunderstanding, hearing the inquisitors cast out a word, that it should be needful for him to talk with the prisoner, and being thereupon more than half persuaded, that at length they meant good faith, did so, and repaired thither about the evening. Immediately upon his coming, the jailer was forthwith charged with him, to shut him up close in such a prison where they appointed him.

The party, hoping at the first that he had been called for about some other matter, and seeing himself, contrary to his expectation, cast into a dark dungeon, perceived at length that the world went with him far otherwise than he supposed it would have done.

But within two or three days after, he was brought into the court, where he began to demand his goods: and because it was a device that well served their turn without any more circumstance, they bid him say his *Ave Maria: Ave Maria gratia plena, Dominus tecum, benedicta tu in mulieribus, et benedictus fructus ventris tui Jesus Amen.*

The same was written word by word as he spake it, and without any more talk of claiming his goods, because it was needless, they commanded him to prison again, and entered an action against him as a heretic, forasmuch as he did not say his *Ave Maria* after the Romish fashion, but ended it very suspiciously, for he should have added moreover; *Sancia Maria mater Dei, ora pro nobis peccatoribus:* by abbreviating whereof, it was evident enough (said they) that he did not allow the mediation of saints.

Thus they picked a quarrel to detain him in prison a longer season, and afterward brought him forth upon their stage disguised after their manner; where sentence was given, that he should lose all the goods which he sued for, though they were not his own, and besides this, suffer a year's imprisonment.

Mark Brughes, an Englishman, master of an English ship called the Minion, was burned in a city in Portugal.

William Hoker, a young man about the age of sixteen years, being an Englishman, was stoned to death by certain young men in the city of Seville, for the same righteous cause.

Some Private Enormities of the Inquisition Laid Open, by a Very Singular Occurrence

When the crown of Spain was contested for in the beginning of the present century, by two princes, who equally pretended to the sovereignty, France espoused the cause of one competitor, and England of the other.

The duke of Berwick, a natural son of James II who abdicated England, commanded the Spanish and French forces, and defeated the English at the celebrated battle of Almanza. The army was then divided into two parts; the one consisting of Spaniards and French, headed by the duke of Berwick, advanced towards Catalonia; the other body, consisting of French troops only, commanded by the duke of Orleans, proceeded to the conquest of Arragon.

As the troops drew near to the city of Arragon, the magistrates came to offer the keys to the duke of Orleans; but he told them haughtily that they were rebels, and that he would not accept the keys, for he had orders to enter the city through a breach.

He accordingly made a breach in the walls with his cannon, and then entered the city through it, together with his whole army. When he had made every necessary regulation here, he departed to subdue other places, leaving a strong garrison at once to overawe and defend, under the command of his lieutenant-general M. de Legal. This gentleman, though brought up a Roman Catholic, was totally free from superstition; he united great talents with great bravery; and was the skilful officer, and accomplished gentleman.

The duke, before his departure, had ordered that heavy contributions should be levied upon the city in the following manner:

1. That the magistrates and principal inhabitants should pay a thousand crowns per month for the duke's table.

2. That every house should pay one pistole, which would monthly amount to 18,000 pistoles.

3. That every convent and monastery should pay a donative, proportionable to its riches and rents.

The two last contributions to be appropriated to the maintenance of the army.

The money levied upon the magistrates and principal inhabitants, and upon every house, was paid as soon as demanded; but when the persons applied to the heads of convents and monasteries, they found that the ecclesiastics were not so willing, as other people, to part with their cash.

Of the donatives to be raised by the clergy:

The College of Jesuits to pay   -   2000 pistoles.
                Carmelites,   -   -   1000
                Augustins,   -   -   1000
                Dominicans,   -   -   1000

M. de Legal sent to the Jesuits a peremptory order to pay the money immediately. The superior of the Jesuits returned for answer that for the clergy to pay money for the army was against all ecclesiastical immunities; and that he knew of no argument which could authorize such a procedure. M. de Legal then sent four companies of dragoons to quarter themselves in the college, with this sarcastic message, "To convince you of the necessity of paying the money, I have sent four substantial arguments to your college, drawn from the system of military logic; and, therefore, hope you will not need any further admonition to direct your conduct."

These proceedings greatly perplexed the Jesuits, who despatched an express to court to the king's confessor, who was of their order; but the dragoons were much more expeditious in plundering and doing mischief, than the courier in his journey: so that the Jesuits, seeing everything going to wreck and ruin, thought proper to adjust the matter amicably, and paid the money before the return of their messenger. The Augustins and Carmelites, taking warning by what had happened to the Jesuits, prudently went and paid the money, and by that means escaped the study of military arguments, and of being taught logic by dragoons.

But the Dominicans, who were all familiars of, or agents dependent on, the Inquisition, imagined that that very circumstance would be their protection; but they were mistaken, for M. de Legal neither feared nor respected the Inquisition. The chief of the Dominicans sent word to the military commander that his order was poor, and had not any money whatever to pay the donative; for, says he, "The whole wealth of the Dominicans consists only in the silver images of the apostles and saints, as large as life, which are placed in our church, and which it would be sacrilege to remove."

This insinuation was meant to terrify the French commander, whom the inquisitors imagined would not dare to be so profane as to wish for the possession of the precious idols.

He, however, sent word that the silver images would make admirable substitutes for money, and would be more in character in his possession, than in that of the Dominicans themselves, "For [said he] while you possess them in the manner you do at present, they stand up in niches, useless and motionless, without being of the least benefit to mankind in general, or even to yourselves; but, when they come into my possession, they shall be useful; I will put them in motion; for I intend to have them coined, when they may travel like the apostles, be beneficial in various places, and circulate for the universal service of mankind."

The inquisitors were astonished at this treatment, which they never expected to receive, even from crowned heads; they therefore determined to deliver their precious images in a solemn procession, that they might excite the people to an insurrection. The Dominican friars were accordingly ordered to march to de Legal's house, with the silver apostles and saints, in a mournful manner, having lighted tapers with them and bitterly crying all the way, "heresy, heresy."

M. de Legal, hearing these proceedings, ordered four companies of grenadiers to line the street which led to his house; each grenadier was ordered to have his loaded fuzee in one hand, and a lighted taper in the other; so that the troops might either repel force with force, or do honor to the farcical solemnity.

The friars did all they could to raise the tumult, but the common people were too much afraid of the troops under arms to obey them; the silver images were, therefore, of necessity delivered up to M. de Legal, who sent them to the mint, and ordered them to be coined immediately.

The project of raising an insurrection having failed, the inquisitors determined to excommunicate M. de Legal, unless he would release their precious silver saints from imprisonment in the mint, before they were melted down, or otherwise mutilated. The French commander absolutely refused to release the images, but said they should certainly travel and do good; upon which the inquisitors drew up the form of excommunication, and ordered their secretary to go and read it to M. de Legal.

The secretary punctually performed his commission, and read the excommunication deliberately and distinctly. The French commander heard it with great patience, and politely told the secretary that he would answer it the next day.

When the secretary of the Inquisition was gone, M. de Legal ordered his own secretary to prepare a form of excommunication, exactly like that sent by the Inquisition; but to make this alteration, instead of his name to put in those of the inquisitors.

The next morning he ordered four regiments under arms, and commanded them to accompany his secretary, and act as he directed.

The secretary went to the Inquisition, and insisted upon admittance, which, after a great deal of altercation, was granted. As soon as he entered, he read, in an audible voice, the excommunication sent by M. de Legal against the inquisitors. The inquisitors were all present, and heard it with astonishment, never having before met with any individual who dared to behave so boldly. They loudly cried out against de Legal, as a heretic; and said, "This was a most daring insult against the Catholic faith." But to surprise them still more, the French secretary told them that they must remove from their present lodgings; for the French commander wanted to quarter the troops in the Inquisition, as it was the most commodious place in the whole city.

The inquisitors exclaimed loudly upon this occasion, when the secretary put them under a strong guard, and sent them to a place appointed by M. de Legal to receive them. The inquisitors, finding how things went, begged that they might be permitted to take their private property, which was granted; and they immediately set out for Madrid, where they made the most bitter complaints to the king; but the monarch told them that he could not grant them any redress, as the injuries they had received were from his grandfather, the king of France's troops, by whose assistance alone he could be firmly established in his kingdom. "Had it been my own troops, [said he] I would have punished them; but as it is, I cannot pretend to exert any authority."

In the mean time, M. de Legal's secretary set open all the doors of the Inquisition, and released the prisoners, who amounted in the whole to four hundred; and among these were sixty beautiful young women, who appeared to form a seraglio for the three principal inquisitors.

This discovery, which laid the enormity of the inquisitors so open, greatly alarmed the archbishop, who desired M. de Legal to send the women to his palace, and he would take proper care of them; and at the same time he published an ecclesiastical censure against all such as should ridicule, or blame, the holy office of the Inquisition.

The French commander sent word to the archbishop, that the prisoners had either run away, or were so securely concealed by their friends, or even by his own officers, that it was impossible for him to send them back again; and, therefore, the Inquisition having committed such atrocious actions, must now put up with their exposure.

Some may suggest, that it is strange crowned heads and eminent nobles did not attempt to crush the power of the Inquisition, and reduce the authority of those ecclesiastical tyrants, from whose merciless fangs neither their families nor themselves were secure.

But astonishing as it is, superstition hath, in this case, always overcome common sense, and custom operated against reason. One prince, indeed, intended to abolish the Inquisition, but he lost his life before he became king, and consequently before he had the power so to do; for the very intimation of his design procured his destruction.

This was that amiable prince Don Carlos, son of Philip the Second, king of Spain, and grandson of the celebrated emperor Charles V. Don Carlos, possessed all the good qualities of his grandfather, without any of the bad ones of his father; and was a prince of great vivacity, admirable learning, and the most amiable disposition. He had sense enough to see into the errors of popery, and abhorred the very name of the Inquisition. He inveighed publicly against the institution, ridiculed the affected piety of the inquisitors, did all he could to expose their atrocious deeds, and even declared, that if he ever came to the crown, he would abolish the Inquisition, and exterminate its agents.

These things were sufficient to irritate the inquisitors against the prince: they, accordingly, bent their minds to vengeance, and determined on his destruction.

The inquisitors now employed all their agents and emissaries to spread abroad the most artful insinuations against the prince; and, at length raised such a spirit of discontent among the people that the king was under the necessity of removing Don Carlos from court. Not content with this, they pursued even his friends, and obliged the king likewise to banish Don John, duke of Austria, his own brother, and consequently uncle to the prince; together with the prince of Parma, nephew to the king, and cousin to the prince, because they well knew that both the duke of Austria, and the prince of Parma, had a most sincere and inviolable attachment to Don Carlos.

Some few years after, the prince having shown great lenity and favor to the Protestants in the Netherlands, the Inquisition loudly exclaimed against him, declaring, that as the persons in question were heretics, the prince himself must necessarily be one, since he gave them countenance. In short, they gained so great an ascendency over the mind of the king, who was absolutely a slave to superstition, that, shocking to relate, he sacrificed the feelings of nature to the force of bigotry, and, for fear of incurring the anger of the Inquisition, gave up his only son, passing the sentence of death on him himself.

The prince, indeed, had what was termed an indulgence; that is, he was permitted to choose the manner of his death. Roman-like, the unfortunate young hero chose bleeding and the hot bath; when the veins of his arms and legs were opened, he expired gradually, falling a martyr to the malice of the inquisitors, and the stupid bigotry of his father.

The Persecution of Dr. Ægidio

Dr. Ægidio was educated at the university of Alcala, where he took his several degrees, and particularly applied himself to the study of the sacred Scriptures and school divinity. When the professor of theology died, he was elected into his place, and acted so much to the satisfaction of every one that his reputation for learning and piety was circulated throughout Europe.

Ægidio, however, had his enemies, and these laid a complaint against him to the inquisitors, who sent him a citation, and when he appeared to it, cast him into a dungeon.

As the greatest part of those who belonged to the cathedral church at Seville, and many persons belonging to the bishopric of Dortois highly approved of the doctrines of Ægidio, which they thought perfectly consonant with true religion, they petitioned the emperor in his behalf. Though the monarch had been educated a Roman Catholic, he had too much sense to be a bigot, and therefore sent an immediate order for his enlargement.

He soon after visited the church of Valladolid, and did every thing he could to promote the cause of religion. Returning home he soon after fell sick, and died in an extreme old age.

The inquisitors having been disappointed of gratifying their malice against him while living, determined (as the emperor's whole thoughts were engrossed by a military expedition) to wreak their vengeance on him when dead. Therefore, soon after he was buried, they ordered his remains to be dug out of the grave; and a legal process being carried on, they were condemned to be burnt, which was executed accordingly.

The Persecution of Dr. Constantine

Dr. Constantine, an intimate acquaintance of the already mentioned Dr. Ægidio, was a man of uncommon natural abilities and profound learning; exclusive of several modern tongues, he was acquainted with the Latin, Greek, and Hebrew languages, and perfectly well knew not only the sciences called abstruse, but those arts which come under the denomination of polite literature.

His eloquence rendered him pleasing, and the soundness of his doctrines a profitable preacher; and he was so popular that he never preached but to a crowded audience. He had many opportunities of rising in the Church, but never would take advantage of them; for if a living of greater value than his own was offered him, he would refuse it, saying, "I am content with what I have"; and he frequently preached so forcibly against simony, that many of his superiors, who were not so delicate upon the subject, took umbrage at his doctrines upon that head.

Having been fully confirmed in Protestantism by Dr. Ægidio, he preached boldly such doctrines only as were agreeable to Gospel purity, and uncontaminated by the errors which had at various times crept into the Romish Church. For these reasons he had many enemies among the Roman Catholics, and some of them were fully determined on his destruction.

A worthy gentleman named Scobaria, having erected a school for divinity lectures, appointed Dr. Constantine to be reader therein. He immediately undertook the task, and read lectures, by portions, on the Proverbs, Ecclesiastes, and Canticles; and was beginning to expound the Book of Job, when he was seized by the inquisitors.

Being brought to examination, he answered with such precaution that they could not find any explicit charge against him, but remained doubtful in what manner to proceed, when the following circumstances occurred to determine them.

Dr. Constantine had deposited with a woman named Isabella Martin, several books, which to him were very valuable, but which he knew, in the eyes of the Inquisition, were exceptionable.

This woman having been informed against as a Protestant, was apprehended, and, after a small process, her goods were ordered to be confiscated. Previous, however, to the officers coming to her house, the woman's son had removed away several chests full of the most valuable articles; among these were Dr. Constantine's books.

A treacherous servant gave intelligence of this to the inquisitors, and an officer was despatched to the son to demand the chests. The son, supposing the officer only came for Constantine's books, said, "I know what you come for, and I will fetch them to you immediately." He then fetched Dr. Constantine's books and papers, when the officer was greatly surprised to find what he did not look for. He, however, told the young man that he was glad these books and papers were produced, but nevertheless he must fulfil the end of his commission, which was to carry him and the goods he had embezzled before the inquisitors, which he did accordingly; for the young man knew it would be in vain to expostulate, or resist, and therefore quietly submitted to his fate.

The inquisitors being thus possessed of Constantine's books and writings, now found matter sufficient to form charges against him. When he was brought to a re-examination, they presented one of his papers, and asked him if he knew the handwriting? Perceiving it was his own, he guessed the whole matter, confessed the writing, and justified the doctrine it contained: saying, "In that, and all my other writings, I have never departed from the truth of the Gospel, but have always kept in view the pure precepts of Christ, as He delivered them to mankind."

After being detained upwards of two years in prison, Dr. Constantine was seized with a bloody flux, which put an end to his miseries in this world. The process, however, was carried on against his body, which, at the ensuing *auto da fé,* was publicly burnt.

The Life of William Gardiner

William Gardiner was born at Bristol, received a tolerable education, and was, at a proper age, placed under the care of a merchant, named Paget.

At the age of twenty-six years, he was, by his master, sent to Lisbon, to act as factor. Here he applied himself to the study of the Portuguese language, executed his business with assiduity and despatch, and behaved with the most engaging affability to all persons with whom he had the least concern. He conversed privately with a few, whom he knew to be zealous Protestants; and, at the same time cautiously avoided giving the least offence to any who were Roman Catholics; he had not, however, hitherto gone into any of the popish churches.

A marriage being concluded between the king of Portugal's son, and the Infanta of Spain, upon the wedding-day the bridegroom, bride, and the whole court went to the cathedral church, attended by multitudes of all ranks of people, and among the rest William Gardiner, who stayed during the whole ceremony, and was greatly shocked at the superstitions he saw.

The erroneous worship which he had seen ran strongly in his mind; he was miserable to see a whole country sunk into such idolatry, when the truth of the Gospel might be so easily obtained. He, therefore, took the inconsiderate, though laudable design, into his head, of making a reform in Portugal, or perishing in the attempt; and determined to sacrifice his prudence to his zeal, though he became a martyr upon the occasion.

To this end, he settled all his worldly affairs, paid his debts, closed his books, and consigned over his merchandise. On the ensuing Sunday he went again to the cathedral church, with a New Testament in his hand, and placed himself near the altar.

The king and the court soon appeared, and a cardinal began Mass, at that part of the ceremony in which the people adore the wafer.

Gardiner could hold out no longer, but springing towards the cardinal, he snatched the host from him, and trampled it under his feet.

This action amazed the whole congregation, and one person, drawing a dagger, wounded Gardiner in the shoulder, and would, by repeating the blow, have finished him, had not the king called to him to desist.

Gardiner, being carried before the king, the monarch asked him what countryman he was: to which he replied, "I am an Englishman by birth, a Protestant by religion, and a merchant by occupation. What I have done is not out of contempt to your royal person, God forbid it should, but out of an honest indignation, to see the ridiculous superstitious and gross idolatries practiced here."

The king, thinking that he had been stimulated by some other person to act as he had done, demanded who was his abetter, to which he replied, "My own conscience alone. I would not hazard what I have done for any man living, but I owe that and all other services to God."

Gardiner was sent to prison, and a general order issued to apprehend all Englishmen in Lisbon. This order was in a great measure put into execution, (some few escaping) and many innocent persons were tortured to make them confess if they knew any thing of the matter; in particular, a person who resided in the same house with Gardiner was treated with unparalleled barbarity to make him confess something which might throw a light upon the affair.

Gardiner himself was then tormented in the most excruciating manner; but in the midst of all his torments he gloried in the deed. Being ordered for death, a large fire was kindled near a gibbet, Gardiner was drawn up to the gibbet by pulleys, and then let down near the fire, but not so close as to touch it; for they burnt or rather roasted him by slow degrees. Yet he bore his sufferings patiently and resigned his soul to the Lord cheerfully.

It is observable that some of the sparks that were blown from the fire, (which consumed Gardiner) towards the haven, burnt one of the king's ships of war, and did other considerable damage. The Englishmen who were taken up on this occasion were, soon after Gardiner's death, all discharged, except the person who resided in the same house with him, who was detained two years before he could procure his liberty.

An Account of the Life and Sufferings of Mr. William Lithgow, a Native of Scotland

This gentleman was descended from a good family, and having a natural propensity for travelling, he rambled, when very young, over the northern and western islands; after which he visited France, Germany, Switzerland, and Spain. He set out on his travels in the month of March, 1609, and the first place he went to was Paris, where he stayed for some time. He then prosecuted his travels through Germany and other parts, and at length arrived at Malaga, in Spain, the seat of all his misfortunes.

During his residence here, he contracted with the master of a French ship for his passage to Alexandria, but was prevented from going by the following circumstances. In the evening of the seventeenth of October, 1620, the English fleet, at that time on a cruise against the Algerine rovers, came to anchor before Malaga, which threw the people of the town into the greatest consternation, as they imagined them to be Turks. The morning, however, discovered the mistake, and the governor of Malaga, perceiving the cross of England in their colors, went on board Sir Robert Mansel's ship, who commanded on that expedition, and after staying some time returned, and silenced the fears of the people.

The next day many persons from on board the fleet came ashore. Among these were several well known by Mr. Lithgow, who, after reciprocal compliments, spent some days together in festivity and the amusements of the town. They then invited Mr. Lithgow to go on board, and pay his respects to the admiral. He accordingly accepted the invitation, was kindly received by him, and detained till the next day when the fleet sailed. The admiral would willingly have taken Mr. Lithgow with him to Algiers; but having contracted for his passage to Alexandria, and his baggage, etc., being in the town, he could not accept the offer.

As soon as Mr. Lithgow got on shore, he proceeded towards his lodgings by a private way, (being to embark the same night for Alexandria) when, in passing through a narrow uninhabited street, he found himself suddenly surrounded by nine sergeants, or officers, who threw a black cloak over him, and forcibly conducted him to the governor's house. After some little time the governor appeared when Mr. Lithgow earnestly begged he might be informed of the cause of such violent treatment. The governor only answered by shaking his head, and gave orders that the prisoner should be strictly watched until he (the governor) returned from his devotions; directing, at the same time, that the captain of the town, the alcade major, and town notary, should be summoned to appear at his examination, and that all this should be done with the greatest secrecy, to prevent the knowledge reaching the ears of the English merchants then residing in the town.

These orders were strictly discharged, and on the governor's return, he, with the officers, having seated themselves, Mr. Lithgow was brought before them for examination. The governor began by asking several questions, namely, of what country he was, whither bound, and how long he had been in Spain. The prisoner, after answering these and other questions, was conducted to a closet, where, in a short space of time, he was visited by the town captain, who inquired whether he had ever been at Seville, or was lately come from thence; and patting his cheeks with an air of friendship, conjured him to tell the truth, "For (said he) your very countenance shows there is some hidden matter in your mind, which prudence should direct you to disclose." Finding himself, however, unable to extort any thing from the prisoner, he left him, and reported the same to the governor and the other officers; on which Mr. Lithgow was again brought before them, a general accusation was laid against him, and he was compelled to swear that he would give true answers to such questions as should be asked him.

The governor proceeded to inquire the quality of the English commander, and the prisoner's opinion what were the motives that prevented his accepting an invitation from him to come on shore. He demanded, likewise, the names of the English captains in the squadron, and what knowledge he had of the embarkation, or preparation for it before his departure from England. The answers given to the several questions asked were set down in writing by the notary; but the junto seemed surprised at his denying any knowledge of the fitting out of the fleet, particularly the governor, who said he lied; that he was a traitor and a spy, and came directly from England to favor and assist the designs that were projected against Spain, and that he had been for that purpose nine months in Seville, in order to procure intelligence of the time the Spanish navy was expected from the Indies. They exclaimed against his familiarity with the officers of the fleet, and many other English gentlemen, between whom, they said, unusual civilities had passed, but all these transactions had been carefully noticed.

Besides to sum up the whole, and put the truth past all doubt, they said he came from a council of war, held that morning on board the admiral's ship, in order to put in execution the orders assigned him. They upbraided him with being accessory to the burning of the island of St. Thomas, in the West Indies. "Wherefore (said they) these Lutherans, and sons of the devil, ought to have no credit given to what they say or swear."

In vain did Mr. Lithgow, endeavor to obviate every accusation laid against him, and to obtain belief from his prejudiced judges. He begged permission to send for his cloak bag which contained his papers, and might serve to show his innocence. This request they complied with, thinking it would discover some things of which they were ignorant. The cloak bag was accordingly brought, and being opened, among other things, was found a license from King James the First, under the sign manual, setting forth the bearer's intention to travel into Egypt; which was treated by the haughty Spaniards with great contempt. The other papers consisted of passports, testimonials, etc., of persons of quality. All these credentials, however, seemed rather to confirm than abate the suspicions of these prejudiced judges, who, after seizing all the prisoner's papers, ordered him again to withdraw.

In the meantime a consultation was held to fix the place where the prisoner should be confined. The alcade, or chief judge, was for putting him into the town prison; but this was objected to, particularly by the corregidor, who said, in Spanish, "In order to prevent the knowledge of his confinement from reaching his countrymen, I will take the matter on myself, and be answerable for the consequences"; upon which it was agreed that he should be confined in the governor's house with the greatest secrecy.

This matter being determined, one of the sergeants went to Mr. Lithgow, and begged his money, with liberty to search him. As it was needless to make any resistance, the prisoner quietly complied, when the sergeant (after rifling his pockets of eleven ducatoons) stripped him to his shirt; and searching his breeches he found, inclosed in the waistband, two canvass bags, containing one hundred and thirty-seven pieces of gold. The sergeant immediately took the money to the corregidor, who, after having told it over, ordered him to clothe the prisoner, and shut him up close until after supper.

About midnight, the sergeant and two Turkish slaves released Mr. Lithgow from his then confinement, but it was to introduce him to one much more horrible. They conducted him through several passages, to a chamber in a remote part of the palace, towards the garden, where they loaded him with irons, and extended his legs by means of an iron bar above a yard long, the weight of which was so great that he could neither stand nor sit, but was obliged to lie continually on his back. They left him in this condition for some time, when they returned with a refreshment of food, consisting of a pound of boiled mutton and a loaf, together with a small quantity of wine; which was not only the first, but the best and last of the kind, during his confinement in this place. After delivering these articles, the sergeant locked the door, and left Mr. Lithgow to his own private contemplations.

The next day he received a visit from the governor, who promised him his liberty, with many other advantages, if he would confess being a spy; but on his protesting that he was entirely innocent, the governor left him in a rage, saying, 'He should see him no more until further torments constrained him to confess'; commanding the keeper, to whose care he was committed, that he should permit no person whatever to have access to, or commune with him; that his sustenance should not exceed three ounces of musty bread, and a pint of water every second day; that he shall be allowed neither bed, pillow, nor coverlid. "Close up (said he) this window in his room with lime and stone, stop up the holes of the door with double mats: let him have nothing that bears any likeness to comfort." These, and several orders of the like severity, were given to render it impossible for his condition to be known to those of the English nation.

In this wretched and melancholy state did poor Lithgow continue without seeing any person for several days, in which time the governor received an answer to a letter he had written, relative to the prisoner, from Madrid; and, pursuant to the instructions given him, began to put in practice the cruelties devised, which were hastened, because Christmas holy-days approached, it being then the forty-seventh day since his imprisonment.

About two o'clock in the morning, he heard the noise of a coach in the street, and sometime after heard the opening of the prison doors, not having had any sleep for two nights; hunger, pain, and melancholy reflections having prevented him from taking any repose.

Soon after the prison doors were opened, the nine sergeants, who had first seized him, entered the place where he lay, and without uttering a word, conducted him in his irons through the house into the street, where a coach waited, and into which they laid him at the bottom on his back, not being able to sit. Two of the sergeants rode with him, and the rest walked by the coach side, but all observed the most profound silence. They drove him to a vinepress house, about a league from the town, to which place a rack had been privately conveyed before; and here they shut him up for that night.

At daybreak the next morning, arrived the governor and the alcade, into whose presence Mr. Lithgow was immediately brought to undergo another examination. The prisoner desired he might have an interpreter, which was allowed to strangers by the laws of that country, but this was refused, nor would they permit him to appeal to Madrid, the superior court of judicature. After a long examination, which lasted from morning until night, there appeared in all his answers so exact a conformity with what he had before said, that they declared he had learned them by heart, there not being the least prevarication. They, however, pressed him again to make a full discovery; that is, to accuse himself of crimes never committed, the governor adding, "You are still in my power; I can set you free if you comply, if not, I must deliver you to the alcade." Mr. Lithgow still persisting in his innocence, the governor ordered the notary to draw up a warrant for delivering him to the alcade to be tortured.

In consequence of this he was conducted by the sergeants to the end of a stone gallery, where the rack was placed. The encarouador, or executioner, immediately struck off his irons, which put him to very great pains, the bolts being so closely riveted that the sledge hammer tore away half an inch of his heel, in forcing off the bolt; the anguish of which, together with his weak condition, (not having the least sustenance for three days) occasioned him to groan bitterly; upon which the merciless alcade said, "Villain, traitor, this is but the earnest of what you shall endure."

When his irons were off, he fell on his knees, uttering a short prayer, that God would be pleased to enable him to be steadfast, and undergo courageously the grievous trial he had to encounter. The alcade and notary having placed themselves in chairs, he was stripped naked, and fixed upon the rack, the office of these gentlemen being to be witness of, and set down the confessions and tortures endured by the delinquent.

It is impossible to describe all the various tortures inflicted upon him. Suffice it to say that he lay on the rack for above five hours, during which time he received above sixty different tortures of the most hellish nature; and had they continued them a few minutes longer, he must have inevitably perished.

These cruel persecutors being satisfied for the present, the prisoner was taken from the rack, and his irons being again put on, he was conducted to his former dungeon, having received no other nourishment than a little warm wine, which was given him rather to prevent his dying, and reserve him for future punishments, than from any principle of charity or compassion.

As a confirmation of this, orders were given for a coach to pass every morning before day by the prison, that the noise made by it might give fresh terrors and alarms to the unhappy prisoner, and deprive him of all possibility of obtaining the least repose.

He continued in this horrid situation, almost starved for want of the common necessaries to preserve his wretched existence, until Christmas day, when he received some relief from Mariane, waiting-woman to the governor's lady. This woman having obtained leave to visit him, carried with her some refreshments, consisting of honey, sugar, raisins, and other articles; and so affected was she at beholding his situation that she wept bitterly, and at her departure expressed the greatest concern at not being able to give him further assistance.

In this loathsome prison was poor Mr. Lithgow kept until he was almost devoured by vermin. They crawled about his beard, lips, eyebrows, etc., so that he could scarce pen his eyes; and his mortification was increased by not having the use of his hands or legs to defend himself, from his being so miserably maimed by the tortures. So cruel was the governor, that he even ordered the vermin to be swept on him twice in every eight days. He, however, obtained some little mitigation of this part of his punishment, from the humanity of a Turkish slave that attended him, who, when he could do it with safety, destroyed the vermin, and contributed every refreshment to him that laid in his power.

From this slave Mr. Lithgow at length received information which gave him little hopes of ever being released, but, on the contrary, that he should finish his life under new tortures. The substance of this information was that an English seminary priest, and a Scotch cooper, had been for some time employed by the governor to translate from the English into the Spanish language, all his books and observations; and that it was commonly said in the governor's house, that he was an arch-heretic.

This information greatly alarmed him, and he began, not without reason, to fear that they would soon finish him, more especially as they could neither by torture or any other means, bring him to vary from what he had all along said at his different examinations.

Two days after he had received the above information, the governor, an inquisitor, and a canonical priest, accompanied by two Jesuits, entered his dungeon, and being seated, after several idle questions, the inquisitor asked Mr. Lithgow if he was a Roman Catholic, and acknowledged the pope's supremacy? He answered that he neither was the one nor did the other, adding that he was surprised at being asked such questions, since it was expressly stipulated by the articles of peace between England and Spain that none of the English subjects should be liable to the Inquisition, or any way molested by them on account of diversity in religion, etc. In the bitterness of his soul he made use of some warm expressions not suited to his circumstances: "As you have almost murdered me (said he) for pretended treason, so now you intend to make a martyr of me for my religion." He also expostulated with the governor on the ill return he made to the king of England, (whose subject he was) for the princely humanity exercised towards the Spaniards in 1588, when their armada was shipwrecked on the Scotch coast, and thousands of the Spaniards found relief, who must otherwise have miserably perished.

The governor admitted the truth of what Mr. Lithgow said, but replied with a haughty air that the king, who then only ruled Scotland, was actuated more by fear than love, and therefore did not deserve any thanks. One of the Jesuits said there was no faith to be kept with heretics. The inquisitor then rising, addressed himself to Mr. Lithgow in the following words: "You have been taken up as a spy, accused of treachery, and tortured, as we acknowledge, innocently: (which appears by the account lately received from Madrid of the intentions of the English) yet it was the divine power that brought those judgments upon you, for presumptuously treating the blessed miracle of Loretto with ridicule, and expressing yourself in your writings irreverently of his holiness, the great agent and Christ's vicar upon earth; therefore you are justly fallen into our hands by their special appointment: thy books and papers are miraculously translated by the assistance of Providence influencing thy own countrymen."

This trumpery being ended, they gave the prisoner eight days to consider and resolve whether he would become a convert to their religion; during which time the inquisitor told him he, with other religious orders, would attend, to give him such assistance thereto as he might want. One of the Jesuits said, (first making the sign of the cross upon his breast), "My son, behold, you deserve to be burnt alive; but by the grace of our lady of Loretto, whom you have blasphemed we will both save your soul and body."

In the morning the inquisitor, with three other ecclesiastics, returned, when the former asked the prisoner what difficulties he had on his conscience that retarded his conversion; to which he answered, 'he had not any doubts in his mind, being confident in the promises of Christ, and assuredly believing his revealed will signified in the Gospels, as professed in the reformed Catholic Church, being confirmed by grace, and having infallible assurance thereby of the Christian faith.' To these words the inquisitor replied, "Thou art no Christian, but an absurd heretic, and without conversion a member of perdition." The prisoner then told him that it was not consistent with the nature and essence of religion and charity to convince by opprobrious speeches, racks, and torments, but by arguments deduced from the Scriptures; and that all other methods would with him be totally ineffectual.

The inquisitor was so enraged at the replies made by the prisoner, that he struck him on the face, used many abusive speeches, and attempted to stab him, which he had certainly done had he not been prevented by the Jesuits; and from this time he never again visited the prisoner.

The next day the two Jesuits returned, and putting on a very grave, supercilious air, the superior asked him what resolution he had taken. To which Mr. Lithgow replied that he was already resolved, unless he could show substantial reasons to make him alter his opinion. The superior, after a pedantic display of their seven sacraments, the intercession of saints, transubstantiation, etc., boasted greatly of their Church, her antiquity, universality, and uniformity; all of which Mr. Lithgow denied: "For (said he) the profession of the faith I hold hath been ever since the first days of the apostles, and Christ had ever his own Church (however obscure) in the greatest time of your darkness."

The Jesuits, finding their arguments had not the desired effect, that torments could not shake his constancy, nor even the fear of the cruel sentence he had reason to expect would be pronounced and executed on him, after severe menaces, left him. On the eighth day after, being the last of their Inquisition, when sentence is pronounced, they returned again, but quite altered both in their words and behavior after repeating much of the same kind of arguments as before, they with seeming tears in their eyes, pretended they were sorry from their heart he must be obliged to undergo a terrible death, but above all, for the loss of his most precious soul; and falling on their knees, cried out, "Convert, convert, O dear brother, for our blessed Lady's sake convert!" To which he answered, "I fear neither death nor fire, being prepared for both."

The first effects Mr. Lithgow felt of the determination of this bloody tribunal was, a sentence to receive that night eleven different tortures, and if he did not die in the execution of them, (which might be reasonably expected from the maimed and disjointed condition he was in) he was, after Easter holy-days, to be carried to Grenada, and there burnt to ashes. The first part of this sentence was executed with great barbarity that night; and it pleased God to give him strength both of body and mind, to stand fast to the truth, and to survive the horrid punishments inflicted on him.

After these barbarians had glutted themselves for the present, with exercising on the unhappy prisoner the most distinguishd cruelties, they again put irons on, and conveyed him to his former dungeon. The next morning he received some little comfort from the Turkish slave before mentioned, who secretly brought him, in his shirt sleeve, some raisins and figs, which he licked up in the best manner his strength would permit with his tongue. It was to this slave Mr. Lithgow attributed his surviving so long in such a wretched situation; for he found means to convey some of these fruits to him twice every week. It is very extraordinary, and worthy of note, that this poor slave, bred up from his infancy, according to the maxims of his prophet and parents, in the greatest detestation of Christians, should be so affected at the miserable situation of Mr. Lithgow that he fell ill, and continued so for upwards of forty days. During this period Mr. Lithgow was attended by a negro woman, a slave, who found means to furnish him with refreshments still more amply than the Turk, being conversant in the house and family. She brought him every day some victuals, and with it some wine in a bottle.

The time was now so far elapsed, and the horrid situation so truly loathsome, that Mr. Lithgow waited with anxious expectation for the day, which, by putting an end to his life, would also end his torments. But his melancholy expectations were, by the interposition of Providence, happily rendered abortive, and his deliverance obtained from the following circumstances.

It happened that a Spanish gentleman of quality came from Grenada to Malaga, who being invited to an entertainment by the governor, informed him of what had befallen Mr. Lithgow from the time of his being apprehended as a spy, and described the various sufferings he had endured. He likewise told him that after it was known the prisoner was innocent, it gave him great concern. That on this account he would gladly have released him, restored his money and papers, and made some atonement for the injuries he had received, but that, upon an inspection into his writings, several were found of a very blasphemous nature, highly reflecting on their religion, that on his refusing to abjure these heretical opinions, he was turned over to the Inquisition, by whom he was finally condemned.

While the governor was relating this tragical tale, a Flemish youth (servant to the Spanish gentleman) who waited at the table, was struck with amazement and pity at the sufferings of the stranger described. On his return to his master's lodgings he began to revolve in his mind what he had heard, which made such an impression on him that he could not rest in his bed. In the short slumbers he had, his imagination pointed to him the person described, on the rack, and burning in the fire. In this anxiety he passed the night; and when the morning came, without disclosing his intentions to any person whatever, he went into the town, and inquired for an English factor. He was directed to the house of a Mr. Wild, to whom he related the whole of what he had heard pass the preceding evening, between his master and the governor, but could not tell Mr. Lithgow's name. Mr. Wild, however, conjectured it was he, by the servant's remembering the circumstance of his being a traveller, and his having had some acquaintance with him.

On the departure of the Flemish servant, Mr. Wild immediately sent for the other English factors, to whom he related all the particulars relative to their unfortunate countryman. After a short consultation it was agreed that an information of the whole affair should be sent, by express, to Sir Walter Aston, the English ambassador to the king of Spain, then at Madrid. This was accordingly done, and the ambassador having presented a memorial to the king and council of Spain, obtained an order for Mr. Lithgow's enlargement, and his delivery to the English factor. This order was directed to the governor of Malaga; and was received with great dislike and surprise by the whole assembly of the bloody Inquisition.

Mr. Lithgow was released from his confinement on the eve of Easter Sunday, when he was carried from his dungeon on the back of the slave who had attended him, to the house of one Mr. Bosbich, where all proper comforts were given him. It fortunately happened that there was at this time a squadron of English ships in the road, commanded by Sir Richard Hawkins, who being informed of the past sufferings and present situation of Mr. Lithgow, came the next day ashore, with a proper guard, and received him from the merchants. He was instantly carried in blankets on board the Vanguard, and three days after was removed to another ship, by direction of the general Sir Robert Mansel, who ordered that he should have proper care taken of him. The factor presented him with clothes, and all necessary provisions, besides which they gave him two hundred reals in silver; and Sir Richard Hawkins sent him two double pistoles.

Before his departure from the Spanish coast, Sir Richard Hawkins demanded the delivery of his papers, money, books, etc., but could not obtain any satisfactory answer on that head.

We cannot help making a pause here to reflect how manifestly Providence interfered in behalf of this poor man, when he was just on the brink of destruction; for by his sentence, from which there was no appeal, he would have been taken, in a few days, to Grenada, and burnt to ashes; and that a poor ordinary servant, who had not the least knowledge of him, nor was any ways interested in his preservation, should risk the displeasure of his master, and hazard his own life, to disclose a thing of so momentous and perilous a nature, to a strange gentleman, on whose secrecy depended his own existence. By such secondary means does Providence frequently interfere in behalf of the virtuous and oppressed; of which this is a most distinguished example.

After lying twelve days in the road, the ship weighed anchor, and in about two months arrived safe at Deptford. The next morning, Mr. Lithgow was carried on a feather bed to Theobalds, in Hertfordshire, where at that time was the king and royal family. His majesty happened to be that day engaged in hunting, but on his return in the evening, Mr. Lithgow was presented to him, and related the particulars of his sufferings, and his happy delivery. The king was so affected at the narrative, that he expressed the deepest concern, and gave orders that he should be sent to Bath, and his wants properly supplied from his royal munificence. By these means, under God, after some time, Mr. Lithgow was restored from the most wretched spectacle, to a great share of health and strength; but he lost the use of his left arm and several of the smaller bones were so crushed and broken, as to be ever after rendered useless.

Notwithstanding that every effort was used, Mr. Lithgow could never obtain any part of his money or effects, although his majesty and the ministers of state interested themselves in his behalf. Gondamore, the Spanish ambassador, indeed, promised that all his effects should be restored, with the addition of £1000 English money, as some atonement for the tortures he had undergone, which last was to be paid him by the governor of Malaga. These engagements, however, were but mere promises; and although the king was a kind of guarantee for the well performance of them, the cunning Spaniard found means to elude the same. He had, indeed, too great a share of influence in the English council during the time of that pacific reign, when England suffered herself to be bullied into slavish compliance by most of the states and kings in Europe.

The Story of Galileo

The most eminent men of science and philosophy of the day did not escape the watchful eye of this cruel despotism. Galileo, the cheif astronomer and mathematician of his age, was the first who used the telescope successfully in solving the movements of the heavenly bodies. He discovered that the sun is the center of motion around which the earth and various planets revolve. For making this great discovery Galileo was brought before the Inquisition, and for a while was in great danger of being put to death.

After a long and bitter review of Galileo's writings, in which many of his most important discoveries were condemned as errors, the charge of the inquisitors went on to declare, "That you, Galileo, have upon account of those things which you have written and confessed, subjected yourself to a strong suspicion of heresy in this Holy Office, by believing, and holding to be true, a doctrine which is false, and contrary to the sacred and divine Scripture— viz., that the sun is the center of the orb of the earth, and does not move from the east to the west; and that the earth moves, and is not the center of the world."

In order to save his life, Galileo admitted that he was wrong in thinking that the earth revolved around the sun, and swore that— "For the future, I will never more say, or assert, either by word or writing, anything that shall give occasion for a like suspicion." But immediately after taking this forced oath he is said to have whispered to a friend standing near, "The earth moves, for all that."

Summary of the Inquisition

Of the multitudes who perished by the Inquisition throughout the world, no authentic record is now discoverable. But wherever popery had power, there was the tribunal. It had been planted even in the east, and the Portuguese Inquisition of Goa was, until within these few years, fed with many an agony. South America was partitioned into provinces of the Inquisition; and with a ghastly mimickry of the crimes of the mother state, the arrivals of viceroys, and the other popular celebrations were thought imperfect without an *auto da fé*. The Netherlands were one scene of slaughter from the time of the decree which planted the Inquisition among them. In Spain the calculation is more attainable. Each of the *seventeen* tribunals during a long period burned annually, on an average, ten miserable beings! We are to recollect that this number was in a country where persecution had for ages abolished all religious differences, and where the difficulty was not to find the stake, but the offering. Yet, even in Spain, thus gleaned of all heresy, the Inquisition could still swell its lists of murders to thirty-two thousand! The numbers burned in effigy, or condemned to penance, punishments generally equivalent to exile, confiscation, and taint of blood, to all ruin but the mere loss of worthless life, amounted to three hundred and nine thousand. But the crowds who perished in dungeons of torture, of confinement, and of broken hearts, the millions of dependent lives made utterly helpless, or hurried to the grave by the death of the victims, are beyond all register; or recorded only before HIM, who has sworn that

"He that leadeth into captivity, shall go into captivity: he that killeth with the sword must be killed with the sword."

Such was the Inquisition, declared by the Spirit of God to be at once the offspring and the *image* of the popedom. To feel the force of the parentage, we must look to the time. In the thirteenth century, the popedom was at the summit of mortal dominion; it was independent of all kingdoms; it ruled with a rank of influence never before or since possessed by a human scepter; it was the acknowledged sovereign of body and soul; to all earthly intents its power was immeasurable for good or evil. It might have spread literature, peace, freedom, and Christianity to the ends of Europe, or the world. But its nature was hostile; its fuller triumph only disclosed its fuller evil; and, to the shame of human reason, and the terror and suffering of human virtue, Rome, in the hour of its consummate grandeur, teemed with the monstrous and horrid birth of the INQUISITION!

CHAPTER VI

An Account of the Persecutions in Italy, Under the Papacy

WE shall now enter on an account of the persecutions in Italy, a country which has been, and still is,

1. The center of popery.
2. The seat of the pontiff.
3. The source of the various errors which have spread themselves over other countries, deluded the minds of thousands, and diffused the clouds of superstition and bigotry over the human understanding.

In pursuing our narrative we shall include the most remarkable persecutions which have happened, and the cruelties which have been practised,

1. By the immediate power of the pope.
2. Through the power of the Inquisition.
3. At the instigation of particular orders of the clergy.
4. By the bigotry of the Italian princes.

In the twelfth century, the first persecutions under the papacy began in Italy, at the time that Adrian, an Englishman, was pope, being occasioned by the following circumstances:

A learned man, and an excellent orator of Brescia, named Arnold, came to Rome, and boldly preached against the corruptions and innovations which had crept into the Church. His discourses were so clear, consistent, and breathed forth such a pure spirit of piety, that the senators and many of the people highly approved of, and admired his doctrines.

This so greatly enraged Adrian that he commanded Arnold instantly to leave the city, as a heretic. Arnold, however, did not comply, for the senators and some of the principal people took his part, and resisted the authority of the pope.

Adrian now laid the city of Rome under an interdict, which caused the whole body of clergy to interpose; and, at length he persuaded the senators and people to give up the point, and suffer Arnold to be banished. This being agreed to, he received the sentence of exile, and retired to Germany, where he continued to preach against the pope, and to expose the gross errors of the Church of Rome.

Adrian, on this account, thirsted for his blood, and made several attempts to get him into his hands; but Arnold, for a long time, avoided every snare laid for him. At length, Frederic Barbarossa arriving at the imperial dignity, requested that the pope would crown him with his own hand. This Adrian complied with, and at the same time asked a favor of the emperor, which was, to put Arnold into his hands. The emperor very readily delivered up the unfortunate preacher, who soon fell a martyr to Adrian's vengeance, being hanged, and his body burnt to ashes, at Apulia. The same fate attended several of his old friends and companions.

Encenas, a Spaniard, was sent to Rome, to be brought up in the Roman Catholic faith; but having conversed with some of the reformed, and having read several treatises which they put into his hands, he became a Protestant. This, at length, being known, one of his own relations informed against him, when he was burnt by order of the pope, and a conclave of cardinals. The brother of Encenas had been taken up much about the same time, for having a New Testament in the Spanish language in his possession; but before the time appointed for his execution, he found means to escape out of prison, and retired to Germany.

Faninus, a learned layman, by reading controversial books, became of the reformed religion. An information being exhibited against him to the pope, he was apprehended, and cast into prison. His wife, children, relations, and friends visited him in his confinement, and so far wrought upon his mind, that he renounced his faith, and obtained his release. But he was no sooner free from confinement than his mind felt the heaviest of chains; the weight of a guilty conscience. His horrors were so great that he found them insupportable, until he had returned from his apostasy, and declared himself fully convinced of the errors of the Church of Rome. To make amends for his falling off, he now openly and strenuously did all he could to make converts to Protestantism, and was pretty successful in his endeavors. These proceedings occasioned his second imprisonment, but he had his life offered him if he would recant again. This proposal he rejected with disdain, saying that he scorned life upon such terms. Being asked why he would obstinately persist in his opinions, and leave his wife and children in distress, he replied, "I shall not leave them in distress; I have recommended them to the care of an excellent trustee." "What trustee?" said the person who had asked the question, with some surprise: to which Faninus answered, "Jesus Christ is the trustee I mean, and I think I could not commit them to the care of a better." On the day of execution he appeared remarkably cheerful, which one observing, said, "It is strange you should appear so merry upon such an occasion, when Jesus Christ himself, just before his death, was in such agonies, that he sweated blood and water." To which Faninus replied: "Christ sustained all manner of pangs and conflicts, with hell and death, on our accounts; and thus, by his sufferings, freed those who really believe in him from the fear of them." He was then strangled, his body was burnt to ashes, and then scattered about by the wind.

Dominicus, a learned soldier, having read several controversial writings, became a zealous Protestant, and retiring to Placentia, he preached the Gospel in its utmost purity, to a very considerable congregation. One day, at the conclusion of his sermon, he said, "If the congregation will attend to-morrow, I will give them a description of Antichrist, and paint him out in his proper colors."

A vast concourse of people attended the next day, but just as Dominicus was beginning his sermon, a civil magistrate went up to the pulpit, and took him into custody. He readily submitted; but as he went along with the magistrate, he made use of this expression: "I wonder the devil hath let me alone so long." When he was brought to examination, this question was put to him: "Will you renounce your doctrines?" To which he replied: "My doctrines! I maintain no doctrines of my own; what I preach are the doctrines of Christ, and for those I will forfeit my blood, and even think myself happy to suffer for the sake of my Redeemer." Every method was taken to make him recant for his faith, and embrace the errors of the Church of Rome; but when persuasions and menaces were found ineffectual, he was sentenced to death, and hanged in the market place.

Galeacius, a Protestant gentleman, who resided near the castle of St. Angelo, was apprehended on account of his faith. Great endeavors being used by his friends he recanted, and subscribed to several of the superstitious doctrines propogated by the Church of Rome. Becoming, however, sensible of his error, he publicly renounced his recantation. Being apprehended for this, he was condemned to be burnt, and agreeable to the order was chained to a stake, where he was left several hours before the fire was put to the fagots, in order that his wife, relations, and friends, who surrounded him, might induce him to give up his opinions. Galeacius, however, retained his constancy of mind, and entreated the executioner to put fire to the wood that was to burn him. This at length he did, and Galeacious was soon consumed in the flames, which burnt with amazing rapidity and deprived him of sensation in a few minutes.

Soon after this gentleman's death, a great number of Protestants were put to death in various parts of Italy, on account of their faith, giving a sure proof of their sincerity in their martyrdoms.

An Account of the Persecutions of Calabria

In the fourteenth century, many of the Waldenses of Pragela and Dauphiny, emigrated to Calabria, and settling some waste lands, by the permission of the nobles of that country, they soon, by the most industrious cultivation, made several wild and barren spots appear with all the beauties of verdure and fertility.

The Calabrian lords were highly pleased with their new subjects and tenants, as they were honest, quiet, and industrious; but the priests of the country exhibited several negative complaints against them; for not being able to accuse them of anything bad which they did do, they founded accusations on what they did not do, and charged them,

With not being Roman Catholics.

With not making any of their boys priests.

With not making any of their girls nuns.

With not going to Mass.

With not giving wax tapers to their priests as offerings.

With not going on pilgrimages.

With not bowing to images.

The Calabrian lords, however, quieted the priests, by telling them that these people were extremely harmless; that they gave no offence to the Roman Catholics, and cheerfully paid the tithes to the priests, whose revenues were considerably increased by their coming into the country, and who, of consequence, ought to be the last persons to complain of them.

Things went on tolerably well after this for a few years, during which the Waldenses formed themselves into two corporate towns, annexing several villages to the jurisdiction of them. At length they sent to Geneva for two clergymen; one to preach in each town, as they determined to make a public profession of their faith. Intelligence of this affair being carried to the pope, Pius the Fourth, he determined to exterminate them from Calabria.

To this end he sent Cardinal Alexandrino, a man of very violent temper and a furious bigot, together with two monks, to Calabria, where they were to act as inquisitors. These authorized persons came to St. Xist, one of the towns built by the Waldenses, and having assembled the people, told them that they should receive no injury, if they would accept of preachers appointed by the pope; but if they would not, they should be deprived both of their properties and lives; and that their intentions might be known, Mass should be publicly said that afternoon, at which they were ordered to attend.

The people of St. Xist, instead of attending Mass, fled into the woods, with their families, and thus disappointed the cardinal and his coadjutors. The cardinal then proceeded to La Garde, the other town belonging to the Waldenses, where, not to be served as he had been at St. Xist, he ordered the gates to be locked, and all avenues guarded. The same proposals were then made to the inhabitants of La Garde, as had previously been offered to those of St. Xist, but with this additional piece of artifice: the cardinal assured them that the inhabitants of St. Xist had immediately come into his proposals, and agreed that the pope should appoint them preachers. This falsehood succeeded; for the people of La Garde, thinking what the cardinal had told them to be the truth, said they would exactly follow the example of their brethren at St. Xist.

The cardinal, having gained his point by deluding the people of one town, sent for troops of soldiers, with a view to murder those of the other. He, accordingly, despatched the soldiers into the woods, to hunt down the inhabitants of St. Xist like wild beasts, and gave them strict orders to spare neither age nor sex, but to kill all they came near. The troops entered the woods, and many fell a prey to their ferocity, before the Waldenses were properly apprised of their design. At length, however, they determined to sell their lives as dear as possible, when several conflicts happened, in which the half-armed Waldenses performed prodigies of valor, and many were slain on both sides. The greatest part of the troops being killed in the different rencontres, the rest were compelled to retreat, which so enraged the cardinal that he wrote to the viceroy of Naples for reinforcements.

The viceroy immediately ordered a proclamation to be made throughout all the Neapolitan territories, that all outlaws, deserters, and other proscribed persons should be surely pardoned for their respective offences, on condition of making a campaign against the inhabitants of St. Xist, and continuing under arms until those people were exterminated.

Many persons of desperate fortunes came in upon this proclamation, and being formed into light companies, were sent to scour the woods, and put to death all they could meet with of the reformed religion. The viceroy himself likewise joined the cardinal, at the head of a body of regular forces; and, in conjunction, they did all they could to harass the poor people in the woods. Some they caught and hanged up upon trees, cut down boughs and burnt them, or ripped them open and left their bodies to be devoured by wild beasts, or birds of prey. Many they shot at a distance, but the greatest number they hunted down by way of sport. A few hid themselves in caves, but famine destroyed them in their retreat; and thus all these poor people perished, by various means, to glut the bigoted malice of their merciless persecutors.

The inhabitants of St. Xist were no sooner exterminated, than those of La Garde engaged the attention of the cardinal and viceroy.

It was offered, that if they should embrace the Roman Catholic persuasion, themselves and families should not be injured, but their houses and properties should be restored, and none would be permitted to molest them; but, on the contrary, if they refused this mercy, (as it was termed) the utmost extremities would be used, and the most cruel deaths the certain consequence of their non-compliance.

Notwithstanding the promises on one side, and menaces on the other, these worthy people unanimously refused to renounce their religion, or embrace the errors of popery. This exasperated the cardinal and viceroy so much, that thirty of them were ordered to be put immediately to the rack, as a terror to the rest.

Those who were put to the rack were treated with such severity that several died under the tortures; one Charlin, in particular, was so cruelly used that his belly burst, his bowels came out, and he expired in the greatest agonies. These barbarities, however, did not answer the purposes for which they were intended; for those who remained alive after the rack, and those who had not felt the rack, remained equally constant in their faith, and boldly declared that no tortures of body, or terrors of mind, should ever induce them to renounce their God, or worship images.

Several were then, by the cardinal's order, stripped stark naked, and whipped to death iron rods; and some were hacked to pieces with large knives; others were thrown down from the top of a large tower, and many were covered over with pitch, and burnt alive.

One of the monks who attended the cardinal, being naturally of a savage and cruel disposition, requested of him that he might shed some of the blood of these poor people with his own hands; when his request being granted, the barbarous man took a large sharp knife, and cut the throats of fourscore men, women, and children, with as little remorse as a butcher would have killed so many sheep. Every one of these bodies were then ordered to be quartered, the quarters placed upon stakes, and then fixed in different parts of the country, within a circuit of thirty miles.

The four principal men of La Garde were hanged, and the clergyman was thrown from the top of his church steeple. He was terribly mangled, but not quite killed by the fall; at which time the viceroy passing by, said, "Is the dog yet living? Take him up, and give him to the hogs," when, brutal as this sentence may appear, it was executed accordingly.

Sixty women were racked so violently, that the cords pierced their arms and legs close to the bone; when, being remanded to prison, their wounds mortified, and they died in the most miserable manner. Many others were put to death by various cruel means;

and if any Roman Catholic, more compassionate than the rest, interceded for any of the reformed, he was immediately apprehended, and shared the same fate as a favorer of heretics.

The viceroy being obliged to march back to Naples, on some affairs of moment which required his presence, and the cardinal being recalled to Rome, the marquis of Butane was ordered to put the finishing stroke to what they had begun; which he at length effected, by acting with such barbarous rigor, that there was not a single person of the reformed religion left living in all Calabria.

Thus were a great number of inoffensive and harmless people deprived of their possessions, robbed of their property, driven from their homes, and at length murdered by various means, only because they would not sacrifice their consciences to the superstitions of others, embrace idolatrous doctrines which they abhorred, and accept of teachers whom they could not believe.

Tyranny is of three kinds, viz., that which enslaves the person, that which seizes the property, and that which prescribes and dictates to the mind. The two first sorts may be termed civil tyranny, and have been practiced by arbitrary sovereigns in all ages, who have delighted in tormenting the persons, and stealing the properties of their unhappy subjects. But the third sort, viz., prescribing and dictating to the mind, may be called ecclesiastical tyranny: and this is the worst kind of tyranny, as it includes the other two sorts; for the Romish clergy not only do torture the body and seize the effects of those they persecute, but take the lives, torment the minds, and, if possible, would tyrannize over the souls of the unhappy victims.

Account of the Persecutions in the Valleys of Piedmont

Many of the Waldenses, to avoid the persecutions to which they were continually subjected in France, went and settled in the valleys of Piedmont, where they increased exceedingly, and flourished very much for a considerable time.

Though they were harmless in their behavior, inoffensive in their conversation, and paid tithes to the Roman clergy, yet the latter could not be contented, but wished to give them some disturbance: they, accordingly, complained to the archbishop of Turin that the Waldenses of the valleys of Piedmont were heretics, for these reasons:

1. That they did not believe in the doctrines of the Church of Rome.

2. That they made no offerings or prayers for the dead.

3. That they did not go to Mass.

4. That they did not confess, and receive absolution.

5. That they did not believe in purgatory, or pay money to get the souls of their friends out of it.

Upon these charges the archbishop ordered a persecution to be commenced, and many fell martyrs to the superstitious rage of the priests and monks.

At Turin, one of the reformed had his bowels torn out, and put in a basin before his face, where they remained in his view until he expired. At Revel, Catelin Girard being at the stake, desired the executioner to give him a stone; which he refused, thinking that he meant to throw it at somebody; but Girard assuring him that he had no such design, the executioner complied; when Girard, looking earnestly at the stone, said, "When it is in the power of a man to eat and digest this solid stone, the religion for which I am about to suffer shall have an end, and not before." He then threw the stone on the ground, and submitted cheerfully to the flames. A great many more of the reformed were oppressed, or put to death, by various means, until the patience of the Waldenses being tired out, they flew to arms in their own defence, and formed themselves into regular bodies.

Exasperated at this, the bishop of Turin procured a number of troops, and sent against them; but in most of the skirmishes and engagements the Waldenses were successful, which partly arose from their being better acquainted with the passes of the valleys of Piedmont than their adversaries, and partly from the desperation with which they fought; for they well knew, if they were taken, they should not be considered as prisoners of war, but tortured to death as heretics.

At length, Philip VII, duke of Savoy, and supreme lord of Piedmont, determined to interpose his authority, and stop these bloody wars, which so greatly disturbed his dominions. He was not willing to disoblige the pope, or affront the archbishop of Turin; nevertheless, he sent them both messages, importing that he could not any longer tamely see his dominions overrun with troops, who were directed by priests instead of officers, and commanded by prelates instead of generals; nor would he suffer his country to be depopulated, while he himself had not been even consulted upon the occasion.

The priests, finding the resolution of the duke, did all they could to prejudice his mind against the Waldenses; but the duke told them, that though he was unacquainted with the religious tenets of these people, yet he had always found them quiet, faithful, and obedient, and therefore he determined they should be no longer persecuted.

The priests now had recourse to the most palpable and absurd falsehoods: they assured the duke that he was mistaken in the Waldenses for they were a wicked set of people, and highly addicted to intemperance, uncleanness, blasphemy, adultery, incest, and many other abominable crimes; and that they were even monsters in nature, for their children were born with black throats, with four rows of teeth, and bodies all over hairy.

The duke was not so devoid of common sense as to give credit to what the priests said, though they affirmed in the most solemn manner the truth of their assertions. He, however, sent twelve very learned and sensible gentlemen into the Piedmontese valleys, to examine into the real character of the inhabitants.

These gentlemen, after travelling through all their towns and villages, and conversing with people of every rank among the Waldenses returned to the duke, and gave him the most favorable account of those people; affirming, before the faces of the priests who vilified them, that they were harmless, inoffensive, loyal, friendly, industrious, and pious: that they abhorred the crimes of which they were accused; and that, should an individual, through his depravity, fall into any of those crimes, he would, by their laws, be punished in the most exemplary manner. "With respect to the children," the gentlemen said, "the priests had told the most gross and ridiculous falsities, for they were neither born with black throats, teeth in their mouths, nor hair on their bodies, but were as fine children as could be seen. And to convince your highness of what we have said, (continued one of the gentlemen) we have brought twelve of the principal male inhabitants, who are come to ask pardon in the name of the rest, for having taken up arms without your leave, though even in their own defence, and to preserve their lives from their merciless enemies. And we have likewise brought several women, with children of various ages, that your highness may have an opportunity of personally examining them as much as you please."

The duke, after accepting the apology of the twelve delegates, conversing with the women, and examining the children, graciously dismissed them. He then commanded the priests, who had attempted to mislead him, immediately to leave the court; and gave strict orders, that the persecution should cease throughout his dominions.

The Waldenses had enjoyed peace many years, when Philip, the seventh duke of Savoy, died, and his successor happened to be a very bigoted papist. About the same time, some of the principal Waldenses proposed that their clergy should preach in public, that every one might know the purity of their doctrines: for hitherto they had preached only in private, and to such congregations as they well knew to consist of none but persons of the reformed religion.

On hearing these proceedings, the new duke was greatly exasperated, and sent a considerable body of troops into the valleys, swearing that if the people would not change their religion, he would have them flayed alive. The commander of the troops soon found the impracticability of conquering them with the number of men he had with him, he, therefore, sent word to the duke that the idea of subjugating the Waldenses, with so small a force, was ridiculous; that those people were better acquainted with the country than any that were with him; that they had secured all the passes, were well armed, and resolutely determined to defend themselves; and, with respect to flaying them alive, he said, that every skin belonging to those people would cost him the lives of a dozen of his subjects.

Terrified at this information, the duke withdrew the troops, determining to act not by force, but by stratagem. He therefore ordered rewards for the taking of any of the Waldenses, who might be found straying from their places of security; and these, when taken, were either flayed alive, or burnt.

The Waldenses had hitherto only had the New Testament and a few books of the Old, in the Waldensian tongue; but they determined now to have the sacred writings complete in their own language. They, therefore, employed a Swiss printer to furnish them with a complete edition of the Old and New Testaments in the Waldensian tongue, which he did for the consideration of fifteen hundred crowns of gold, paid him by those pious people.

Pope Paul the third, a bigoted papist, ascending the pontifical chair, immediately solicited the parliament of Turin to persecute the Waldenses, as the most pernicious of all heretics.

The parliament readily agreed, when several were suddenly apprehended and burnt by their order. Among these was Bartholomew Hector, a bookseller and stationer of Turin, who was brought up a Roman Catholic, but having read some treatises written by the reformed clergy, was fully convinced of the errors of the Church of Rome; yet his mind was, for some time, wavering, and he hardly knew what persuasion to embrace.

At length, however, he fully embraced the reformed religion, and was apprehended, as we have already mentioned, and burnt by order of the parliament of Turin.

A consultation was now held by the parliament of Turin, in which it was agreed to send deputies to the valleys of Piedmont, with the following propositions:

1. That if the Waldenses would come to the bosom of the Church of Rome, and embrace the Roman Catholic religion, they should enjoy their houses, properties, and lands, and live with their families, without the least molestation.

2. That to prove their obedience, they should send twelve of their principal persons, with all their ministers and schoolmasters, to Turin, to be dealt with at discretion.

3. That the pope, the king of France, and the duke of Savoy, approved of, and authorized the proceedings of the parliament of Turin, upon this occasion.

4. That if the Waldenses of the valleys of Piedmont refused to comply with these propositions, persecution should ensue, and certain death be their portion.

To each of these propositions the Waldenses nobly replied in the following manner, answering them respectively:

1. That no considerations whatever should make them renounce their religion.

2. That they would never consent to commit their best and most respectable friends, to the custody and discretion of their worst and most inveterate enemies.

3. That they valued the approbation of the King of kings, who reigns in heaven, more than any temporal authority.

4. That their souls were more precious than their bodies.

These pointed and spirited replies greatly exasperated the parliament of Turin; they continued, with more avidity than ever, to kidnap such Waldenses as did not act with proper precaution, who were sure to suffer the most cruel deaths. Among these, it unfortunately happened, that they got hold of Jeffery Varnagle, minister of Angrogne, whom they committed to the flames as a heretic.

They then solicited a considerable body of troops of the king of France, in order to exterminate the reformed entirely from the valleys of Piedmont; but just as the troops were going to march, the Protestant princes of Germany interposed, and threatened to send troops to assist the Waldenses, if they should be attacked. The king of France, not caring to enter into a war, remanded the troops, and sent word to the parliament of Turin that he could not spare any troops at present to act in Piedmont. The members of the parliament were greatly vexed at this disappointment, and the persecution gradually ceased, for as they could only put to death such of the reformed as they caught by chance, and as the Waldenses daily grew more cautious, their cruelty was obliged to subside, for want of objects on whom to exercise it.

After the Waldenses had enjoyed a few years tranquillity, they were again disturbed by the following means: the pope's nuncio coming to Turin to the duke of Savoy upon business, told that prince he was astonished he had not yet either rooted out the Waldenses from the valleys of Piedmont entirely, or compelled them to enter into the bosom of the Church of Rome. That he could not help looking upon such conduct with a suspicious eye, and that he really thought him a favorer of those heretics, and should report the affair accordingly to his holiness the pope.

Stung by this reflection, and unwilling to be misrepresented to the pope, the duke determined to act with the greatest severity, in order to show his zeal, and to make amends for former neglect by future cruelty. He, accordingly, issued express orders for all the Waldenses to attend Mass regularly on pain of death. This they absolutely refused to do, on which he entered the Piedmontese valleys, with a formidable body of troops, and began a most furious persecution, in which great numbers were hanged, drowned, ripped open, tied to trees, and pierced with prongs, thrown from precipices, burnt, stabbed, racked to death, crucified with their heads downwards, worried by dogs, etc.

Those who fled had their goods plundered, and their houses burnt to the ground: they were particularly cruel when they caught a minister or a schoolmaster, whom they put to such exquisite tortures, as are almost incredible to conceive. If any whom they took seemed wavering in their faith, they did not put them to death, but sent them to the galleys, to be made converts by dint of hardships.

The most cruel persecutors, upon this occasion, that attended the duke, were three in number, viz. 1. Thomas Incomel, an apostate, for he was brought up in the reformed religion, but renounced his faith, embraced the errors of popery, and turned monk. He was a great libertine, given to unnatural crimes, and sordidly solicitous for plunder of the Waldenses. 2. Corbis, a man of a very ferocious and cruel nature, whose business was to examine the prisoners. 3. The provost of justice, who was very anxious for the execution of the Waldenses, as every execution put money in his pocket.

These three persons were unmerciful to the last degree; and wherever they came, the blood of the innocent was sure to flow. Exclusive of the cruelties exercised by the duke, by these three persons, and the army, in their different marches, many local barbarities were committed. At Pignerol, a town in the valleys, was a monastery, the monks of which, finding they might injure the reformed with impunity, began to plunder the houses and pull down the churches of the Waldenses. Not meeting with any opposition, they seized upon the persons of those unhappy people, murdering the men, confining the women, and putting the children to Roman Catholic nurses.

The Roman Catholic inhabitants of the valley of St. Martin, likewise, did all they could to torment the neighboring Waldenses: they destroyed their churches, burnt their houses, seized their properties, stole their cattle, converted their lands to their own use, committed their ministers to the flames, and drove the Waldenses to the woods, where they had nothing to subsist on but wild fruits, roots, the bark of trees, etc.

Some Roman Catholic ruffians having seized a minister as he was going to preach, determined to take him to a convenient place, and burn him. His parishioners having intelligence of this affair, the men armed themselves, pursued the ruffians, and seemed determined to rescue their minister; which the ruffians no sooner perceived than they stabbed the poor gentleman, and leaving him weltering in his blood, made a precipitate retreat. The astonished parishioners did all they could to recover him, but in vain: for the weapon had touched the vital parts, and he expired as they were carrying him home.

The monks of Pignerol having a great inclination to get the minister of a town in the valleys, called St. Germain, into their power, hired a band of ruffians for the purpose of apprehending him. These fellows were conducted by a treacherous person, who had formerly been a servant to the clergyman, and who perfectly well knew a secret way to the house, by which he could lead them without alarming the neighborhood. The guide knocked at the door, and being asked who was there, answered in his own name. The clergyman, not expecting any injury from a person on whom he had heaped favors, immediately opened the door; but perceiving the ruffians, he started back, and fled to a back door; but they rushed in, followed, and seized him. Having murdered all his family, they made him proceed towards Pignerol, goading him all the way with pikes, lances, swords, etc. He was kept a considerable time in prison, and then fastened to the stake to be burnt; when two women of the Waldenses, who had renounced their religion to save their lives, were ordered to carry fagots to the stake to burn him; and as they laid them down, to say, "Take these, thou wicked heretic, in recompense for the pernicious doctrines thou hast taught us." These words they both repeated to him; to which he calmly replied, "I formerly taught you well, but you have since learned ill." The fire was then put to the fagots, and he was speedily consumed, calling upon the name of the Lord as long as his voice permitted.

As the troops of ruffians, belonging to the monks, did great mischief about the town of St. Germain, murdering and plundering many of the inhabitants, the reformed of Lucerne and Angrogne, sent some bands of armed men to the assistance of their brethren of St. Germain. These bodies of armed men frequently attacked the ruffians, and often put them to the rout, which so terrified the monks, that they left the monastery of Pignerol for some time, until they could procure a body of regular troops to guard them.

The duke not thinking himself so successful as he at first imagined he should be, greatly augmented his forces; he ordered the bands of ruffians, belonging to the monks, to join him, and commanded that a general jail-delivery should take place, provided the persons released would bear arms, and form themselves into light companies, to assist in the extermination of the Waldenses.

The Waldenses, being informed of the proceedings, secured as much of their properties as they could, and quitted the valleys, retired to the rocks and caves among the Alps; for it is to be understood that the valleys of Piedmont are situated at the foot of those prodigious mountains called the Alps, or the Alpine hills.

The army now began to plunder and burn the towns and villages wherever they came; but the troops could not force the passes to the Alps, which were gallantly defended by the Waldenses, who always repulsed their enemies: but if any fell into the hands of the troops, they were sure to be treated with the most barbarous severity.

A soldier having caught one of the Waldenses, bit his right ear off, saying, "I will carry this member of that wicked heretic with me into my own country, and preserve it as a rarity." He then stabbed the man and threw him into a ditch.

A party of the troops found a venerable man, upwards of a hundred years of age, together with his granddaughter, a maiden, of about eighteen, in a cave. They butchered the poor old man in the most inhuman manner, and then attempted to ravish the girl, when she started away and fled from them; but they pursuing her, she threw herself from a precipice and perished.

The Waldenses, in order the more effectually to be able to repel force by force, entered into a league with the Protestant powers of Germany, and with the reformed of Dauphiny and Pragela. These were respectively to furnish bodies of troops; and the Waldenses determined, when thus reinforced, to quit the mountains of the Alps, (where they must soon have perished, as the winter was coming on,) and to force the duke's army to evacuate their native valleys.

The duke of Savoy was now tired of the war; it had cost him great fatigue and anxiety of mind, a vast number of men, and very considerable sums of money. It had been much more tedious and bloody than he expected, as well as more expensive than he could at first have imagined, for he thought the plunder would have discharged the expenses of the expedition; but in this he was mistaken, for the pope's nuncio, the bishops, monks, and other ecclesiastics, who attended the army and encouraged the war, sunk the greatest part of the wealth that was taken under various pretences. For these reasons, and the death of his duchess, of which he had just received intelligence, and fearing that the Waldenses, by the treaties they had entered into, would become more powerful than ever, he determined to return to Turin with his army, and to make peace with the Waldenses.

This resolution he executed, though greatly against the will of the ecclesiastics, who were the chief gainers, and the best pleased with revenge. Before the articles of peace could be ratified, the duke himself died, soon after his return to Turin; but on his deathbed he strictly enjoined his son to perform what he intended, and to be as favorable as possible to the Waldenses.

The duke's son, Charles Emmanuel, succeeded to the dominions of Savoy, and gave a full ratification of peace to the Waldenses, according to the last injunctions of his father, though the ecclesiastics did all they could to persuade him to the contrary.

An Account of the Persecutions in Venice

While the state of Venice was free from inquisitors, a great number of Protestants fixed their residence there, and many converts

6672

were made by the purity of the doctrines they professed, and the inoffensiveness of the conversation they used.

The pope being informed of the great increase of Protestantism, in the year 1542 sent inquisitors to Venice to make an inquiry into the matter, and apprehend such as they might deem obnoxious persons. Hence a severe persecution began, and many worthy persons were martyred for serving God with purity, and scorning the trappings of idolatry.

Various were the modes by which the Protestants were deprived of life; but one particular method, which was first invented upon this occasion, we shall describe; as soon as sentence was passed, the prisoner had an iron chain which ran through a great stone fastened to his body. He was then laid flat upon a plank, with his face upwards, and rowed between two boats to a certain distance at sea, when the two boats separated, and he was sunk to the bottom by the weight of the stone.

If any denied the jurisdiction of the inquisitors at Venice, they were sent to Rome, where, being committed purposely to damp prisons, and never called to a hearing, their flesh mortified, and they died miserably in jail.

A citizen of Venice, Anthony Ricetti, being apprehended as a Protestant, was sentenced to be drowned in the manner we have already described. A few days previous to the time appointed for his execution, his son went to see him, and begged him to recant, that his life might be saved, and himself not left fatherless. To which the father replied, "A good Christian is bound to relinquish not only goods and children, but life itself, for the glory of his Redeemer: therefore I am resolved to sacrifice every thing in this transitory world, for the sake of salvation in a world that will last to eternity."

The lords of Venice likewise sent him word, that if he would embrace the Roman Catholic religion, they would not only give him his life, but redeem a considerable estate which he had mortgaged, and freely present him with it. This, however, he absolutely refused to comply with, sending word to the nobles that he valued his soul beyond all other considerations; and being told that a fellow-prisoner, named Francis Sega, had recanted, he answered, "If he has forsaken God, I pity him; but I shall continue steadfast in my duty." Finding all endeavors to persuade him to renounce his faith ineffectual, he was executed according to his sentence, dying cheerfully, and recommending his soul fervently to the Almighty.

What Ricetti had been told concerning the apostasy of Francis Sega, was absolutely false, for he had never offered to recant, but steadfastly persisted in his faith, and was executed, a few days after Ricetti, in the very same manner.

Francis Spinola, a Protestant gentleman of very great learning, being apprehended by order of the inquisitors, was carried before

LINCOLN BIBLE INSTITUTE

their tribunal. A treatise on the Lord's Supper was then put into his hands and he was asked if he knew the author of it. To which he replied, "I confess myself to be the author of it, and at the same time solemnly affirm, that there is not a line in it but what is authorized by, and consonant to, the holy Scriptures." On this confession he was committed close prisoner to a dungeon for several days.

Being brought to a second examination, he charged the pope's legate, and the inquisitors, with being merciless barbarians, and then represented the superstitions and idolatries practised by the Church of Rome in so glaring a light, that not being able to refute his arguments, they sent him back to his dungeon, to make him repent of what he had said.

On his third examination, they asked him if he would recant his error. To which he answered that the doctrines he maintained were not erroneous, being purely the same as those which Christ and his apostles had taught, and which were handed down to us in the sacred writings. The inquisitors then sentenced him to be drowned, which was executed in the manner already described. He went to meet death with the utmost serenity, seemed to wish for dissolution, and declaring that the prolongation of his life did but tend to retard that real happiness which could only be expected in the world to come.

An Account of Several Remarkable Individuals, Who Were Martyred in Different Parts of Italy, on Account of Their Religion

John Mollius was born at Rome, of reputable parents. At twelve years of age they placed him in the monastery of Gray Friars, where he made such a rapid progress in arts, sciences, and languages that at eighteen years of age he was permitted to take priest's orders.

He was then sent to Ferrara, where, after pursuing his studies six years longer, he was made theological reader in the university of that city. He now, unhappily, exerted his great talents to disguise the Gospel truths, and to varnish over the errors of the Church of Rome. After some years residence in Ferrara, he removed to the university of Bononia, where he became a professor. Having read some treatises written by ministers of the reformed religion, he grew fully sensible of the errors of popery, and soon became a zealous Protestant in his heart.

He now determined to expound, accordingly to the purity of the Gospel, St. Paul's Epistle to the Romans, in a regular course of sermons. The concourse of people that continually attended his preaching was surprising, but when the priests found the tenor of his doctrines, they despatched an account of the affair to Rome; when the pope sent a monk, named Cornelius, to Bononia, to expound the same epistle, according to the tenets of the Church of Rome. The people, however, found such a disparity between the two preachers that the audience of Mollius increased, and Cornelius was forced to preach to empty benches.

Cornelius wrote an account of his bad success to the pope, who immediately sent an order to apprehend Mollius, who was seized upon accordingly, and kept in close confinement. The bishop of Bononia sent him word that he must recant, or be burnt; but he appealed to Rome, and was removed thither.

At Rome he begged to have a public trial, but that the pope absolutely denied him, and commanded him to give an account of his opinions in writing, which he did under the following heads:

Original sin. Free-will. The infallibility of the church of Rome. The infallibility of the pope. Justification by faith. Purgatory. Transubstantiation. Mass. Auricular confession. Prayers for the dead. The host. Prayers for saints. Going on pilgrimages. Extreme unction. Performing services in an unknown tongue, etc., etc.

All these he confirmed from Scripture authority. The pope, upon this occasion, for political reasons, spared him for the present, but soon after had him apprehended, and put to death, he being first hanged, and his body burnt to ashes, A. D. 1553.

The year after, Francis Gamba, a Lombard, of the Protestant persuasion, was apprehended, and condemned to death by the senate of Milan. At the place of execution, a monk presented a cross to him, to whom he said, "My mind is so full of the real merits and goodness of Christ that I want not a piece of senseless stick to put me in mind of Him." For this expression his tongue was bored through, and he was afterward burnt.

A. D. 1555, Algerius, a student in the university of Padua, and a man of great learning, having embraced the reformed religion, did all he could to convert others. For these proceedings he was accused of heresy to the pope, and being apprehended, was committed to the prison at Venice.

The pope, being informed of Algerius's great learning, and surprising natural abilities, thought it would be of infinite service to the Church of Rome if he could induce him to forsake the Protestant cause. He, therefore, sent for him to Rome, and tried, by the most profane promises, to win him to his purpose. But finding his endeavors ineffectual, he ordered him to be burnt, which sentence was executed accordingly.

A. D. 1559, John Alloysius, being sent from Geneva to preach in Calabria, was there apprehended as a Protestant, carried to Rome, and burnt by order of the pope; and James Bovellus, for the same reason, was burnt at Messina.

A. D. 1560, Pope Pius the Fourth, ordered all the Protestants to be severely persecuted throughout the Italian states, when great numbers of every age, sex, and condition, suffered martyrdom. Concerning the cruelties practiced upon this occasion, a learned and humane Roman Catholic thus spoke of them, in a letter to a noble lord:

"I cannot, my lord, forbear disclosing my sentiments, with respect to the persecution now carrying on: I think it cruel and unnecessary; I tremble at the manner of putting to death, as it resembles more the slaughter of calves and sheep, than the execution of human beings. I will relate to your lordship a dreadful scene, of which I was myself an eye witness: seventy Protestants were cooped up in one filthy dungeon together; the executioner went in among them, picked out one from among the rest, blindfolded him, led him out to an open place before the prison, and cut his throat with the greatest composure. He then calmly walked into the prison again, bloody as he was, and with the knife in his hand selected another, and despatched him in the same manner; and this, my lord, he repeated until the whole number were put to death. I leave it to your lordship's feelings to judge of my sensations upon this occasion; my tears now wash the paper upon which I give you the recital. Another thing I must mention—the patience with which they met death: they seemed all resignation and piety, fervently praying to God, and cheerfully encountering their fate. I cannot reflect without shuddering, how the executioner held the bloody knife between his teeth; what a dreadful figure he appeared, all covered with blood. and with what unconcern he executed his barbarous office."

A young Englishman who happened to be at Rome, was one day passing by a church, when the procession of the host was just coming out. A bishop carried the host, which the young man perceiving, he snatched it from him, threw it upon the ground, and trampled it under his feet, crying out, "Ye wretched idolaters, who neglect the true God, to adore a morsel of bread." This action so provoked the people that they would have torn him to pieces on the spot; but the priests persuaded them to let him abide by the sentence of the pope.

When the affair was represented to the pope, he was so greatly exasperated that he ordered the prisoner to be burnt immediately; but a cardinal dissuaded him from this hasty sentence, saying that it was better to punish him by slow degrees, and to torture him, that they might find out if he had been instigated by any particular person to commit so atrocious an act.

This being approved, he was tortured with the most exemplary severity, notwithstanding which they could only get these words from him, "It was the will of God that I should do as I did."

The pope then passed this sentence upon him.

1. That he should be led by the executioner, naked to the middle, through the streets of Rome.

2. That he should wear the image of the devil upon his head.

3. That his breeches should be painted with the representation of flames.

4. That he should have his right hand cut off.

5. That after having been carried about thus in procession, he should be burnt.

When he heard this sentence pronounced, he implored God to give him strength and fortitude to go through it. As he passed through the streets he was greatly derided by the people, to whom he said some severe things respecting the Romish superstition. But a cardinal, who attended the procession, overhearing him, ordered him to be gagged.

When he came to the church door, where he trampled on the host, the hangman cut off his right hand, and fixed it on a pole. Then two tormentors, with flaming torches, scorched and burnt his flesh all the rest of the way. At the place of execution he kissed the chains that were to bind him to the stake. A monk presenting the figure of a saint to him, he struck it aside, and then being chained to the stake, fire was put to the fagots, and he was soon burnt to ashes.

A little after the last-mentioned execution, a venerable old man, who had long been a prisoner in the Inquisition, was condemned to be burnt, and brought out for execution. When he was fastened to the stake, a priest held a crucifix to him, on which he said, "If you do not take that idol from my sight, you will constrain me to spit upon it." The priest rebuked him for this with great severity; but he bade him remember the First and Second Commandments, and refrain from idolatry, as God himself had commanded. He was then gagged, that he should not speak any more, and fire being put to the fagots, he suffered martyrdom in the flames.

An Account of the Persecutions in the Marquisate of Saluces

The Marquisate of Saluces, on the south side of the valleys of Piedmont, was in A. D. 1561, principally inhabited by Protestants, when the marquis, who was proprietor of it, began a persecution against them at the instigation of the pope. He began by banishing the ministers, and if any of them refused to leave their flocks, they were sure to be imprisoned, and severely tortured; however, he did not proceed so far as to put any to death.

Soon after the marquisate fell into the possession of the duke of Savoy, who sent circular letters to all the towns and villages, that he expected the people should all conform to go to Mass.

The inhabitants of Saluces, upon receiving this letter, returned a general epistle, in answer.

The duke, after reading the letter, did not interrupt the Protestants for some time; but, at length, he sent them word that they must either conform to the Mass, or leave his dominions in fifteen days. The Protestants, upon this unexpected edict, sent a deputy to the duke to obtain its revocation, or at least to have it moderated. But their remonstrances were in vain, and they were given to understand that the edict was absolute.

Some were weak enough to go to Mass, in order to avoid banishment, and preserve their property; others removed, with all their effects, to different countries; and many neglected the time so long that they were obliged to abandon all they were worth, and leave the marquisate in haste. Those, who unhappily stayed behind, were seized, plundered, and put to death.

An Account of the Persecutions in the Valleys of Piedmont, in the Seventeenth Century

Pope Clement the Eighth, sent missionaries into the valleys of Piedmont, to induce the Protestants to renounce their religion; and these missionaries having erected monasteries in several parts of the valleys, became exceedingly troublesome to those of the reformed, where the monasteries appeared, not only as fortresses to curb, but as sanctuaries for all such to fly to, as had any ways injured them.

The Protestants petitioned the duke of Savoy against these missionaries, whose insolence and ill-usage were become intolerable; but instead of getting any redress, the interest of the missionaries so far prevailed, that the duke published a decree, in which he declared, that one witness should be sufficient in a court of law against a Protestant, and that any witness, who convicted a Protestant of any crime whatever, should be entitled to one hundred crowns.

It may be easily imagined, upon the publication of a decree of this nature, that many Protestants fell martyrs to perjury and avarice; for several villainous papists would swear any thing against the Protestants for the sake of the reward, and then fly to their own priests for absolution from their false oaths. If any Roman Catholic, of more conscience than the rest, blamed these fellows for their atrocious crimes, they themselves were in danger of being informed against and punished as favorers of heretics.

The missionaries did all they could to get the books of the Protestants into their hands, in order to burn them; when the Protestants doing their utmost endeavors to conceal their books, the missionaries wrote to the duke of Savoy, who, for the heinous crime of not surrendering their Bibles, prayer books, and religious treatises, sent a number of troops to be quartered on them. These military gentry did great mischief in the houses of the Protestants, and destroyed such quantities of provisions, that many families were thereby ruined.

To encourage, as much as possible, the apostasy of the Protestants, the duke of Savoy published a proclamation wherein he said, "To encourage the heretics to turn Catholics, it is our will and pleasure, and we do hereby expressly command, that all such as shall embrace the holy Roman Catholic faith, shall enjoy an exemption, from all and every tax for the space of five years, commencing from the day of their conversion." The duke of Savoy, likewise established a court, called the council for extirpating the heretics. This court was to enter into inquiries concerning the ancient privileges of the Protestant churches, and the decrees which had been, from time to time, made in favor of the Protestants. But the investigation of these things was carried on with the most manifest partiality; old charters were wrested to a wrong sense, and sophistry was used to pervert the meaning of everything, which tended to favor the reformed.

As if these severities were not sufficient, the duke, soon after, published another edict, in which he strictly commanded, that no Protestant should act as a schoolmaster, or tutor, either in public or private, or dare to teach any art, science, or language, directly or indirectly, to persons of any persuasion whatever.

This edict was immediately followed by another, which decreed that no Protestant should hold any place of profit, trust, or honor; and to wind up the whole, the certain token of an approaching persecution came forth in a final edict, by which it was positively ordered, that all Protestants should diligently attend Mass.

The publication of an edict, containing such an injunction, may be compared to unfurling the bloody flag; for murder and rapine were sure to follow. One of the first objects that attracted the notice of the papists was Mr. Sebastian Basan, a zealous Protestant, who was seized by the missionaries, confined, tormented for fifteen months, and then burnt.

Previous to the persecution, the missionaries employed kidnappers to steal away the Protestants' children, that they might privately be brought up Roman Catholics; but now they took away the children by open force, and if they met with any resistance, they murdered the parents.

To give greater vigor to the persecution, the duke of Savoy called a general assembly of the Roman Catholic nobility and gentry when a solemn edict was published against the reformed, containing many heads, and including several reasons for extirpating the Protestants, among which were the following:

1. For the preservation of the papal authority.

2. That the church livings may be all under one mode of government.

3. To make a union among all parties.

4. In honor of all the saints, and of the ceremonies of the Church of Rome.

This severe edict was followed by a most cruel order, published on January 25, A. D. 1655, under the duke's sanction, by Andrew Gastaldo, doctor of civil laws. This order set forth, "That every head of a family, with the individuals of that family, of the reformed religion, of what rank, degree, or condition soever, none excepted inhabiting and possessing estates in Lucerne, St. Giovanni, Bibiana, Campiglione, St. Secondo, Lucernetta, La Torre, Fenile, and Brich-erassio, should, within three days after the publication thereof, withdraw and depart, and be withdrawn out of the said places, and translated into the places and limits tolerated by his highness during his pleasure; particularly Bobbio, Angrogne, Vilario, Rorata, and the county of Bonetti.

"And all this to be done on pain of death, and confiscation of house and goods, unless within the limited time they turned Roman Catholics."

A flight with such speed, in the midst of winter, may be conceived as no agreeable task, especially in a country almost surrounded by mountains. The sudden order affected all, and things, which would have been scarcely noticed at another time, now appeared in the most conspicuous light. Women with child, or women just lain-in, were not objects of pity on this order for sudden removal, for all were included in the command; and it unfortunately happened, that the winter was remarkably severe and rigorous.

The papists, however, drove the people from their habitations at the time appointed, without even suffering them to have sufficient clothes to cover them; and many perished in the mountains through the severity of the weather, or for want of food. Some, however, who remained behind after the decree was published, met with the severest treatment, being murdered by the popish inhabitants, or shot by the troops who were quartered in the valleys. A particular description of these cruelties is given in a letter, written by a Protestant, who was upon the spot, and who happily escaped the carnage. "The army (says he) having got footing, became very numerous, by the addition of a multitude of the neighboring popish inhabitants, who finding we were the destined prey of the plunderers, fell upon us with an impetuous fury. Exclusive of the duke of Savoy's troops, and the popish inhabitants, there were several regiments of French auxiliaries, some companies belonging to the Irish brigades, and several bands formed of outlaws, smugglers, and prisoners, who had been promised pardon and liberty in this world, and absolution in the next, for assisting to exterminate the Protestants from Piedmont.

"This armed multitude being encouraged by the Roman Catholic bishops and monks fell upon the Protestants in a most furious manner. Nothing now was to be seen but the face of horror and despair, blood stained the floors of the houses, dead bodies bestrewed the streets, groans and cries were heard from all parts. Some armed themselves, and skirmished with the troops; and many, with their families, fled to the mountains. In one village they cruelly tormented one hundred and fifty women and children after the men were fled, beheading the women, and dashing out the brains of the children. In the towns of Vilario and Bobbio, most of those who refused to go to Mass, who were upwards of fifteen years of age, they crucified with their heads downwards; and the greatest number of those who were under that age were strangled."

Sarah Rastignole des Vignes, a woman of sixty years of age, being seized by some soldiers, they ordered her to say a prayer to some saints, which she refusing, they thrust a sickle into her belly, ripped her up, and then cut off her head.

Martha Constantine, a handsome young woman, was treated with great indecency and cruelty by several of the troops, who first ravished, and then killed her by cutting off her breasts. These they fried, and set before some of their comrades, who ate them without knowing what they were. When they had done eating, the others told them what they had made a meal of, in consequence of which a quarrel ensued, swords were drawn, and a battle took place. Several were killed in the fray, the greater part of whom were those concerned in the horrid massacre of the woman, and who had practiced such an inhuman deception on their companions.

Some of the soldiers seized a man of Thrassiniere, and ran the points of their swords through his ears, and through his feet. They then tore off the nails of his fingers and toes with red-hot pincers, tied him to the tail of an ass, and dragged him about the streets; they finally fastened a cord around his head, which they twisted with a stick in so violent a manner as to wring it from his body.

Peter Symonds, a Protestant, of about eighty years of age, was tied neck and heels, and then thrown down a precipice. In the fall the branch of a tree caught hold of the ropes that fastened him, and suspended him in the midway, so that he languished for several days, and at length miserably perished of hunger.

Esay Garcino, refusing to renounce his religion, was cut into small pieces; the soldiers, in ridicule, saying, they had minced him. A woman, named Armand, had every limb separated from each other, and then the respective parts were hung upon a hedge. Two old women were ripped open, and then left in the fields upon the snow, where they perished; and a very old woman, who was deformed, had her nose and hands cut off, and was left, to bleed to death in that manner.

A great number of men, women, and children, were flung from the rocks, and dashed to pieces. Magdalen Bertino, a Protestant woman of La Torre, was stripped stark naked, her head tied between her legs, and thrown down one of the precipices; and Mary Raymondet, of the same town, had the flesh sliced from her bones until she expired.

Magdalen Pilot, of Vilario, was cut to pieces in the cave of Castolus; Ann Charboniere had one end of a stake thrust up her body; and the other being fixed in the ground, she was left in that manner to perish, and Jacob Perrin the elder, of the church of Vilario, and David, his brother, were flayed alive.

An inhabitant of La Torre, named Giovanni Andrea Michialm, was apprehended, with four of his children, three of them were hacked to pieces before him, the soldiers asking him, at the death of every child, if he would renounce his religion; this he constantly refused. One of the soldiers then took up the last and youngest by the legs, and putting the same question to the father, he replied as before, when the inhuman brute dashed out the child's brains. The father, however, at the same moment started from them, and fled; the soldiers fired after him, but missed him; and he, by the swiftness of his heels, escaped, and hid himself in the Alps.

Further Persecutions in the Valleys of Piedmont, in the Seventeenth Century

Giovanni Pelanchion, for refusing to turn papist, was tied by one leg to the tail of a mule, and dragged through the streets of Lucerne, amidst the acclamations of an inhuman mob, who kept stoning him, and crying out, "He is possessed with the devil, so that, neither stoning, nor dragging him through the streets, will kill him, for the devil keeps him alive." They then took him to the river side, chopped off his head, and left that and his body unburied, upon the bank of the stream.

Magdalen, the daughter of Peter Fontaine, a beautiful child of ten years of age, was ravished and murdered by the soldiers. Another girl of about the same age, they roasted alive at Villa Nova; and a poor woman, hearing that the soldiers were coming toward her house, snatched up the cradle in which her infant son was asleep, and fled toward the woods. The soldiers, however, saw and pursued her; when she lightened herself by putting down the cradle and child, which the soldiers no sooner came to, than they murdered the infant, and continuing the pursuit, found the mother in a cave, where they first ravished, and then cut her to pieces.

Jacob Michelino, chief elder of the church of Bobbio, and several other Protestants, were hung up by means of hooks fixed in their bellies, and left to expire in the most excruciating tortures.

Giovanni Rostagnal, a venerable Protestant, upwards of fourscore years of age, had his nose and ears cut off, and slices cut from the fleshy parts of his body, until he bled to death.

Seven persons, viz. Daniel Seleagio and his wife, Giovanni Durant, Lodwich Durant, Bartholomew Durant, Daniel Revel, and Paul Reynaud, had their mouths stuffed with gunpowder, which being set fire to, their heads were blown to pieces.

Jacob Birone, a schoolmaster of Rorata, for refusing to change his religion, was stripped quite naked; and after having been very indecently exposed, had the nails of his toes and fingers torn off with red-hot pincers, and holes bored through his hands with the point of a dagger. He then had a cord tied round his middle, and was led through the streets with a soldier on each side of him. At every turning the soldier on his right hand side cut a gash in his flesh, and the soldier on his left hand side struck him with a bludgeon, both saying, at the same instant, "Will you go to Mass? will you go to Mass?" He still replied in the negative to these interrogatories, and being at length taken to the bridge, they cut off his head on the balustrades, and threw both that and his body into the river.

Paul Garnier, a very pious Protestant, had his eyes put out, was then flayed alive, and being divided into four parts, his quarters were placed on four of the principal houses of Lucerne. He bore all his sufferings with the most exemplary patience, praised God as long as he could speak, and plainly evinced, what confidence and resignation a good conscience can inspire.

Daniel Cardon, of Rocappiata, being apprehended by some soldiers, they cut his head off, and having fried his brains, ate them. Two poor old blind women, of St. Giovanni, were burnt alive; and a widow of La Torre, with her daughter, were driven into the river, and there stoned to death.

Paul Giles, on attempting to run away from some soldiers, was shot in the neck: they then slit his nose, sliced his chin, stabbed him, and gave his carcass to the dogs.

Some of the Irish troops having taken eleven men of Garcigliana prisoners, they made a furnace red hot, and forced them to push each other in until they came to the last man, whom they pushed in themselves.

Michael Gonet, a man of ninety, was burnt to death; Baptista Oudri, another old man, was stabbed; and Bartholomew Frasche had holes made in his heels, through which ropes were put; then he was dragged by them to the jail, where his wounds mortified and killed him.

Magdalene de la Piere being pursued by some of the soldiers, and taken, was thrown down a precipice, and dashed to pieces. Margaret Revella, and Mary Pravillerin, two very old women, were burnt alive; and Michael Bellino, with Ann Bochardno, were beheaded.

The son and the daughter of a counsellor of Giovanni were rolled down a steep hill together, and suffered to perish in a deep pit at the bottom. A tradesman's family, viz.: himself, his wife, and an infant in her arms, were cast from a rock, and dashed to pieces; and Joseph Chairet and Paul Carniero were flayed alive.

Cypriania Bustia, being asked if he would renounce his religion and turn Roman Catholic, replied, "I would rather renounce life, or turn dog"; to which a priest answered, "For that expression you shall both renounce life, and be given to the dogs." They, accordingly, dragged him to prison, where he continued a considerable time without food, until he was famished; after which they threw his corpse into the street before the prison, and it was devoured by dogs in the most shocking manner.

Margaret Saretta was stoned to death, and then thrown into the river; Antonio Bartina had his head cleft asunder; and Joseph Pont was cut through the middle of his body.

Daniel Maria, and his whole family, being ill of a fever, several papist ruffians broke into his house, telling him they were practical physicians, and would give them all present ease, which they did by knocking the whole family on the head.

Three infant children of a Protestant, named Peter Fine, were covered with snow, and stifled; an elderly widow, named Judith, was beheaded, and a beautiful young woman was stripped naked, and had a stake driven through her body, of which she expired.

Lucy, the wife of Peter Besson, a woman far gone in her pregnancy, who lived in one of the villages of the Piedmontese valleys, determined, if possible, to escape from such dreadful scenes as everywhere surrounded her: she, accordingly took two young children, one in each hand, and set off towards the Alps. But on the third day of the journey she was taken in labor among the mountains, and delivered of an infant, who perished through the extreme inclemency of the weather, as did the two other children; for all three were found dead by her, and herself just expiring, by the person to whom she related the above particulars.

Francis Gros, the son of a clergyman, had his flesh slowly cut from his body into small pieces, and put into a dish before him; two of his children were minced before his sight; and his wife was fastened to a post, that she might behold all these cruelties practiced on her husband and offspring. The tormentors at length being tired of exercising their cruelties, cut off the heads of both husband and wife, and then gave the flesh of the whole family to the dogs.

The sieur Thomas Margher fled to a cave, when the soldiers shut up the mouth, and he perished with famine. Judith Revelin, and seven children, were barbarously murdered in their beds; and a widow of near fourscore years of age, was hewn to pieces by soldiers.

Jacob Roseno was ordered to pray to the saints, which he absolutely refused to do: some of the soldiers beat him violently with bludgeons to make him comply, but he still refusing, several of them fired at him, and lodged a great many balls in his body. As he was almost expiring, they cried to him, "Will you call upon the saints? Will you pray to the saints?" To which he answered "No! No! No!" when one of the soldiers, with a broadsword, clove his head asunder, and put an end to his sufferings in this world; for which undoubtedly, he is gloriously rewarded in the next.

A soldier, attempting to ravish a young woman, named Susanna Gacquin, she made a stout resistance, and in the struggle pushed him over a precipice, when he was dashed to pieces by the fall. His comrades, instead of admiring the virtue of the young woman, and applauding her for so nobly defending her chastity, fell upon her with their swords, and cut her to pieces.

Giovanni Pulhus, a poor peasant of La Torre, being apprehended as a Protestant by the soldiers, was ordered, by the marquis of Pianesta, to be executed in a place near the convent. When he came to the gallows, several monks attended, and did all they could to persuade him to renounce his religion. But he told them he never would embrace idolatry, and that he was happy at being thought worthy to suffer for the name of Christ. They then put him in mind of what his wife and children, who depended upon his labor, would suffer after his decease; to which he replied, "I would have my wife and children, as well as myself, to consider their souls more than their bodies, and the next world before this; and with respect to the distress I may leave them in, God is merciful, and will provide for them while they are worthy of his protection." Finding the inflexibility of this poor man, the monks cried, "Turn him off! turn him off!" which the executioner did almost immediately, and the body being afterward cut down, was flung into the river.

Paul Clement, an elder of the church of Rossana, being apprehended by the monks of a neighboring monastery, was carried to the market place of that town, where some Protestants had just been executed by the soldiers. He was shown the dead bodies, in order that the sight might intimidate him. On beholding the shocking subjects, he said, calmly, "You may kill the body, but you cannot prejudice the soul of a true believer; but with respect to the dreadful spectacles which you have here shown me, you may rest assured, that God's vengeance will overtake the murderers of those poor people, and punish them for the innocent blood they have spilt." The monks were so exasperated at this reply that they ordered him to be hanged directly; and while he was hanging, the soldiers amused themselves in standing at a distance, and shooting at the body as at a mark.

Daniel Rambaut, of Vilario, the father of a numerous family, was apprehended, and, with several others, committed to prison, in the jail of Paysana. Here he was visited by several priests, who with continual importunities did all they could to persuade him to renounce the Protestant religion and turn papist; but this he peremptorily refused, and the priests finding his resolution, pretended to pity his numerous family, and told him that he might yet have his life, if he would subscribe to the belief of the following articles:

1. The real presence in the host.
2. Transubstantiation.
3. Purgatory.
4. The pope's infallibility.

5. That Masses said for the dead will release souls from purgatory.

6. That praying to saints will procure the remission of sins.

M. Rambaut told the priests that neither his religion, his understanding, nor his conscience, would suffer him to subscribe to any of the articles, for the following reasons:

1. That to believe the real presence in the host, is a shocking union of both blasphemy and idolatry.

2. That to fancy the words of consecration perform what the papists call transubstantiation, by converting the wafer and wine into the real and identical body and blood of Christ, which was crucified, and which afterward ascended into heaven, is too gross an absurdity for even a child to believe, who was come to the least glimmering of reason; and that nothing but the most blind superstition could make the Roman Catholics put a confidence in anything so completely ridiculous.

3. That the doctrine of purgatory was more inconsistent and absurd than a fairy tale.

4. That the pope's being infallible was an impossibility, and the pope arrogantly laid claim to what could belong to God only, as a perfect being.

5. That saying Masses for the dead was ridiculous, and only meant to keep up a belief in the fable of purgatory, as the fate of all is finally decided, on the departure of the soul from the body.

6. That praying to saints for the remission of sins is misplacing adoration; as the saints themselves have occasion for an intercessor in Christ. Therefore, as God only can pardon our errors, we ought to sue to him alone for pardon.

The priests were so highly offended at M. Rambaut's answers to the articles to which they would have had him subscribe, that they determined to shake his resolution by the most cruel method imaginable: they ordered one joint of his finger to be cut off every day until all his fingers were gone: they then proceeded in the same manner with his toes; afterward they alternately cut off, daily, a hand and a foot; but finding that he bore his sufferings with the most admirable patience, increased both in fortitude and resignation, and maintained his faith with steadfast resolution and unshaken constancy they stabbed him to the heart, and then gave his body to be devoured by the dogs.

Peter Gabriola, a Protestant gentleman of considerable eminence, being seized by a troop of soldiers, and refusing to renounce his religion, they hung a great number of little bags of gunpowder about his body, and then setting fire to them, blew him up.

Anthony, the son of Samuel Catieris, a poor dumb lad who was extremely inoffensive, was cut to pieces by a party of the troops; and soon after the same ruffians entered the house of Peter Moniriat, and cut off the legs of the whole family, leaving them to bleed to death, as they were unable to assist themselves, or to help each other.

Daniel Benech being apprehended, had his nose slit, his ears cut off, and was then divided into quarters, each quarter being hung upon a tree, and Mary Monino had her jaw bones broke and was then left to anguish till she was famished.

Mary Pelanchion, a handsome widow, belonging to the town of Vilario, was seized by a party of the Irish brigades, who having beat her cruelly, and ravished her, dragged her to a high bridge which crossed the river, and stripped her naked in a most indecent manner, hung her by the legs to the bridge, with her head downwards towards the water, and then going into boats, they fired at her until she expired.

Mary Nigrino, and her daughter who was an idiot, were cut to pieces in the woods, and their bodies left to be devoured by wild beasts: Susanna Bales, a widow of Vilario, was immured until she perished through hunger; and Susanna Calvio running away from some soldiers and hiding herself in a barn, they set fire to the straw and burnt her.

Paul Armand was hacked to pieces; a child named Daniel Bertino was burnt; Daniel Michialino had his tongue plucked out, and was left to perish in that condition; and Andreo Bertino, a very old man, who was lame, was mangled in a most shocking manner, and at length had his belly ripped open, and his bowels carried about on the point of a halbert.

Constantia Bellione, a Protestant lady, being apprehended on account of her faith, was asked by a priest if she would renounce the devil and go to Mass; to which she replied, "I was brought up in a religion by which I was always taught to renounce the devil; but should I comply with your desire, and go to Mass, I should be sure to meet him there in a variety of shapes." The priest was highly incensed at what she said, and told her to recant, or she would suffer cruelly. The lady, however, boldly answered that she valued not any sufferings he could inflict, and in spite of all the torments he could invent, she would keep her conscience pure and her faith inviolate. The priest then ordered slices of her flesh to be cut off from several parts of her body, which cruelty she bore with the most singular patience, only saying to the priest, "What horrid and lasting torments will you suffer in hell, for the trifling and temporary pains which I now endure." Exasperated at this expression, and willing to stop her tongue, the priest ordered a file of musqueteers to draw up and fire upon her, by which she was soon despatched, and sealed her martyrdom with her blood.

A young woman named Judith Mandon, for refusing to change her religion and embrace popery, was fastened to a stake, and sticks thrown at her from a distance, in the very same manner as that barbarous custom which was formerly practiced on Shrove-Tuesday, of shying at rocks, as it was termed. By this inhuman proceeding, the poor creature's limbs were beat and mangled in a terrible manner, and her brains were at last dashed out by one of the bludgeons.

David Paglia and Paul Genre, attempting to escape to the Alps, with each his son, were pursued and overtaken by the soldiers in a large plain. Here they hunted them for their diversion, goading them with their swords, and making them run about until they dropped down with fatigue. When they found that their spirits were quite exhausted, and that they could not afford them any more barbarous sport by running, the soldiers hacked them to pieces, and left their mangled bodies on the spot.

A young man of Bobbio, named Michael Greve, was apprehended in the town of La Torre, and being led to the bridge, was thrown over into the river. As he could swim very well, he swam down the stream, thinking to escape, but the soldiers and the mob followed on both sides of the river, and kept stoning him, until receiving a blow on one of his temples, he was stunned, and consequently sunk and was drowned.

David Armand was ordered to lay his head down on a block, when a soldier, with a large hammer, beat out his brains. David Baridona being apprehended at Vilario, was carried to La Torre, where, refusing to renounce his religion, he was tormented by means of brimstone matches being tied between his fingers and toes, and set fire to; and afterward, by having his flesh plucked off with red-hot pincers, until he expired; and Giovanni Barolina, with his wife, were thrown into a pool of stagnant water, and compelled, by means of pitchforks and stones, to duck down their heads until they were suffocated.

A number of soldiers went to the house of Joseph Garniero, and before they entered, fired in at the window, to give notice of their approach. A musket ball entered one of Mrs. Garniero's breasts, as she was suckling an infant with the other. On finding their intentions, she begged hard that they would spare the life of the infant, which they promised to do, and sent it immediately to a Roman Catholic nurse. They then took the husband and hanged him at his own door, and having shot the wife through the head, they left her body weltering in its blood, and her husband hanging on the gallows.

Isaiah Mondon, an elderly man, and a pious Protestant, fled from the merciless persecutors to a cleft in a rock, where he suffered the most dreadful hardships; for, in the midst of the winter he was forced to lie on the bare stone, without any covering; his food was the roots he could scratch up near his miserable habitation; and the only way by which he could procure drink, was to put snow in his mouth until it melted. Here, however, some of the inhuman soldiers found him, and after having beaten him unmercifully, they drove him towards Lucerne, goading him with the points of their swords.

Being exceedingly weakened by his manner of living, and his spirits exhausted by the blows he had received, he fell down in the road. They again beat him to make him proceed: when on his knees, he implored them to put him out of his misery, by despatching him. This they at last agreed to do; and one of them stepping up to him shot him through the head with a pistol, saying, "There, heretic, take thy request."

Mary Revol, a worthy Protestant, received a shot in her back, as she was walking along the street. She dropped down with the wound, but recovering sufficient strength, she raised herself upon her knees, and lifting her hands towards heaven, prayed in a most fervent manner to the Almighty, when a number of soldiers, who were near at hand, fired a whole volley of shot at her, many of which took effect, and put an end to her miseries in an instant.

Several men, women, and children secreted themselves in a large cave, where they continued for some weeks in safety. It was the custom for two of the men to go when it was necessary, and by stealth, procure provisions. These were, however, one day watched, by which the cave was discovered, and soon after, a troop of Roman Catholics appeared before it. The papists that assembled upon this occasion were neighbors and intimate acquaintances of the Protestants in the cave; and some were even related to each other. The Protestants, therefore, came out, and implored them, by the ties of hospitality, by the ties of blood, and as old acquaintances and neighbors, not to murder them. But superstition overcomes every sensation of nature and humanity; so that the papists, blinded by bigotry, told them they could not show any mercy to heretics, and, therefore, bade them prepare to die. Hearing this, and knowing the fatal obstinacy of the Roman Catholics, the Protestants all fell prostrate, lifted their hands and hearts to heaven, prayed with great sincerity and fervency, and then bowing down, put their faces close to the ground, and patiently waited their fate, which was soon decided, for the papists fell upon them with unremitting fury, and having cut them to pieces, left the mangled bodies and limbs in the cave.

Giovanni Salvagiot, passing by a Roman Catholic church, and not taking off his hat, was followed by some of the congregation, who fell upon and murdered him; and Jacob Barrel and his wife, having been taken prisoners by the earl of St. Secondo, one of the duke of Savoy's officers, he delivered them up to the soldiery. who cut off the woman's breasts, and the man's nose, and then shot them both through the head.

Anthony Guigo, a Protestant, of a wavering disposition, went to Periero, with an intent to renounce his religion and embrace popery. This design he communicated to some priests, who highly commended it, and a day was fixed upon for his public recantation. In the meantime, Anthony grew fully sensible of his perfidy, and his conscience tormented him so much night and day that he determined not to recant, but to make his escape. This he effected, but being soon missed and pursued, he was taken. The troops on the way did all they could to bring him back to his design of recantation; but finding their endeavors ineffectual, they beat him violently on the road. When coming near a precipice, he took an opportunity of leaping down it and was dashed to pieces.

A Protestant gentleman, of considerable fortune, at Bobbio, being nightly provoked by the insolence of a priest, retorted with great severity; and among other things, said, that the pope was Antichrist, Mass idolatry, purgatory a farce, and absolution a cheat. To be revenged, the priest hired five desperate ruffians, who, the same evening, broke into the gentleman's house, and seized upon him in a violent manner. The gentleman was terribly frightened, fell on his knees, and implored mercy; but the desperate ruffians despatched him without the least hesitation.

A Narrative of the Piedmontese War

The massacres and murders already mentioned to have been committed in the valleys of Piedmont, nearly depopulated most of the towns and villages. One place only had not been assaulted, and that was owing to the difficulty of approaching it; this was the little commonalty of Roras, which was situated upon a rock.

As the work of blood grew slack in other places, the earl of Christople, one of the duke of Savoy's officers, determined, if possible, to make himself master of it; and, with that view, detached three hundred men to surprise it secretly.

The inhabitants of Roras, however, had intelligence of the approach of these troops, when captain Joshua Gianavel, a brave Protestant officer, put himself at the head of a small body of the citizens, and waited in ambush to attack the enemy in a small defile.

When the troops appeared, and had entered the defile, which was the only place by which the town could be approached, the Protestants kept up a smart and well-directed fire against them, and still kept themselves concealed behind bushes from the sight of the enemy. A great number of the soldiers were killed, and the remainder receiving a continued fire, and not seeing any to whom they might return it, thought proper to retreat.

The members of this little community then sent a memorial to the marquis of Pianessa, one of the duke's general officers, setting forth, 'That they were sorry, upon any occasion, to be under the necessity of taking up arms; but that the secret approach of a body of troops, without any reason assigned, or any previous notice sent of the purpose of their coming, had greatly alarmed them; that as it was their custom never to suffer any of the military to enter their little community, they had repelled force by force, and should do so again; but in all other respects, they professed themselves dutiful, obedient, and loyal subjects to their sovereign, the duke of Savoy.'

The marquis of Pianessa, that he might have the better opportunity of deluding and surprising the Protestants of Roras, sent them word in answer, 'That he was perfectly satisfied with their behavior, for they had done right, and even rendered a service to their country, as the men who had attempted to pass the defile were not his troops, or sent by him, but a band of desperate robbers, who had, for some time, infested those parts, and been a terror to the neighboring country.' To give a greater color to his treachery, he then published an ambiguous proclamation seemingly favorable to the inhabitants.

Yet, the very day after this plausible proclamation, and specious conduct, the marquis sent five hundred men to possess themselves of Roras, while the people, as he thought, were lulled into perfect security by his specious behavior.

Captain Gianavel, however, was not to be deceived so easily: he, therefore, laid an ambuscade for this body of troops, as he had for the former, and compelled them to retire with very considerable loss.

Though foiled in these two attempts, the marquis of Pianessa determined on a third, which should be still more formidable; but first he imprudently published another proclamation, disowning any knowledge of the second attempt.

Soon after, seven hundred chosen men were sent upon the expedition, who, in spite of the fire from the Protestants, forced the defile, entered Roras, and began to murder every person they met with, without distinction of age or sex. The Protestant captain Gianavel, at the head of a small body, though he had lost the defile, determined to dispute their passage through a fortified pass that led to the richest and best part of the town. Here he was successful, by keeping up a continual fire, and by means of his men being all complete marksmen. The Roman Catholic commander was greatly staggered at this opposition, as he imagined that he had surmounted all difficulties. He, however, did his endeavors to force the pass, but being able to bring up only twelve men in front at a time, and the Protestants being secured by a breastwork, he found he should be baffled by the handful of men who opposed him.

Enraged at the loss of so many of his troops, and fearful of disgrace if he persisted in attempting what appeared so impracticable, he thought it the wisest thing to retreat. Unwilling, however, to withdraw his men by the defile at which he had entered, on account of the difficulty and danger of the enterprise, he determined to retreat towards Vilario, by another pass called Piampra, which though hard of access, was easy of descent. But in this he met with disappointment, for Captain Gianavel having posted his little band here, greatly annoyed the troops as they passed, and even pursued their rear until they entered the open country.

The marquis of Pianessa, finding that all his attempts were frustrated, and that every artifice he used was only an alarm signal to the inhabitants of Roras, determined to act openly, and therefore proclaimed that ample rewards should be given to any one who would bear arms against the obstinate heretics of Roras, as he called them; and that any officer who would exterminate them should be rewarded in a princely manner.

This engaged Captain Mario, a bigoted Roman Catholic, and a desperate ruffian, to undertake the enterprise. He, therefore, obtained leave to raise a regiment in the following six towns: Lucerne, Borges, Famolas, Bobbio, Begnal, and Cavos.

Having completed his regiment, which consisted of one thousand men, he laid his plan not to go by the defiles or the passes, but to attempt gaining the summit of a rock, whence he imagined he could pour his troops into the town without much difficulty or opposition.

The Protestants suffered the Roman Catholic troops to gain almost the summit of the rock, without giving them any opposition, or ever appearing in their sight: but when they had almost reached the top they made a most furious attack upon them; one party keeping up a well-directed and constant fire, and another party rolling down huge stones.

This stopped the career of the papist troops: many were killed by the musketry, and more by the stones, which beat them down the precipices. Several fell sacrifices to their hurry, for by attempting a precipitate retreat they fell down, and were dashed to pieces; and Captain Mario himself narrowly escaped with his life, for he fell from a craggy place into a river which washed the foot of the rock. He was taken up senseless, but afterwards recovered, though he was ill of the bruises for a long time; and, at length he fell into a decline at Lucerne, where he died.

Another body of troops was ordered from the camp at Vilario, to make an attempt upon Roras; but these were likewise defeated, by means of the Protestants' ambush fighting, and compelled to retreat again to the camp at Vilario.

After each of these signal victories, Captain Gianavel made a suitable discourse to his men, causing them to kneel down, and return thanks to the Almighty for his providential protection; and usually concluded with the Eleventh Psalm, where the subject is placing confidence in God.

The marquis of Pianessa was greatly enraged at being so much baffled by the few inhabitants of Roras: he, therefore, determined to attempt their expulsion in such a manner as could hardly fail of success.

With this view he ordered all the Roman Catholic militia of Piedmont to be raised and disciplined. When these orders were completed, he joined to the militia eight thousand regular troops, and dividing the whole into three distinct bodies, he designed that three formidable attacks should be made at the same time, unless the people of Roras, to whom he sent an account of his great preparations, would comply with the following conditions:

1. To ask pardon for taking up arms. 2. To pay the expenses of all the expeditions sent against them. 3. To acknowledge the infallibility of the pope. 4. To go to Mass. 5. To pray to the saints. 6. To wear beards. 7. To deliver up their ministers. 8. To deliver up their schoolmasters. 9. To go to confession. 10. To pay loans for the delivery of souls from purgatory. 11. To give up Captain Gianavel at discretion. 12. To give up the elders of their church at discretion.

The inhabitants of Roras, on being acquainted with these conditions, were filled with an honest indignation, and, in answer, sent word to the marquis that sooner than comply with them they would suffer three things, which, of all others, were the most obnoxious to mankind, viz.

1. Their estates to be seized. 2. Their houses to be burned. 3. Themselves to be murdered.

Exasperated at this message, the marquis sent them this laconic epistle.

To the Obstinate Heretics Inhabiting Roras

You shall have your request, for the troops sent against you have strict injunctions to plunder, burn, and kill.

PIANESSA.

The three armies were then put in motion, and the attacks ordered to be made thus: the first by the rocks of Vilario; the second by the pass of Bagnol; and the third by the defile of Lucerne.

The troops forced their way by the superiority of numbers, and having gained the rocks, pass, and defile, began to make the most horrid depredations, and exercise the greatest cruelties. Men they hanged, burned, racked to death, or cut to pieces; women they ripped open, crucified, drowned, or threw from the precipices; and children they tossed upon spears, minced, cut their throats, or dashed out their brains. One hundred and twenty-six suffered in this manner on the first day of their gaining the town.

Agreeable to the marquis of Pianessa's orders, they likewise plundered the estates, and burned the houses of the people. Several Protestants, however, made their escape, under the conduct of Captain Gianavel, whose wife and children were unfortunately made prisoners and sent under a strong guard to Turin.

The marquis of Pianessa wrote a letter to Captain Gianavel, and released a Protestant prisoner that he might carry it him. The contents were, that if the captain would embrace the Roman Catholic religion, he should be indemnified for all his losses since the commencement of the war; his wife and children should be immediately released, and himself honorably promoted in the duke of Savoy's army; but if he refused to accede to the proposals made him, his wife and children should be put to death; and so large a reward should be given to take him, dead or alive, that even some of his own confidential friends should be tempted to betray him, from the greatness of the sum.

To this epistle, the brave Gianavel sent the following answer.

My Lord Marquis,
There is no torment so great or death so cruel, but what I would prefer to the abjuration of my religion: so that promises lose their effects, and menaces only strengthen me in my faith.

With respect to my wife and children, my lord, nothing can be more afflicting to me than the thought of their confinement, or more dreadful to my imagination, than their suffering a violent and cruel death. I keenly feel all the tender sensations of husband and parent; my heart is replete with every sentiment of humanity; I would suffer any torment to rescue them from danger; I would die to preserve them.

But having said thus much, my lord, I assure you that the purchase of their lives must not be the price of my salvation. You have them in your power it is true; but my consolation is that your power is only a temporary authority over their bodies: you may destroy the mortal part, but their immortal souls are out of your reach, and will live hereafter to bear testimony against you for your cruelties. I therefore recommend them and myself to God, and pray for a reformation in your heart.

JOSHUA GIANAVEL.

This brave Protestant officer, after writing the above letter, retired to the Alps, with his followers; and being joined by a great number of other fugitive Protestants, he harassed the enemy by continual skirmishes.

Meeting one day with a body of papist troops near Bibiana, he, though inferior in numbers, attacked them with great fury, and put them to the rout without the loss of a man, though himself was shot through the leg in the engagement, by a soldier who had hid himself behind a tree; but Gianavel perceiving whence the shot came, pointed his gun to the place, and despatched the person who had wounded him.

Captain Gianavel hearing that a Captain Jahier had collected together a considerable body of Protestants, wrote him a letter, proposing a junction of their forces. Captain Jahier immediately agreed to the proposal, and marched directly to meet Gianavel.

The junction being formed, it was proposed to attack a town, (inhabited by Roman Catholics) called Garcigliana. The assault was given with great spirit, but a reinforcement of horse and foot having lately entered the town, which the Protestants knew nothing of, they were repulsed; yet made a masterly retreat, and only lost one man in the action.

The next attempt of the Protestant forces was upon St. Secondo, which they attacked with great vigor, but met with a strong resistance from the Roman Catholic troops, who had fortified the streets and planted themselves in the houses, from whence they poured musket balls in prodigious numbers. The Protestants, however, advanced, under cover of a great number of planks, which some held over their heads, to secure them from the shots of the enemy from the houses, while others kept up a well-directed fire; so that the houses and entrenchments were soon forced, and the town taken.

In the town they found a prodigious quantity of plunder, which had been taken from Protestants at various times, and different places, and which were stored up in the warehouses, churches, dwelling houses, etc. This they removed to a place of safety, to be distributed, with as much justice as possible, among the sufferers.

This successful attack was made with such skill and spirit that it cost very little to the conquering party, the Protestants having only seventeen killed, and twenty-six wounded; while the papists suffered a loss of no less than four hundred and fifty killed, and five hundred and eleven wounded.

Five Protestant officers, viz., Gianavel, Jahier, Laurentio, Genolet and Benet, laid a plan to surprise Biqueras. To this end they marched in five respective bodies, and by agreement were to make the attack at the same time. The captains, Jahier and Laurentio, passed through two defiles in the woods, and came to the place in safety, under covert; but the other three bodies made their approaches through an open country, and, consequently, were more exposed to an attack.

The Roman Catholics taking the alarm, a great number of troops were sent to relieve Biqueras from Cavors, Bibiana, Feline, Campiglione, and some other neighboring places. When these were united, they determined to attack the three Protestant parties, that were marching through the open country.

The Protestant officers perceiving the intent of the enemy, and not being at a great distance from each other, joined forces with the utmost expedition, and formed themselves in order of battle.

In the meantime, the captains, Jahier and Laurentio, had assaulted the town of Biqueras, and burnt all the out houses, to make their approaches with the greater ease; but not being supported as they expected by the other three Protestant captains, they sent a messenger, on a swift horse, towards the open country, to inquire the reason.

The messenger soon returned and informed them that it was not in the power of the three Protestant captains to support their proceedings, as they were themselves attacked by a very superior force in the plain, and could scarce sustain the unequal conflict.

The captains, Jahier and Laurentio, on receiving this intelligence, determined to discontinue the assault on Biqueras, and to proceed, with all possible expedition, to the relief of their friends on the plain. This design proved to be of the most essential service, for just as they arrived at the spot where the two armies were engaged, the papist troops began to prevail, and were on the point of flanking the left wing, commanded by Captain Gianavel. The arrival of these troops turned the scale in favor of the Protestants: and the papist forces, though they fought with the most obstinate intrepidity, were totally defeated. A great number were killed and wounded, on both sides, and the baggage, military stores, etc., taken by the Protestants were very considerable.

Captain Gianavel, having information that three hundred of the enemy were to convoy a great quantity of stores, provisions, etc., from La Torre to the castle of Mirabac, determined to attack them on the way. He, accordingly, began the assault at Malbec, though with a very inadequate force. The contest was long and bloody, but the Protestants at length were obliged to yield to the superiority of numbers, and compelled to make a retreat, which they did with great regularity, and but little loss.

Captain Gianavel advanced to an advantageous post, situated near the town of Vilario, and then sent the following information and commands to the inhabitants.

1. That he should attack the town in twenty-four hours.

2. That with respect to the Roman Catholics who had borne arms, whether they belonged to the army or not, he should act by the law of retaliation, and put them to death, for the numerous depredations and many cruel murders they had committed.

3. That all women and children, whatever their religion might be, should be safe.

4. That he commanded all male Protestants to leave the town and join him.

5. That all apostates, who had, through weakness, abjured their religion, should be deemed enemies, unless they renounced their abjuration.

6. That all who returned to their duty to God, and themselves, should be received as friends.

The Protestants, in general, immediately left the town, and joined Captain Gianavel with great satisfaction, and the few, who through weakness or fear, had abjured their faith, recanted their abjuration and were received into the bosom of the Church. As the marquis of Pianessa had removed the army, and encamped in quite a different part of the country, the Roman Catholics of Vilario thought it would be folly to attempt to defend the place with the small force they had. They, therefore, fled with the utmost precipitation, leaving the town and most of their property to the discretion of the Protestants.

The Protestant commanders having called a council of war, resolved to make an attempt upon the town of La Torre.

The papists being apprised of the design, detached some troops to defend a defile, through which the Protestants must make their approach; but these were defeated, compelled to abandon the pass, and forced to retreat to La Torre.

The Protestants proceeded on their march, and the troops of La Torre, on their approach, made a furious sally, but were repulsed with great loss, and compelled to seek shelter in the town. The governor now only thought of defending the place, which the Protestants began to attack in form; but after many brave attempts, and furious assaults, the commanders determined to abandon the enterprise for several reasons, particularly, because they found the place itself too strong, their own number too weak, and their cannon not adequate to the task of battering down the walls.

This resolution taken, the Protestant commanders began a masterly retreat, and conducted it with such regularity that the enemy did not choose to pursue them, or molest their rear, which they might have done, as they passed the defiles.

The next day they mustered, reviewed the army, and found the whole to amount to four hundred and ninety-five men. They then held a council of war, and planned an easier enterprise: this was to make an attack on the commonalty of Crusol, a place inhabited by a number of the most bigoted Roman Catholics, and who had exercised, during the persecutions, the most unheard-of cruelties on the Protestants.

The people of Crusol, hearing of the design against them, fled to a neighboring fortress, situated on a rock, where the Protestants could not come to them, for a very few men could render it inaccessible to a numerous army. Thus they secured their persons, but were in too much hurry to secure their property, the principal part of which, indeed, had been plundered from the Protestants, and now luckily fell again to the possession of the right owners. It consisted of many rich and valuable articles, and what, at that time, was of much more consequence, viz., a great quantity of military stores.

The day after the Protestants were gone with their booty, eight hundred troops arrived to the assistance of the people of Crusol, having been despatched from Lucerne, Biqueras, Cavors, etc. But finding themselves too late, and that pursuit would be vain, not to return empty handed, they began to plunder the neighboring villages, though what they took was from their friends. After collecting a tolerable booty, they began to divide it, but disagreeing about the different shares, they fell from words to blows, did a great deal of mischief, and then plundered each other.

On the very same day in which the Protestants were so successful at Crusol, some papists marched with a design to plunder and burn the little Protestant village of Rocappiatta, but by the way they met with the Protestant forces belonging to the captains, Jahier and Laurentio, who were posted on the hill of Angrogne. A trivial engagement ensued, for the Roman Catholics, on the very first attack, retreated in great confusion, and were pursued with much slaughter. After the pursuit was over, some straggling papist troops meeting with a poor peasant, who was a Protestant, tied a cord round his head, and strained it until his skull was quite crushed.

Captain Gianavel and Captain Jahier concerted a design together to make an attack upon Lucerne; but Captain Jahier, not bringing up his forces at the time appointed, Captain Gianavel determined to attempt the enterprise himself.

He, therefore, by a forced march, proceeded towards that place during the whole, and was close to it by break of day. His first care was to cut the pipes that conveyed water into the town, and then to break down the bridge, by which alone provisions from the country could enter.

He then assaulted the place, and speedily possessed himself of two of the outposts; but finding he could not make himself master of the place, he prudently retreated with very little loss, blaming, however, Captain Jahier, for the failure of the enterprise.

The papists being informed that Captain Gianavel was at Angrogne with only his own company, determined if possible to surprise him. With this view, a great number of troops were detached from La Torre and other places: one party of these got on top of a mountain, beneath which he was posted; and the other party intended to possess themselves of the gate of St. Bartholomew.

The papists thought themselves sure of taking Captain Gianavel and every one of his men, as they consisted but of three hundred, and their own force was two thousand five hundred. Their design, however, was providentially frustrated, for one of the popish soldiers imprudently blowing a trumpet before the signal for attack was given, Captain Gianavel took the alarm, and posted his little company so advantageously at the gate of St. Bartholomew and at the defile by which the enemy must descend from the mountains, that the Roman Catholic troops failed in both attacks, and were repulsed with very considerable loss.

Soon after, Captain Jahier came to Angrogne, and joined his forces to those of Captain Gianavel, giving sufficient reasons to excuse his before-mentioned failure. Captain Jahier now made several secret excursions with great success, always selecting the most active troops, belonging both to Gianavel and himself. One day he had put himself at the head of forty-four men, to proceed upon an expedition, when entering a plain near Ossac, he was suddenly surrounded by a large body of horse. Captain Jahier and his men fought desperately, though oppressed by odds, and killed the commander-in-chief, three captains, and fifty-seven private men, of the enemy. But Captain Jahier himself being killed, with thirty-five of his men, the rest surrendered. One of the soldiers cut off Captain Jahier's head, and carrying it to Turin, presented it to the duke of Savoy, who rewarded him with six hundred ducatoons.

The death of this gentleman was a signal loss to the Protestants, as he was a real friend to, and companion of, the reformed Church. He possessed a most undaunted spirit, so that no difficulties could deter him from undertaking an enterprise, or dangers terrify him in its execution. He was pious without affectation, and humane without weakness; bold in a field, meek in a domestic life, of a penetrating genius, active in spirit, and resolute in all his undertakings.

To add to the affliction of the Protestants, Captain Gianavel was, soon after, wounded in such a manner that he was obliged to keep his bed. They, however, took new courage from misfortunes, and determining not to let their spirits droop attacked a body of popish troops with great intrepidity; the Protestants were much inferior in numbers, but fought with more resolution than the papists, and at length routed them with considerable slaughter. During the action, a sergeant named Michael Bertino was killed; when his son, who was close behind him, leaped into his place, and said, "I have lost my father; but courage, fellow soldiers, God is a father to us all."

Several skirmishes likewise happened between the troops of La Torre and Tagliaretto, and the Protestant forces, which in general terminated in favor of the latter.

A Protestant gentleman, named Andrion, raised a regiment of horse, and took the command of it himself. The sieur John Leger persuaded a great number of Protestants to form themselves into volunteer companies; and an excellent officer, named Michelin, instituted several bands of light troops. These being all joined to the remains of the veteran Protestant troops, (for great numbers had been lost in the various battles, skirmishes, sieges, etc.) composed a respectable army, which the officers thought proper to encamp near St. Giovanni.

The Roman Catholic commanders, alarmed at the formidable appearance and increased strength of the Protestant forces, determined, if possible, to dislodge them from their encampment. With this view they collected together a large force, consisting of the principal part of the garrisons of the Roman Catholic towns, the draft from the Irish brigades, a great number of regulars sent by the marquis of Pianessa, the auxiliary troops, and the independent companies.

These, having formed a junction, encamped near the Protestants, and spent several days in calling councils of war, and disputing on the most proper mode of proceeding. Some were for plundering the country, in order to draw the Protestants from their camp; others were for patiently waiting till they were attacked; and a third party were for assaulting the Protestant camp, and trying to make themselves master of everything in it.

The last of them prevailed, and the morning after the resolution had been taken was appointed to put it into execution. The Roman Catholic troops were accordingly separated into four divisions, three of which were to make an attack in different places; and the fourth to remain as a body of reserve to act as occasion might require.

One of the Roman Catholic officers, previous to the attack, thus harangued his men:

"Fellow-soldiers, you are now going to enter upon a great action, which will bring you fame and riches. The motives of your acting with spirit are likewise of the most important nature; namely, the honor of showing your loyalty to your sovereign, the pleasure of spilling heretic blood, and the prospect of plundering the Protestant camp. So, my brave fellows, fall on, give no quarter, kill all you meet, and take all you come near."

After this inhuman speech the engagement began, and the Protestant camp was attacked in three places with inconceivable fury. The fight was maintained with great obstinacy and perseverance on both sides, continuing without intermission for the space of four hours: for the several companies on both sides relieved each other alternately, and by that means kept up a continual fire during the whole action.

During the engagement of the main armies, a detachment was sent from the body of reserve to attack the post of Castelas, which, if the papists had carried, it would have given them the command of the valleys of Perosa, St. Martino, and Lucerne; but they were repulsed with great loss, and compelled to return to the body of reserve, from whence they had been detached.

Soon after the return of this detachment, the Roman Catholic troops, being hard pressed in the main battle, sent for the body of reserve to come to their support. These immediately marched to their assistance, and for some time longer held the event doubtful, but at length the valor of the Protestants prevailed, and the papists were totally defeated, with the loss of upwards of three hundred men killed, and many more wounded.

When the Syndic of Lucerne, who was indeed a papist, but not a bigoted one, saw the great number of wounded men brought into that city, he exclaimed, "Ah! I thought the wolves used to devour the heretics, but now I see the heretics eat the wolves." This expression being reported to M. Marolles, the Roman Catholic commander-in-chief at Lucerne, he sent a very severe and threatening letter to the Syndic, who was so terrified, that the fright threw him into a fever, and he died in a few days.

This great battle was fought just before the harvest was got in, when the papists, exasperated at their disgrace, and resolved on any kind of revenge, spread themselves by night in detached parties over the finest corn fields of the Protestants, and set them on fire in sundry places. Some of these straggling parties, however, suffered for their conduct; for the Protestants, being alarmed in the night by the blazing of the fire among the corn, pursued the fugitives early in the morning, and overtaking many, put them to death. The Protestant captain Bellin, likewise, by way of retaliation, went with a body of light troops, and burnt the suburbs of La Torre, making his retreat afterward with very little loss.

A few days after, Captain Bellin, with a much stronger body of troops, attacked the town of La Torre itself, and making a breach in the wall of the convent, his men entered, driving the garrison into the citadel and burning both town and convent. After having effected this, they made a regular retreat, as they could not reduce the citadel for want of cannon.

An Account of the Persecutions of Michael de Molinos, a Native of Spain

Michael de Molinos, a Spaniard of a rich and honorable family, entered, when young, into priest's orders, but would not accept of any preferment in the Church. He possessed great natural abilities, which he dedicated to the service of his fellow creatures, without any view of emolument to himself. His course of life was pious and uniform; nor did he exercise those austerities which are common among the religious orders of the Church of Rome.

Being of a contemplative turn of mind, he pursued the track of the mystical divines, and having acquired great reputation in Spain, and being desirous of propagating his sublime mode of devotion, he left his own country, and settled at Rome. Here he soon connected himself with some of the most distinguished among the literati, who so approved of his religious maxims, that they concurred in assisting him to propagate them; and, in a short time, he obtained a great number of followers, who, from the sublime mode of their religion, were distinguished by the name of Quietists.

In 1675, Molinos published a book entitled "Il Guida Spirituale," to which were subjoined recommendatory letters from several great personages. One of these was by the archbishop of Reggio; a second by the general of the Franciscans; and a third by Father Martin de Esparsa, a Jesuit, who had been divinity-professor both at Salamanca and Rome.

No sooner was the book published than it was greatly read, and highly esteemed, both in Italy and Spain; and this so raised the reputation of the author that his acquaintance was coveted by the most respectable characters. Letters were written to him from numbers of people, so that a correspondence was settled between him, and those who approved of his method in different parts of Europe. Some secular priests, both at Rome and Naples, declared themselves openly for it, and consulted him, as a sort of oracle, on many occasions. But those who attached themselves to him with the greatest sincerity were some of the fathers of the Oratory; in particular three of the most eminent, namely, Caloredi, Ciceri, and Petrucci. Many of the cardinals also courted his acquaintance, and thought themselves happy in being reckoned among the number of his friends. The most distinguished of them was the Cardinal d'Estrees, a man of very great learning, who so highly approved of Molinos' maxims that he entered into a close connection with him. They conversed together daily, and notwithstanding the distrust a Spaniard has naturally of a Frenchman, yet Molinos, who was sincere in his principles, opened his mind without reserve to the cardinal; and by this means a correspondence was settled between Molinos and some distinguished characters in France.

Whilst Molinos was thus laboring to propagate his religious mode, Father Petrucci wrote several treatises relative to a contemplative life; but he mixed in them so many rules for the devotions of the Romish Church, as mitigated that censure he might have otherwise incurred. They were written chiefly for the use of the nuns, and therefore the sense was expressed in the most easy and familiar style.

Molinos had now acquired such reputation, that the Jesuits and Dominicans began to be greatly alarmed, and determined to put a stop to the progress of this method. To do this, it was necessary to decry the author of it; and as heresy is an imputation that makes the strongest impression at Rome, Molinos and his followers were given out to be heretics. Books were also written by some of the Jesuits against Molinos and his method; but they were all answered with spirit by Molinos.

These disputes occasioned such disturbance in Rome that the whole affair was taken notice of by the Inquisition. Molinos and his book, and Father Petrucci, with his treatises and letters, were brought under a severe examination; and the Jesuits were considered as the accusers. One of the society had, indeed, approved of Molinos' book, but the rest took care he should not be again seen at Rome. In the course of the examination both Molinos and Petrucci acquitted themselves so well, that their books were again approved, and the answers which the Jesuits had written were censured as scandalous.

Petrucci's conduct on this occasion was so highly approved that it not only raised the credit of the cause, but his own emolument; for he was soon after made bishop of Jesis, which was a new declaration made by the pope in their favor. Their books were now esteemed more than ever, their method was more followed, and the novelty of it, with the new approbation given after so vigorous an accusation by the Jesuits, all contributed to raise the credit, and increase the number of the party.

The behavior of Father Petrucci in his new dignity greatly contributed to increase his reputation, so that his enemies were unwilling to give him any further disturbance; and, indeed, there was less occasion given for censure by his writings than those of Molinos. Some passages in the latter were not so cautiously expressed, but there was room to make exceptions to them; while, on the other hand Petrucci so fully explained himself, as easily to remove the objections made to some parts of his letter.

The great reputation acquired by Molinos and Petrucci occasioned a daily increase of the Quietists. All who were thought sincerely devout, or at least affected the reputation of it, were reckoned among the number. If these persons were observed to become more strict in their lives and mental devotions, yet there appeared less zeal in their whole deportment at the exterior parts of the Church ceremonies. They were not so assiduous at Mass, nor so earnest to procure Masses to be said for their friends; nor were they so frequently either at confession, or in processions.

Though the new approbation given to Molinos' book by the Inquisition had checked the proceedings of his enemies; yet they were still inveterate against him in their hearts, and determined if possible to ruin him. They insinuated that he had ill designs, and was, in his heart, an enemy to the Christian religion: that under pretence of raising men to a sublime strain of devotion, he intended to erase from their minds a sense of the mysteries of Christianity. And because he was a Spaniard, they gave out that he was descended from a Jewish or Mahometan race, and that he might carry in his blood, or in his first education, some seeds of those religions which he had since cultivated with no less art than zeal. This last calumny gained but little credit at Rome, though it was said an order was sent to examine the registers of the place where Molinos was baptized.

Molinos finding himself attacked with great vigor, and the most unrelenting malice, took every necessary precaution to prevent these imputations being credited. He wrote a treatise, entitled "Frequent and Daily Communion," which was likewise approved by some of the most learned of the Romish clergy. This was printed with his Spiritual Guide, in the year 1675; and in the preface to it he declared that he had not written it with any design to engage himself in matters of controversy, but that it was drawn from him by the earnest solicitations of many pious people.

The Jesuits, failing in their attempts of crushing Molinos' power in Rome, applied to the court of France, when, in a short time, they

10

so far succeeded that an order was sent to Cardinal d'Estrees, commanding him to prosecute Molinos with all possible rigor. The cardinal, though so strongly attached to Molinos, resolved to sacrifice all that is sacred in friendship to the will of his master. Finding, however, there was not sufficient matter for an accusation against him, he determined to supply that defect himself. He therefore went to the inquisitors, and informed them of several particulars, not only relative to Molinos, but also Petrucci, both of whom, together with several of their friends, were put into the Inquisition.

When they were brought before the inquisitors, (which was the beginning of the year 1684) Petrucci answered the respective questions put to him with so much judgment and temper that he was soon dismissed; and though Molinos' examination was much longer, it was generally expected he would have been likewise discharged: but this was not the case. Though the inquisitors had not any just accusation against him, yet they strained every nerve to find him guilty of heresy. They first objected to his holding a correspondence in different parts of Europe; but of this he was acquitted, as the matter of that correspondence could not be made criminal. They then directed their attention to some suspicious papers found in his chamber; but Molinos so clearly explained their meaning that nothing could be made of them to his prejudice. At length, Cardinal d'Estrees, after producing the order sent him by the king of France for prosecuting Molinos, said he could prove against him more than was necessary to convince them he was guilty of heresy. To do this he perverted the meaning of some passages in Molinos' books and papers, and related many false and aggravating circumstances relative to the prisoner. He acknowledged he had lived with him under the appearance of friendship, but that it was only to discover his principles and intentions: that he had found them to be of a bad nature, and that dangerous consequences were likely to ensue; but in order to make a full discovery, he had assented to several things, which, in his heart, he detested; and that, by these means, he saw into the secrets of Molinos, but determined not to take any notice, until a proper opportunity should offer of crushing him and his followers.

In consequence of d'Estree's evidence, Molinos was closely confined by the Inquisition, where he continued for some time, during which period all was quiet, and his followers prosecuted their mode without interruption. But on a sudden the Jesuits determined to extirpate them, and the storm broke out with the most inveterate vehemence.

The Count Vespiniani and his lady, Don Paulo Rocchi, confessor to the prince Borghese, and some of his family, with several others, (in all seventy persons) were put into the Inquisition, among whom many were highly esteemed for their learning and piety. The accusation laid against the clergy was their neglecting to say the breviary; and the rest were accused of going to the Communion without first attending confession. In a word, it was said, they neglected all the exterior parts of religion, and gave themselves up wholly to solitude and inward prayer.

The Countess Vespiniani exerted herself in a very particular manner on her examination before the inquisitors. She said she had never revealed her method of devotion to any mortal but her confessor, and that it was impossible they should know it without his discovering the secret; that, therefore it was time to give over going to confession, if priests made this use of it, to discover the most secret thoughts intrusted to them; and that, for the future, she would only make her confession to God.

From this spirited speech, and the great noise made in consequence of the countess's situation, the inquisitors thought it most prudent to dismiss both her and her husband, lest the people might be incensed. and what she said might lessen the credit of confession. They were, therefore, both discharged, but bound to appear whenever they should be called upon.

Besides those already mentioned, such was the inveteracy of the Jesuits against the Quietists, that, within the space of a month, upwards of two hundred persons were put into the Inquisition; and that method of devotion which had passed in Italy as the most elevated to which mortals could aspire, was deemed heretical, and the chief promoters of it confined in a wretched dungeon.

In order, if possible, to extirpate Quietism, the inquisitors sent a circular letter to Cardinal Cibo, as the chief minister, to disperse it through Italy. It was addressed to all prelates, informed them, that whereas many schools and fraternities were established in several parts of Italy, in which some persons, under the pretence of leading people into the ways of the Spirit, and to the prayer of quietness, instilled into them many abominable heresies, therefore a strict charge was given to dissolve all those societies, and to oblige the spiritual guide to tread in the known paths; and, in particular, to take care that none of that sort should be suffered to have the direction of the nunneries. Orders were likewise given to proceed, in the way of justice, against those who should be found guilty of these abominable errors.

After this a strict inquiry was made into all the nunneries in Rome, when most of their directors and confessors were discovered to be engaged in this new method. It was found that the Carmelites, the nuns of the Conception, and those of several other convents, were wholly given up to prayer and contemplation, and that, instead of their beads, and the other devotions to saints, or images, they were much alone, and often in the exercise of mental prayer; that when they were asked why they had laid aside the use of their beads and their ancient forms, their answer was that their directors had advised them so to do. Information of this being given to the Inquisition, they sent orders that all books written in the same strain with those of Molinos and Petrucci should be taken from them, and that they should be compelled to return to their original form of devotion.

The circular letter sent to Cardinal Cibo, produced but little effect, for most of the Italian bishops were inclined to Molinos' method. It was intended that this, as well as all other orders from the inquisitors, should be kept secret; but notwithstanding all their care, copies of it were printed, and dispersed in most of the principal towns in Italy. This gave great uneasiness to the inquisitors, who used every method they could to conceal their proceedings from the knowledge of the world. They blamed the cardinal, and accused him of being the cause of it; but he retorted on them, and his secretary laid the fault on both.

During these transactions, Molinos suffered great indignities from the officers of the Inquisition; and the only comfort he received was from being sometimes visited by Father Petrucci.

Though he had lived in the highest reputation in Rome for some years, he was now as much despised as he had been admired, being generally considered as one of the worst of heretics.

The greater part of Molinos' followers, who had been placed in the Inquisition, having abjured his mode, were dismissed; but a harder fate awaited Molinos, their leader.

After lying a considerable time in prison, he was at length brought again before the inquisitors to answer to a number of articles exhibited against him from his writings. As soon as he appeared in court, a chain was put round his body, and a wax light in his hand, when two friars read aloud the articles of accusation. Molinos answered each with great steadiness and resolution; and notwithstanding his arguments totally defeated the force of all, yet he was found guilty of heresy, and condemned to imprisonment for life.

When he left the court he was attended by a priest, who had borne him the greatest respect. On his arrival at the prison he entered the cell allotted for his confinement with great tranquillity; and on taking leave of the priest, thus addressed him: "Adieu, father, we shall meet again at the Day of Judgment, and then it will appear on which side the truth is, whether on my side, or on yours."

During his confinement, he was several times tortured in the most cruel manner, until, at length, the severity of the punishments overpowered his strength, and finished his existence.

The death of Molinos struck such an impression on his followers that the greater part of them soon abjured his mode; and by the assiduity of the Jesuits, Quietism was totally extirpated throughout the country.

CHAPTER VII

An Account of the Life and Persecutions of John Wickliffe

IT will not be inappropriate to devote a few pages of this work to a brief detail of the lives of some of those men who first stepped forward, regardless of the bigoted power which opposed all reformation ,to stem the time of papal corruption, and to seal the pure doctrines of the Gospel with their blood. Among these, Great Britain has the honor of taking the lead, and first maintaining that freedom in religious controversy which astonished Europe, and demonstrated that political and religious liberty are equally the growth of that favored island. Among the earliest of these eminent persons was

John Wickliffe

This celebrated reformer, denominated the "Morning Star of the Reformation," was born about the year 1324, in the reign of Edward II. Of his extraction we have no certain account. His parents designing him for the Church, sent him to Queen's College, Oxford. about that period founded by Robert Eaglesfield, confessor to Queen Philippi. But not meeting with the advantages for study in that newly established house which he expected, he removed to Merton College, which was then esteemed one of the most learned societies in Europe.

The first thing which drew him into public notice, was his defence of the university against the begging friars, who about this time, from their settlement in Oxford in 1230, had been troublesome neighbors to the university. Feuds were continually fomented; the friars appealing to the pope, the scholars to the civil power; and sometimes one party, and sometimes, the other, prevailed. The friars became very fond of a notion that Christ was a common beggar; that his disciples were beggars also; and that begging was of Gospel institution. This doctrine they urged from the pulpit and wherever they had access.

Wickliffe had long held these religious friars in contempt for the laziness of their lives, and had now a fair opportunity of exposing them. He published a treatise against able beggary, in which he lashed the friars, and proved that they were not only a reproach to religion, but also to human society. The university began to consider him one of her first champions, and he was soon promoted to the mastership of Baliol College.

About this time, Archbishop Islip founded Canterbury Hall, in Oxford, where he established a warden and eleven scholars. To this wardenship Wickliffe was elected by the archbishop, but upon his demise, he was displaced by his successor, Stephen Langham, bishop of Ely. As there was a degree of flagrant injustice in the affair, Wickliffe appealed to the pope, who subsequently gave it against him from the following cause: Edward III, then king of England, had withdrawn the tribune, which from the time of King John had been paid to the pope. The pope menaced; Edward called a parliament. The parliament resolved that King John had done an illegal thing, and given up the rights of the nation, and advised the king not to submit, whatever consequences might follow.

The clergy now began to write in favor of the pope, and a learned monk published a spirited and plausible treatise, which had many advocates. Wickliffe, irritated at seeing so bad a cause so well defended, opposed the monk, and did it in so masterly a way that he was considered no longer as unanswerable. His suit at Rome was immediately determined against him; and nobody doubted but his opposition to the pope, at so critical a period, was the true cause of his being non-suited at Rome.

Wickliffe was afterward elected to the chair of the divinity professor: and now fully convinced of the errors of the Romish Church, and the vileness of its monastic agents, he determined to expose them. In public lectures he lashed their vices and opposed their follies. He unfolded a variety of abuses covered by the darkness of superstition. At first he began to loosen the prejudices of the vulgar, and proceeded by slow advances; with the metaphysical disquisitions of the age, he mingled opinions in divinity apparently novel. The usurpations of the court of Rome was a favorite topic. On these he expatiated with all the keenness of argument, joined to logical reasoning. This soon procured him the clamor of the clergy, who, with the archbishop of Canterbury, deprived him of his office.

At this time the administration of affairs was in the hands of the duke of Lancaster, well known by the name of John of Gaunt. This prince had very free notions of religion, and was at enmity with the clergy. The exactions of the court of Rome having become very burdensome, he determined to send the bishop of Bangor and Wickliffe to remonstrate against these abuses, and it was agreed that the pope should no longer dispose of any benefices belonging to the Church of England. In this embassy, Wickliffe's observant mind penetrated into the constitution and policy of Rome, and he returned more strongly than ever determined to expose its avarice and ambition.

Having recovered his former situation, he inveighed, in his lectures, against the pope—his usurpation—his infallibility—his pride—his avarice—and his tyranny. He was the first who termed the pope Antichrist. From the pope, he would turn to the pomp, the luxury, and trappings of the bishops, and compared them with the simplicity of primitive bishops. Their superstitions and deceptions were topics that he urged with energy of mind and logical precision.

From the patronage of the duke of Lancaster, Wickliffe received a good benefice; but he was no sooner settled in his parish, than his enemies and the bishops began to persecute him with renewed vigor. The duke of Lancaster was his friend in this persecution, and by his presence and that of Lord Percy, earl marshal of England, he so overawed the trial, that the whole ended in disorder.

After the death of Edward III his grandson Richard II succeeded, in the eleventh year of his age. The duke of Lancaster not obtaining to be the sole regent, as he expected, his power began to decline, and the enemies of Wickliffe, taking advantage of the circumstance, renewed their articles of accusation against him. Five bulls were despatched in consequence by the pope to the king and certain bishops, but the regency and the people manifested a spirit of contempt at the haughty proceedings of the pontiff, and the former at that time wanting money to oppose an expected invasion of the French, proposed to apply a large sum, collected for the use of the pope, to that purpose. The question was submitted to the decision of Wickliffe. The bishops, however, supported by the papal authority, insisted upon bringing Wickliffe to trial, and he was actually undergoing examination at Lambeth, when, from the riotous behavior of the populace without, and awed by the command of Sir Lewis Clifford, a gentleman of the court, that they should not proceed to any definitive sentence, they terminated the whole affair in a prohibition to Wickliffe, not to preach those doctrines which were obnoxious to the pope; but this was laughed at by our reformer, who, going about barefoot, and in a long frieze gown, preached more vehemently than before.

In the year 1378, a contest arose between two popes, Urban VI and Clement VII which was the lawful pope, and true vicegerent of God. This was a favorable period for the exertion of Wickliffe's talents: he soon produced a tract against popery, which was eagerly read by all sorts of people.

About the end of the year, Wickliffe was seized with a violent disorder, which it was feared might prove fatal. The begging friars, accompanied by four of the most eminent citizens of Oxford, gained admittance to his bed chamber, and begged of him to retract, for his soul's sake, the unjust things he had asserted of their order. Wickliffe, surprised at the solemn message, raised himself in his bed, and with a stern countenance replied, "I shall not die, but live to declare the evil deeds of the friars."

When Wickliffe recovered, he set about a most important work, the translation of the Bible into English. Before this work appeared, he published a tract, wherein he showed the necessity of it. The zeal of the bishops to suppress the Scriptures greatly promoted its sale, and they who were not able to purchase copies, procured transcripts of particular Gospels or Epistles. Afterward, when Lollardy increased, and the flames kindled, it was a common practice to fasten about the neck of the condemned heretic such of these scraps of Scripture as were found in his possession, which generally shared his fate.

Immediately after this transaction, Wickliffe ventured a step further, and affected the doctrine of transubstantiation. This strange opinion was invented by Paschade Radbert, and asserted with amazing boldness. Wickliffe, in his lecture before the University of Oxford, 1381, attacked this doctrine, and published a treatise on the subject. Dr. Barton, at this time vice-chancellor of Oxford, calling together the heads of the university, condemned Wickliffe's doctrines as heretical, and threatened their author with excommunication. Wickliffe could now derive no support from the duke of Lancaster, and being cited to appear before his former adversary, William Courteney, now made archbishop of Canterbury, he sheltered himself under the plea, that, as a member of the university, he was exempt from episcopal jurisdiction. This plea was admitted, as the university were determined to support their member.

The court met at the appointed time, determined, at least to sit in judgment upon his opinions, and some they condemned as erroneous, others as heretical. The publication on this subject was immediately answered by Wickliffe, who had become a subject of the archbishop's determined malice. The king, solicited by the archbishop, granted a license to imprison the teacher of heresy, but the commons made the king revoke this act as illegal. The primate, however, obtained letters from the king, directing the head of the University of Oxford to search for all heresies and the books published by Wickliffe; in consequence of which order, the university became a scene of tumult. Wickliffe is supposed to have retired from the storm, into an obscure part of the kingdom. The seeds, however, were scattered, and Wickliffe's opinions were so prevalent that it was said if you met two persons upon the road, you might be sure that one was a Lollard. At this period, the disputes between the two popes continued. Urban published a bull, in which he earnestly called upon all who had any regard for religion, to exert themselves in its cause; and to take up arms against Clement and his adherents in defence of the holy see.

A war, in which the name of religion was so vilely prostituted, roused Wickliffe's inclination, even in his declining years. He took up his pen once more, and wrote against it with the greatest acrimony. He expostulated with the pope in a very free manner, and asks him boldly: 'How he durst make the token of Christ on the cross (which is the token of peace, mercy and charity) a banner to lead us to slay Christian men, for the love of two false priests, and to oppress Christiandom worse than Christ and his apostles were oppressed by the Jews? 'When', said he, 'will the proud priest of Rome grant indulgences to mankind to live in peace and charity, as he now does to fight and slay one another?'

This severe piece drew upon him the resentment of Urban, and was likely to have involved him in greater troubles than he had before experienced, but providentially he was delivered out of their hands. He was struck with the palsy, and though he lived some time, yet it was in such a way that his enemies considered him as a person below their resentment.

Wickliffe returning within short space, either from his banishment, or from some other place where he was secretly kept, repaired to his parish of Lutterworth, where he was parson; and there, quietly departing this mortal life, slept in peace in the Lord, in the end of the year 1384, upon Silvester's day. It appeared that he was well aged before he departed, "and that the same thing pleased him in his old age, which did please him being young."

Wickliffe had some cause to give them thanks, that they would at least spare him until he was dead, and also give him so long respite after his death, forty-one years to rest in his sepulchre before they ungraved him, and turned him from earth to ashes; which ashes they also took and threw into the river. And so was he resolved into three elements, earth, fire, and water, thinking thereby utterly to extinguish and abolish both the name and doctrine of Wickliffe forever. Not much unlike the example of the old Pharisees and sepulchre knights, who, when they had brought the Lord unto the grave, thought to make him sure never to rise again. But these and all others must know that, as there is no counsel against the Lord, so there is no keeping down of verity, but it will spring up and come out of dust and ashes, as appeared right well in this man; for though they dug up his body, burned his bones, and drowned his ashes, yet the Word of God and the truth of his doctrine, with the fruit and success thereof, they could not burn.

CHAPTER VIII

An Account of the Persecutions in Bohemia Under the Papacy

THE Roman pontiffs having usurped a power over several churches were particularly severe on the Bohemians, which occasioned them to send two ministers and four lay-brothers to Rome, in the year 977, to obtain redress of the pope. After some delay, their request was granted, and their grievances redressed. Two things in particular they were permitted to do, viz., to have divine service performed in their own language, and to give the cup to the laity in the Sacrament.

The disputes, however, soon broke out again, the succeeding popes exerting their whole power to impose on the minds of the Bohemians: and the latter, with great spirit, aiming to preserve their religious liberties.

In A. D. 1375, some zealous friends of the Gospel applied to Charles, king of Bohemia, to call an ecumenical Council, for an inquiry into the abuses that had crept into the Church, and to make a full and thorough reformation. The king, not knowing how to proceed, sent to the pope for directions how to act; but the pontiff was so incensed at this affair that his only reply was, "Severely punish those rash and profane heretics." The monarch, accordingly banished every one who had been concerned in the application, and, to oblige the pope, laid a great number of additional restraints upon the religious liberties of the people.

The victims of persecution, however, were not so numerous in Bohemia, until after the burning of John Huss and Jerome of Prague. These two eminent reformers were condemned and executed at the instigation of the pope and his emissaries, as the reader will perceive by the following short sketches of their lives.

Persecution of John Huss

John Huss was born at Hussenitz, a village in Bohemia, about the year 1380. His parents gave him the best education their circumstances would admit; and having acquired a tolerable knowledge of the classics at a private school, he was removed to the university of Prague, where he soon gave strong proofs of his mental powers, and was remarkable for his diligence and application to study.

In 1398, Huss commenced bachelor of divinity, and was after successively chosen pastor of the Church of Bethlehem, in Prague, and dean and rector of the university. In these stations he discharged his duties with great fidelity; and became, at length, so conspicuous for his preaching, which was in conformity with the doctrines of Wickliffe, that it was not likely he could long escape the notice of the pope and his adherents, against whom he inveighed with no small degree of asperity.

The English reformist, Wickliffe, had so kindled the light of reformation, that it began to illumine the darkest corners of popery and ignorance. His doctrines spread into Bohemia, and were well received by great numbers of people, but by none so particularly as John Huss, and his zealous friend and fellow martyr, Jerome of Prague.

The archbishop of Prague, finding the reformists daily increasing, issued a decree to suppress the further spreading of Wickliffe's writings: but this had an effect quite different to what he expected, for it stimulated the friends of those doctrines to greater zeal, and almost the whole university united to propagate them.

Being strongly attached to the doctrines of Wickliffe, Huss opposed the decree of the archbishop, who, however, at length, obtained a bull from the pope, giving him commission to prevent the publishing of Wickliffe's doctrines in his province. By virtue of this bull, the archbishop condemned the writings of Wickliffe: he also proceeded against four doctors, who had not delivered up the copies of that divine, and prohibited them, notwithstanding their privileges, to preach to any congregation. Dr. Huss, with some other members of the university, protested against these proceedings, and entered an appeal from the sentence of the archbishop.

The affair being made known to the pope, he granted a commission to Cardinal Colonna, to cite John Huss to appear personally at the court of Rome, to answer the accusations laid against him, of preaching both errors and heresies. Dr. Huss desired to be excused from a personal appearance, and was so greatly favored in Bohemia, that King Winceslaus, the queen, the nobility, and the university, desired the pope to dispense with such an appearance; as also that he would not suffer the kingdom of Bohemia to lie under the accusation of heresy, but permit them to preach the Gospel with freedom in their places of worship.

Three proctors appeared for Dr. Huss before Cardinal Colonna. They endeavored to excuse his absence, and said they were ready to answer in his behalf. But the cardinal declared Huss contumacious, and excommunicated him accordingly. The proctors appealed to the pope, and appointed four cardinals to examine the process: these commissioners confirmed the former sentence, and extended the excommunication not only to Huss but to all his friends and followers.

From this unjust sentence Huss appealed to a future Council, but without success; and, notwithstanding so severe a decree, and an expulsion in consequence from his church in Prague, he retired to Hussenitz, his native place, where he continued to promulgate his new doctrine, both from the pulpit and with the pen.

The letters which he wrote at this time were very numerous; and he compiled a treatise in which he maintained, that reading the books of Protestants could not be absolutely forbidden. He wrote in defence of Wickliffe's book on the Trinity; and boldly declared against the vices of the pope, the cardinals, and clergy, of those corrupt times. He wrote also many other books, all of which were penned with a strength of argument that greatly facilitated the spreading of his doctrines.

In the month of November, 1414, a general Council was assembled at Constance, in Germany, in order, as was pretended, for the sole purpose of determining a dispute then pending between three persons who contended for the papacy; but the real motive was to crush the progress of the Reformation.

John Huss was summoned to appear at this Council; and, to encourage him, the emperor sent him a safe-conduct: the civilities, and even reverence, which Huss met with on his journey were beyond imagination. The streets, and sometimes the very roads, were lined with people, whom respect, rather than curiosity, had brought together.

He was ushered into the town with great acclamations, and it may be said that he passed through Germany in a kind of triumph. He could not help expressing his surprise at the treatment he received: "I thought (said he) I had been an outcast. I now see my worst friends are in Bohemia."

As soon as Huss arrived at Constance, he immediately took lodgings in a remote part of the city. A short time after his arrival, came one Stephen Paletz, who was employed by the clergy at Prague to manage the intended prosecution against him. Paletz was afterwards joined by Michael de Cassis, on the part of the court of Rome. These two declared themselves his accusers, and drew up a set of articles against him, which they presented to the pope and the prelates of the Council.

When it was known that he was in the city he was immediately arrested, and committed prisoner to a chamber in the palace. This violation of common law and justice was particularly noticed by one of Huss's friends, who urged the imperial safe-conduct; but the pope replied he never granted any safe-conduct, nor was he bound by that of the emperor.

While Huss was in confinement, the Council acted the part of inquisitors. They condemned the doctrines of Wickliffe, and even ordered his remains to be dug up and burned to ashes; which orders were strictly complied with. In the meantime, the nobility of Bohemia and Poland strongly interceded for Huss; and so far prevailed as to prevent his being condemned unheard, which had been resolved on by the commissioners appointed to try him.

When he was brought before the Council, the articles exhibited against him were read: they were upwards of forty in number, and chiefly extracted from his writings.

John Huss's answer was this: "I did appeal unto the pope; who being dead, and the cause of my matter remaining undetermined, I appealed likewise unto his successor John XXIII: before whom when, by the space of two years, I could not be admitted by my advocates to defend my cause, I appealed unto the high judge Christ."

When John Huss had spoken these words, it was demanded of him whether he had received absolution of the pope or no? He answered, "No." Then again, whether it were lawful for him to appeal unto Christ or no? Whereunto John Huss answered: "Verily I do affirm here before you all, that there is no more just or effectual appeal, than that appeal which is made unto Christ, forasmuch as the law doth determine, that to appeal is no other thing than in a cause of grief or wrong done by an inferior judge, to implore and require aid at a higher Judge's hand. Who is then a higher Judge than Christ? Who, I say, can know or judge the matter more justly, or with more equity? when in Him there is found no deceit, neither can He be deceived; or, who can better help the miserable and oppressed than He?" While John Huss, with a devout and sober countenance, was speaking and pronouncing those words, he was derided and mocked by all the whole Council.

These excellent sentences were esteemed as so many expressions of treason, and tended to inflame his adversaries. Accordingly, the bishops appointed by the Council stripped him of his priestly garments, degraded him, put a paper miter on his head, on which was painted devils, with this inscription, "A ringleader of heretics." Which when he saw, he said: "My Lord Jesus Christ, for my sake, did wear a crown of thorns; why should not I then, for His sake, again wear this light crown, be it ever so ignominious? Truly I will do it, and that willingly." When it was set upon his head, the bishop said: "Now we commit thy soul unto the devil." "But I," said John Huss, lifting his eyes up towards the heaven, "do commend into Thy hands, O Lord Jesus Christ! my spirit which Thou hast redeemed."

When the chain was put about him at the stake, he said, with a smiling countenance, "My Lord Jesus Christ was bound with a harder chain than this for my sake, and why then should I be ashamed of this rusty one?"

When the fagots were piled up to his very neck, the duke of Bavaria was so officious as to desire him to abjure. "No, (said Huss;) I never preached any doctrine of an evil tendency; and what I taught with my lips I now seal with my blood." He then said to the executioner, "You are now going to burn a goose, (Huss signifying goose in the Bohemian language:) but in a century you will have a swan which you can neither roast nor boil." If he were prophetic, he must have meant Martin Luther, who shone about a hundred years after, and who had a swan for his arms.

The flames were now applied to the fagots, when our martyr sung a hymn with so loud and cheerful a voice that he was heard through all the cracklings of the combustibles, and the noise of the multitude At length his voice was interrupted by the severity of the flames, which soon closed his existence.

Then, with great diligence, gathering the ashes together, they cast them into the river Rhine, that the least remnant of that man should not be left upon the earth, whose memory, notwithstanding, cannot be abolished out of the minds of the godly, neither by fire, neither by water, neither by any kind of torment.

Persecution of Jerome of Prague

This reformer, who was the companion of Dr. Huss, and may be said to be a co-martyr with him, was born at Prague, and educated in that university, where he particularly distinguished himself for his great abilities and learning. He likewise visited several other learned seminaries in Europe, particularly the universities of Paris, Heidelburg, Cologne and Oxford. At the latter place he became acquainted with the works of Wickliffe, and being a person of uncommon application, he translated many of them into his native language, having, with great pains, made himself master of the English tongue.

On his return to Prague, he professed himself an open favorer of Wickliffe, and finding that his doctrines had made considerable progress in Bohemia, and that Huss was the principal promoter of them, he became an assistant to him in the great work of reformation.

On the fourth of April, 1415, Jerome arrived at Constance, about three months before the death of Huss. He entered the town privately, and consulting with some of the leaders of his party, whom he found there, was easily convinced he could not be of any service to his friends.

Finding that his arrival in Constance was publicly known, and that the Council intended to seize him, he thought it most prudent to retire. Accordingly, the next day he went to Iberling, an imperial town, about a mile from Constance. From this place he wrote to the emperor, and proposed his readiness to appear before the Council, if he would give him a safe-conduct; but this was refused. He then applied to the Council, but met with an answer no less unfavorable than that from the emperor.

After this, he set out on his return to Bohemia. He had the precaution to take with him a certificate, signed by several of the Bohemian nobility, then at Constance, testifying that he had used all prudent means in his power to procure a hearing.

Jerome, however, did not thus escape. He was seized at Hirsaw by an officer belonging to the duke of Sultsbach, who, though unauthorized so to act, made little doubt of obtaining thanks from the Council for so acceptable a service.

The duke of Sultsbach, having Jerome now in his power, wrote to the Council for directions how to proceed. The Council, after expressing their obligations to the duke, desired him to send the prisoner immediately to Constance. The elector palatine met him on the way, and conducted him into the city, himself riding on horseback, with a numerous retinue, who led Jerome in fetters by a long chain; and immediately on his arrival he was committed to a loathsome dungeon.

Jerome was treated nearly in the same manner as Huss had been, only that he was much longer confined, and shifted from one prison to another. At length, being brought before the Council, he desired that he might plead his own cause, and exculpate himself: which being refused him, he broke out into the following exclamation:

"What barbarity is this! For three hundred and forty days have I been confined in a variety of prisons. There is not a misery, there is not a want, that I have not experienced. To my enemies you have allowed the fullest scope of accusation: to me you deny the least opportunity of defence. Not an hour will you now indulge me in preparing for my trial. You have swallowed the blackest calumnies against me. You have represented me as a heretic, without knowing my doctrine; as an enemy of the faith, before you knew what faith I professed: as a persecutor of priests before you could have an opportunity of understanding my sentiments on that head. You are a General Council: in you center all this world can communicate of gravity, wisdom, and sanctity: but still you are men, and men are seducible by appearances. The higher your character is for wisdom, the greater ought your care to be not to deviate into folly. The cause I now plead is not my own cause: it is the cause of men, it is the cause of Christians; it is a cause which is to affect the rights of posterity, however the experiment is to be made in my person."

This speech had not the least effect; Jerome was obliged to hear the charge read, which was reduced under the following heads: 1. That he was a derider of the papal dignity. 2. An opposer of the pope. 3. An enemy to the cardinals. 4. A persecutor of the prelates. 5. A hater of the Christian religion.

The trial of Jerome was brought on the third day after his accusation and witnesses were examined in support of the charge. The prisoner was prepared for his defence, which appears almost incredible, when we consider he had been three hundred and forty days shut up in loathsome prisons, deprived of daylight, and almost starved for want of common necessaries. But his spirit soared above these disadvantages, under which a man less animated would have sunk; nor was he more at a loss of quotations from the fathers and ancient authors than if he had been furnished with the finest library.

The most bigoted of the assembly were unwilling he should be heard, knowing what effect eloquence is apt to have on the minds of the most prejudiced. At length, however, it was carried by the majority that he should have liberty to proceed in his defence, which he began in such an exalted strain of moving elocution that the heart of obdurate zeal was seen to melt, and the mind of superstition seemed to admit a ray of conviction. He made an admirable distinction between evidence as resting upon facts, and as supported by malice and calumny. He laid before the assembly the whole tenor of his life and conduct. He observed that the greatest and most holy men had been known to differ in points of speculation, with a view to distinguish truth, not to keep it concealed. He expressed a noble contempt of all his enemies, who would have induced him to retract the cause of virtue and truth. He entered upon a high encomium of Huss; and declared he was ready to follow him in the glorious track of martyrdom. He then touched upon the most defensible doctrines of Wickliffe; and concluded with observing that it was far from his intention to advance anything against the state of the Church of God; that it was only against the abuse of the clergy he complained; and that he could not help saying, it was certainly impious that the patrimony of the Church, which was originally intended for the purpose of charity and universal benevolence, should be prostituted to the pride of the eye, in feasts, foppish vestments, and other reproaches to the name and profession of Christianity.

The trial being over, Jerome received the same sentence that had been passed upon his martyred countryman. In consequence of this, he was, in the usual style of popish affectation, delivered over to the civil power: but as he was a layman, he had not to undergo the ceremony of degradation. They had prepared a cap of paper painted with red devils, which being put upon his head, he said, "Our Lord Jesus Christ, when He suffered death for me a most miserable sinner, did wear a crown of thorns upon His head, and for His sake will I wear this cap."

Two days were allowed him in hopes that he would recant; in which time the cardinal of Florence used his utmost endeavors to bring him over. But they all proved ineffectual. Jerome was resolved to seal the doctrine with his blood; and he suffered death with the most distinguished magnanimity.

In going to the place of execution he sang several hymns, and when he came to the spot, which was the same where Huss had been burnt, he knelt down, and prayed fervently. He embraced the stake with great cheerfulness, and when they went behind him to set fire to the fagots, he said, "Come here, and kindle it before my eyes; for if I had been afraid of it, I had not come to this place." The fire being kindled, he sang a hymn, but was soon interrupted by the flames; and the last words he was heard to say these, "This soul in flames I offer Christ, to Thee."

The elegant Pogge, a learned gentleman of Florence, secretary to two popes, and a zealous but liberal Catholic, in a letter to Leonard Arotin, bore ample testimony of the extraordinary powers and virtues of Jerome whom he emphatically styles, A prodigious man!

Persecution of Zisca

The real name of this zealous servant of Christ was John de Trocznow, that of Zisca is a Bohemian word, signifying one-eyed, as he had lost an eye. He was a native of Bohemia, of a good family and left the court of Winceslaus, to enter into the service of the king of Poland against the Teutonic knights. Having obtained a badge of honor and a purse of ducats for his gallantry, at the close of the war, he returned to the court of Winceslaus, to whom he boldly avowed the deep interest he took in the bloody affront offered to his majesty's subjects at Constance in the affair of Huss. Winceslaus lamented it was not in his power to revenge it; and from this moment Zisca is said to have formed the idea of asserting the religious liberties of his country. In the year 1418, the Council was dissolved, having done more mischief than good, and in the summer of that year a general meeting was held of the friends of religious reformation, at the castle of Wisgrade, who, conducted by Zisca, repaired to the emperor with arms in their hands, and offered to defend him against his enemies. The king bid them use their arms properly, and this stroke of policy first insured to Zisca the confidence of his party.

Winceslaus was succeeded by Sigismond, his brother, who rendered himself odious to the reformers; and removed all such as were obnoxious to his government. Zisca and his friends, upon this, immediately flew to arms, declared war against the emperor and the pope, and laid siege to Pilsen with 40,000 men. They soon became masters of the fortress, and in a short time all the southwest part of Bohemia submitted, which greatly increased the army of the reformers. The latter having taken the pass of Muldaw, after a severe conflict of five days and nights, the emperor became alarmed, and withdrew his troops from the confines of Turkey, to march them into Bohemia. At Berne in Moravia, he halted, and sent despatches to treat of peace, as a preliminary to which Zisca gave up Pilsen and all the fortresses he had taken. Sigismond proceeding in a manner that clearly manifested he acted on the Roman doctrine, that no faith was to be kept with heretics, and treating some of the authors of the late disturbances with severity, the alarm-bell of revolt was sounded from one end of Bohemia to the other. Zisca took the castle of Prague by the power of money, and on August 19, 1420, defeated the small army the emperor had hastily got together to oppose him. He next took Ausea by assault, and destroyed the town with a barbarity that disgraced the cause in which he fought.

Winter approaching, Zisca fortified his camp on a strong hill about forty miles from Prague, which he called Mount Tabor, whence he surprised a body of horse at midnight, and made a thousand men prisoners. Shortly after, the emperor obtained possession of the strong fortress of Prague, by the same means that Zisca had before done: it was soon blockaded by the latter, and want began to threaten the emperor, who saw the necessity of a retreat.

Determined to make a desperate effort, Sigismond attacked the fortified camp of Zisca on Mount Tabor, and carried it with great slaughter. Many other fortresses also fell, and Zisca withdrew to a craggy hill, which he strongly fortified, and whence he so annoyed the emperor in his approaches against the town of Prague, that he found he must either abandon the siege or defeat his enemy. The marquis of Misnia was deputed to effect this with a large body of troops, but the event was fatal to the imperialists; they were defeated, and the emperor having lost nearly one third of his army, retreated from the siege of Prague, harassed in his rear by the enemy.

In the spring of 1421, Zisca commenced the campaign, as before, by destroying all the monasteries in his way. He laid siege to the castle of Wisgrade, and the emperor coming to relieve it, fell into a snare, was defeated with dreadful slaughter, and this important fortress was taken. Our general had now leisure to attend to the work of reformation, but he was much disgusted with the gross ignorance and superstition of the Bohemian clergy, who rendered themselves contemptible in the eyes of the whole army. When he saw any symptoms of uneasiness in his camp, he would spread alarm in order to divert them, and draw his men into action. In one of these expeditions, he encamped before the town of Rubi, and while pointing out the place for an assault, an arrow shot from the wall struck him in the eye. At Prague it was extracted, but, being barbed, it tore the eye out with it. A fever succeeded, and his life was with difficulty preserved. He was now totally blind, but still desirous of attending the army. The emperor, having summoned the states of the empire to assist him, resolved, with their assistance, to attack Zisca in the winter, when many of his troops departed until the return of spring.

The confederate princes undertook the siege of Soisin, but at the approach merely of the Bohemian general, they retreated. Sigismond nevertheless advanced with his formidable army, consisting of 15,000 Hungarian horse and 25,000 infantry, well equipped for a winter campaign. This army spread terror through all the east of Bohemia. Wherever Sigismond marched, the magistrates laid their keys at his feet, and were treated with severity or favor, according to their merits in his cause. Zisca, however, with speedy marches, approached, and the emperor resolved to try his fortune once more with that invincible chief. On the thirteenth of January, 1422, the two armies met on a spacious plain near Kremnitz. Zisca appeared in the center of his front line, guarded, or rather conducted, by a horseman on each side, armed with a pole-axe. His troops having sung a hymn, with a determined coolness drew their swords, and waited for a signal. When his officers had informed him that the ranks were all well closed, he waved his sabre round his head, which was the sign of battle.

This battle is described as a most awful sight. The extent of the plain was one continued scene of disorder. The imperial army fled towards the confines of Moravia, the Taborites, without intermission, galling their rear. The river Igla, then frozen opposed their flight. The enemy pressing furiously, many of the infantry and in a manner the whole body of the cavalry, attempted the river. The ice gave way, and not fewer than two thousand were swallowed up in the water. Zisca now returned to Tabor, laden with all the spoils and trophies which the most complete victory could give.

Zisca now began again to pay attention to the Reformation; he forbid all the prayers for the dead, images, sacerdotal vestments, fasts, and festivals. Priests were to be preferred according to their merits, and no one to be persecuted for religious opinions. In everything Zisca consulted the liberal minded, and did nothing without general concurrence. An alarming disagreement now arose at Prague between the magistrates who were Calixtans, or receivers of the Sacraments in both kinds, and the Taborites, nine of the chiefs of whom were privately arraigned, and put to death. The populace, enraged, sacrificed the magistrates, and the affair terminated without any particular consequence. The Calixtans having sunk into contempt, Zisca was solicited to assume the crown of Bohemia; but this he nobly refused, and prepared for the next campaign, in which Sigismond resolved to make his last effort. While the marquis of Misnia penetrated into Upper Saxony, the emperor proposed to enter Moravia, on the side of Hungary. Before the marquis had taken the field, Zisca sat down before the strong town of Aussig, situated on the Elbe. The marquis flew to its relief with a superior army, and, after an obstinate engagement, was totally defeated and Aussig capitulated. Zisca then went to the assistance of Procop, a young general whom he had appointed to keep Sigismond in check, and whom he compelled to abandon the siege of Pernitz, after laying eight weeks before it.

Zisca, willing to give his troops some respite from fatigue, now entered Prague, hoping his presence would quell any uneasiness that might remain after the late disturbance: but he was suddenly attacked by the people; and he and his troop having beaten off the citizens, effected a retreat to his army, whom he acquainted with the treacherous conduct of the Calixtans. Every effort of address was necessary to appease their vengeful animosity, and at night, in a private interview between Roquesan, an ecclesiastic of great eminence in Prague, and Zisca, the latter became reconciled, and the intended hostilities were done away.

Mutually tired of the war, Sigismond sent to Zisca, requesting him to sheath his sword, and name his conditions. A place of congress being appointed, Zisca, with his chief officers, set out to meet the emperor. Compelled to pass through a part of the country where the plague raged, he was seized with it at the castle of Briscaw, and departed this life, October 6, 1424. Like Moses, he died in view of the completion of his labors, and was buried in the great

Church of Czaslow, in Bohemia, where a monument is erected to his memory, with this inscription on it—"Here lies John Zisca, who, having defended his country against the encroachments of papal tyranny, rests in this hallowed place, in despite of the pope."

After the death of Zisca, Procop was defeated, and fell with the liberties of his country.

After the death of Huss and Jerome, the pope, in conjunction with the Council of Constance, ordered the Roman clergy everywhere to excommunicate such as adopted their opinions, or commiserated their fate.

These orders occasioned great contentions between the papists and reformed Bohemians, which was the cause of a violent persecution against the latter. At Prague, the persecution was extremely severe, until, at length, the reformed being driven to desperation, armed themselves, attacked the senate-house, and threw twelve senators, with the speaker, out of the senate-house windows, whose bodies fell upon spears, which were held up by others of the reformed in the street, to receive them.

Being informed of these proceedings, the pope came to Florence, and publicly excommunicated the reformed Bohemians, exciting the emperor of Germany, and all kings, princes, dukes, etc., to take up arms, in order to extirpate the whole race; and promising, by way of encouragement, full remission of all sins whatever, to the most wicked person, if he did but kill one Bohemian Protestant.

This occasioned a bloody war; for several popish princes undertook the extirpation, or at least expulsion, of the proscribed people; and the Bohemians, arming themselves, prepared to repel force by force, in the most vigorous and effectual manner. The popish army prevailing against the Protestant forces at the battle of Cuttenburgh, the prisoners of the reformed were taken to three deep mines near that town, and several hundreds were cruelly thrown into each, where they miserably perished.

A merchant of Prague, going to Breslau, in Silesia, happened to lodge in the same inn with several priests. Entering into conversation upon the subject of religious controversy, he passed many encomiums upon the martyred John Huss, and his doctrines. The priests taking umbrage at this, laid an information against him the next morning, and he was committed to prison as a heretic. Many endeavors were used to persuade him to embrace the Roman Catholic faith, but he remained steadfast to the pure doctrines of the reformed Church. Soon after his imprisonment, a student of the university was committed to the same jail; when, being permitted to converse with the merchant, they mutually comforted each other. On the day appointed for execution, when the jailer began to fasten ropes to their feet, by which they were to be dragged through the streets, the student appeared quite terrified, and offered to abjure his faith, and turn Roman Catholic if he might be saved. The offer was accepted, his abjuration was taken by a priest, and he was set at liberty. A priest applying to the merchant to follow the example of the student, he nobly said, "Lose no time in hopes of my recantation, your expectations will be vain; I sincerely pity that poor wretch, who has miserably sacrificed his soul for a few more uncertain years of a troublesome life; and, so far from having the least idea of following his example, I glory in the very thoughts of dying for the sake of Christ." On hearing these words, the priest ordered the executioner to proceed, and the merchant being drawn through the city was brought to the place of execution, and there burnt.

Pichel, a bigoted popish magistrate, apprehended twenty-four Protestants, among whom was his daughter's husband. As they all owned they were of the reformed religion, he indiscriminately condemned them to be drowned in the river Abbis. On the day appointed for the execution, a great concourse of people attended, among whom was Pichel's daughter. This worthy wife threw herself at her father's feet, bedewed them with tears, and in the most pathetic manner, implored him to commiserate her sorrow, and pardon her husband. The obdurate magistrate sternly replied, "Intercede not for him, child, he is a heretic, a vile heretic." To which she nobly answered, "Whatever his faults may be, or however his opinions may differ from yours, he is still my husband, a name which, at a time like this, should alone employ my whole consideration." Pichel flew into a violent passion and said, "You are mad! cannot you, after the death of this, have a much worthier husband?" "No, sir, (replied she) my affections are fixed upon this, and death itself shall not dissolve my marriage vow." Pichel, however, continued inflexible, and ordered the prisoners to be tied with their hands and feet behind them, and in that manner be thrown into the river. As soon as this was put into execution, the young lady watched her opportunity, leaped into the waves, and embracing the body of her husband, both sank together into one watery grave. An uncommon instance of conjugal love in a wife, and of an inviolable attachment to, and personal affection for, her husband.

The emperor Ferdinand, whose hatred to the Bohemian Protestants was without bounds, not thinking he had sufficiently oppressed them, instituted a high court of reformers, upon the plan of the Inquisition, with this difference, that the reformers were to remove from place to place, and always to be attended by a body of troops.

These reformers consisted chiefly of Jesuits, and from their decision, there was no appeal, by which it may be easily conjectured, that it was a dreadful tribunal indeed.

This bloody court, attended by a body of troops, made the tour of Bohemia, in which they seldom examined or saw a prisoner, suffering the soldiers to murder the Protestants as they pleased, and then to make a report of the matter to them afterward.

The first victim of their cruelty was an aged minister, whom they killed as he lay sick in his bed; the next day they robbed and murdered another, and soon after shot a third, as he was preaching in his pulpit.

A nobleman and clergyman, who resided in a Protestant village, hearing of the approach of the high court of reformers and the troops, fled from the place, and secreted themselves. The soldiers, however, on their arrival, seized upon a schoolmaster, asked him where the lord of that place and the minister were concealed, and where they had hidden their treasures. The schoolmaster replied that he could not answer either of the questions. They then stripped him naked, bound him with cords, and beat him most unmercifully with cudgels. This cruelty not extorting any confession from him, they scorched him in various parts of his body; when, to gain a respite from his torments, he promised to show them where the treasures were hid. The soldiers gave ear to this with pleasure, and the schoolmaster led them to a ditch full of stones, saying, "Beneath these stones are the treasures ye seek for." Eager after money, they went to work, and soon removed those stones, but not finding what they sought after, they beat the schoolmaster to death, buried him in the ditch, and covered him with the very stones he had made them remove.

Some of the soldiers ravished the daughters of a worthy Protestant before his face, and then tortured him to death. A minister and his wife they tied back to back and burnt. Another minister they hung upon a cross beam, and making a fire under him, broiled him to death. A gentleman they hacked into small pieces, and they filled a young man's mouth with gunpowder, and setting fire to it, blew his head to pieces.

As their principal rage was directed against the clergy, they took a pious Protestant minister, and tormenting him daily for a month together, in the following manner, making their cruelty regular, systematic, and progressive.

They placed him amidst them, and made him the subject of their derision and mockery, during a whole day's entertainment, trying to exhaust his patience, but in vain, for he bore the whole with true Christian fortitude. They spit in his face, pulled his nose, and pinched him in most parts of his body. He was hunted like a wild beast, until ready to expire with fatigue. They made him run the gauntlet between two ranks of them, each striking him with a twig. He was beat with their fists. He was beat with ropes. They scourged him with wires. He was beat with cudgels. They tied him up by the heels with his head downwards, until the blood started out of his nose, mouth, etc. They hung him by the right arm until it was dislocated, and then had it set again. The same was repeated with his left arm. Burning papers dipped in oil were placed between his fingers and toes. His flesh was torn with red-hot pincers. He was put to the rack. They pulled off the nails of his right hand. The same repeated with his left hand. He was bastinadoed on his feet. A slit was made in his right ear. The same repeated on his left ear. His nose was slit. They whipped him through the town upon an ass. They made several incisions in his flesh. They pulled off the toe nails of his right foot. The same they repeated with his left foot. He was tied up by the loins, and suspended for a considerable time. The teeth of his upper jaw were pulled out. The same was repeated with his lower jaw. Boiling lead was poured upon his fingers. The same was repeated with his toes. A knotted cord was twisted about his forehead in such a manner as to force out his eyes.

During the whole of these horrid cruelties, particular care was taken that his wounds should not mortify, and not to injure him mortally until the last day, when the forcing out of his eyes proved his death.

Innumerable were the other murders and depredations committed by those unfeeling brutes, and shocking to humanity were the cruelties which they inflicted on the poor Bohemian Protestants. The winter being far advanced, however, the high court of reformers, with their infernal band of military ruffians, thought proper to return to Prague; but on their way, meeting with a Protestant pastor, they could not resist the temptation of feasting their barbarous eyes with a new kind of cruelty, which had just suggested itself to the diabolical imagination of one of the soldiers. This was to strip the minister naked, and alternately to cover him with ice and burning coals. This novel mode of tormenting a fellow creature was immediately put into practice, and the unhappy victim expired beneath the torments, which seemed to delight his inhuman persecutors.

A secret order was soon after issued by the emperor, for apprehending all noblemen and gentlemen, who had been principally concerned in supporting the Protestant cause, and in nominating Frederic elector Palatine of the Rhine, to be king of Bohemia. These, to the number of fifty, were apprehended in one night, and at one hour, and brought from the places where they were taken, to the castle of Prague, and the estates of those who were absent from the kingdom were confiscated, themselves were made outlaws, and their names fixed upon a gallows, as marks of public ignominy.

The high court of reformers then proceeded to try the fifty, who had been apprehended, and two apostate Protestants were appointed to examine them. These examinants asked a great number of unnecessary and impertinent questions, which so exasperated one of the noblemen, who was naturally of a warm temper, that he exclaimed, opening his breast at the same time, "Cut here, search my heart, you shall find nothing but the love of religion and liberty; those were the motives for which I drew my sword, and for those I am willing to suffer death."

As none of the prisoners would change their religion, or acknowledge they had been in error, they were all pronounced guilty; but the sentence was referred to the emperor. When that monarch had read their names, and an account of the respective accusations against them, he passed judgment on all, but in a different manner, as his sentences were of four kinds, viz. death, banishment, imprisonment for life, and imprisonment during pleasure.

Twenty being ordered for execution, were informed they might send for Jesuits, monks, or friars, to prepare for the awful change they were to undergo; but that no Protestants should be permitted to come near them. This proposal they rejected, and strove all they could to comfort and cheer each other upon the solemn occasion.

On the morning of the day appointed for the execution, a cannon was fired as a signal to bring the prisoners from the castle to the principal market place, in which scaffolds were erected, and a body of troops were drawn up to attend the tragic scene.

The prisoners left the castle with as much cheerfulness as if they had been going to an agreeable entertainment, instead of a violent death.

Exclusive of soldiers, Jesuits, priests, executioners, attendants, etc., a prodigious concourse of people attended, to see the exit of these devoted martyrs, who were executed in the following order.

Lord Schilik was about fifty years of age, and was possessed of great natural and acquired abilities. When he was told he was to be quartered, and his parts scattered in different places, he smiled with great serenity, saying, "The loss of a sepulchre is but a trifling consideration." A gentleman who stood by, crying, "Courage, my lord!" he replied, "I have God's favor, which is sufficient to inspire any one with courage: the fear of death does not trouble me; formerly I have faced him in fields of battle to oppose Antichrist; and now dare face him on a scaffold, for the sake of Christ." Having said a short prayer, he told the executioner he was ready. He cut off his right hand and his head, and then quartered him. His hand and his head were placed upon the high tower of Prague, and his quarters distributed in different parts of the city.

Lord Viscount Winceslaus, who had attained the age of seventy years, was equally respectable for learning, piety, and hospitality. His temper was so remarkably patient that when his house was broken open, his property seized, and his estates confiscated, he only said, with great composure, "The Lord hath given, and the Lord hath taken away." Being asked why he could engage in so dangerous a cause as that of attempting to support the elector Palatine

Frederic against the power of the emperor, he replied, "I acted strictly according to the dictates of my conscience, and, to this day, deem him my king. I am now full of years, and wish to lay down life, that I may not be a witness of the further evils which are to attend my country. You have long thirsted for my blood, take it, for God will be my avenger." Then approaching the block, he stroked his long, grey beard, and said, "Venerable hairs, the greater honor now attends ye, a crown of martyrdom is your portion." Then laying down his head, it was severed from his body at one stroke, and placed upon a pole in a conspicuous part of the city.

Lord Harant was a man of good sense, great piety, and much experience gained by travel, as he had visited the principal places in Europe, Asia, and Africa. Hence he was free from national prejudices and had collected much knowledge.

The accusations against this nobleman, were, his being a Protestant, and having taken an oath of allegiance to Frederic, elector Palatine of the Rhine, as king of Bohemia. When he came upon the scaffold he said, "I have travelled through many countries, and traversed various barbarous nations, yet never found so much cruelty as at home. I have escaped innumerable perils both by sea and land, and surmounted inconceivable difficulties, to suffer innocently in my native place. My blood is likewise sought by those for whom I, and my forefathers, have hazarded our estates; but, Almighty God! forgive them, for they know not what they do." He then went to the block, kneeled down, and exclaimed with great energy, "Into Thy hands, O Lord! I commend my spirit; in Thee have I always trusted; receive me, therefore, my blessed Redeemer." The fatal stroke was then given, and a period put to the temporary pains of this life.

Lord Frederic de Bile suffered as a Protestant, and a promoter of the late war; he met his fate with serenity, and only said he wished well to the friends whom he left behind, forgave the enemies who caused his death, denied the authority of the emperor in that country, acknowledged Frederic to be the only true king of Bohemia, and hoped for salvation in the merits of his blessed Redeemer.

Lord Henry Otto, when he first came upon the scaffold, seemed greatly confounded, and said, with some asperity, as if addressing himself to the emperor, "Thou tyrant Ferdinand, your throne is established in blood; but if you will kill my body, and disperse my members, they shall still rise up in judgment against you." He then was silent, and having walked about for some time, seemed to recover his fortitude, and growing calm, said to a gentleman who stood near, "I was, a few minutes since, greatly discomposed, but now I feel my spirits revive; God be praised for affording me such comfort; death no longer appears as the king of terrors, but seems to invite me to participate of some unknown joys." Kneeling before the block, he said, "Almighty God! to Thee I commend my soul, receive it for the sake of Christ, and admit it to the glory of Thy presence." The executioner put this nobleman to considerable pain, by making several strokes before he severed the head from the body.

The earl of Rugenia was distinguished for his superior abilities, and unaffected piety. On the scaffold he said, "We who drew our swords fought only to preserve the liberties of the people, and to keep our consciences sacred: as we were overcome, I am better pleased at the sentence of death, than if the emperor had given me life; for I find that it pleases God to have his truth defended, not by our swords, but by our blood." He then went boldly to the block, saying, "I shall now be speedily with Christ," and received the crown of martyrdom with great courage.

Sir Gaspar Kaplitz was eighty-six years of age. When he came to the place of execution, he addressed the principal officer thus: "Behold a miserable ancient man, who hath often entreated God to take him out of this wicked world, but could not until now obtain his desire, for God reserved me until these years to be a spectacle to the world, and a sacrifice to himself; therefore God's will be done." One of the officers told him, in consideration of his great age, that if he would only ask pardon, he would immediately receive it. "Ask pardon, (exclaimed he) I will ask pardon of God, whom I have frequently offended; but not of the emperor, to whom I never gave any offence; should I sue for pardon, it might be justly suspected I had committed some crime for which I deserved this condemnation. No, no, as I die innocent, and with a clear conscience, I would not be separated from this noble company of martyrs:" so saying, he cheerfully resigned his neck to the block.

Procopius Dorzecki on the scaffold said, "We are now under the emperor's judgment; but in time he shall be judged, and we shall appear as witnesses against him." Then taking a gold medal from his neck, which was struck when the elector Frederic was crowned king of Bohemia, he presented it to one of the officers, at the same time uttering these words, "As a dying man, I request, if ever King Frederic is restored to the throne of Bohemia, that you will give him this medal. Tell him, for his sake, I wore it until death, and that now I willingly lay down my life for God and my king." He then cheerfully laid down his head and submitted to the fatal blow.

Dionysius Servius was brought up a Roman Catholic, but had embraced the reformed religion for some years. When upon the scaffold the Jesuits used their utmost endeavors to make him recant, and return to his former faith, but he paid not the least attention to their exhortations. Kneeling down he said, "They may destroy my body, but cannot injure my soul, that I commend to my Redeemer"; and then patiently submitted to martyrdom, being at that time fifty-six years of age.

Valentine Cockan, was a person of considerable fortune and eminence, perfectly pious and honest, but of trifling abilities; yet his imagination seemed to grow bright, and his faculties to improve on death's approach, as if the impending danger refined the understanding. Just before he was beheaded, he expressed himself with such eloquence, energy, and precision as greatly amazed those who knew his former deficiency in point of capacity.

Tobias Steffick was remarkable for his affability and serenity of temper. He was perfectly resigned to his fate, and a few minutes before his death spoke in this singular manner, "I have received, during the whole course of my life, many favors from God; ought I not therefore cheerfully to take one bitter cup, when He thinks proper to present it? Or rather, ought I not to rejoice that it is his will I should give up a corrupted life for that of immortality!"

Dr. Jessenius, an able student of physic, was accused of having spoken disrespectful words of the emperor, of treason in swearing allegiance to the elector Frederic, and of heresy in being a Protestant. For the first accusation he had his tongue cut out; for the second he was beheaded; and for the third, and last, he was quartered, and the respective parts exposed on poles.

Christopher Chober, as soon as he stepped upon the scaffold said, "I come in the name of God, to die for His glory; I have fought the good fight, and finished my course; so, executioner, do your office." The executioner obeyed, and he instantly received the crown of martyrdom.

No person ever lived more respected or died more lamented than John Shultis. The only words he spoke, before receiving the fatal stroke, were, "The righteous seem to die in the eyes of fools, but they only go to rest. Lord Jesus! Thou hast promised that those who come to Thee shall not be cast off. Behold, I am come; look on me, pity me, pardon my sins, and receive my soul."

Maximilian Hostialick was famed for his learning, piety, and humanity. When he first came on the scaffold, he seemed exceedingly terrified at the approach of death. The officer taking notice of his agitation, Hostialick said, "Ah! sir, now the sins of my youth crowd upon my mind, but I hope God will enlighten me, lest I sleep the sleep of death and lest mine enemies say we have prevailed." Soon after he said, "I hope my repentance is sincere, and will be accepted, in which case the blood of Christ will wash me from my crimes." He then told the officer he should repeat the Song of Simeon; at the conclusion of which the executioner might do his duty. He accordingly, said, "Lord, now lettest Thou Thy servant depart in peace, according to Thy word: For mine eyes have seen Thy salvation;" at which words his head was struck off at one blow.

When John Kutnaur came to the place of execution, a Jesuit said to him. "Embrace the Roman Catholic faith, which alone can save and arm you against the terrors of death." To which he replied, "Your superstitious faith I abhor, it leads to perdition, and I wish for no other arms against the terrors of death than a good conscience." The Jesuit turned away, saying, sarcastically, "The Protestants are impenetrable rocks." "You are mistaken," said Kutnaur, "it is Christ that is the Rock, and we are firmly fixed upon Him."

This person not being born independent, but having acquired a fortune by a mechanical employment, was ordered to be hanged. Just before he was turned off, he said, "I die, not for having committed any crime, but for following the dictates of my own conscience, and defending my country and religion."

Simeon Sussickey was father-in-law to Kutnaur, and like him, was ordered to be executed on a gallows. He went cheerfully to death, and appeared impatient to be executed, saying, "Every moment delays me from entering into the Kingdom of Christ."

Nathaniel Wodnianskey was hanged for having supported the Protestant cause, and the election of Frederic to the crown of Bohemia. At the gallows, the Jesuits did all in their power to induce him to renounce his faith. Finding their endeavors ineffectual, one of them said, "If you will not abjure your heresy, at least repent of your rebellion?" To which Wodnianskey replied, "You take away our lives under a pretended charge of rebellion; and, not content with that, seek to destroy our souls; glut yourselves with blood, and be satisfied; but tamper not with our consciences."

Wodnianskey's own son then approached the gallows, and said to his father, "Sir, if life should be offered to you on condition of apostasy, I entreat you to remember Christ, and reject such pernicious overtures." To this the father replied, "It is very acceptable, my son, to be exhorted to constancy by you; but suspect me not; rather endeavor to confirm in their faith your brothers, sisters, and children, and teach them to imitate that constancy of which I shall leave them an example." He had so sooner concluded these words than he was turned off, receiving the crown of martyrdom with great fortitude.

Winceslaus Gisbitzkey, during his whole confinement, had great hopes of life given him, which made his friends fear for the safety of his soul. He, however, continued steadfast in his faith, prayed fervently at the gallows, and met his fate with singular resignation.

Martin Foster was an ancient cripple; the accusations against whom were, being charitable to heretics, and lending money to the elector Frederic. His great wealth, however, seemed to have been his principal crime; and that he might be plundered of his treasures was the occasion of his being ranked in this illustrious list of martyrs.

CHAPTER IX

An Account of the Life and Persecutions of Martin Luther

THIS illustrious German divine and reformer of the Church was the son of John Luther and Margaret Ziegler, and born at Isleben, a town of Saxony, in the county of Mansfield, November 10, 1483. His father's extraction and condition were originally but mean, and his occupation that of a miner; it is probable, however, that by his application and industry he improved the fortunes of his family, as he afterward became a magistrate of rank and dignity. Luther was early initiated into letters, and at the age of thirteen was sent to school at Magdeburg, and thence to Eisenach, in Thuringia, where he remained four years, producing the early indications of his future eminence.

In 1501 he was sent to the University of Erfurt, where he went through the usual courses of logic and philosophy. When twenty, he took a master's degree, and then lectured on Aristotle's physics, ethics, and other parts of philosophy. Afterward, at the instigation of his parents, he turned himself to the civil law, with a view of advancing himself to the bar, but was diverted from this pursuit by the following accident. Walking out into the fields one day, he was struck by lightning so as to fall to the ground, while a companion was killed by his side; and this affected him so sensibly, that, without communicating his purpose to any of his friends, he withdrew himself from the world, and retired into the order of the hermits of St. Augustine.

Here he employed himself in reading St. Augustine and the schoolmen; but in turning over the leaves of the library, he accidentally found a copy of the Latin Bible, which he had never seen before. This raised his curiosity to a high degree: he read it over very greedily, and was amazed to find what a small portion of the Scriptures was rehearsed to the people.

He made his profession in the monastery of Erfurt, after he had been a novice one year; and he took priest's orders, and celebrated his first Mass in 1507. The year after, he was removed from the convent of Erfurt to the University of Wittenberg; for this university being just founded, nothing was thought more likely to bring it into immediate repute and credit, than the authority and presence of a man so celebrated, for his great parts and learning, as Luther.

In this University of Erfurt, there was a certain aged man in the convent of the Augustines with whom Luther, being then of the same order, a friar Augustine, had conference upon divers things, especially touching remission of sins; which article the said aged father opened unto Luther; declaring that God's express commandment is that every man should particularly believe his sins to be forgiven him in Christ: and further said that this interpretation was confirmed by St. Bernard: "This is the testimony that the Holy Ghost giveth thee in thy heart, saying, thy sins are forgiven thee. For this is the opinion of the apostle, that man is freely justified by faith."

By these words Luther was not only strengthened, but was also instructed of the full meaning of St. Paul, who repeateth so many times this sentence, "We are justified by faith." And having read the expositions of many upon this place, he then perceived, as well by the discourse of the old man, as by the comfort he received in his spirit, the vanity of those interpretations, which he had read before, of the schoolmen. And so, by little and little, reading and comparing the sayings and examples of the prophets and apostles, with continual invocation of God, and the excitation of faith by force of prayer, he perceived that doctrine most evidently. Thus continued he his study at Erfurt the space of four years in the convent of the Augustines.

In 1512, seven convents of his order having a quarrel with their vicar-general, Luther was chosen to go to Rome to maintain their cause. At Rome he saw the pope and the court, and had an opportunity of observing also the manners of the clergy, whose hasty, superficial, and impious way of celebrating Mass, he has severely noted. As soon as he had adjusted the dispute which was the business of his journey, he returned to Wittenberg, and was created doctor of divinity, at the expense of Frederic, elector of Saxony; who had often heard him preach, was perfectly acquainted with his merit, and reverenced him highly.

He continued in the University of Wittenberg, where, as professor of divinity, he employed himself in the business of his calling. Here then he began in the most earnest manner to read lectures upon the sacred books: he explained the Epistle to the Romans, and the Psalms, which he cleared up and illustrated in a manner so entirely new, and so different from what had been pursued by former commentators, that "there seemed, after a long and dark night, a new day to arise, in the judgment of all pious and prudent men."

Luther diligently reduced the minds of men to the Son of God: as John the Baptist demonstrated the Lamb of God that took away the sins of the world, even so Luther, shining in the Church as the bright daylight after a long and dark night, expressly showed that sins are freely remitted for the love of the Son of God, and that we ought faithfully to embrace this bountiful gift.

His life was correspondent to his profession; and it plainly appeared that his words were no lip-labor, but proceeded from the very heart. This admiration of his holy life much allured the hearts of his auditors.

The better to qualify himself for the task he had undertaken, he applied himself attentively to the Greek and Hebrew languages; and in this manner was he employed, when the general indulgences were published in 1517.

Leo X who succeeded Julius II in March, 1513, formed a design of building the magnificent Church of St. Peter's at Rome, which was, indeed, begun by Julius, but still required very large sums to be finished. Leo, therefore, in 1517 published general indulgences throughout all Europe, in favor of those who contribute any sum to the building of St. Peter's; and appointed persons in different countries to preach up these indulgences, and to receive money for them. These strange proceedings gave vast offence at Wittenberg, and particularly inflamed the pious zeal of Luther; who, being naturally warm and active, and in the present case unable to contain himself, was determined to declare against them at all adventures.

Upon the eve of All-saints, therefore, in 1517, he publicly fixed up, at the church next to the castle of that town, a thesis upon indulgences; in the beginning of which he challenged any one to oppose it either by writing or disputation. Luther's propositions about indulgences were no sooner published, than Tetzel, the Dominican friar, and commissioner for selling them, maintained and published at Frankfort, a thesis, containing a set of propositions directly contrary to them. He did more; he stirred up the clergy of his order against Luther; anathematized him from the pulpit, as a most damnable heretic; and burnt his thesis publicly at Frankfort. Tetzel's thesis was also burnt, in return, by the Lutherans at Wittenberg; but Luther himself disowned having had any hand in that procedure.

In 1518, Luther, though dissuaded from it by his friends, yet, to show obedience to authority, went to the monastery of St. Augustine, at Heidelberg, while the chapter was held; and here maintained, April 26, a dispute concerning "justification by faith"; which Bucer, who was present at, took down in writing, and afterward communicated to Beatus Rhenanus, not without the highest commendations.

In the meantime, the zeal of his adversaries grew every day more and more active against him; and he was at length accused to Leo X as a heretic. As soon as he returned therefore from Heidelberg, he wrote a letter to that pope, in the most submissive terms; and sent him, at the same time, an explication of his propositions about indulgences. This letter is dated on Trinity Sunday, 1518, and was accompanied with a protestation, wherein he declared, that 'he did not pretend to advance or defend anything contrary to the Holy Scriptures, or to the doctrine of the fathers, received and observed by the Church of Rome, or to the canons and decretals of the popes: nevertheless, he thought he had the liberty either to approve or disapprove the opinions of St. Thomas, Bonaventure, and other school-men and canonists, which are not grounded upon any text.'

The emperor Maximilian was equally solicitous, with the pope about putting a stop to the propagation of Luther's opinions in Saxony; troublesome both to the Church and empire. Maximilian, therefore, applied to Leo, in a letter dated August 5, 1518, and begged him to forbid, by his authority, these useless, rash, and dangerous disputes; assuring him also that he would strictly execute in the empire whatever his holiness should enjoin.

In the meantime Luther, as soon as he understood what was transacting about him at Rome, used all imaginable means to prevent his being carried thither, and to obtain a hearing of his cause in Germany. The elector was also against Luther's going to Rome, and desired of Cardinal Cajetan, that he might be heard before him, as the pope's legate in Germany. Upon these addresses, the pope consented that the cause should be tried before Cardinal Cajetan, to whom he had given power to decide it.

Luther, therefore, set off immediately for Augsburg, and carried with him letters from the elector. He arrived here in October, 1518, and, upon an assurance of his safety, was admitted into the cardinal's presence. But Luther was soon convinced that he had more to fear from the cardinal's power than from disputations of any kind; and, therefore, apprehensive of being seized if he did not submit, withdrew from Augsburg upon the twentieth. But, before his departure, he published a formal appeal to the pope, and finding himself protected by the elector, continued to teach the same doctrines at Wittenberg, and sent a challenge to all the inquisitors to come and dispute with him.

As to Luther, Miltitius, the pope's chamberlain, had orders to require the elector to oblige him to retract, or to deny him his protection: but things were not now to be carried with so high a hand, Luther's credit being too firmly established. Besides, the emperor Maximilian happened to die upon the twelfth of this month, whose death greatly altered the face of affairs, and made the elector more able to determine Luther's fate. Miltitius thought it best, therefore, to try what could be done by fair and gentle means, and to that end came to some conference with Luther.

During all these treaties, the doctrine of Luther spread, and prevailed greatly; and he himself received great encouragement at home and abroad. The Bohemians about this time sent him a book of the celebrated John Huss, who had fallen a martyr in the work of reformation; and also letters, in which they exhorted him to constancy and perseverance, owning that the divinity which he taught was the pure, sound, and orthodox divinity. Many great and learned men had joined themselves to him.

In 1519, he had a famous dispute at Leipsic with John Eccius.

But this dispute ended at length like all others, the parties not the least nearer in opinion, but more at enmity with each other's persons.

About the end of this year, Luther published a book, in which he contended for the Communion being celebrated in both kinds; which was condemned by the bishop of Misnia, January 24, 1520.

While Luther was laboring to excuse himself to the new emperor and the bishops of Germany, Eccius had gone to Rome, to solicit his condemnation; which, it may easily be conceived, was now become not difficult to be attained. Indeed the continual importunities of Luther's adversaries with Leo, caused him at length to publish a formal condemnation of him, and he did so accordingly, in a bull, dated June 15, 1520. This was carried into Germany, and published there by Eccius, who had solicited it at Rome; and who, together with Jerome Alexander, a person eminent for his learning and eloquence, was intrusted by the pope with the execution of it. In the meantime, Charles V of Spain, after he had set things to rights in the Low Countries, went into Germany, and was crowned emperor, October the twenty-first at Aix-la-Chapelle.

Martin Luther, after he had been first accused at Rome upon Maunday Thursday by the pope's censure, shortly after Easter speedeth his journey toward Worms, where the said Luther, appearing before the emperor and all the states of Germany, constantly stuck to the truth, defended himself, and answered his adversaries.

Luther was lodged, well entertained, and visited by many earls, barons, knights of the order, gentlemen, priests, and the commonalty, who frequented his lodging until night.

He came, contrary to the expectation of many, as well adversaries as others. His friends deliberated together, and many persuaded him not to adventure himself to such a present danger, considering how these beginnings answered not the faith of promise made. Who, when he had heard their whole persuasion and advice, answered in this wise: "As touching me, since I am sent for, I am resolved and certainly determined to enter Worms, in the name of our Lord Jesus Christ; yea, although I knew there were as many devils to resist me as there are tiles to cover the houses in Worms."

The next day, the herald brought him from his lodging to the emperor's court, where he abode until six o'clock, for that the princes were occupied in grave consultations; abiding there, and being environed with a great number of people, and almost smothered for the press that was there. Then after, when the princes were set, and Luther entered, Eccius, the official, spake in this manner: "Answer now to the Emperor's demand. Wilt thout maintain all thy books which thou hast acknowledged, or revoke any part of them, and submit thyself?"

Martin Luther answered modestly and lowly, and yet not without some stoutness of stomach, and Christian constancy. "Considering your sovereign majesty, and your honors, require a plain answer; this I say and profess as resolutely as I may, without doubting or sophistication, that if I be not convinced by testimonies of the Scriptures (for I believe not the pope, neither his general Councils, which have erred many times, and have been contrary to themselves), my conscience is so bound and captivated in these Scriptures and the Word of God, that I will not, nor may not revoke any manner of thing; considering it is not godly or lawful to do anything against conscience. Hereupon I stand and rest: I have not what else to say. God have mercy upon me!"

The princes consulted together upon this answer given by Luther; and when they had diligently examined the same, the prolocutor began to repel him thus: "The Emperor's majesty requireth of thee a simple answer, either negative or affirmative, whether thou mindest to defend all thy works as Christian, or no?"

Then Luther, turning to the emperor and the nobles, besought them not to force or compel him to yield against his conscience, confirmed with the Holy Scriptures, without manifest arguments alleged to the contrary by his adversaries. "I am tied by the Scriptures."

Before the Diet of Worms was dissolved, Charles V caused an edict to be drawn up, which was dated the eighth of May, and decreed that Martin Luther be, agreeably to the sentence of the pope, henceforward looked upon as a member separated from the Church, a schismatic, and an obstinate and notorious heretic. While the bull of Leo X executed by Charles V was thundering throughout the empire, Luther was safely shut up in the castle of Wittenberg; but weary at length of his retirement, he appeared publicly again at Wittenberg, March 6, 1522, after he had been absent about ten months.

Luther now made open war with the pope and bishops; and, that he might make the people despise their authority as much as possible, he wrote one book against the pope's bull, and another against the order falsely called "The Order of Bishops." He published also a translation of the New Testament in the German tongue, which was afterward corrected by himself and Melancthon.

Affairs were now in great confusion in Germany; and they were not less so in Italy, for a quarrel arose between the pope and the emperor, during which Rome was twice taken, and the pope imprisoned. While the princes were thus employed in quarrelling with each other, Luther persisted in carrying on the work of the Reformation, as well by opposing the papists, as by combating the Anabaptists and other fanatical sects; which, having taken the advantage of his contest with the Church of Rome, had sprung up and established themselves in several places.

In 1527, Luther was suddenly seized with a coagulation of the blood about the heart, which had like to have put an end to his life. The troubles of Germany being not likely to have any end, the emperor was forced to call a diet at Spires, in 1529, to require the assistance of the princes of the empire against the Turks. Fourteen cities, viz., Strassburg, Nuremberg, Ulm, Constance, Retlingen, Windsheim, Memmingen, Lindow, Kempten, Hailbron, Isny, Weissemburg, Nortlingen, S. Gal, joined against the decree of the Diet protestation, which was put into writing, and published April, 1529. This was the famous protestation, which gave the name of "Protestants" to the reformers in Germany.

After this, the Protestant princes labored to make a firm league and enjoined the elector of Saxony and his allies to approve of what the Diet had done; but the deputies drew up an appeal, and the Protestants afterwards presented an apology for their "Confession"— that famous confession which was drawn up by the temperate Melancthon, as also the apology. These were signed by a variety of princes, and Luther had now nothing else to do, but to sit down and contemplate the mighty work he had finished: for that a single monk should be able to give the Church of Rome so rude a shock, that there needed but such another entirely to overthrow it, may be well esteemed a mighty work.

In 1533, Luther wrote a consolatory epistle to the citizens of Oschatz, who had suffered some hardships for adhering to the Augsburg confession of faith: and in 1534, the Bible translated by him into German was first printed, as the old privilege, dated at Bibliopolis, under the elector's own hand, shows; and it was published in the year after. He also published this year a book, "Against Masses and the Consecration of Priests."

In February, 1537, an assembly was held at Smalkald about matters of religion, to which Luther and Melancthon were called. At this meeting Luther was seized with so grievous an illness that there was no hope of his recovery. As he was carried along he made his will, in which he bequeathed his detestation of popery to his friends and brethren. In this manner was he employed until his death, which happened in 1546.

That year, accompanied by Melancthon, he paid a visit to his own country, which he had not seen for many years, and returned again in safety. But soon after, he was called thither again by the earls of Mansfelt, to compose some differences which had arisen about their boundaries, where he was received by one hundred horsemen, or more, and conducted in a very honorable manner; but was at the same time so very ill that it was feared he would die. He said that these fits of sickness often came upon him, when he had any great business to undertake. Of this, however, he did not recover, but died in February 18, in his sixty-third year. A little before he expired, he admonished those that were about him to pray to God for the propagation of the Gospel, "Because," said he, "the Council of Trent, which had sat once or twice, and the pope, will devise strange things against it." Feeling his fatal hour to approach, before nine o'clock in the morning, he commended himself to God with this devout prayer: "My heavenly Father, eternal and merciful God! Thou hast manifested unto me Thy dear Son, our Lord Jesus Christ. I have taught Him, I have known Him; I love Him as my life, my health and my redemption; Whom the wicked have persecuted, maligned, and with injury afflicted. Draw my soul to Thee."

After this he said as ensueth, thrice: "I commend my spirit into Thy hands, Thou hast redeemed me, O God of Truth! 'God so loved the world, that He gave His only begotten Son, that whosoever believeth in Him should not perish, but have life everlasting.'" Having repeated oftentimes his prayers, he was called to God. So praying, his innocent ghost peaceably was separated from the earthly body.

CHAPTER X

General Persecutions in Germany

THE general persecutions in Germany were principally occasioned by the doctrines and ministry of Martin Luther. Indeed, the pope was so terrified at the success of that courageous reformer, that he determined to engage the emperor, Charles V, at any rate, in the scheme to attempt their extirpation

To this end

1. He gave the emperor two hundred thousand crowns in ready money.

2. He promised to maintain twelve thousand foot, and five thousand horse, for the space of six months, or during a campaign.

3. He allowed the emperor to receive one half the revenues of the clergy of the empire during the war.

4. He permitted the emperor to pledge the abbey lands for five hundred thousand crowns, to assist in carrying on hostilities against the Protestants.

Thus prompted and supported, the emperor undertook the extirpation of the Protestants, against whom, indeed, he was particularly enraged himself; and, for this purpose, a formidable army was raised in Germany, Spain, and Italy.

The Protestant princes, in the meantime, formed a powerful confederacy, in order to repel the impending blow. A great army was raised, and the command given to the elector of Saxony, and the landgrave of Hesse. The imperial forces were commanded by the emperor of Germany in person, and the eyes of all Europe were turned on the event of the war.

At length the armies met, and a desperate engagement ensued, in which the Protestants were defeated, and the elector of Saxony and the landgrave of Hesse both taken prisoners. This fatal blow was succeeded by a horrid persecution, the severities of which were such that exile might be deemed a mild fate, and concealment in a dismal wood pass for happiness. In such times a cave is a palace, a rock a bed of down, and wild roots delicacies.

Those who were taken experienced the most cruel tortures that infernal imaginations could invent; and by their constancy evinced that a real Christian can surmount every difficulty, and despite every danger acquire a crown of martyrdom.

Henry Voes and John Esch, being apprehended as Protestants, were brought to examination. Voes, answering for himself and the other, gave the following answers to some questions asked by a priest, who examined them by order of the magistracy.

Priest. Were you not both, some years ago, Augustine friars?

Voes. Yes.

Priest. How came you to quit the bosom of the Church of Rome?

Voes. On account of her abominations.

Priest. In what do you believe?

Voes. In the Old and New Testaments.

Priest. Do you believe in the writings of the fathers, and the decrees of the Councils?

Voes. Yes, if they agree with Scripture.

Priest. Did not Martin Luther seduce you both?

Voes. He seduced us even in the very same manner as Christ seduced the apostles; that is, he made us sensible of the frailty of our bodies, and the value of our souls.

This examination was sufficient. They were both condemned to the flames, and soon after suffered with that manly fortitude which becomes Christians when they receive a crown of martyrdom.

Henry Sutphen, an eloquent and pious preacher, was taken out of his bed in the middle of the night, and compelled to walk barefoot a considerable way, so that his feet were terribly cut. He desired a horse, but his conductors said, in derision, "A horse for a heretic! no no, heretics may go barefoot." When he arrived at the place of his destination, he was condemned to be burnt; but, during the execution, many indignities were offered him, as those who attended not content with what he suffered in the flames, cut and slashed him in a most terrible manner.

Many were murdered at Halle; Middleburg being taken by storm all the Protestants were put to the sword, and great numbers were burned at Vienna.

An officer being sent to put a minister to death, pretended, when he came to the clergyman's house, that his intentions were only to pay him a visit. The minister, not suspecting the intended cruelty, entertained his supposed guest in a very cordial manner. As soon as dinner was over, the officer said to some of his attendants, "Take this clergyman, and hang him." The attendants themselves were so shocked after the civility they had seen, that they hesitated to perform the commands of their master; and the minister said, "Think what a sting will remain on your conscience, for thus violating the laws of hospitality." The officer, however, insisted upon being obeyed, and the attendants, with reluctance, performed the execrable office of executioners.

Peter Spengler, a pious divine, of the town of Schalet, was thrown into the river, and drowned. Before he was taken to the banks of the stream which was to become his grave, they led him to the market place that his crimes might be proclaimed; which were, not going to Mass, not making confession, and not believing in transubstantiation. After this ceremony was over, he made a most excellent discourse to the people, and concluded with a kind hymn, of a very edifying nature.

A Protestant gentleman being ordered to lose his head for not renouncing his religion, went cheerfully to the place of execution. A friar came to him, and said these words in a low tone of voice, "As you have a great reluctance publicly to abjure your faith, whisper your confession in my ear, and I will absolve your sins." To this the gentleman loudly replied, "Trouble me not, friar, I have confessed my sins to God, and obtained absolution through the merits of Jesus Christ." Then turning to the executioner, he said, "Let me not be pestered with these men, but perform your duty," on which his head was struck off at a single blow.

Wolfgang Scuch, and John Huglin, two worthy ministers, were burned, as was Leonard Keyser, a student of the University of Wertembergh; and George Carpenter, a Bavarian, was hanged for refusing to recant Protestantism.

The persecutions in Germany having subsided many years, again broke out in 1630, on account of the war between the emperor and the king of Sweden, for the latter was a Protestant prince, and consequently the Protestants of Germany espoused his cause, which greatly exasperated the emperor against them.

The imperialists having laid siege to the town of Passewalk, (which was defended by the Swedes) took it by storm, and committed the most horrid cruelties on the occasion. They pulled down the churches, burnt the houses, pillaged the properties, massacred the ministers, put the garrison to the sword, hanged the townsmen, ravished the women, smothered the children, etc., etc.

A most bloody tragedy was transacted at Magdeburg, in the year 1631. The generals Tilly and Pappenheim, having taken that Protestant city by storm, upwards of twenty thousand persons, without distinction of rank, sex, or age, were slain during the carnage, and six thousand were drowned in attempting to escape over the river Elbe. After this fury had subsided, the remaining inhabitants were stripped naked, severely scourged, had their ears cropped, and being yoked together like oxen were turned adrift.

The town of Hoxter was taken by the popish army, and all the inhabitants as well as the garrison were put to the sword; the houses even were set on fire, the bodies being consumed in the flames.

At Griphenberg, when the imperial forces prevailed, they shut up the senators in the senate chamber, and surrounding it by lighted straw suffocated them.

Franhendal surrendered upon articles of capitulation, yet the inhabitants were as cruelly used as at other places; and at Heidelberg many were shut up in prison and starved.

The cruelties used by the imperial troops, under Count Tilly in Saxony, are thus enumerated.

Half strangling, and recovering the persons again repeatedly. Rolling sharp wheels over the fingers and toes. Pinching the thumbs in a vice. Forcing the most filthy things down the throat, by which many were choked. Tying cords round the head so tightly that the blood gushed out of the eyes, nose, ears, and mouth. Fastening burning matches to the fingers, toes, ears, arms, legs, and even the tongue. Putting powder in the mouth and setting fire to it, by which the head was shattered to pieces. Tying bags of powder to all parts of the body, by which the person was blown up. Drawing cords backwards and forwards through the fleshy parts. Making incisions with bodkins and knives in the skin. Running wires through the nose, ears, lips, etc. Hanging Protestants up by the legs, with their heads over a fire, by which they were smoke dried. Hanging up by one arm until it was dislocated. Hanging upon hooks by the ribs. Forcing people to drink until they burst. Baking many in hot ovens. Fixing weights to the feet, and drawing up several with pulleys. Hanging, stifling, roasting, stabbing, frying, racking, ravishing, ripping open, breaking the bones, rasping off the flesh, tearing with wild horses, drowning, strangling, burning, broiling, crucifying, immuring, poisoning, cutting off tongues, noses, ears, etc., sawing off the limbs, hacking to pieces, and drawing by the heels through the streets.

The enormous cruelties will be a perpetual stain on the memory of Count Tilly, who not only committed, but even commanded the troops to put them in practice. Wherever he came, the most horrid barbarities and cruel depredations ensued: famine and conflagration marked his progress: for he destroyed all the provisions he could not take with him, and burnt all the towns before he left them; so that the full result of his conquests were murder, poverty, and desolation.

An aged and pious divine they stripped naked, tied him on his back upon a table, and fastened a large, fierce cat upon his belly. They then pricked and tormented the cat in such a manner that the creature with rage tore his belly open, and gnawed his bowels.

Another minister and his family were seized by these inhuman monsters; they ravished his wife and daughter before his face; stuck his infant son upon the point of a lance, and then surrounding him with his whole library of books, they set fire to them, and he was consumed in the midst of the flames.

In Hesse-Cassel some of the troops entered an hospital, in which were principally mad women, when stripping all the poor wretches naked, they made them run about the streets for their diversion, and then put them all to death.

In Pomerania, some of the imperial troops entering a small town, seized upon all the young women, and girls of upwards of ten years, and then placing their parents in a circle, they ordered them to sing Psalms, while they ravished their children, or else they swore they would cut them to pieces afterward. They then took all the married women who had young children, and threatened, if they did not consent to the gratification of their lusts, to burn their children before their faces in a large fire, which they had kindled for that purpose.

A band of Count Tilly's soldiers meeting a company of merchants belonging to Basel, who were returning from the great market of Strassburg, attempted to surround them; all escaped, however, but ten, leaving their properties behind. The ten who were taken begged hard for their lives: but the soldiers murdered them saying, "You must die because you are heretics, and have got no money."

The same soldiers met with two countesses, who, together with some young ladies, the daughters of one of them, were taking an airing in a landau. The soldiers spared their lives, but treated them with the greatest indecency, and having stripped them all stark naked, bade the coachman drive on.

By means and mediation of Great Britain, peace was at length restored to Germany, and the Protestants remained unmolested for several years, until some new disturbances broke out in the Palatinate, which were thus occasioned:

The great Church of the Holy Ghost, at Heidelberg, had, for many years, been shared equally by the Protestants and Roman Catholics in this manner: the Protestants performed divine service in the nave or body of the church; and the Roman Catholics celebrated Mass in the choir. Though this had been the custom from time immemorial, the elector of the Palatinate, at length, took it into his head not to suffer it any longer, declaring, that as Heidelberg was the place of his residence, and the Church of the Holy Ghost the cathedral of his principal city, divine service ought to be performed only according to the rites of the Church of which he was a member. He then forbade the Protestants to enter the church, and put the papists in possession of the whole.

The aggrieved people applied to the Protestant powers for redress, which so much exasperated the elector, that he suppressed the Heidelberg catechism. The Protestant powers, however, unanimously agreed to demand satisfaction, as the elector, by this conduct, had broken an article of the treaty of Westphalia; and the courts of Great Britain, Prussia, Holland, etc., sent deputies to the elector, to represent the injustice of his proceedings, and to threaten, unless he changed his behavior to the Protestants in the Palatinate, that they would treat their Roman Catholic subjects with the greatest severity. Many violent disputes took place between the Protestant powers and those of the elector, and these were greatly augmented by the following incident: the coach of the Dutch minister standing before the door of the resident sent by the prince of Hesse, the host was by chance being carried to a sick person; the coachman took not the least notice, which those who attended the host observing, pulled him from his box, and compelled him to kneel; this violence to the domestic of a public minister was highly resented by all the Protestant deputies; and still more to heighten these differences, the Protestants presented to the deputies three additional articles of complaint.

1. That military executions were ordered against all Protestant shoemakers who should refuse to contribute to the Masses of St. Crispin.

2. That the Protestants were forbid to work on popish holy days, even in harvest time, under very heavy penalties, which occasioned great inconveniences, and considerably prejudiced public business.

3. That several Protestant ministers had been dispossessed of their churches, under pretence of their having been originally founded and built by Roman Catholics.

The Protestant deputies at length became so serious as to intimate to the elector, that force of arms should compel him to do the justice he denied to their representations. This menace brought him to reason, as he well knew the impossibility of carrying on a war against the powerful states who threatened him. He therefore agreed that the body of the Church of the Holy Ghost should be restored to the Protestants. He restored the Heidelberg catechism, put the Protestant ministers again in possession of the churches of which they had been dispossessed, allowed the Protestants to work on popish holy days, and, ordered, that no person should be molested for not kneeling when the host passed by.

These things he did through fear; but to show his resentment to his Protestant subjects, in other circumstances where Protestant states had no right to interfere, he totally abandoned Heidelberg, removing all the courts of justice to Mannheim, which was entirely inhabited by Roman Catholics. He likewise built a new palace there, making it his place of residence; and, being followed by the Roman Catholics of Heidelberg, Mannheim became a flourishing place.

In the meantime the Protestants of Heidelberg sunk into poverty and many of them became so distressed as to quit their native country, and seek an asylum in Protestant states. A great number of these coming into England, in the time of Queen Anne, were cordially received there, and met with a most humane assistance, both by public and private donations.

In 1732, above thirty thousand Protestants were, contrary to the treaty of Westphalia, driven from the archbishopric of Salzburg. They went away in the depth of winter, with scarcely enough clothes to cover them, and without provisions, not having permission to take anything with them. The cause of these poor people not being publicly espoused by such states as could obtain them redress, they emigrated to various Protestant countries, and settled in places where they could enjoy the free exercise of their religion, without hurting their consciences, and live free from the trammels of popish superstition, and the chains of papal tyranny.

CHAPTER XI

An Account of the Persecutions in the Netherlands

THE light of the Gospel having successfully spread over the Netherlands, the pope instigated the emperor to commence a persecution against the Protestants; when many thousand fell martyrs to superstitious malice and barbarous bigotry, among whom the most remarkable were the following:

Wendelinuta, a pious Protestant widow, was apprehended on account of her religion, when several monks, unsuccessfully, endeavored to persuade her to recant. As they could not prevail, a Roman Catholic lady of her acquaintance desired to be admitted to the dungeon in which she was confined, and promised to exert herself strenuously towards inducing the prisoner to abjure the reformed religion. When she was admitted to the dungeon, she did her utmost to perform the task she had undertaken; but finding her endeavors ineffectual, she said, "Dear Wendelinuta, if you will not embrace our faith, at least keep the things which you profess secret within your own bosom, and strive to prolong your life." To which the widow replied, "Madam, you know not what you say; for with the heart we believe to righteousness, but with the tongue confession is made unto salvation." As she positively refused to recant, her goods were confiscated, and she was condemned to be burnt. At the place of execution a monk held a cross to her, and bade her kiss and worship God. To which she answered, "I worship no wooden god, but the eternal God who is in heaven." She was then executed, but through the before-mentioned Roman Catholic lady, the favor was granted that she should be strangled before fire was put to the fagots.

Two Protestant clergymen were burnt at Colen; a tradesman of Antwerp, named Nicholas, was tied up in a sack, thrown into the river, and drowned; and Pistorius, a learned student, was carried to the market of a Dutch village in a fool's coat, and committed to the flames.

Sixteen Protestants, having received sentence to be beheaded, a Protestant minister was ordered to attend the execution. This gentleman performed the function of his office with great propriety, exhorted them to repentance, and gave them comfort in the mercies of their Redeemer. As soon as the sixteen were beheaded, the magistrate cried out to the executioner, "There is another stroke remaining yet; you must behead the minister; he can never die at a better time than with such excellent precepts in his mouth, and such laudable examples before him." He was accordingly beheaded, though even many of the Roman Catholics themselves reprobated this piece of treacherous and unnecessary cruelty.

George Scherter, a minister of Salzburg, was apprehended and committed to prison for instructing his flock in the knowledge of the Gospel. While he was in confinement he wrote a confession of his faith; soon after which he was condemned, first to be beheaded, and afterward to be burnt to ashes. On his way to the place of execution he said to the spectators, "That you may know I die a true Christian, I will give you a sign." This was indeed verified in a most singular manner; for after his head was cut off, the body lying a short space of time with the belly to the ground, it suddenly turned upon the back, when the right foot crossed over the left, as did also the right arm over the left: and in this manner it remained until it was committed to the flames.

In Louviana, a learned man, named Percinal, was murdered in prison; and Justus Insparg was beheaded, for having Luther's sermons in his possession.

Giles Tilleman, a cutler of Brussels, was a man of great humanity and piety. Among others he was apprehended as a Protestant, and many endeavors were made by the monks to persuade him to recant. He had once, by accident, a fair opportunity of escaping from prison and being asked why he did not avail himself of it, he replied, "I would not do the keepers so much injury, as they must have answered for my absence, had I gone away." When he was sentenced to be burnt, he fervently thanked God for granting him an opportunity, by martyrdom, to glorify His name. Perceiving, at the place of execution, a great quantity of fagots, he desired the principal part of them might be given to the poor, saying, "A small quantity will suffice to consume me." The executioner offered to strangle him before the fire was lighted, but he would not consent, telling him that he defied the flames; and, indeed, he gave up the ghost with such composure amidst them, that he hardly seemed sensible of their effects.

In the year 1543 and 1544, the persecution was carried on throughout all Flanders in a most violent and cruel manner. Some were condemned to perpetual imprisonment, others to perpetual banishment; but most were put to death either by hanging, drowning, immuring, burning, the rack, or burying alive.

John de Boscane, a zealous Protestant, was apprehended on account of his faith, in the city of Antwerp. On his trial, he steadfastly professed himself to be of the reformed religion, which occasioned his immediate condemnation. The magistrate, however, was afraid to put him to death publicly, as he was popular through his great generosity, and almost universally beloved for his inoffensive life, and exemplary piety. A private execution being determined on, an order was given to drown him in prison. The executioner, accordingly, put him in a large tub; but Boscane struggling, and getting his head above the water, the executioner stabbed him with a dagger in several places, until he expired.

John de Buisons, another Protestant, was, about the same time, secretly apprehended, and privately executed at Antwerp. The numbers of Protestants being great in that city, and the prisoner much respected, the magistrates feared an insurrection, and for that reason ordered him to be beheaded in prison.

A. D. 1568, three persons were apprehended in Antwerp, named Scoblant, Hues, and Coomans. During their confinement they behaved with great fortitude and cheerfulness, confessing that the hand of God appeared in what had befallen them, and bowing down before the throne of his providence. In an epistle to some worthy Protestants, they expressed themselves in the following words: "Since it is the will of the Almighty that we should suffer for His name, and be persecuted for the sake of His Gospel, we patiently submit, and are joyful upon the occasion; though the flesh may rebel against the spirit, and hearken to the council of the old serpent, yet the truths of the Gospel shall prevent such advice from being taken, and Christ shall bruise the serpent's head. We are not comfortless in confinement, for we have faith; we fear not affliction, for we have hope; and we forgive our enemies, for we have charity. Be not under apprehensions for us, we are happy in confinement through the promises of God, glory in our bonds, and exult in being thought worthy to suffer for the sake of Christ. We desire not to be released, but to be blessed with fortitude; we ask not liberty, but the power of perseverance; and wish for no change in our condition, but that which places a crown of martyrdom upon our heads."

Scoblant was first brought to his trial; when, persisting in the profession of his faith, he received sentence of death. On his return to prison, he earnestly requested the jailer not to permit any friar to come near him; saying, "They can do me no good, but may greatly disturb me. I hope my salvation is already sealed in heaven, and that the blood of Christ, in which I firmly put my trust, hath washed me from my iniquities. I am now going to throw off this mantle of clay, to be clad in robes of eternal glory, by whose celestial brightness I shall be freed from all errors. I hope I may be the last martyr to papal tyranny, and the blood already spilt found sufficient to quench the thirst of popish cruelty; that the Church of Christ may have rest here, as his servants will hereafter." On the day of execution, he took a pathetic leave of his fellow prisoners. At the stake he fervently said the Lord's Prayer, and sung the Fortieth Psalm; then commending his soul to God, he was burnt alive.

Hues, soon after died in prison; upon which occasion Coomans wrote thus to his friends: "I am now deprived of my friends and companions; Scoblant is martyred, and Hues dead, by the visitation of the Lord: yet I am not alone, I have with me the God of Abraham, of Isaac, and of Jacob; He is my comfort, and shall be my reward. Pray unto God to strengthen me to the end, as I expect every hour to be freed from this tenement of clay."

On his trial he freely confessed himself of the reformed religion, answered with a manly fortitude to every charge against him, and proved the Scriptural part of his answers from the Gospel. The judge told him the only alternatives were recantation or death; and concluded by saying, "Will you die for the faith you profess?" To which Coomans replied, "I am not only willing to die, but to suffer the most excruciating torments for it; after which my soul shall receive its confirmation from God Himself, in the midst of eternal glory." Being condemned, he went cheerfully to the place of execution, and died with the most manly fortitude, and Christian resignation.

William of Nassau fell a sacrifice to treachery, being assassinated in the fifty-first year of his age, by Beltazar Gerard, a native of Franche Compte, in the province of Burgundy. This murderer, in hopes of a reward here and hereafter, for killing an enemy to the king of Spain and an enemy to the Catholic religion, undertook to destroy the prince of Orange. Having procured firearms, he watched him as he passed through the great hall of his palace to dinner, and demanded a passport. The princess of Orange, observing that the assassin spoke with a hollow and confused voice, asked who he was, saying that she did not like his countenance. The prince answered that it was one that demanded a passport, which he should presently have.

Nothing further passed before dinner, but on the return of the prince and princess through the same hall, after dinner was over, the assassin, standing concealed as much as possible by one of the pillars, fired at the prince, the balls entering at the left side, and passing through the right, wounding in their passage the stomach and vital parts. On receiving the wounds, the prince only said, "Lord, have mercy upon my soul, and upon these poor people," and then expired immediately.

The lamentations throughout the United Provinces were general, on account of the death of the prince of Orange; and the assassin, who was immediately taken, received sentence to be put to death in the most exemplary manner, yet such was his enthusiasm, or folly, that when his flesh was torn by red-hot pincers, he coolly said, "If I was at liberty, I would commit such an action over again."

The prince of Orange's funeral was the grandest ever seen in the Low Countries, and perhaps the sorrow for his death the most sincere, as he left behind him the character he honestly deserved, viz., that of father of his people.

To conclude, multitudes were murdered in different parts of Flanders; in the city of Valence, in particular, fifty-seven of the principal inhabitants were butchered in one day, for refusing to embrace the Romish superstition; and great numbers were suffered to languish in confinement, until they perished through the inclemency of their dungeons.

CHAPTER XII

The Life and Story of the True Servant and Martyr of God, William Tyndale

WE have now to enter into the story of the good martyr of God, William Tyndale; which William Tyndale, as he was a special organ of the Lord appointed, and as God's mattock to shake the inward roots and foundation of the pope's proud prelacy, so the great prince of darkness, with his impious imps, having a special malice against him, left no way unsought how craftily to entrap him, and falsely to betray him, and maliciously to spill his life, as by the process of his story here following may appear.

William Tyndale, the faithful minister of Christ, was born about the borders of Wales, and brought up from a child in the University of Oxford, where he, by long continuance, increased as well in the knowledge of tongues, and other liberal arts, as especially in the knowledge of the Scriptures, whereunto his mind was singularly addicted; insomuch that he, lying then in Magdalen Hall, read privily to certain students and fellows of Magdalen College some parcel of divinity; instructing them in the knowledge and truth of the Scriptures. His manners and conversation being correspondent to the same, were such that all they that knew him reputed him to be a man of most virtuous disposition, and of life unspotted.

Thus he, in the University of Oxford, increasing more and more in learning, and proceeding in degrees of the schools, spying his time, removed from thence to the University of Cambridge, where he likewise made his abode a certain space. Being now further ripened in the knowledge of God's Word, leaving that university, he resorted to one Master Welch, a knight of Gloucestershire, and was there schoolmaster to his children, and in good favor with his master. As this gentleman kept a good ordinary commonly at his table, there resorted to him many times sundry abbots, deans, archdeacons, with divers other doctors, and great beneficed men; who there, together with Master Tyndale sitting at the same table, did use many times to enter communication, and talk of learned men, as of Luther and of Erasmus; also of divers other controversies and questions upon the Scripture.

Then Master Tyndale, as he was learned and well practiced in God's matters, spared not to show unto them simply and plainly his judgment, and when they at any time did vary from Tyndale in opinions, he would show them in the Book, and lay plainly before them the open and manifest places of the Scriptures, to confute their errors, and confirm his sayings. And thus continued they for a certain season, reasoning and contending together divers times, until at length they waxed weary, and bare a secret grudge in their hearts against him.

As this grew on, the priests of the country, clustering together, began to grudge and storm against Tyndale, railing against him in alehouses and other places, affirming that his sayings were heresy; and accused him secretly to the chancellor, and others of the bishop's officers.

It followed not long after this that there was a sitting of the bishop's chancellor appointed, and warning was given to the priests to appear, amongst whom Master Tyndale was also warned to be there. And whether he had any misdoubt by their threatenings, or knowledge given him that they would lay some things to his charge, it is uncertain; but certain this is (as he himself declared), that he doubted their privy accusations; so that he by the way, in going thitherwards, cried in his mind heartily to God, to give him strength fast to stand in the truth of His Word.

When the time came for his appearance before the chancellor, he threatened him grievously, reviling and rating him as though he had been a dog, and laid to his charge many things whereof no accuser could be brought forth, notwithstanding that the priests of the country were there present. Thus Master Tyndale, escaping out of their hands, departed home, and returned to his master again.

There dwelt not far off a certain doctor, that had been chancellor to a bishop, who had been of old, familiar acquaintance with Master Tyndale, and favored him well; unto whom Master Tyndale went and opened his mind upon divers questions of the Scripture: for to him he durst be bold to disclose his heart. Unto whom the doctor said, "Do you not know that the pope is very Antichrist, whom the Scripture speaketh of? But beware what you say; for if you shall be perceived to be of that opinion, it will cost you your life."

Not long after, Master Tyndale happened to be in the company of a certain divine, recounted for a learned man, and, in communing and disputing with him, he drove him to that issue, that the said great doctor burst out into these blasphemous words, "We were better to be without God's laws than the pope's." Master Tyndale, hearing this, full of godly zeal, and not bearing that blasphemous saying, replied, "I defy the pope, and all his laws;" and added, 'if God spared him life, ere many years he would cause a boy that driveth the plough to know more of the Scripture than he did.'

The grudge of the priests increasing still more and more against Tyndale, they never ceased barking and rating at him, and laid many things sorely to his charge, saying that he was a heretic. Being so molested and vexed, he was constrained to leave that country, and to seek another place; and so coming to Master Welch, he desired him, of his good will, that he might depart from him, saying: "Sir, I perceive that I shall not be suffered to tarry long here in this country, neither shall you be able, though you would, to keep me out of the hands of the spirituality; what displeasure might grow to you by keeping me, God knoweth; for the which I should be right sorry."

So that in fine, Master Tyndale, with the good will of his master, departed, and eftsoons came up to London, and there preached a while, as he had done in the country.

Bethinking himself of Cuthbert Tonstal, then bishop of London, and especially of the great commendation of Erasmus, who, in his annotations, so extolleth the said Tonstal for his learning, Tyndale thus cast with himself, that if he might attain unto his service, he were a happy man. Coming to Sir Henry Guilford, the king's comptroller, and bringing with him an oration of Isocrates, which he had translated out of Greek into English, he desired him to speak to the said bishop of London for him; which he also did; and willed him moreover to write an epistle to the bishop, and to go himself with him. This he did, and delivered his epistle to a servant of his, named William Hebilthwait, a man of his old acquaintance. But God, who secretly disposeth the course of things, saw that was not best for Tyndale's purpose, nor for the profit of His Church, and therefore gave him to find little favor in the bishop's sight; the answer of whom was this: his house was full; he had more than he could well find: and he advised him to seek in London abroad, where, he said, he could lack no service.

Being refused of the bishop he came to Humphrey Mummuth, alderman of London, and besought him to help him: who the same time took him into his house, where the said Tyndale lived (as Mummuth said) like a good priest, studying both night and day. He would eat but sodden meat by his good will, nor drink but small single beer. He was never seen in the house to wear linen about him, all the space of his being there.

And so remained Master Tyndale in London almost a year, marking with himself the course of the world, and especially the demeanor of the preachers, how they boasted themselves, and set up their authority; beholding also the pomp of the prelates, with other things more, which greatly misliked him; insomuch that he understood not only that there was no room in the bishop's house for him to translate the New Testament, but also that there was no place to do it in all England.

Therefore, having by God's providence some aid ministered unto him by Humphrey Mummuth, and certain other good men, he took his leave of the realm, and departed into Germany, where the good man, being inflamed with a tender care and zeal of his country, refused no travail nor diligence, how, by all means possible, to reduce his brethren and countrymen of England to the same taste and understanding of God's holy Word and verity, which the Lord had endued him withal. Whereupon, considering in his mind, and conferring also with John Frith, Tyndale thought with himself no way more to conduce thereunto, than if the Scripture were turned into the vulgar speech, that the poor people might read and see the simple plain Word of God. He perceived that it was not possible to establish the lay people in any truth, except the Scriptures were so plainly laid before their eyes in their mother tongue that they might see the meaning of the text; for else, whatsoever truth should be taught them, the enemies of the truth would quench it, either with reasons of sophistry, and traditions of their own making, founded without all ground of Scripture; or else juggling with the text, expounding it in such a sense as it were impossible to gather of the text, if the right meaning thereof were seen.

Master Tyndale considered this only, or most chiefly, to be the cause of all mischief in the Church, that the Scriptures of God were hidden from the people's eyes; for so long the abominable doings and idolatries maintained by the pharisaical clergy could not be espied; and therefore all their labor was with might and main to keep it down, so that either it should not be read at all, or if it were, they

13

would darken the right sense with the mist of their sophistry, and so entangle those who reguked or despised their abominations; wresting the Scripture unto their own purpose, contrary unto the meaning of the text, they would so delude the unlearned lay people, that though thou felt in thy heart, and wert sure that all were false that they said, yet couldst thou not solve their subtle riddles.

For these and such other considerations this good man was stirred up of God to translate the Scripture into his mother tongue, for the profit of the simple people of his country; first setting in hand with the New Testament, which came forth in print about A. D. 1525. Cuthbert Tonstal, bishop of London, with Sir Thomas More, being sore aggrieved, devised how to destroy that false erroneous translation, as they called it.

It happened that one Augustine Packington, a mercer, was then at Antwerp, where the bishop was. This man favored Tyndale, but showed the contrary unto the bishop. The bishop, being desirous to bring his purpose to pass, communed how that he would gladly buy the New Testaments. Packington hearing him say so, said, "My lord! I can do more in this matter than most merchants that be here, if it be your pleasure; for I know the Dutchmen and strangers that have bought them of Tyndale, and have them here to sell; so that if it be your lordship's pleasure, I must disburse money to pay for them, or else I cannot have them: and so I will assure you to have every book of them that is printed and unsold." The bishop, thinking he had God "by the toe," said, "Do your diligence, gentle Master Packington! get them for me, and I will pay whatsoever they cost; for I intend to burn and destroy them all at Paul's Cross." This Augustine Packington went unto William Tyndale, and declared the whole matter, and so, upon compact made between them, the bishop of London had the books, Packington had the thanks, and Tyndale had the money.

After this, Tyndale corrected the same New Testaments again, and caused them to be newly imprinted, so that they came thick and threefold over into England. When the bishop perceived that, he sent for Packington, and said to him, "How cometh this, that there are so many New Testaments abroad? You promised me that you would buy them all." Then answered Packington, "Surely, I bought all that were to be had, but I perceive they have printed more since. I see it will never be better so long as they have letters and stamps: wherefore you were best to buy the stamps too, and so you shall be sure," at which answer the bishop smiled, and so the matter ended.

In short space after, it fortuned that George Constantine was apprehended by Sir Thomas More, who was then chancellor of England, as suspected of certain heresies. Master More asked of him, saying, "Constantine! I would have thee be plain with me in one thing that I will ask; and I promise thee I will show thee favor in all other things whereof thou art accused. There is beyond the sea, Tyndale, Joye, and a great many of you: I know they cannot live without help. There are some that succor them with money; and thou, being one of them, hadst thy part thereof, and therefore knowest whence it came. I pray thee, tell me, who be they that help them thus?" "My lord," quoth Constantine, "I will tell you truly: it is the bishop of London that hath holpen us, for he hath bestowed among us a great deal of money upon New Testaments to burn them; and that hath been, and yet is, our only succor and comfort." "Now by my troth," quoth More, "I think even the same; for so much I told the bishop before he went about it."

After that, Master Tyndale took in hand to translate the Old Testament, finishing the five books of Moses, with sundry most learned and godly prologues most worthy to be read and read again by all good Christians. These books being sent over into England, it cannot be spoken what a door of light they opened to the eyes of the whole English nation, which before were shut up in darkness.

At his first departing out of the realm he took his journey into Germany, where he had conference with Luther and other learned men; after he had continued there a certain season he came down into the Netherlands, and had his most abiding in the town of Antwerp.

The godly books of Tyndale, and especially the New Testament of his translation, after that they began to come into men's hands, and to spread abroad, wrought great and singular profit to the godly; but the ungodly (envying and disdaining that the people should be anything wiser than they and, fearing lest by the shining beams of truth, their works of darkness should be discerned) began to stir with no small ado.

At what time Tyndale had translated Deuteronomy, minding to print the same at Hamburg, he sailed thitherward; upon the coast of Holland he suffered shipwreck, by which he lost all his books, writings, and copies, his money and his time, and so was compelled to begin all again. He came in another ship to Hamburg, where, at his appointment, Master Coverdale tarried for him, and helped him in the translating of the whole five books of Moses, from Easter until December, in the house of a worshipful widow, Mistress Margaret Van Emmerson, A. D. 1529; a great sweating sickness being at the same time in the town. So, having dispatched his business at Hamburg, he returned to Antwerp.

When God's will was, that the New Testament in the common tongue should come abroad, Tyndale, the translator thereof, added to the latter end a certain epistle, wherein he desired them that were learned to amend, if ought were found amiss. Wherefore if there had been any such default deserving correction, it had been the part of courtesy and gentleness, for men of knowledge and judgment to have showed their learning therein, and to have redressed what was to be amended. But the clergy, not willing to have that book prosper, cried out upon it, that there were a thousand heresies in it, and that it was not to be corrected, but utterly to be suppressed. Some said it was not possible to translate the Scriptures into English; some that it was not lawful for the lay people to have it in their mother tongue; some, that it would make them all heretics. And to the intent to induce the temporal rulers unto their purpose, they said it would make the people to rebel against the king.

All this Tyndale himself, in his prologue before the first book of Moses, declareth; showing further what great pains were taken in examining that translation, and comparing it with their own imaginations, that with less labor, he supposeth, they might have translated a great part of the Bible; showing moreover that they scanned and examined every title and point in such sort, and so narrowly, that there was not one *i* therein, but if it lacked a prick over his head, they did note it, and numbered it unto the ignorant people for a heresy.

So great were then the froward devices of the English clergy (who should have been the guides of light unto the people), to drive the people from the knowledge of the Scripture, which neither they would translate themselves, nor yet abide it to be translated of others; to the intent (as Tyndale saith) that the world being kept still in darkness, they might sit in the consciences of the people through vain superstition and false doctrine, to satisfy their ambition, and insatiable covetousness, and to exalt their own honor above king and emperor.

The bishops and prelates never rested before they had brought the king to their consent; by reason whereof, a proclamation in all haste was devised and set forth under public authority, that the Testament of Tyndale's translation was inhibited—which was about A. D. 1537. And not content herewith, they proceeded further, how to entangle him in their nets, and to bereave him of his life; which how they brought to pass, now it remaineth to be declared.

In the registers of London it appeareth manifest how that the bishops and Sir Thomas More having before them such as had been at Antwerp, most studiously would search and examine all things belonging to Tyndale, where and with whom he hosted, whereabouts stood the house, what was his stature, in what apparel he went, what resort he had; all which things when they had diligently learned then began they to work their feats.

William Tyndale, being in the town of Antwerp, had been lodged about one whole year in the house of Thomas Pointz, an Englishman, who kept a house of English merchants. Came thither one out of England, whose name was Henry Philips, his father being customer of Poole, a comely fellow, like as he had been a gentleman having a servant with him: but wherefore he came, or for what purpose he was sent thither, no man could tell.

Master Tyndale divers times was desired forth to dinner and supper amongst merchants; by means whereof this Henry Philips became acquainted with him, so that within short space Master Tyndale had a great confidence in him, and brought him to his lodging, to the house of Thomas Pointz; and had him also once or twice with him to dinner and supper, and further entered such friendship with him, that through his procurement he lay in the same house of the said Pointz; to whom he showed moreover his books, and other secrets of his study, so little did Tyndale then mistrust this traitor.

But Pointz, having no great confidence in the fellow, asked Master Tyndale how he came acquainted with this Philips. Master Tyndale answered, that he was an honest man, handsomely learned, and very conformable. Pointz, perceiving that he bare such favor to him, said no more, thinking that he was brought acquainted with him by some friend of his. The said Philips, being in the town three or four days, upon a time desired Pointz to walk with him forth of the town to show him the commodities thereof, and in walking together without the town, had communication of divers things, and some of the king's affairs; by which talk Pointz as yet suspected nothing. But after, when the time was past, Pointz perceived this to be the mind of Philips, to feel whether the said Pointz might, for lucre of money, help him to his purpose, for he perceived before that Philips was monied, and would that Pointz should think no less. For he had desired Pointz before to help him to divers things; and such things as he named, he required might be of the best, "for," said he, "I have money enough."

Philips went from Antwerp to the court of Brussels, which is from thence twenty-four English miles, whence he brought with him to Antwerp, the procurator-general, who is the emperor's attorney, with certain other officers.

Within three or four days, Pointz went forth to the town of Barrois, being eighteen English miles from Antwerp, where he had business to do for the space of a month or six weeks; and in the time of his absence Henry Philips came again to Antwerp, to the house of Pointz, and coming in, spake with his wife, asking whether Master Tyndale were within. Then went he forth again and set the officers whom he had brought with him from Brussels, in the street, and about the door. About noon he came again, and went to Master Tyndale, and desired him to lend him forty shillings; "for," said he, "I lost my purse this morning, coming over at the passage between this and Mechlin." So Master Tyndale took him forty shillings, which was easy to be had of him, if he had it; for in the wily subtleties of this world he was simple and inexpert. Then said Philips, "Master Tyndale! you shall be my guest here this day." "No," said Master

Tyndale, "I go forth this day to dinner, and you shall go with me, and be my guest, where you shall be welcome."

So when it was dinner time, Master Tyndale went forth with Philips, and at the going forth of Pointz's house, was a long narrow entry, so that two could not go in front. Master Tyndale would have put Philips before him, but Philips would in no wise, but put Master Tyndale before, for that he pretended to show great humanity. So Master Tyndale, being a man of no great stature, went before, and Philips, a tall, comely person, followed behind him; who had set officers on either side of the door upon two seats, who might see who came in the entry. Philips pointed with his finger over Master Tyndale's head down to him, that the officers might see that it was he whom they should take. The officers afterwards told Pointz, when they had laid him in prison, that they pitied to see his simplicity. They brought him to the emperor's attorney, where he dined. Then came the procurator-general to the house of Pointz, and sent away all that was there of Master Tyndale's, as well his books as other things; and from thence Tyndale was had to the castle of Vilvorde, eighteen English miles from Antwerp.

Master Tyndale, remaining in prison, was proffered an advocate and a procurator; the which he refused, saying that he would make answer for himself. He had so preached to them who had him in charge, and such as was there conversant with him in the Castle that they reported of him, that if he were not a good Christian man, they knew not whom they might take to be one.

At last, after much reasoning, when no reason would serve, although he deserved no death, he was condemned by virtue of the emperor's decree, made in the assembly at Augsburg. Brought forth to the place of execution, he was tied to the stake, strangled by the hangman, and afterwards consumed with fire, at the town of Vilvorde, A. D. 1536; crying at the stake with a fervent zeal, and a loud voice, "Lord! open the king of England's eyes."

Such was the power of his doctrine, and the sincerity of his life, that during the time of his imprisonment (which endured a year and a half), he converted, it is said, his keeper, the keeper's daughter, and others of his household.

As touching his translation of the New Testament, because his enemies did so much carp at it, pretending it to be full of heresies, he wrote to John Frith, as followeth, "I call God to record against the day we shall appear before our Lord Jesus, that I never altered one syllable of God's Word against my conscience, nor would do this day, if all that is in earth, whether it be honor, pleasure, or riches, might be given me."

CHAPTER XIII

An Account of the Life of John Calvin

THIS reformer was born at Noyon in Picardy, July 10, 1509. He was instructed in grammar, learning at Paris under Maturinus Corderius, and studied philosophy in the College of Montaign under a Spanish professor.

His father, who discovered many marks of his early piety, particularly in his reprehensions of the vices of his companions, designed him at first for the Church, and got him presented, May 21, 1521, to the chapel of Notre Dame de la Gesine, in the Church of Noyon. In 1527 he was presented to the rectory of Marseville, which he exchanged in 1529 for the rectory of Pont l'Eveque, near Noyon. His father afterward changed his resolution, and would have him study law; to which Calvin, who, by reading the Scriptures, had conceived a dislike to the superstitions of popery, readily consented, and resigned the chapel of Gesine and the rectory of Pont l'Eveque, in 1534. He made a great progress in that science, and improved no less in the knowledge of divinity by his private studies. At Bourges he applied to the Greek tongue, under the direction of Professor Wolmar.

His father's death having called him back to Noyon, he stayed there a short time, and then went to Paris, where a speech of Nicholas Cop, rector of the University of Paris, of which Calvin furnished the materials, having greatly displeased the Sorbonne and the parliament, gave rise to a persecution against the Protestants, and Calvin, who narrowly escaped being taken in the College of Forteret, was forced to retire to Xaintonge, after having had the honor to be introduced to the queen of Navarre, who had raised this first storm against the Protestants.

Calvin returned to Paris in 1534. This year the reformed met with severe treatment, which determined him to leave France, after publishing a treatise against those who believed that departed souls are in a kind of sleep. He retired to Basel, where he studied Hebrew: at this time he published his Institutions of the Christian Religion; a work well adapted to spread his fame, though he himself was desirous of living in obscurity. It is dedicated to the French king, Francis I. Calvin next wrote an apology for the Protestants who were burnt for their religion in France. After the publication of this work, Calvin went to Italy to pay a visit to the duchess of Ferrara, a lady of eminent piety, by whom he was very kindly received.

From Italy he came back to France, and having settled his private affairs, he proposed to go to Strassburg or Basel, in company with his sole surviving brother, Antony Calvin; but as the roads were not safe on account of the war, except through the duke of Savoy's territories, he chose that road. "This was a particular direction of Providence," says Bayle; "it was his destiny that he should settle at Geneva, and when he was wholly intent upon going farther, he found himself detained by an order from heaven, if I may so speak."

At Geneva, Calvin therefore was obliged to comply with the choice which the consistory and magistrates made of him, with the consent of the people, to be one of their ministers, and professor of divinity. He wanted to undertake only this last office, and not the other; but in the end he was obliged to take both upon him, in August, 1536. The year following, he made all the people declare, upon oath, their assent to the confession of faith, which contained a renunciation of popery. He next intimated that he could not submit to a regulation which the canton of Berne had lately made. Whereupon the syndics of Geneva summoned an assembly of the people; and it was ordered that Calvin, Farel, and another minister should leave the town in a few days, for refusing to administer the Sacrament.

Calvin retired to Strassburg, and established a French church in that city, of which he was the first minister: he was also appointed to be professor of divinity there. Meanwhile the people of Geneva entreated him so earnestly to return to them that at last he consented, and arrived September 13, 1541, to the great satisfaction both of the people and the magistrates; and the first thing he did, after his arrival, was to establish a form of church discipline, and a consistorial jurisdiction, invested with power of inflicting censures and canonical punishments, as far as excommunication, inclusively.

It has long been the delight of both infidels and some professed Christians, when they wish to bring odium upon the opinions of Calvin, to refer to his agency in the death of Michael Servetus. This action is used on all occasions by those who have been unable to overthrow his opinions, as a conclusive argument against his whole system. "Calvin burnt Servetus!—Calvin burnt Servetus!" is a good proof with a certain class of reasoners, that the doctrine of the Trinity is not true—that divine sovereignty is Antiscriptural,—and Christianity a cheat.

We have no wish to palliate any act of Calvin's which is manifestly wrong. All his proceedings, in relation to the unhappy affair of Servetus, we think, cannot be defended. Still it should be remembered that the true principles of religious toleration were very little understood in the time of Calvin. All the other reformers then living approved of Calvin's conduct. Even the gentle and amiable Melancthon expressed himself in relation to this affair, in the following manner. In a letter addressed to Bullinger, he says, "I have read your statement respecting the blasphemy of Servetus, and praise your piety and judgment; and am persuaded that the Council of Geneva has done right in putting to death this obstinate man, who would never have ceased his blasphemies. I am astonished that any one can be found to disapprove of this proceeding." Farel expressly says, that "Servetus deserved a capital punishment." Bucer did not hesitate to declare, that "Servetus deserved something worse than death."

The truth is, although Calvin had some hand in the arrest and imprisonment of Servetus, he was unwilling that he should be burnt at all. "I desire," says he, "that the severity of the punishment should be remitted." "We endeavored to commute the kind of death, but in vain." "By wishing to mitigate the severity of the punishment," says Farel to Calvin, "you discharge the office of a friend towards your greatest enemy." "That Calvin was the instigator of the magistrates that Servetus might be burned," says Turritine, "historians neither anywhere affirm, nor does it appear from any considerations. Nay, it is certain, that he, with the college of pastors, dissuaded from that kind of punishment."

It has been often asserted, that Calvin possessed so much influence with the magistrates of Geneva that he might have obtained the release of Servetus, had he not been desirous of his destruction. This however, is not true. So far from it, that Calvin was himself once banished from Geneva, by these very magistrates, and often opposed their arbitrary measures in vain. So little desirous was Calvin of procuring the death of Servetus that he warned him of his danger, and suffered him to remain several weeks at Geneva, before he was arrested. But his language, which was then accounted blasphemous, was the cause of his imprisonment. When in prison, Calvin visited him, and used every argument to persuade him to retract his horrible blasphemies, without reference to his peculiar sentiments. This was the extent of Calvin's agency in this unhappy affair.

It cannot, however, be denied, that in this instance, Calvin acted contrary to the benignant spirit of the Gospel. It is better to drop a tear over the inconsistency of human nature, and to bewail those infirmities which cannot be justified. He declared he acted conscientiously, and publicly justified the act.

It was the opinion, that *erroneous religious principles are punishable by the civil magistrate,* that did the mischief, whether at Geneva, in Transylvania, or in Britain; and to this, rather than to Trinitarianism, or Unitarianism, it ought to be imputed.

After the death of Luther, Calvin exerted great sway over the men of that notable period. He was influential in France, Italy, Germany, Holland, England, and Scotland. Two thousand one hundred and fifty reformed congregations were organized, receiving from him their preachers.

Calvin, triumphant over all his enemies, felt his death drawing near. Yet he continued to exert himself in every way with youthful energy. When about to lie down in rest, he drew up his will, saying: "I do testify that I live and purpose to die in this faith which God has given me through His Gospel, and that I have no other dependence for salvation than the free choice which is made of me by Him. With my whole heart I embrace His mercy, through which all my sins are covered, for Christ's sake, and for the sake of His death and sufferings. According to the measure of grace granted unto me, I have taught this pure, simple Word, by sermons, by deeds, and by expositions of this Scripture. In all my battles with the enemies of the truth I have not used sophistry, but have fought the good fight squarely and directly."

May 27, 1564, was the day of his release and blessed journey home. He was in his fifty-fifth year.

That a man who had acquired so great a reputation and such an authority, should have had but a salary of one hundred crowns, and refuse to accept more; and after living fifty-five years with the utmost frugality should leave but three hundred crowns to his heirs, including the value of his library, which sold very dear, is something so heroical, that one must have lost all feeling not to admire. When Calvin took his leave of Strassburg, to return to Geneva, they wanted to continue to him the privileges of a freeman of their town, and the revenues of a prebend, which had been assigned to him; the former he accepted, but absolutely refused the other. He carried one of the brothers with him to Geneva, but he never took any pains to get him preferred to an honorable post, as any other possessed of his credit would have done. He took care indeed of the honor of his brother's family, by getting him freed from an adultress, and obtaining leave for him to marry again; but even his enemies relate that he made him learn the trade of a bookbinder, which he followed all his life after.

Calvin as a Friend of Civil Liberty

The Rev. Dr. Wisner, in his late discourse at Plymouth, on the anniversary of the landing of the Pilgrims, made the following assertion: "Much as the name of Calvin has been scoffed at and loaded with reproach by many sons of freedom, there is not an historical proposition more susceptible of complete demonstration than this, that *no man has lived to whom the world is under greater obligations for the freedom it now enjoys, than John Calvin.*"

CHAPTER XIV

An Account of the Persecutions in Great Britain and Ireland, Prior to the Reign of Queen Mary I

GILDAS, the most ancient British writer extant, who lived about the time that the Saxons left the island of Great Britain, has drawn a most shocking instance of the barbarity of those people.

The Saxons, on their arrival, being heathens like the Scots and Picts, destroyed the churches and murdered the clergy wherever they came: but they could not destroy Christianity, for those who would not submit to the Saxon yoke, went and resided beyond the Severn. Neither have we the names of those Christian sufferers transmitted to us, especially those of the clergy.

The most dreadful instance of barbarity under the Saxon government, was the massacre of the monks of Bangor, A. D. 586. These monks were in all respects different from those men who bear the same name at present.

In the eighth century, the Danes, a roving crew of barbarians, landed in different parts of Britain, both in England and Scotland. At first they were repulsed, but in A. D. 857, a party of them landed somewhere near Southampton, and not only robbed the people but burned down the churches, and murdered the clergy.

In A. D. 868, these barbarians penetrated into the center of England, and took up their quarters at Nottingham; but the English, under their king, Ethelred, drove them from their posts, and obliged them to retire to Northumberland.

In 870, another body of these barbarians landed at Norfolk, and engaged in battle with the English at Hertford. Victory declared in favor of the pagans, who took Edmund, king of the East Angles, prisoner, and after treating him with a thousand indignities, transfixed his body with arrows, and then beheaded him.

In Fifeshire, in Scotland, they burned many of the churches, and among the rest that belonging to the Culdees, at St. Andrews. The piety of these men made them objects of abhorrence to the Danes, who, wherever they went singled out the Christian priests for destruction, of whom no less than two hundred were massacred in Scotland.

It was much the same in that part of Ireland now called Leinster, there the Danes murdered and burned the priests alive in their own churches; they carried destruction along with them wherever they went, sparing neither age nor sex, but the clergy were the most obnoxious to them, because they ridiculed their idolatry, and persuaded their people to have nothing to do with them.

In the reign of Edward III the Church of England was extremely corrupted with errors and superstition; and the light of the Gospel of Christ was greatly eclipsed and darkened with human inventions, burthensome ceremonies and gross idolatry.

The followers of Wickliffe, then called Lollards, were become extremely numerous, and the clergy were so vexed to see them increase; whatever power or influence they might have to molest them in an underhand manner, they had no authority by law to put them to death. However, the clergy embraced the favorable opportunity, and prevailed upon the king to suffer a bill to be brought into parliament, by which all Lollards who remained obstinate, should be delivered over to the secular power, and burnt as heretics. This act was the first in Britain for the burning of people for their religious sentiments; it passed in the year 1401, and was soon after put into execution.

The first person who suffered in consequence of this cruel act was William Santree, or Sawtree, a priest, who was burnt to death in Smithfield.

Soon after this, Sir John Oldcastle, Lord Cobham, in consequence of his attachment to the doctrines of Wickliffe, was accused of heresy, and being condemned to be hanged and burnt, was accordingly executed in Lincoln's Inn Fields, A. D. 1419. In his written defense Lord Cobham said:

"As for images, I understand that they be not of belief, but that they were ordained since the belief of Christ was given by sufferance of the Church, to represent and bring to mind the passion of our Lord Jesus Christ, and martyrdom and good living of other saints: and that whoso it be, that doth the worship to dead images that is due to God, or putteth such hope or trust in help of them, as he should do to God, or hath affection in one more than in another, he doth in that, the greatest sin of idol worship.

"Also I suppose this fully, that every man in this earth is a pilgrim toward bliss, or toward pain; and that he that knoweth not, we will not know, we keep the holy commandments of God in his living here (albeit that he go on pilgrimages to all the world, and he die so), he shall be damned: he that knoweth the holy commandments of God, and keepeth them to his end, he shall be saved, though he never in his life go on pilgrimage, as men now use, to Canterbury, or to Rome, or to any other place."

Upon the day appointed, Lord Cobham was brought out of the Tower with his arms bound behind him, having a very cheerful countenance. Then was he laid upon a hurdle, as though he had been a most heinous traitor to the crown, and so drawn forth into St. Giles's field. As he was come to the place of execution, and was taken from the hurdle, he fell down devoutly upon his knees, desiring Almighty God to forgive his enemies. Then stood he up and beheld the multitude, exhorting them in most godly manner to follow the laws of God written in the Scriptures, and to beware of such teachers as they see contrary to Christ in their conversation and living. Then was he hanged up by the middle in chains of iron, and so consumed alive in the fire, praising the name of God so long as his life lasted; the people, there present, showing great dolor. And this was done A. D. 1418.

How the priests that time fared, blasphemed, and accursed, requiring the people not to pray for him, but to judge him damned in hell, for that he departed not in the obedience of their pope, it were too long to write.

Thus resteth this valiant Christian knight, Sir John Oldcastle, under the altar of God, which is Jesus Christ, among that godly company, who, in the kingdom of patience, suffered great tribulation with the death of their bodies, for His faithful word and testimony.

In August, 1473, one Thomas Granter was apprehended in London; he was accused of professing the doctrines of Wickliffe, for which he was condemned as an obstinate heretic. This pious man, being brought to the sheriff's house, on the morning of the day appointed for his execution, desired a little refreshment, and having ate some, he said to the people present, "I eat now a very good meal, for I have a strange conflict to engage with before I go to supper"; and having eaten, he returned thanks to God for the bounties of His all-gracious providence, requesting that he might be instantly led to the place of execution, to bear testimony to the truth of those principles which he had professed. Accordingly he was chained to a stake on Tower-hill, where he was burnt alive, professing the truth with his last breath.

In the year 1499, one Badram, a pious man, was brought before the bishop of Norwich, having been accused by some of the priests, with holding the doctrines of Wickliffe. He confessed he did believe everything that was objected against him. For this, he was condemned as an obstinate heretic, and a warrant was granted for his execution; accordingly he was brought to the stake at Norwich, where he suffered with great constancy.

In 1506, one William Tilfrey, a pious man, was burnt alive at Amersham, in a close called Stoneyprat, and at the same time, his daughter, Joan Clarke, a married woman, was obliged to light the fagots that were to burn her father.

This year also one Father Roberts, a priest, was convicted of being a Lollard before the bishop of Lincoln, and burnt alive at Buckingham.

In 1507, one Thomas Norris was burnt alive for the testimony of the truth of the Gospel, at Norwich. This man was a poor, inoffensive, harmless person, but his parish priest conversing with him one day, conjectured he was a Lollard. In consequence of this supposition he gave information to the bishop, and Norris was apprehended.

In 1508, one Lawrence Guale, who had been kept in prison two years, was burnt alive at Salisbury, for denying the real presence in the Sacrament. It appeared that this man kept a shop in Salisbury, and entertained some Lollards in his house; for which he was informed against to the bishop; but he abode by his first testimony, and was condemned to suffer as a heretic.

A pious woman was burnt at Chippen Sudburne, by order of the chancellor, Dr. Whittenham. After she had been consumed in the flames, and the people were returning home, a bull broke loose from a butcher and singling out the chancellor from all the rest of the company, he gored him through the body, and on his horns carried his entrails. This was seen by all the people, and it is remarkable that the animal did not meddle with any other person whatever.

October 18, 1511, William Succling and John Bannister, who had formerly recanted, returned again to the profession of the faith, and were burnt alive in Smithfield.

In the year 1517, one John Brown (who had recanted before in the reign of Henry VII and borne a fagot round St. Paul's,) was condemned by Dr. Wonhaman, archbishop of Canterbury, and burnt alive at Ashford. Before he was chained to the stake, the archbishop Wonhaman, and Yester, bishop of Rochester, caused his feet to be burnt in a fire until all the flesh came off, even to the bones. This was done in order to make him again recant, but he persisted in his attachment to the truth to the last.

Much about this time one Richard Hunn, a merchant tailor of the city of London, was apprehended, having refused to pay the priest his fees for the funeral of a child; and being conveyed to the Lollards' Tower, in the palace of Lambeth, was there privately murdered by some of the servants of the archbishop.

September 24, 1518, John Stilincen, who had before recanted, was apprehended, brought before Richard Fitz-James, bishop of London, and on the twenty-fifth of October was condemned as a heretic. He was chained to the stake in Smithfield amidst a vast crowd of spectators, and sealed his testimony to the truth with his blood. He declared that he was a Lollard, and that he had always believed the opinions of Wickliffe; and although he had been weak enough to recant his opinions, yet he was now willing to convince the world that he was ready to die for the truth.

In the year 1519, Thomas Mann was burnt in London, as was one Robert Celin, a plain, honest man for speaking against image worship and pilgrimages.

Much about this time, was executed in Smithfield, in London, James Brewster, a native of Colchester. His sentiments were the same as the rest of the Lollards, or those who followed the doctrines of Wickliffe; but notwithstanding the innocence of his life, and the regularity of his manners, he was obliged to submit to papal revenge.

During this year, one Christopher, a shoemaker, was burnt alive at Newbury, in Berkshire, for denying those popish articles which we have already mentioned. This man had gotten some books in English, which were sufficient to render him obnoxious to the Romish clergy.

Robert Silks, who had been condemned in the bishop's court as a heretic, made his escape out of prison, but was taken two years afterward, and brought back to Coventry, where he was burnt alive. The sheriffs always seized the goods of the martyrs for their own use, so that their wives and children were left to starve.

In 1532, Thomas Harding, who with his wife, had been accused of heresy, was brought before the bishop of Lincoln, and condemned for denying the real presence in the Sacrament. He was then chained to a stake, erected for the purpose, at Chesham in the Pell, near Botely; and when they had set fire to the fagots, one of the spectators dashed out his brains with a billet. The priests told the people that whoever brought fagots to burn heretics would have an indulgence to commit sins for forty days.

During the latter end of this year, Worham, archbishop of Canterbury, apprehended one Hitten, a priest at Maidstone; and after he had been long tortured in prison, and several times examined by the archbishop, and Fisher, bishop of Rochester, he was condemned as a heretic, and burnt alive before the door of his own parish church.

Thomas Bilney, professor of civil law at Cambridge, was brought before the bishop of London, and several other bishops, in the Chapter house, Westminster, and being several times threatened with the stake and flames, he was weak enough to recant; but he repented severely afterward.

For this he was brought before the bishop a second time, and condemned to death. Before he went to the stake he confessed his adherence to those opinions which Luther held; and, when at it, he smiled, and said, "I have had many storms in this world, but now my vessel will soon be on shore in heaven." He stood unmoved in the flames, crying out, "Jesus, I believe"; and these were the last words he was heard to utter.

A few weeks after Bilney had suffered, Richard Byfield was cast into prison, and endured some whipping, for his adherence to the doctrines of Luther: this Mr. Byfield had been some time a monk, at Barnes, in Surrey, but was converted by reading Tyndale's version of the New Testament. The sufferings this man underwent for the truth were so great that it would require a volume to contain them. Sometimes he was shut up in a dungeon, where he was almost suffocated by the offensive and horrid smell of filth and stagnant water. At other times he was tied up by the arms, until almost all his joints were dislocated. He was whipped at the post several times, until scarcely any flesh was left on his back; and all this was done to make him recant. He was then taken to the Lollard's Tower in Lambeth palace, where he was chained by the neck to the wall, and once every day beaten in the most cruel manner by the archbishop's servants. At last he was condemned, degraded, and burnt in Smithfield.

The next person that suffered was John Tewkesbury. This was a plain, simple man, who had been guilty of no other offence against what was called the holy Mother Church, than that of reading Tyndale's translation of the New Testament. At first he was weak enough to abjure, but afterward repented, and acknowledged the truth. For this he was brought before the bishop of London, who condemned him as an obstinate heretic. He suffered greatly during the time of his imprisonment, so that when they brought him out to execution, he was almost dead. He was conducted to the stake in Smithfield, where he was burned, declaring his utter abhorrence of popery, and professing a firm belief that his cause was just in the sight of God.

The next person that suffered in this reign was James Baynham, a reputable citizen in London, who had married the widow of a gentleman in the Temple. When chained to the stake he embraced the fagots, and said, "Oh, ye papists, behold! ye look for miracles; here now may you see a miracle; for in this fire I feel no more pain than if I were in bed; for it is as sweet to me as a bed of roses." Thus he resigned his soul into the hands of his Redeemer.

Soon after the death of this martyr, one Traxnal, an inoffensive countryman, was burned alive at Bradford in Wiltshire, because he would not acknowledge the real presence in the Sacrament, nor own the papal supremacy over the consciences of men.

In the year 1533, John Frith, a noted martyr, died for the truth. When brought to the stake in Smithfield, he embraced the fagots, and exhorted a young man named Andrew Hewit, who suffered with him, to trust his soul to that God who had redeemed it. Both these sufferers endured much torment, for the wind blew the flames away from them, so that they were above two hours in agony before they expired.

In the year 1538, one Collins, a madman, suffered death with his dog in Smithfield. The circumstances were as follows: Collins happened to be in church when the priest elevated the host; and Collins, in derision of the sacrifice of the Mass, lifted up his dog above his head. For this crime Collins, who ought to have been sent to a madhouse, or whipped at the cart's tail, was brought before the bishop of London; and although he was really mad, yet such was the force of popish power, such the corruption in Church and state, that the poor madman, and his dog, were both carried to the stake in Smithfield, where they were burned to ashes, amidst a vast crowd of spectators.

There were some other persons who suffered the same year, of whom we shall take notice in the order they lie before us.

One Cowbridge suffered at Oxford; and although he was reputed to be a madman, yet he showed great signs of piety when he was fastened to the stake, and after the flames were kindled around him.

About the same time one Purderve was put to death for saying privately to a priest, after he had drunk the wine, "He blessed the hungry people with the empty chalice."

At the same time was condemned William Letton, a monk of great age, in the county of Suffolk, who was burned at Norwich for speaking against an idol that was carried in procession; and for asserting, that the Sacrament should be administered in both kinds.

Sometime before the burning of these men, Nicholas Peke was executed at Norwich; and when the fire was lighted, he was so scorched that he was as black as pitch. Dr. Reading standing before him, with Dr. Hearne and Dr. Spragwell, having a long white wand in his hand, struck him upon the right shoulder, and said, "Peke, recant, and believe in the Sacrament." To this he answered, "I despise thee and it also;" and with great violence he spit blood, occasioned by the anguish of his sufferings. Dr. Reading granted forty days' indulgence for the sufferer, in order that he might recant his opinions. But he persisted in his adherence to the truth, without paying any regard to the malice of his enemies; and he was burned alive, rejoicing that Christ had counted him worthy to suffer for His name's sake.

On July 28, 1540, or 1541, (for the chronology differs) Thomas Cromwell, earl of Essex, was brought to a scaffold on Tower-hill, where he was executed with some striking instances of cruelty. He made a short speech to the people, and then meekly resigned himself to the axe.

It is, we think, with great propriety, that this nobleman is ranked among the martyrs; for although the accusations preferred against him, did not relate to anything in religion, yet had it not been for his zeal to demolish popery, he might have to the last retained the king's favor. To this may be added, that the papists plotted his destruction, for he did more towards promoting the Reformation, than any man in that age, except the good Dr. Cranmer.

Soon after the execution of Cromwell, Dr. Cuthbert Barnes, Thomas Garnet, and William Jerome, were brought before the ecclesiastical court of the bishop of London, and accused of heresy.

Being before the bishop of London, Dr. Barnes was asked whether the saints prayed for us? To this he answered, that 'he would leave that to God; but (said he) I will pray for you.'

On the thirteenth of July, 1541, these men were brought from the Tower to Smithfield, where they were all chained to one stake; and there suffered death with a constancy that nothing less than a firm faith in Jesus Christ could inspire.

One Thomas Sommers, an honest merchant, with three others,

was thrown into prison, for reading some of Luther's books, and they were condemned to carry those books to a fire in Cheapside; there they were to throw them in the flames; but Sommers threw his over, for which he was sent back to the Tower, where he was stoned to death.

Dreadful persecutions were at this time carried on at Lincoln, under Dr. Longland, the bishop of that diocese. At Buckingham, Thomas Bainard, and James Moreton, the one for reading the Lord's Prayer in English, and the other for reading St. James' Epistles in English, were both condemned and burnt alive.

Anthony Parsons, a priest, together with two others, was sent to Windsor, to be examined concerning heresy; and several articles were tendered to them to subscribe, which they refused. This was carried on by the bishop of Salisbury, who was the most violent persecutor of any in that age, except Bonner. When they were brought to the stake, Parsons asked for some drink, which being brought him, he drank to his fellow-sufferers, saying, "Be merry, my brethren, and lift up your hearts to God; for after this sharp breakfast I trust we shall have a good dinner in the Kingdom of Christ, our Lord and Redeemer." At these words Eastwood, one of the sufferers, lifted up his eyes and hands to heaven, desiring the Lord above to receive his spirit. Parsons pulled the straw near to him, and then said to the spectators, "This is God's armor, and now I am a Christian soldier prepared for battle: I look for no mercy but through the merits of Christ; He is my only Savior, in Him do I trust for salvation;" and soon after the fires were lighted, which burned their bodies, but could not hurt their precious and immortal souls. Their constancy triumphed over cruelty, and their sufferings will be held in everlasting remembrance.

Thus were Christ's people betrayed every way, and their lives bought and sold. For, in the said parliament, the king made this most blasphemous and cruel act, to be a law forever: that whatsoever they were that should read the Scriptures in the mother-tongue (which was then called "Wickliffe's learning"), they should forfeit land, cattle, body, life, and goods, from their heirs for ever, and so be condemned for heretics to God, enemies to the crown, and most arrant traitors to the land.

CHAPTER XV

An Account of the Persecutions in Scotland During the Reign of King Henry VIII

Like as there was no place, either of Germany, Italy, or France, wherein there were not some branches sprung out of that most fruitful root of Luther; so likewise was not this isle of Britain without his fruit and branches. Amongst whom was Patrick Hamilton, a Scotchman born of high and noble stock, and of the king's blood, of excellent towardness, twenty-three years of age, called abbot of Ferne. Coming out of his country with three companions to seek godly learning, he went to the University of Marburg in Germany, which university was then newly erected by Philip, Landgrave of Hesse.

During his residence here, he became intimately acquainted with those eminent lights of the Gospel, Martin Luther and Philip Melancthon; from whose writings and doctrines he strongly attached himself to the Protestant religion.

The archbishop of St. Andrews (who was a rigid papist) learning of Mr. Hamilton's proceedings, caused him to be seized, and being brought before him, after a short examination relative to his religious principles, he committed him a prisoner to the castle, at the same time ordering him to be confined in the most loathsome part of the prison.

The next morning Mr. Hamilton was brought before the bishop, and several others, for examination, when the principal articles exhibited against him were, his publicly disapproving of pilgrimages, purgatory, prayers to saints, for the dead, etc.

These articles Mr. Hamilton acknowledged to be true, in consequence of which he was immediately condemned to be burnt; and that his condemnation might have the greater authority, they caused it to be subscribed by all those of any note who were present, and to make the number as considerable as possible, even admitted the subscription of boys who were sons of the nobility.

So anxious was this bigoted and persecuting prelate for the destruction of Mr. Hamilton, that he ordered his sentence to be put in execution on the afternoon of the very day it was pronounced. He was accordingly led to the place appointed for the horrid tragedy, and was attended by a prodigious number of spectators. The greatest part of the multitude would not believe it was intended he should be put to death, but that it was only done to frighten him, and thereby bring him over to embrace the principles of the Romish religion. But they soon found themselves mistaken.

When he arrived at the stake, he kneeled down, and, for some time prayed with great fervency. After this he was fastened to the stake, and the fagots placed round him. A quantity of gunpowder having been placed under his arms was first set on fire which scorched his left hand and one side of his face, but did no material injury, neither did it communicate with the fagots. In consequence of this, more powder and combustible matter were brought, which being set on fire took effect, and the fagots being kindled, he called out, with an audible voice: "Lord Jesus, receive my spirit! How long shall darkness overwhelm this realm? And how long wilt Thou suffer the tyranny of these men?"

The fire burning slow put him to great torment; but he bore it with Christian magnanimity. What gave him the greatest pain was, the clamor of some wicked men set on by the friars, who frequently cried, "Turn, thou heretic; call upon our Lady; say, Salve Regina, etc." To whom he replied, "Depart from me, and trouble me not, ye messengers of Satan." One Campbell, a friar, who was the ringleader, still continuing to interrupt him by opprobrious language; he said to him, "Wicked man, God forgive thee." After which, being prevented from further speech by the violence of the smoke, and the rapidity of the flames, he resigned up his soul into the hands of Him who gave it.

This steadfast believer in Christ suffered martyrdom in the year 1527.

One Henry Forest, a young inoffensive Benedictine, being charged with speaking respectfully of the above Patrick Hamilton, was thrown into prison; and, in confessing himself to a friar, owned that he thought Hamilton a good man; and that the articles for which he was sentenced to die, might be defended. This being revealed by the friar, it was received as evidence; and the poor Benedictine was sentenced to be burnt.

Whilst consultation was held, with regard to the manner of his execution, John Lindsay, one of the archbishop's gentlemen, offered his advice, to burn Friar Forest in some cellar; "for," said he, "the smoke of Patrick Hamilton hath infected all those on whom it blew."

This advice was taken, and the poor victim was rather suffocated, than burnt.

The next who fell victims for professing the truth of the Gospel, were David Stratton and Norman Gourlay.

When they arrived at the fatal spot, they both kneeled down, and prayed for some time with great fervency. They then arose, when Stratton, addressing himself to the spectators, exhorted them to lay aside their superstitious and idolatrous notions, and employ their time in seeking the true light of the Gospel. He would have said more, but was prevented by the officers who attended.

Their sentence was then put into execution, and they cheerfully resigned up their souls to that God who gave them, hoping, through the merits of the great Redeemer, for a glorious resurrection to life immortal. They suffered in the year 1534.

The martyrdoms of the two before-mentioned persons, were soon followed by that of Mr. Thomas Forret, who, for a considerable time, had been dean of the Romish Church; Killor and Beverage, two blacksmiths; Duncan Simson, a priest; and Robert Forrester, a gentleman. They were all burnt together, on the Castle-hill at Edinburgh, the last day of February, 1538.

The year following the martyrdoms of the before-mentioned persons, viz. 1539, two others were apprehended on a suspicion of heresy; namely, Jerome Russell and Alexander Kennedy, a youth about eighteen years of age.

These two persons, after being some time confined in prison, were brought before the archbishop for examination. In the course of which Russell, being a very sensible man, reasoned learnedly against his accusers; while they in return made use of very opprobrious language.

The examination being over, and both of them deemed heretics, the archbishop pronounced the dreadful sentence of death, and they were immediately delivered over to the secular power in order for execution.

The next day they were led to the place appointed for them to suffer; in their way to which, Russell, seeing his fellow-sufferer have the appearance of timidity in his countenance, thus addressed him: "Brother, fear not; greater is He that is in us, than He that is in the world. The pain that we are to suffer is short, and shall be light; but our joy and consolation shall never have an end. Let us, therefore, strive to enter into our Master and Savior's joy, by the same straight way which He hath taken before us. Death cannot hurt us, for it is already destroyed by Him, for whose sake we are now going to suffer."

When they arrived at the fatal spot, they both kneeled down and prayed for some time; after which being fastened to the stake, and the fagots lighted, they cheerfully resigned their souls into the hands of Him who gave them, in full hopes of an everlasting reward in the heavenly mansions.

An Account of the Life, Sufferings, and Death of Mr. George Wishart, Who Was Strangled and Afterward Burned, in Scotland, for Professing the Truth of the Gospel

About the year of our Lord 1543, there was, in the University of Cambridge, one Master George Wishart, commonly called Master George of Benet's College, a man of tall stature, polled-headed, and on the same a round French cap of the best; judged to be of melancholy complexion by his physiognomy, black-haired, long-bearded, comely of personage, well spoken after his country of Scotland, courteous, lowly, lovely, glad to teach, desirous to learn, and well travelled; having on him for his clothing a frieze gown to the shoes, a black millian fustian doublet, and plain black hosen, coarse new canvas for his shirts, and white falling bands and cuffs at his hands.

He was a man modest, temperate, fearing God, hating covetousness; for his charity had never end, night, noon, nor day; he forbare one meal in three, one day in four for the most part, except something to comfort nature. He lay hard upon a puff of straw and coarse, new canvas sheets, which, when he changed, he gave away. He had commonly by his bedside a tub of water, in the which (his people being in bed, the candle put out and all quiet) he used to bathe himself. He loved me tenderly, and I him. He taught with great modesty and gravity, so that some of his people thought him severe, and would have slain him; but the Lord was his defence. And he, after due correction for their malice, by good exhortation amended them and went his way. Oh, that the Lord had left him to me, his poor boy, that he might have finished what he had begun! for he went into Scotland with divers of the nobility, that came for a treaty to King Henry.

In 1543, the archbishop of St. Andrews made a visitation into various parts of his diocese, where several persons were informed against at Perth for heresy. Among those the following were condemned to die, viz. William Anderson, Robert Lamb, James Finlayson, James Hunter, James Raveleson, and Helen Stark.

The accusations laid against these respective persons were as follow: The four first were accused of having hung up the image of St. Francis, nailing ram's horns on his head, and fastening a cow's tail to his rump; but the principal matter on which they were condemned was having regaled themselves with a goose on fast day.

James Raveleson was accused of having ornamented his house with the three crowned diadem of Peter, carved in wood, which the archbishop conceived to be done in mockery to his cardinal's cap.

Helen Stark was accused of not having accustomed herself to pray to the Virgin Mary, more especially during the time she was in childbed.

On these respective accusations they were all found guilty, and immediately received sentence of death; the four men, for eating the goose, to be hanged; James Raveleson to be burnt; and the woman, with her sucking infant, to be put into a sack and drowned.

The four men, with the woman and the child, suffered at the same time, but James Ravelson was not executed until some days after.

The martyrs were carried by a great band of armed men (for they feared rebellion in the town except they had their men of war) to the place of execution, which was common to all thieves, and that to make their cause appear more odious to the people. Every one comforting another, and assuring themselves that they should sup together in the Kingdom of Heaven that night, they commended themselves to God, and died constantly in the Lord.

The woman desired earnestly to die with her husband, but she was not suffered; yet, following him to the place of execution, she gave him comfort, exhorting him to perseverance and patience for

Christ's sake, and, parting from him with a kiss, said, "Husband, rejoice, for we have lived together many joyful days; but this day, in which we must die, ought to be most joyful unto us both, because we must have joy forever; therefore I will not bid you good night, for we shall suddenly meet with joy in the Kingdom of Heaven." The woman, after that, was taken to a place to be drowned, and albeit she had a child sucking on her breast, yet this moved nothing in the unmerciful hearts of the enemies. So, after she had commended her children to the neighbors of the town for God's sake, and the sucking bairn was given to the nurse, she sealed up the truth by her death.

Being desirous of propagating the true Gospel in his own country George Wishart left Cambridge in 1544, and on his arrival in Scotland he first preached at Montrose, and afterwards at Dundee. In this last place he made a public exposition of the Epistle to the Romans, which he went through with such grace and freedom, as greatly alarmed the papists.

In consequence of this, (at the instigation of Cardinal Beaton, the archbishop of St. Andrews) one Robert Miln, a principal man at Dundee, went to the church where Wishart preached, and in the middle of his discourse publicly told him not to trouble the town any more, for he was determined not to suffer it.

This sudden rebuff greatly surprised Wishart, who, after a short pause, looking sorrowfully on the speaker and the audience, said: "God is my witness, that I never minded your trouble but your comfort; yea, your trouble is more grievous to me than it is to yourselves: but I am assured to refuse God's Word, and to chase from you His messenger, shall not preserve you from trouble, but shall bring you into it: for God shall send you ministers that shall fear neither burning nor banishment. I have offered you the Word of salvation. With the hazard of my life I have remained among you; now you yourselves refuse me; and I must leave my innocence to be declared by my God. If it be long prosperous with you, I am not led by the Spirit of truth; but if unlooked-for troubles come upon you, acknowledge the cause and turn to God, who is gracious and merciful. But if you turn not at the first warning, He will visit you with fire and sword." At the close of this speech he left the pulpit, and retired.

After this he went into the west of Scotland, where he preached God's Word, which was gladly received by many.

A short time after this Mr. Wishart received intelligence that the plague had broken out in Dundee. It began four days after he was prohibited from preaching there, and raged so extremely that it was almost beyond credit how many died in the space of twenty-four hours. This being related to him, he, notwithstanding the importunity of his friends to detain him, determined to go there, saying: "They are now in troubles, and need comfort. Perhaps this hand of God will make them now to magnify and reverence the Word of God, which before they lightly esteemed."

Here he was with joy received by the godly. He chose the east gate for the place of his preaching; so that the healthy were within, and the sick without the gate. He took his text from these words, "He sent His word and healed them," etc. In this sermon he chiefly dwelt upon the advantage and comfort of God's Word, the judgments that ensue upon the contempt or rejection of it, the freedom of God's grace to all His people, and the happiness of those of His elect, whom He takes to Himself out of this miserable world. The hearts of his hearers were so raised by the divine force of this discourse, as not to regard death, but to judge them the more happy who should then be called, not knowing whether he should have such comfort again with them.

After this the plague abated; though, in the midst of it, Wishart constantly visited those that lay in the greatest extremity, and comforted them by his exhortations.

When he took his leave of the people of Dundee, he said that God had almost put an end to that plague, and that he was now called to another place. He went from thence to Montrose; where he sometimes preached, but he spent most of his time in private meditation and prayer.

It is said that before he left Dundee, and while he was engaged in the labors of love to the bodies as well as to the souls of those poor afflicted people, Cardinal Beaton engaged a desperate popish priest, called John Weighton, to kill him; the attempt to execute which was as follows: one day, after Wishart had finished his sermon, and the people departed, a priest stood waiting at the bottom of the stairs, with a naked dagger in his hand under his gown. But Mr. Wishart, having a sharp, piercing eye, and seeing the priest as he came from the pulpit, said to him, "My friend, what would you have?" and immediately clapping his hand upon the dagger, took it from him. The priest being terrified, fell to his knees, confessed his intention, and craved pardon. A noise was hereupon raised, and it coming to the ears of those who were sick, they cried, "Deliver the traitor to us, we will take him by force"; and they burst in at the gate. But Wishart, taking the priest in his arms, said, "Whatsoever hurts him shall hurt me; for he hath done me no mischief, but much good, by teaching more heedfulness for the time to come." By this conduct he appeased the people and saved the life of the wicked priest.

Soon after his return to Montrose, the cardinal again conspired his death, causing a letter to be sent him as if it had been from his familiar friend, the laird of Kennier, in which it was desired with all possible speed to come to him, as he was taken with a sudden sickness. In the meantime the cardinal had provided sixty men armed to lie in wait within a mile and a half of Montrose, in order to murder him as he passed that way.

The letter came to Wishart's hand by a boy, who also brought him a horse for the journey. Wishart, accompanied by some honest men, his friends, set forward; but something particular striking his mind by the way, he returned, which they wondering at, asked him the cause; to whom he said, "I will not go; I am forbidden of God; I am assured there is treason. Let some of you go to yonder place, and tell me what you find." Which doing, they made the discovery; and hastily returning, they told Mr. Wishart; whereupon he said, "I know I shall end my life by that bloodthirsty man's hands, but it will not be in this manner."

A short time after this he left Montrose, and proceeded to Edinburgh, in order to propagate the Gospel in that city. By the way he lodged with a faithful brother, called James Watson of Inner-Goury. In the middle of the night he got up, and went into the yard, which two men hearing they privately followed him. While in the yard, he fell on his knees, and prayed for some time with the greatest fervency, after which he arose, and returned to his bed. Those who attended him, appearing as though they were ignorant of all, came and asked him where he had been. But he would not answer them. The next day they importuned him to tell them, saying "Be plain with us, for we heard your mourning, and saw your gestures."

On this he with a dejected countenance, said, "I had rather you had been in your beds." But they still pressing upon him to know something, he said, "I will tell you; I am assured that my warfare is near at an end, and therefore pray to God with me, that I shrink not when the battle waxeth most hot."

Soon after, Cardinal Beaton, archbishop of St. Andrews, being informed that Mr. Wishart was at the house of Mr. Cockburn, of Ormiston, in East Lothian, applied to the regent to cause him to be apprehended; with which, after great persuasion, and much against his will, he complied.

In consequence of this the cardinal immediately proceeded to the trial of Wishart, against whom no less than eighteen articles were exhibited. Mr. Wishart answered the respective articles with great composure of mind, and in so learned and clear a manner as greatly surprised most of those who were present.

After the examination was finished, the archbishop endeavored to prevail on Mr. Wishart to recant; but he was too firmly fixed in his religious principles and too much enlightened with the truth of the Gospel, to be in the least moved.

On the morning of his execution there came to him two friars from the cardinal; one of whom put on him a black linen coat, and the other brought several bags of gunpowder, which they tied about different parts of his body.

As soon as he arrived at the stake, the executioner put a rope round his neck and a chain about his middle, upon which he fell on his knees and thus exclaimed:

"O thou Savior of the world, have mercy upon me! Father of heaven, I commend my spirit into Thy holy hands."

After this he prayed for his accusers, saying, "I beseech thee, Father of heaven, forgive them that have, from ignorance or an evil mind, forged lies of me: I forgive them with all my heart. I beseech Christ to forgive them that have ignorantly condemned me."

He was then fastened to the stake, and the fagots being lighted immediately set fire to the powder that was tied about him, which blew into a flame and smoke.

The governor of the castle, who stood so near that he was singed with the flame, exhorted the martyr, in a few words, to be of good cheer, and to ask the pardon of God for his offences. To which he replied, "This flame occasions trouble to my body, indeed, but it hath in nowise broken my spirit. But he who now so proudly looks down upon me from yonder lofty place (pointing to the cardinal) shall, ere long, be ignominiously thrown down, as now he proudly lolls at his ease." Which prediction was soon after fulfilled.

The hangman, that was his tormentor, sat down upon his knees, and said, "Sir, I pray you to forgive me, for I am not guilty of your death." To whom he answered, "Come hither to me." When that he was come to him, he kissed his cheek, and said: "Lo, here is a token that I forgive thee. My heart, do thine office." And then he was put upon the gibbet and hanged, and burned to powder. When that the people beheld the great tormenting, they might not withhold from piteous mourning and complaining of this innocent lamb's slaughter.

It was not long after the martyrdom of this blessed man of God, Master George Wishart, who was put to death by David Beaton, the bloody archbishop and cardinal of Scotland, A. D. 1546, the first day of March, that the said David Beaton, by the just revenge of God's mighty judgment, was slain within his own castle of St. Andrews, by the hands of one Leslie and other gentlemen, who, by the Lord stirred up, brake in suddenly upon him, and in his bed murdered him the said year, the last day of May, crying out, "Alas! alas! slay me not! I am a priest!" And so, like a butcher he lived, and like a butcher he died, and lay seven months and more unburied, and at last like a carrion was buried in a dunghill.

The last who suffered martyrdom in Scotland, for the cause of Christ, was one Walter Mill, who was burnt at Edinburgh in the year 1558.

This person, in his younger years, had travelled in Germany, and on his return was installed a priest of the Church of Lunan in Angus, but, on an information of heresy, in the time of Cardinal Beaton, he was forced to abandon his charge and abscond. But he was soon apprehended, and committed to prison.

Being interrogated by Sir Andrew Oliphant, whether he would recant his opinions, he answered in the negative, saying that he would 'sooner forfeit ten thousand lives, than relinquish a particle of those heavenly principles he had received from the suffrages of his blessed Redeemer.'

In consequence of this, sentence of condemnation was immediately passed on him, and he was conducted to prison in order for execution the following day.

This steadfast believer in Christ was eighty-two years of age, and exceedingly infirm; whence it was supposed that he could scarcely be heard. However, when he was taken to the place of execution, he expressed his religious sentiments with such courage, and at the same time composure of mind, as astonished even his enemies. As soon as he was fastened to the stake and the fagots lighted, he addressed the spectators as follows: "The cause why I suffer this day is not for any crime, (though I acknowledge myself a miserable sinner) but only for the defence of the truth as it is in Jesus Christ; and I praise God who hath called me, by His mercy, to seal the truth with my life; which, as I received it from Him, so I willingly and joyfully offer it up to His glory. Therefore, as you would escape eternal death, be no longer seduced by the lies of the seat of Antichrist: but depend solely on Jesus Christ, and His mercy, that you may be delivered from condemnation." And then added that he trusted he should be the last who would suffer death in Scotland upon a religious account.

Thus did this pious Christian cheerfully give up his life in defence of the truth of Christ's Gospel, not doubting but he should be made partaker of his heavenly Kingdom.

CHAPTER XVI

Persecutions in England During the Reign of Queen Mary

THE premature death of that celebrated young monarch, Edward VI, occasioned the most extraordinary and wonderful occurrences, which had ever existed from the times of our blessed Lord and Savior's incarnation in human shape. This melancholy event became speedily a subject of general regret. The succession to the British throne was soon made a matter of contention; and the scenes which ensued were a demonstration of the serious affliction in which the kingdom was involved. As his loss to the nation was more and more unfolded, the remembrance of his government was more and more the basis of grateful recollection. The very awful prospect, which was soon presented to the friends of Edward's administration, under the direction of his counsellors and servants, was a contemplation which the reflecting mind was compelled to regard with most alarming apprehensions. The rapid approaches which were made towards a total reversion of the proceedings of the young king's reign, denoted the advances which were thereby represented to an entire resolution in the management of public affairs both in Church and state.

Alarmed for the condition in which the kingdom was likely to be involved by the king's death, an endeavor to prevent the consequences, which were but too plainly foreseen, was productive of the most serious and fatal effects. The king, in his long and lingering affliction, was induced to make a will, by which he bequeathed the English crown to Lady Jane, the daughter of the duke of Suffolk, who had been married to Lord Guilford, the son of the duke of Northumberland, and was the granddaughter of the second sister of King Henry, by Charles, duke of Suffolk. By this will, the succession of Mary and Elizabeth, his two sisters, was entirely superseded, from an apprehension of the returning system of popery; and the king's council, with the chief of the nobility, the lord-mayor of the city of London, and almost all the judges and the principal lawyers of the realm, subscribed their names to this regulation, as a sanction to the measure. Lord Chief Justice Hale, though a true Protestant and an upright judge, alone declined to unite his name in favor of the Lady Jane, because he had already signified his opinion that Mary was entitled to assume the reins of government. Others objected to Mary's being placed on the throne, on account of their fears that she might marry a foreigner, and thereby bring the crown into considerable danger. Her partiality to popery also left little doubt on the minds of any, that she would be induced to revive the dormant interests of the pope, and change the religion which had been used both in the days of her father, King Henry, and in those of her brother Edward: for in all his time she had manifested the greatest stubbornness and inflexibility of temper, as must be obvious from her letter to the lords of the council, whereby she put in her claim to the crown, on her brother's decease.

When this happened, the nobles, who had associated to prevent Mary's succession, and had been instrumental in promoting, and, perhaps, advising the measures of Edward, speedily proceeded to proclaim Lady Jane Gray, to be queen of England, in the city of London and various other populous cities of the realm. Though young, she possessed talents of a very superior nature, and her improvements under a most excellent tutor had given her many very great advantages.

Her reign was of only five days' continuance, for Mary, having succeeded by false promises in obtaining the crown, speedily commenced the execution of her avowed intention of extirpating and burning every Protestant. She was crowned at Westminster in the usual form, and her elevation was the signal for the commencement of the bloody persecution which followed.

Having obtained the sword of authority, she was not sparing in its exercise. The supporters of Lady Jane Gray were destined to feel its force. The duke of Northumberland was the first who experienced her savage resentment. Within a month after his confinement in the Tower, he was condemned, and brought to the scaffold, to suffer as a traitor. From his varied crimes, resulting out of a sordid and inordinate ambition, he died unpitied and unlamented.

The changes, which followed with rapidity, unequivocally declared that the queen was disaffected to the present state of religion. Dr. Poynet was displaced to make room for Gardiner to be bishop of Winchester, to whom she also gave the important office of lord-chancellor. Dr. Ridley was dismissed from the see of London, and Bonne introduced. J. Story was put out of the bishopric of Chichester, to admit Dr. Day. J. Hooper was sent prisoner to the Fleet, and Dr. Heath put into the see of Worcester. Miles Coverdale was also excluded from Exeter, and Dr. Vesie placed in that diocese. Dr. Tonstall was also promoted to the see of Durham. These things being marked and perceived, great heaviness and discomfort grew more and more to all good men's hearts; but to the wicked great rejoicing. They that could dissemble took no great care how the matter went; but such, whose consciences were joined with the truth, perceived already coals to be kindled, which after should be the destruction of many a true Christian.

The Words and Behavior of the Lady Jane upon the Scaffold

The next victim was the amiable Lady Jane Gray, who, by her acceptance of the crown at the earnest solicitations of her friends, incurred the implacable resentment of the bloody Mary. When she first mounted the scaffold, she spoke to the spectators in this manner: "Good people, I am come hither to die, and by a law I am condemned to the same. The fact against the queen's highness was unlawful, and the consenting thereunto by me: but, touching the procurement and desire thereof by me, or on my behalf, I do wash my hands thereof in innocency before God, and the face of you, good Christian people, this day:" and therewith she wrung her hands, wherein she had her book. Then said she, "I pray you all, good Christian people, to bear me witness, that I die a good Christian woman, and that I do look to be saved by no other mean, but only by the mercy of God in the blood of His only Son Jesus Christ: and I confess that when I did know the Word of God, I neglected the same, loved myself and the world, and therefore this plague and punishment is happily and worthily happened unto me for my sins; and yet I thank God, that of His goodness He hath thus given me a time and a respite to repent. And now, good people, while I am alive, I pray you assist me with your prayers." And then, kneeling down, she turned to Feckenham, saying, "Shall I say this Psalm?" and he said, "Yea." Then she said the Psalm of *Miserere mei Deus,* in English, in a most devout manner throughout to the end; and then she stood up, and gave her maid, Mrs. Ellen, her gloves and handkerchief, and her book to Mr. Bruges; and then she untied her gown, and the executioner pressed upon her to help her off with it: but she, desiring him to let her alone, turned towards her two gentlewomen, who helped her off therewith, and also with her frowes, paaft, and neckerchief, giving to her a fair handkerchief to put about her eyes.

Then the executioner kneeled down, and asked her forgiveness, whom she forgave most willingly. Then he desired her to stand upon the straw, which doing, she saw the block. Then she said, "I pray you, despatch me quickly." Then she kneeled down, saying, "Will you take it off before I lay me down?" And the executioner said, "No, madam." Then she tied a handkerchief about her eyes, and feeling for the block, she said, "What shall I do? Where is it? Where is it?" One of the standers-by guiding her thereunto, she laid her head upon the block, and then stretched forth her body, and said, "Lord, into Thy hands I commend my spirit;" and so finished her life, in the year of our Lord 1554, the twelfth day of February, about the seventeenth year of her age.

Thus died Lady Jane; and on the same day Lord Guilford, her husband, one of the duke of Northumberland's sons, was likewise beheaded, two innocents in comparison with them that sat upon them. For they were both very young, and ignorantly accepted that which others had contrived, and by open proclamation consented to take from others, and give to them.

Touching the condemnation of this pious lady, it is to be noted that Judge Morgan, who gave sentence against her, soon after he had condemned her, fell mad, and in his raving cried out continually to have the Lady Jane taken away from him, and so he ended his life.

On the twenty-first day of the same month, Henry, duke of Suffolk, was beheaded on Tower-hill, the fourth day after his condemnation: about which time many gentlemen and yeomen were condemned, whereof some were executed at London, and some in the country. In the number of whom was Lord Thomas Gray, brother to the said duke, being apprehended not long after in North Wales, and executed for the same. Sir Nicholas Throgmorton, also, very narrowly escaped.

John Rogers, Vicar of St. Sepulchre's, and Reader of St. Paul's, London

John Rogers was educated at Cambridge, and was afterward many years chaplain to the merchant adventurers at Antwerp in Brabant. Here he met with the celebrated martyr William Tyndale, and Miles Coverdale, both voluntary exiles from their country for their aversion to popish superstition and idolatry. They were the instruments of his conversion; and he united with them in that translation of the Bible into English, entitled "The Translation of Thomas Matthew." From the Scriptures he knew that unlawful vows may be lawfully broken; hence he married, and removed to Wittenberg in Saxony, for the improvement of learning; and he there learned the Dutch language, and received the charge of a congregation, which he faithfully executed for many years. On King Edward's accession, he left Saxony to promote the work of reformation in England; and, after some time, Nicholas Ridley, then bishop of London, gave him a prebend in St. Paul's Cathedral, and the dean and chapter appointed him reader of the divinity lesson there. Here he continued until Queen Mary's succession to the throne, when the Gospel and true religion were banished, and the Antichrist of Rome, with his superstition and idolatry, introduced.

The circumstance of Mr. Rogers having preached at Paul's cross, after Queen Mary arrived at the Tower, has been already stated. He confirmed in his sermon the true doctrine taught in King Edward's time, and exhorted the people to beware of the pestilence of popery, idolatry, and superstition. For this he was called to account, but so ably defended himself that, for that time, he was dismissed. The proclamation of the queen, however, to prohibit true preaching, gave his enemies a new handle against him. Hence he was again summoned before the council, and commanded to keep his house. He did so, though he might have escaped; and though he perceived the state of the true religion to be desperate. He knew he could not want a living in Germany; and he could not forget a wife and ten children, and to seek means to succor them. But all these things were insufficient to induce him to depart, and, when once called to answer in Christ's cause, he stoutly defended it, and hazarded his life for that purpose.

After long imprisonment in his own house, the restless Bonner, bishop of London, caused him to be committed to Newgate, there to be lodged among thieves and murderers.

After Mr. Rogers had been long and straitly imprisoned, and lodged in Newgate among thieves, often examined, and very uncharitably entreated, and at length unjustly and most cruelly condemned by Stephen Gardiner, bishop of Winchester, the fourth day of February, in the year of our Lord 1555, being Monday in the morning, he was suddenly warned by the keeper of Newgate's wife, to prepare himself for the fire; who, being then sound asleep, could scarce be awaked. At length being raised and awaked, and bid to make haste, then said he, "If it be so, I need not tie my points." And so was had down, first to bishop Bonner to be degraded: which being done, he craved of Bonner but one petition; and Bonner asked what that should be. Mr. Rogers replied that he might speak a few words with his wife before his burning, but that could not be obtained of him.

When the time came that he should be brought out of Newgate to Smithfield, the place of his execution, Mr. Woodroofe, one of the sheriffs, first came to Mr. Rogers, and asked him if he would revoke his abominable doctrine, and the evil opinion of the Sacrament of the altar. Mr. Rogers answered, "That which I have preached I will seal with my blood." Then Mr. Woodroofe said, "Thou art an heretic." "That shall be known," quoth Mr. Rogers, "at the Day of Judgment." "Well," said Mr. Woodroofe, "I will never pray for thee." "But I will pray for you," said Mr. Rogers; and so was brought the same day, the fourth of February, by the sheriffs, towards Smithfield, saying the Psalm *Miserere* by the way, all the people wonderfully rejoicing at his constancy; with great praises and thanks to God for the same. And there in the presence of Mr. Rochester, comptroller of the queen's household, Sir Richard Southwell, both the sheriffs, and a great number of people, he was burnt to ashes, washing his hands in the flame as he was burning. A little before his burning, his pardon was brought, if he would have recanted; but he utterly refused it. He was the first martyr of all the blessed company that suffered in Queen Mary's time that gave the first adventure upon the fire. His wife and children, being eleven in number, ten able to go, and one sucking at her breast, met him by the way, as he went towards Smithfield. This sorrowful sight of his own flesh and blood could nothing move him, but that he constantly and cheerfully took his death with wonderful patience, in the defence and quarrel of the Gospel of Christ."

The Rev. Lawrence Saunders

Mr. Saunders, after passing some time in the school of Eaton, was chosen to go to King's College in Cambridge, where he continued three years, and profited in knowledge and learning very much for that time. Shortly after he quitted the university, and went to his parents, but soon returned to Cambridge again to his study, where he began to add to the knowledge of the Latin, the study of the Greek and Hebrew tongues, and gave himself up to the study of the Holy Scriptures, the better to qualify himself for the office of preacher.

In the beginning of King Edward's reign, when God's true religion was introduced, after license obtained, he began to preach, and was so well liked of them who then had authority that they appointed him to read a divinity lecture in the College of Fothringham. The College of Fothringham being dissolved, he was placed to be a reader in the minster at Litchfield. After a certain space, he departed from Litchfield to a benefice in Leicestershire, called Church-langton, where he held a residence, taught diligently, and kept a liberal house. Thence he was orderly called to take a benefice in the city of London, namely, All-hallows in Bread-street. After this he preached at Northhampton, nothing meddling with the state, but boldly uttering his conscience against the popish doctrines which were likely to spring up again in England, as a just plague for the little love which the English nation then bore to the blessed Word of God, which had been so plentifully offered unto them.

The queen's party who were there, and heard him, were highly displeased with him for his sermon, and for it kept him among them as a prisoner. But partly for love of his brethren and friends, who were chief actors for the queen among them, and partly because there was no law broken by his preaching, they dismissed him.

Some of his friends, perceiving such fearful menacing, counselled him to fly out of the realm, which he refused to do. But seeing he was with violence kept from doing good in that place, he returned towards London, to visit his flock.

In the afternoon of Sunday, October 15, 1554, as he was reading in his church to exhort his people, the bishop of London interrupted him, by sending an officer for him.

His treason and sedition the bishop's charity was content to let slip until another time, but a heretic he meant to prove him, and all those, he said, who taught and believed that the administration of the Sacraments, and all orders of the Church, are the most pure, which come the nearest to the order of the primitive Church.

After much talk concerning this matter, the bishop desired him to write what he believed of transubstantiation. Lawrence Saunders did so, saying, "My Lord, you seek my blood, and you shall have it: I pray God that you may be so baptized in it that you may ever after loathe blood-sucking, and become a better man." Upon being closely charged with contumacy, the severe replies of Mr. Saunders to the bishop, (who had before, to get the favor of Henry VIII written and set forth in print, a book of true obedience, wherein he had openly declared Queen Mary to be a bastard) so irritated him that he exclaimed, "Carry away this frenzied fool to prison."

After this good and faithful martyr had been kept in prison one year and a quarter, the bishops at length called him, as they did his fellow-prisoners, openly to be examined before the queen's council.

His examination being ended, the officers led him out of the place, and stayed until the rest of his fellow-prisoners were likewise examined, that they might lead them all together to prison.

After his excommunication and delivery over to the secular power, he was brought by the sheriff of London to the Compter, a prison in his own parish of Bread-street, at which he rejoiced greatly, both because he found there a fellow-prisoner, Mr. Cardmaker, with whom he had much Christian and comfortable discourse; and because out of prison, as before in his pulpit, he might have an opportunity of preaching to his parishioners. On the fourth of February, Bonner, bishop of London, came to the prison to degrade him; the day following, in the morning the sheriff of London delivered him to certain of the queen's guard, who were appointed to carry him to the city of Coventry, there to be burnt.

When they had arrived at Coventry, a poor shoemaker, who used to serve him with shoes, came to him, and said, "O my good master, God strengthen and comfort you." "Good shoemaker," Mr. Saunders replied, "I desire thee to pray for me, for I am the most unfit man for this high office, that ever was appointed to it; but my gracious God and dear Father is able to make me strong enough." The next day, being the eighth of February, 1555, he was led to the place of execution, in the park, without the city. He went in an old gown and a shirt, barefooted, and oftentimes fell flat on the ground, and prayed. When he was come to nigh the place, the officer, appointed to see the execution done, said to Mr. Saunders that he was one of them who marred the queen's realm, but if he would recant, there was pardon for him. "Not I," replied the holy martyr, "but such as you have injured the realm. The blessed Gospel of Christ is what I hold; that do I believe, that have I taught, and that will I never revoke!" Mr. Saunders then slowly moved towards the fire, sank to the earth and prayed; he then rose up, embraced the stake, and frequently said, "Welcome, thou cross of Christ! welcome everlasting life!" Fire was then put to the fagots, and, he was overwhelmed by the dreadful flames, and sweetly slept in the Lord Jesus.

The History, Imprisonment, and Examination of Mr. John Hooper, Bishop of Worcester and Gloucester

John Hooper, student and graduate in the University of Oxford, was stirred with such fervent desire to the love and knowledge of the Scriptures that he was compelled to move from thence, and was retained in the house of Sir Thomas Arundel, as his steward, until Sir Thomas had intelligence of his opinions and religion, which he in no case did favor, though he exceedingly favored his person and condition and wished to be his friend. Mr. Hooper now prudently left Sir Thomas' house and arrived at Paris, but in a short time returned to England, and was retained by Mr. Sentlow, until the time that he was again molested and sought for, when he passed through France to the higher parts of Germany; where, commencing acquaintance with learned men, he was by them free and lovingly entertained, both at Basel, and especially at Zurich, by Mr. Bullinger, who was his singular friend; here also he married his wife, who was a Burgonian, and applied very studiously to the Hebrew tongue.

At length, when God saw it good to stay the bloody time of the six articles, and to give us King Edward to reign over this realm, with some peace and rest unto the Church, amongst many other English exiles, who then repaired homeward, Mr. Hooper also, moved in conscience, thought not to absent himself, but seeing such a time and occasion, offered to help forward the Lord's work, to the utter-most of his ability.

When Mr. Hooper had taken his farewell of Mr. Bullinger, and his friends in Zurich, he repaired again to England in the reign of King Edward VI, and coming to London, used continually to preach, most times twice, or at least once a day.

In his sermons, according to his accustomed manner, he corrected sin, and sharply inveighed against the iniquity of the world and the corrupt abuses of the Church. The people in great flocks and com-panies daily came to hear his voice, as the most melodious sound and tune of Orpheus' harp, insomuch, that oftentimes when he was preaching, the church would be so full that none could enter farther than the doors thereof. In his doctrine he was earnest, in tongue eloquent, in the Scriptures perfect, in pains indefatigable, in his life exemplary.

Having preached before the king's majesty, he was soon after made bishop of Gloucester. In that office he continued two years, and be-haved himself so well that his very enemies could find no fault with him, and after that he was made bishop of Worcester.

Dr. Hooper executed the office of a most careful and vigilant pastor, for the space of two years and more, as long as the state of religion in King Edward's time was sound and flourishing.

After he had been cited to appear before Bonner and Dr. Heath, he was led to the Council, accused falsely of owing the queen money, and in the next year, 1554, he wrote an account of his severe treat-ment during near eighteen months' confinement in the Fleet, and after his third examination, January 28, 1555, at St. Mary Overy's, he, with the Rev. Mr. Rogers, was conducted to the Compter in Southwark, there to remain until the next day at nine o'clock, to see whether they would recant. "Come, Brother Rogers," said Dr. Hooper, "must we two take this matter first in hand, and begin to fry in these fagots?" "Yes, Doctor," said Mr. Rogers, "by God's grace." "Doubt not," said Dr. Hooper, "but God will give us strength;" and the people so applauded their constancy that they had much ado to pass.

January 29, Bishop Hooper was degraded and condemned, and the Rev. Mr. Rogers was treated in like manner. At dark, Dr. Hooper was led through the city to Newgate; notwithstanding this secrecy, many people came forth to their doors with lights, and saluted him, praising God for his constancy.

During the few days he was in Newgate, he was frequently visited by Bonner and others, but without avail. As Christ was tempted, so they tempted him, and then maliciously reported that he had recanted. The place of his martyrdom being fixed at Gloucester, he rejoiced very much, lifting up his eyes and hands to heaven, and praising God that he saw it good to send him among the people over whom he was pastor, there to confirm with his death the truth which he had before taught them.

On February 7, he came to Gloucester, about five o'clock, and lodged at one Ingram's house. After his first sleep, he continued in prayer until morning; and all the day, except a little time at his meals, and when conversing such as the guard kindly permitted to speak to him, he spent in prayer.

Sir Anthony Kingston, at one time Dr. Hooper's good friend, was appointed by the queen's letters to attend at his execution. As soon as he saw the bishop he burst into tears. With tender entreaties he exhorted him to live. "True it is," said the bishop, "that death is bitter, and life is sweet; but alas! consider that the death to come is more bitter, and the life to come is more sweet."

The same day a blind boy obtained leave to be brought into Dr. Hooper's presence. The same boy, not long before, had suffered imprisonment at Gloucester for confessing the truth. "Ah! poor boy," said the bishop, "though God hath taken from thee thy outward sight, for what reason He best knoweth, yet He hath endued thy soul with the eye of knowledge and of faith. God give thee grace continually to pray unto Him, that thou lose not that sight, for then wouldst thou indeed be blind both in body and soul."

When the mayor waited upon him preparatory to his execution, he expressed his perfect obedience, and only requested that a quick fire might terminate his torments. After he had got up in the morning, he desired that no man should be suffered to come into the chamber, that he might be solitary until the hour of execution.

About eight o'clock, on February 9, 1555, he was led forth, and many thousand persons were collected, as it was market-day. All the way, being straitly charged not to speak, and beholding the people, who mourned bitterly for him, he would sometimes lift up his eyes towards heaven, and look very cheerfully upon such as he knew: and he was never known, during the time of his being among them, to look with so cheerful and ruddy a countenance as he did at that time. When he came to the place appointed where he should die, he smilingly beheld the stake and preparation made for him, which was near unto the great elm tree over against the college of priests, where he used to preach.

Now, after he had entered into prayer, a box was brought and laid before him upon a stool, with his pardon from the queen, if he would turn. At the sight whereof he cried, "If you love my soul, away with it!" The box being taken away, Lord Chandois said, "Seeing there is no remedy; despatch him quickly."

Command was now given that the fire should be kindled. But because there were not more green fagots than two horses could carry, it kindled not speedily, and was a pretty while also before it took the reeds upon the fagots. At length it burned about him, but the wind having full strength at that place, and being a lowering cold morning, it blew the flame from him, so that he was in a manner little more than touched by the fire.

Within a space after, a few dry fagots were brought, and a new fire kindled with fagots, (for there were no more reeds) and those burned at the nether parts, but had small power above, because of the wind, saving that it burnt his hair and scorched his skin a little. In the time of which fire, even as at the first flame, he prayed, saying mildly, and not very loud, but as one without pain, "O Jesus, Son of David, have mercy upon me, and receive my soul!" After the second fire was spent, he wiped both his eyes with his hands, and beholding the people, he said with an indifferent, loud voice, "For God's love, good people, let me have more fire!" and all this while his nether parts did burn; but the fagots were so few that the flame only singed his upper parts.

The third fire was kindled within a while after, which was more extreme than the other two. In this fire he prayed with a loud voice, "Lord Jesus, have mercy upon me! Lord Jesus receive my spirit!" And these were the last words he was heard to utter. But when he was black in the mouth, and his tongue so swollen that he could not speak, yet his lips went until they were shrunk to the gums: and he knocked his breast with his hands until one of his arms fell off, and then knocked still with the other, while the fat, water, and blood dropped out at his fingers' ends, until by renewing the fire, his strength was gone, and his hand clave fast in knocking to the iron upon his breast. Then immediately bowing forwards, he yielded up his spirit.

Thus was he three quarters of an hour or more in the fire. Even as a lamb, patiently he abode the extremity thereof, neither moving forwards, backwards, nor to any side; but he died as quietly as a child in his bed. And he now reigneth, I doubt not, as a blessed martyr in the joys of heaven, prepared for the faithful in Christ before the foundations of the world; for whose constancy all Christians are bound to praise God.

The Life and Conduct of Dr. Rowland Taylor of Hadley

Dr. Rowland Taylor, vicar of Hadley, in Suffolk, was a man of eminent learning, and had been admitted to the degree of doctor of the civil and canon law.

His attachment to the pure and uncorrupted principles of Christianity recommended him to the favor and friendship of Dr. Cranmer, archbishop of Canterbury, with whom he lived a considerable time, until through his interest he obtained the living at Hadley.

Not only was his word a preaching unto them, but all his life and conversation was an example of unfeigned Christian life and true holiness. He was void of all pride, humble and meek as any child: so that none were so poor but they might boldly, as unto their father, resort unto him; neither was his lowliness childish or fearful, but, as occasion, time, and place required, he would be stout in rebuking the sinful and evildoers; so that none was so rich but he would tell them plainly his fault, with such earnest and grave rebukes as became a good curate and pastor. He was a man very mild, void of all rancor, grudge or evil will; ready to do good to all men; readily forgiving his enemies; and never sought to do evil to any.

To the poor that were blind, lame, sick, bedrid, or that had many children, he was a very father, a careful patron, and diligent provider, insomuch that he caused the parishioners to make a general provision for them; and he himself (beside the continual relief that they always found at his house) gave an honest portion yearly to the common almsbox. His wife also was an honest, discreet, and sober matron, and his children well nurtured, brought up in the fear of God and good learning.

He was a good salt of the earth, savorly biting the corrupt manners of evil men; a light in God's house, set upon a candlestick for all good men to imitate and follow.

Thus continued this good shepherd among his flock, governing and leading them through the wilderness of this wicked world, all the days of the most innocent and holy king of blessed memory, Edward VI. But on his demise, and the succession of Queen Mary to the throne, he escaped not the cloud that burst on so many beside; for two of his parishioners, Foster, an attorney, and Clark, a tradesman, out of blind zeal, resolved that Mass should be celebrated, in all its superstitious forms, in the parish church of Hadley, on Monday before Easter. This Dr. Taylor, entering the church, strictly forbade; but Clark forced the Doctor out of the church, celebrated Mass, and immediately informed the lord-chancellor, bishop of Winchester of his behavior, who summoned him to appear, and answer the complaints that were alleged against him.

The doctor upon the receipt of the summons, cheerfully prepared to obey the same; and rejected the advice of his friends to fly beyond sea. When Gardiner saw Dr. Taylor, he, according to his common custom, reviled him. Dr. Taylor heard his abuse patiently, and when the bishop said, "How darest thou look me in the face! knowest thou not who I am?" Dr. Taylor replied, "You are Dr. Stephen Gardiner, bishop of Winchester, and lord-chancellor, and yet but a mortal man. But if I should be afraid of your lordly looks, why fear ye not God, the Lord of us all? With what countenance will you appear before the judgment seat of Christ, and answer to your oath made first unto King Henry VIII, and afterward unto King Edward VI, his son?"

A long conversation ensued, in which Dr. Taylor was so piously collected and severe upon his antagonist, that he exclaimed: "Thou art a blasphemous heretic! Thou indeed blasphemist the blessed Sacrament, (here he put off his cap) and speakest against the holy Mass, which is made a sacrifice for the quick and the dead." The bishop afterward committed him into the king's bench.

When Dr. Taylor came there, he found the virtuous and vigilant preacher of God's Word, Mr. Bradford; who equally thanked God that He had provided him with such a comfortable fellow-prisoner; and they both together praised God, and continued in prayer, reading and exhorting one another.

After Dr. Taylor had lain some time in prison, he was cited to appear in the arches of Bow-church.

Dr. Taylor being condemned, was committed to the Clink, and the keepers were charged to treat him roughly; at night he was removed to the Poultry Compter.

When Dr. Taylor had lain in the Compter about a week on the fourth of February, Bonner came to degrade him, bringing with him such ornaments as appertained to the massing mummery; but the Doctor refused these trappings until they were forced upon him.

The night after he was degraded his wife came with John Hull, his servant, and his son Thomas, and were by the gentleness of the keepers permitted to sup with him.

After supper, walking up and down, he gave God thanks for His grace, that had given him strength to abide by His holy Word. With tears they prayed together, and kissed one another. Unto his son Thomas he gave a Latin book, containing the notable sayings of the old martyrs, and in the end of that he wrote his testament:

"I say to my wife, and to my children, The Lord gave you unto me, and the Lord hath taken me from you, and you from me: blessed be the name of the Lord! I believe that they are blessed which die in the Lord. God careth for sparrows, and for the hairs of our heads. I have ever found Him more faithful and favorable, than is any father or husband. Trust ye therefore in Him by the means of our dear Savior Christ's merits: believe, love, fear, and obey Him: pray to Him, for He hath promised to help. Count me not dead, for I shall certainly live, and never die. I go before, and you shall follow after, to our long home."

On the morrow the sheriff of London with his officers came to the Compter by two o'clock in the morning, and brought forth Dr. Taylor; and without any light led him to the Woolsack, an inn without Aldgate. Dr. Taylor's wife, suspecting that her husband should that night be carried away, watched all night in St. Botolph's church-porch beside Aldgate, having her two children, the one named Elizabeth, of thirteen years of age (whom, being left without father or mother, Dr. Taylor had brought up of alms from three years old), the other named Mary, Dr. Taylor's own daughter.

Now, when the sheriff and his company came against St. Botolph's church, Elizabeth cried, saying, "O my dear father! mother, mother, here is my father led away." Then his wife cried, "Rowland, Rowland, where art thou?"—for it was a very dark morning, that the one could not well see the other. Dr. Taylor answered, "Dear wife, I am here"; and stayed. The sheriff's men would have led him forth, but the sheriff said, "Stay a little, masters, I pray you; and let him speak to his wife"; and so they stayed.

Then came she to him, and he took his daughter Mary in his arms; and he, his wife, and Elizabeth kneeled down and said the Lord's Prayer, at which sight the sheriff wept apace, and so did divers others of the company. After they had prayed, he rose up and kissed his wife, and shook her by the hand, and said, "Farewell, my dear wife; be of good comfort, for I am quiet in my conscience. God shall stir up a father for my children."

All the way Dr. Taylor was joyful and merry, as one that accounted himself going to a most pleasant banquet or bridal. He spake many notable things to the sheriff and yeomen of the guard that conducted him, and often moved them to weep, through his much earnest calling upon them to repent, and to amend their evil and wicked living. Oftentimes also he caused them to wonder and rejoice, to see him so constant and steadfast, void of all fear, joyful in heart, and glad to die.

When Dr. Taylor had arrived at Aldham Common, the place where he should suffer, seeing a great multitude of people, he asked, "What place is this, and what meaneth it that so much people are gathered hither?" It was answered, "It is Aldham Common, the place where you must suffer; and the people have come to look upon you." Then he said, "Thanked be God, I am even at home"; and he alighted from his horse and with both hands rent the hood from his head.

His head had been notched and clipped like as a man would clip a fool's; which cost the good bishop Bonner had bestowed upon him. But when the people saw his reverend and ancient face, with a long white beard, they burst out with weeping tears, and cried, saying: "God save thee, good Dr. Taylor! Jesus Christ strengthen thee, and help thee! the Holy Ghost comfort thee!" with such other like good wishes.

When he had prayed, he went to the stake and kissed it, and set himself into a pitch barrel, which they had put for him to stand in, and stood with his back upright against the stake, with his hands folded together, and his eyes towards heaven, and continually prayed.

They then bound him with the chains, and having set up the fagots, one Warwick cruelly cast a fagot at him, which struck him on his head, and cut his face, so that the blood ran down. Then said Dr. Taylor, "O friend, I have harm enough; what needed that?"

Sir John Shelton standing by, as Dr. Taylor was speaking, and saying the Psalm *Miserere* in English, struck him on the lips: "You knave," he said, "speak Latin: I will make thee." At last they kindled the fire; and Dr. Taylor holding up both his hands, calling upon God, and said, "Merciful Father of heaven! for Jesus Christ, my Savior's sake, receive my soul into Thy hands!" So he stood still without either crying or moving, with his hands folded together, until Soyce, with a halberd struck him on the head until his brains fell out, and the corpse fell down into the fire.

Thus rendered up this man of God his blessed soul into the hands of his merciful Father, and to his most dear Savior Jesus Christ, whom he most entirely loved, faithfully and earnestly preached, obediently followed in living, and constantly glorified in death.

Martyrdom of William Hunter

William Hunter had been trained to the doctrines of the Reformation from his earliest youth, being descended from religious parents, who carefully instructed him in the principles of true religion.

Hunter, then nineteen years of age, refusing to receive the communion at Mass, was threatened to be brought before the bishop; to whom this valiant young martyr was conducted by a constable.

Bonner caused William to be brought into a chamber, where he began to reason with him, promising him security and pardon if he would recant. Nay, he would have been content if he would have gone only to receive and to confession, but William would not do so for all the world.

Upon this the bishop commanded his men to put William in the stocks in his gate house, where he sat two days and nights, with a crust of brown bread and a cup of water only, which he did not touch.

At the two days' end, the bishop came to him, and finding him steadfast in the faith, sent him to the convict prison, and commanded the keeper to lay irons upon him as many as he could bear. He continued in prison three quarters of a year, during which time he had been before the bishop five times, besides the time when he was condemned in the consistory in St. Paul's, February 9, at which time his brother, Robert Hunter, was present.

Then the bishop, calling William, asked him if he would recant, and finding he was unchangeable, pronounced sentence upon him, that he should go from that place to Newgate for a time, and thence to Brentwood, there to be burned.

About a month afterward, William was sent down to Brentwood, where he was to be executed. On coming to the stake, he knelt down and read the Fifty-first Psalm, until he came to these words, "The sacrifices of God are a broken spirit; a broken and a contrite heart, O God, Thou wilt not despise." Steadfast in refusing the queen's pardon, if he would become an apostate, at length one Richard Ponde, a bailiff, came, and made the chain fast about him.

William now cast his psalter into his brother's hand, who said, "William, think on the holy passion of Christ, and be not afraid of death." "Behold," answered William, "I am not afraid." Then he lifted up his hands to heaven, and said, "Lord, Lord, Lord, receive my spirit;" and casting down his head again into the smothering smoke, he yielded up his life for the truth, sealing it with his blood to the praise of God.

Dr. Robert Farrar

This worthy and learned prelate, the bishop of St. David's in Wales, having in the former reign, as well as since the accession of Mary, been remarkably zealous in promoting the reformed doctrines, and exploding the errors of popish idolatry, was summoned, among others, before the persecuting bishop of Winchester, and other commissioners set apart for the abominable work of devastation and massacre.

His principal accusers and persecutors, on a charge of præmunire in the reign of Edward VI were George Constantine Walter, his servant; Thomas Young, chanter of the cathedral, afterward bishop of Bangor, etc. Dr. Farrar ably replied to the copies of information laid against him, consisting of fifty-six articles. The whole process of this trial was long and tedious. Delay succeeded delay, and after that Dr. Farrar had been long unjustly detained in custody under sureties, in the reign of King Edward, because he had been promoted by the duke of Somerset, whence after his fall he found fewer friends to support him against such as wanted his bishopric by the coming in of Queen Mary, he was accused and examined not for any matter of præmunire, but for his faith and doctrine; for which he was called before the bishop of Winchester with Bishop Hooper, Mr. Rogers, Mr. Bradford, Mr. Saunders, and others, February 4, 1555; on which day he would also with them have been condemned, but his condemnation was deferred, and he sent to prison again, where he continued until February 14, and then was sent into

Wales to receive sentence. He was six times brought up before Henry Morgan, bishop of St. David's, who demanded if he would abjure; from which he zealously dissented, and appealed to Cardinal Pole; notwithstanding which, the bishop, proceeding in his rage, pronounced him a heretic excommunicate, and surrendered him to the secular power.

Dr. Farrar, being condemned and degraded, was not long after brought to the place of execution in the town of Carmathen, in the market-place of which, on the south side of the market-cross, March 30, 1555, being Saturday next before Passion Sunday, he most constantly sustained the torments of the fire.

Concerning his constancy, it is said that one Richard Jones, a knight's son, coming to Dr. Farrar a little before his death, seemed to lament the painfulness of the death he had to suffer; to whom the bishop answered that if he saw him once stir in the pains of his burning, he might then give no credit to his doctrine; and as he said, so did he maintain his promise, patiently standing without emotion, until one Richard Gravell with a staff struck him down.

Martyrdom of Rawlins White

Rawlins White was by his calling and occupation a fisherman, living and continuing in the said trade for the space of twenty years at least, in the town of Cardiff, where he bore a very good name amongst his neighbors.

Though the good man was altogether unlearned, and withal very simple, yet it pleased God to remove him from error and idolatry to a knowledge of the truth, through the blessed Reformation in Edward's reign. He had his son taught to read English, and after the little boy could read pretty well, his father every night after supper, summer and winter, made the boy read a portion of the Holy Scriptures, and now and then a part of some other good book.

When he had continued in his profession the space of five years, King Edward died, upon whose decease Queen Mary succeeded and with her all kinds of superstition crept in. White was taken by the officers of the town, as a man suspected of heresy, brought before the Bishop Llandaff, and committed to prison in Chepstow, and at last removed to the castle of Cardiff, where he continued for the space of one whole year. Being brought before the bishop in his chapel, he counselled him by threats and promises. But as Rawlins would in no wise recant his opinions, the bishop told him plainly that he must proceed against him by law, and condemn him as a heretic.

Before they proceeded to this extremity, the bishop proposed that prayer should be said for his conversion. "This," said White, "is like a godly bishop, and if your request be godly and right, and you pray as you ought, no doubt God will hear you; pray you, therefore, to your God, and I will pray to my God." After the bishop and his party had done praying, he asked Rawlins if he would now revoke. "You find," said the latter, "your prayer is not granted, for I remain the same; and God will strengthen me in support of this truth." After this, the bishop tried what saying Mass would do; but Rawlins called all the people to witness that he did not bow down to the host. Mass being ended, Rawlins was called for again; to whom the bishop used many persuasions; but the blessed man continued so steadfast in his former profession that the bishop's discourse was to no purpose. The bishop now caused the definitive sentence to be read, which being ended, Rawlins was carried again to Cardiff, to a loathsome prison in the town, called Cockmarel, where he passed his time in prayer, and in the singing of Psalms. In about three weeks the order came from town for his execution.

When he came to the place, where his poor wife and children stood weeping, the sudden sight of them so pierced his heart, that the tears trickled down his face. Being come to the altar of his sacrifice, in going toward the stake, he fell down upon his knees, and kissed the ground; and in rising again, a little earth sticking on his face, he said these words. "Earth unto earth, and dust unto dust; thou art my mother, and unto thee I shall return."

When all things were ready, directly over against the stake, in the face of Rawlins White, there was a stand erected, whereon stepped up a priest, addressing himself to the people, but, as he spoke of the Romish doctrines of the Sacraments, Rawlins cried out, "Ah! thou wicked hypocrite, dost thou presume to prove thy false doctrine by Scripture? Look in the text that followeth; did not Christ say, 'Do this in remembrance of me?'"

Then some that stood by cried out, "Put fire! set on fire!" which being done, the straw and reeds cast up a great and sudden flame. In which flame this good man bathed his hands so long, until such time as the sinews shrank, and the fat dropped away, saving that once he did, as it were, wipe his face with one of them. All this while, which was somewhat long, he cried with a loud voice, "O Lord, receive my spirit!" until he could not open his mouth. At last the extremity of the fire was so vehement against his legs that they were consumed almost before the rest of his body was hurt, which made the whole body fall over the chains into the fire sooner than it would have done. Thus died this good old man for his testimony of God's truth, and is now rewarded, no doubt, with the crown of eternal life.

The Rev. George Marsh

George Marsh, born in the parish of Deane, in the county of Lancaster, received a good education and trade from his parents; about his twenty-fifth year he married, and lived, blessed with several children, on his farm until his wife died. He then went to study at Cambridge, and became the curate of Rev. Lawrence Saunders, in which duty he constantly and zealously set forth the truth of God's Word, and the false doctrines of the modern Antichrist.

Being confined by Dr. Coles, the bishop of Chester, within the precincts of his own house, he was kept from any intercourse with his friends during four months; his friends and mother, earnestly wished him to have flown from "the wrath to come;" but Mr. Marsh thought that such a step would ill agree with that profession he had during nine years openly made. He, however, secreted himself, but he had much struggling, and in secret prayer begged that God would direct him, through the advice of his best friends, for his own glory and to what was best. At length, determined by a letter he received, boldly to confess the faith of Christ, he took leave of his mother-in-law and other friends, recommending his children to their care and departed for Smethehills, whence he was, with others, conducted to Lathum, to undergo examination before the earl of Derby, Sir William Nores, Mr. Sherburn, the parson of Grapnal, and others. The various questions put to him he answered with a good conscience, but when Mr. Sherburn interrogated him upon his belief of the Sacrament of the altar, Mr. Marsh answered like a true Protestant that the essence of the bread and wine was not at all changed, hence, after receiving dreadful threats from some, and fair words from others, for his opinions, he was remanded to ward, where he lay two nights without any bed.

On Palm Sunday he underwent a second examination, and Mr. Marsh much lamented that his fear should at all have induced him to prevaricate, and to seek his safety, as long as he did not openly deny Christ; and he again cried more earnestly to God for strength that he might not be overcome by the subtleties of those who strove to overrule the purity of his faith. He underwent three examinations before Dr. Coles, who, finding him steadfast in the Protestant faith, began to read his sentence; but he was interrupted by the chancellor, who prayed the bishop to stay before it was too late. The priest then prayed for Mr. Marsh, but the latter, upon being again solicited to recant, said he durst not deny his Savior Christ, lest he lose His everlasting mercy, and so obtain eternal death. The bishop then proceeded in the sentence. He was committed to a dark dungeon, and lay deprived of the consolation of any one (for all were afraid to relieve or communicate with him) until the day appointed came that he should suffer. The sheriffs of the city, Amry and Couper, with their officers, went to the north gate, and took out Mr. George Marsh, who walked all the way with the Book in his hand, looking upon the same, whence the people said, "This man does not go to his death as a thief, nor as one that deserveth to die."

When he came to the place of execution without the city, near Spittal-Boughton, Mr. Cawdry, deputy chamberlain of Chester, showed Mr. Marsh a writing under a great seal, saying that it was a pardon for him if he would recant. He answered that he would gladly accept the same did it not tend to pluck him from God.

After that, he began to speak to the people, showing the cause of his death, and would have exhorted them to stick unto Christ, but one of the sheriffs prevented him. Kneeling down, he then said his prayers, put off his clothes unto his shirt, and was chained to the post, having a number of fagots under him, and a thing made like a firkin, with pitch and tar in it, over his head. The fire being unskilfully made, and the wind driving it in eddies, he suffered great extremity, which notwithstanding he bore with Christian fortitude.

When he had been a long time tormented in the fire without moving, having his flesh so broiled and puffed up that they who stood before him could not see the chain wherewith he was fastened, and therefore supposed that he had been dead, suddenly he spread abroad his arms, saying, "Father of heaven have mercy upon me!" and so yielded his spirit into the hands of the Lord. Upon this, many of the people said he was a martyr, and died gloriously patient. This caused the bishop shortly after to make a sermon in the cathedral church, and therein he affirmed, that the said 'Marsh was a heretic, burnt as such, and is a firebrand in hell.' Mr. Marsh suffered April 24, 1555.

William Flower

William Flower, otherwise Branch, was born at Snow-hill, in the county of Cambridge, where he went to school some years, and then came to the abby of Ely. After he had remained a while he became a professed monk, was made a priest in the same house, and there celebrated and sang Mass. After that, by reason of a visitation, and certain injunctions by the authority of Henry VIII he took upon him the habit of a secular priest, and returned to Snow-hill, where he was born, and taught children about half a year.

He then went to Ludgate, in Suffolk, and served as a secular priest about a quarter of a year; from thence to Stoniland; at length to Tewksbury, where he married a wife, with whom he ever after faithfully and honestly continued. After marriage he resided at Tewksbury about two years, and thence went to Brosley, where he practiced physic and surgery; but departing from those parts he came to London, and finally settled at Lambeth, where he and his wife dwelt together. However, he was generally abroad, excepting once or twice in a month, to visit and see his wife. Being at home upon Easter Sunday morning, he came over the water from Lambeth into St. Margaret's Church at Westminster; when seeing a priest, named John Celtham, administering and giving the Sacrament of the altar to the people, and being greatly offended in his conscience with the priest for the same, he struck and wounded him upon the head, and also upon the arm and hand, with his wood knife, the priest having at the same time in his hand a chalice with the consecrated host therein, which became sprinkled with blood.

Mr. Flower, for this injudicious zeal, was heavily ironed, and put into the gatehouse at Westminster; and afterward summoned before bishop Bonner and his ordinary, where the bishop, after he had sworn him upon a Book, ministered articles and interrogatories to him.

After examination, the bishop began to exhort him again to return to the unity of his mother the Catholic Church, with many fair promises. These Mr. Flower steadfastly rejecting, the bishop ordered him to appear in the same place in the afternoon, and in the meantime to consider well his former answer; but he, neither apologizing for having struck the priest, nor swerving from his faith, the bishop assigned him the next day, April 20, to receive sentence if he would not recant. The next morning, the bishop accordingly proceeded to the sentence, condemning and excommunicating him for a heretic, and after pronouncing him to be degraded, committed him to the secular power.

On April 24, St. Mark's eve, he was brought to the place of martyrdom, in St. Margaret's churchyard, Westminster, where the fact was committed: and there coming to the stake, he prayed to Almighty God, made a confession of his faith, and forgave all the world.

This done, his hand was held up against the stake, and struck off, his left hand being fastened behind him. Fire was then set to him, and he burning therein, cried with a loud voice, "O Thou Son of God receive my soul!" three times. His speech being now taken from him, he spoke no more, but notwithstanding he lifted up the stump with his other arm as long as he could.

Thus he endured the extremity of the fire, and was cruelly tortured, for the few fagots that were brought being insufficient to burn him they were compelled to strike him down into the fire, where lying along upon the ground, his lower part was consumed in the fire, whilst his upper part was little injured, his tongue moving in his mouth for a considerable time.

The Rev. John Cardmaker and John Warne

May 30, 1555, the Rev. John Cardmaker, otherwise called Taylor, prebendary of the Church of Wells, and John Warne, upholsterer, of St. John's, Walbrook, suffered together in Smithfield. Mr. Cardmaker, who first was an observant friar before the dissolution of the abbeys, afterward was a married minister, and in King Edward's time appointed to be a reader in St. Paul's; being apprehended in the beginning of Queen Mary's reign, with Dr. Barlow, bishop of Bath, he was brought to London, and put in the Fleet prison, King Edward's laws being yet in force. In Mary's reign, when brought before the bishop of Winchester, the latter offered them the queen's mercy, if they would recant.

Articles having been preferred against Mr. John Warne, he was examined upon them by Bonner, who earnestly exhorted him to recant his opinions, to whom he answered, "I am persuaded that I am in the right opinion, and I see no cause to recant; for all the filthiness and idolatry lies in the Church of Rome."

The bishop then, seeing that all his fair promises and terrible threatenings could not prevail, pronounced the definitive sentence of condemnation, and ordered May 30, 1555, for the execution of John Cardmaker and John Warne, who were brought by the sheriffs to Smithfield. Being come to the stake, the sheriffs called Mr. Cardmaker aside, and talked with him secretly, during which Mr. Warne prayed, was chained to the stake, and had wood and reeds set about him.

The people were greatly afflicted, thinking that Mr. Cardmaker would recant at the burning of Mr. Warne. At length Mr. Cardmaker departed from the sheriffs, and came towards the stake, knelt down, and made a long prayer in silence to himself. He then arose up, put off his clothes to his shirt, and went with a bold courage unto the stake and kissed it; and taking Mr. Warne by the hand, he heartily comforted him, and was bound to the stake, rejoicing. The people seeing this so suddenly done, contrary to their previous expectation, cried out, "God be praised! the Lord strengthen thee, Cardmaker! the Lord Jesus receive thy spirit!" And this continued while the executioner put fire to them, and both had passed through the fire to the blessed rest and peace among God's holy saints and martyrs, to enjoy the crown of triumph and victory prepared for the elect soldiers and warriors of Christ Jesus in His blessed Kingdom, to whom be glory and majesty forever. Amen.

John Simpson and John Ardeley

John Simpson and John Ardeley were condemned on the same day with Mr. Cardmaker and John Warne, which was the twenty-fifth of May. They were shortly after sent down from London to Essex, where they were burnt in one day, John Simpson at Rochford, and John Ardeley at Railey, glorifying God in His beloved Son, and rejoicing that they were accounted worthy to suffer.

Thomas Haukes, Thomas Watts, and Anne Askew

Thomas Haukes, with six others, was condemned on the ninth of February, 1555. In education he was erudite; in person, comely, and of good stature; in manners, a gentleman, and a sincere Christian. A little before death, several of Mr. Hauke's friends, terrified by the sharpness of the punishment he was going to suffer, privately desired that in the midst of the flames he should show them some token, whether the pains of burning were so great that a man might not collectedly endure it. This he promised to do; and it was agreed that if the rage of the pain might be suffered, then he should lift up his hands above his head towards heaven, before he gave up the ghost.

Not long after, Mr. Haukes was led away to the place appointed for slaughter by Lord Rich, and being come to the stake, mildly and patiently prepared himself for the fire, having a strong chain cast about his middle, with a multitude of people on every side compassing him about, unto whom after he had spoken many things, and poured out his soul unto God, the fire was kindled.

When he had continued long in it, and his speech was taken away by violence of the flame, his skin drawn together, and his fingers consumed with the fire, so that it was thought that he was gone, suddenly and contrary to all expectation, this good man being mindful of his promise, reached up his hands burning in flames over his head to the living God, and with great rejoicings as it seemed, struck or clapped them three times together. A great shout followed this wonderful circumstance, and then this blessed martyr of Christ, sinking down in the fire, gave up his spirit, June 10, 1555.

Thomas Watts, of Billerica, in Essex, of the diocese of London, was a linen draper. He had daily expected to be taken by God's adversaries, and this came to pass on the fifth of April, 1555, when he was brought before Lord Rich, and other commissioners at Chelmsford, and accused for not coming to the church.

Being consigned over to the bloody bishop, who gave him several hearings, and, as usual, many arguments, with much entreaty, that he would be a disciple of Antichrist, but his preaching availed not, and he resorted to his last revenge—that of condemnation.

At the stake, after he had kissed it, he spake to Lord Rich, charging him to repent, for the Lord would revenge his death. Thus did this good martyr offer his body to the fire, in defence of the true Gospel of the Savior.

Thomas Osmond, William Bamford, and Nicholas Chamberlain, all of the town of Coxhall, being sent up to be examined, Bonner, after several hearings, pronounced them obstinate heretics, and delivered them to the sheriffs, in whose custody they remained until they were delivered to the sheriff of Essex county, and by him were executed, Chamberlain at Colchester, the fourteenth of June; Thomas Osmond at Maningtree, and William Bamford, alias Butler, at Harwich, the fifteenth of June, 1555; all dying full of the glorious hope of immortality.

Then Wriotheseley, lord chancellor, offered Anne Askew the king's pardon if she would recant; who made this answer, that she came not thither to deny her Lord and Master. And thus the good Anne Askew, being compassed in with flames of fire, as a blessed sacrifice unto God, slept in the Lord, A. D. 1546, leaving behind her a singular example of Christian constancy for all men to follow.

Rev. John Bradford, and John Leaf, an Apprentice

Rev. John Bradford was born at Manchester, in Lancashire; he was a good Latin scholar, and afterward became a servant of Sir John Harrington, knight.

He continued several years in an honest and thriving way; but the Lord had elected him to a better function. Hence he departed from his master, quitting the Temple, at London, for the University of Cambridge, to learn, by God's law, how to further the building of the Lord's temple. In a few years after, the university gave him the degree of master of arts, and he became a fellow of Pembroke Hall.

Martin Bucer first urged him to preach, and when he modestly doubted his ability, Bucer was wont to reply, "If thou hast not fine wheat bread, yet give the poor people barley bread, or whatsoever else the Lord hath committed unto thee." Dr. Ridley, that worthy bishop of London, and glorious martyr of Christ, first called him to take the degree of a deacon and gave him a prebend in his cathedral Church of St. Paul.

In this preaching office Mr. Bradford diligently labored for the space of three years. Sharply he reproved sin, sweetly he preached Christ crucified, ably he disproved heresies and errors, earnestly he persuaded to godly life. After the death of blessed King Edward VI Mr. Bradford still continued diligent in preaching, until he was suppressed by Queen Mary.

An act now followed of the blackest ingratitude, and at which a pagan would blush. It has been recited, that a tumult was occasioned by Mr. Bourne's (then bishop of Bath) preaching at St. Paul's Cross; the indignation of the people placed his life in imminent danger; indeed a dagger was thrown at him. In this situation he entreated Mr. Bradford, who stood behind him, to speak in his place, and assuage the tumult. The people welcomed Mr. Bradford, and the latter afterward kept close to him, that his presence might prevent the populace from renewing their assaults.

The same Sunday in the afternoon, Mr. Bradford preached at Bow Church in Cheapside, and reproved the people sharply for their seditious misdemeanor. Notwithstanding this conduct, within three days after, he was sent for to the Tower of London, where the queen then was, to appear before the Council. There he was charged with this act of saving Mr. Bourne, which was called seditious, and they also objected against him for preaching. Thus he was committed, first to the Tower, then to other prisons, and, after his condemnation, to the Poultry Compter, where he preached twice a day continually, unless sickness hindered him. Such was his credit with the keeper of the king's Bench, that he permitted him in an evening to visit a poor, sick person near the steel-yard, upon his promise to return in time, and in this he never failed.

The night before he was sent to Newgate, he was troubled in his sleep by foreboding dreams, that on Monday after he should be burned in Smithfield. In the afternoon the keeper's wife came up and announced this dreadful news to him, but in him it excited only thankfulness to God. At night half a dozen friends came, with whom he spent all the evening in prayer and godly exercises.

When he was removed to Newgate, a weeping crowd accompanied him, and a rumor having been spread that he was to suffer at four the next morning, an immense multitude attended. At nine o'clock Mr. Bradford was brought into Smithfield. The cruelty of the sheriff deserves notice; for his brother-in-law, Roger Beswick, having taken him by the hand as he passed, Mr. Woodroffe, with his staff, cut his head open.

Mr. Bradford, being come to the place, fell flat on the ground, Church of St. Paul.

and putting off his clothes unto the shirt, he went to the stake, and there suffered with a young man of twenty years of age, whose name was John Leaf, an apprentice to Mr. Humphrey Gaudy, tallow-chandler, of Christ-church, London. Upon Friday before Palm Sunday, he was committed to the Compter in Bread-street, and afterward examined and condemned by the bloody bishop.

It is reported of him, that, when the bill of his confession was read unto him, instead of pen, he took a pin, and pricking his hand, sprinkled the blood upon the said bill, desiring the reader thereof to show the bishop that he had sealed the same bill with his blood already.

They both ended this mortal life, July 12, 1555, like two lambs, without any alteration of their countenances, hoping to obtain that prize they had long run for; to which may Almighty God conduct us all, through the merits of Christ our Savior!

We shall conclude this article with mentioning that Mr. Sheriff Woodroffe, it is said, within half a year after, was struck on the right side with a palsy, and for the space of eight years after, (until his dying day,) he was unable to turn himself in his bed; thus he became at last a fearful object to behold.

The day after Mr. Bradford and John Leaf suffered in Smithfield William Minge, priest, died in prison at Maidstone. With as great constancy and boldness he yielded up his life in prison, as if it had pleased God to have called him to suffer by fire, as other godly men had done before at the stake, and as he himself was ready to do, had it pleased God to have called him to this trial.

Rev. John Bland, Rev. John Frankesh, Nicholas Shetterden, and Humphrey Middleton

These Christian persons were all burnt at Canterbury for the same cause. Frankesh and Bland were ministers and preachers of the Word of God, the one being parson of Adesham, and the other vicar of Rolvenden. Mr. Bland was cited to answer for his opposition to antichristianism, and underwent several examinations before Dr. Harpsfield, archdeacon of Canterbury, and finally on the twenty-fifth of June, 1555, again withstanding the power of the pope, he was condemned, and delivered to the secular arm. On the same day were condemned John Frankesh, Nicholas Shetterden, Humphrey Middleton, Thacker, and Crocker, of whom Thacker only recanted.

Being delivered to the secular power, Mr. Bland, with the three former, were all burnt together at Canterbury, July 12, 1555, at two several stakes, but in one fire, when they, in the sight of God and His angels, and before men, like true soldiers of Jesus Christ, gave a constant testimony to the truth of His holy Gospel.

Dirick Carver and John Launder

The twenty-second of July, 1555, Dirick Carver, brewer, of Brighthelmstone, aged forty, was burnt at Lewes. And the day following John Launder, husbandman, aged twenty-five, of God-stone, Surrey, was burnt at Stening.

Dirick Carver was a man whom the Lord had blessed as well with temporal riches as with his spiritual treasures. At his coming into the town of Lewes to be burnt, the people called to him, beseeching God to strengthen him in the faith of Jesus Christ; and, as he came to the stake, he knelt down, and prayed earnestly. Then his Book was thrown into the barrel, and when he had stripped himself, he too, went into a barrel. As soon as he was in, he took the Book, and threw it among the people, upon which the sheriff commanded, in the name of the king and queen, on pain of death, to throw in the Book again. And immediately the holy martyr began to address the people. After he had prayed a while, he said, "O Lord my God, Thou hast written, he that will not forsake wife, children, house, and every thing that he hath, and take up Thy cross and follow Thee, is not worthy of Thee! but Thou, Lord, knowest that I have forsaken all to come unto Thee. Lord, have mercy upon me, for unto Thee I commend my spirit! and my soul doth rejoice in Thee!" These were the last words of this faithful servant of Christ before enduring the fire. And when the fire came to him, he cried, "O Lord, have mercy upon me!" and sprang up in the fire, calling upon the name of Jesus, until he gave up the ghost.

James Abbes. This young man wandered about to escape apprehension, but was at last informed against, and brought before the bishop of Norwich, who influenced him to recant; to secure him further in apostasy, the bishop afterward gave him a piece of money; but the interference of Providence is here remarkable. This bribe lay so heavily upon his conscience, that he returned, threw back the money, and repented of his conduct. Like Peter, he was contrite, steadfast in the faith, and sealed it with his blood at Bury, August 2, 1555, praising and glorifying God.

John Denley, John Newman, and Patrick Packingham

Mr. Denley and Newman were returning one day to Maidstone, the place of their abode, when they were met by E. Tyrrel, Esq., a bigoted justice of the peace in Essex, and a cruel persecutor of the Protestants. He apprehended them merely on suspicion. On the fifth of July, 1555, they were condemned, and consigned to the sheriffs, who sent Mr. Denley to Uxbridge, where he perished, August eighth, 1555. While suffering in agony, and singing a Psalm, Dr. Story inhumanly ordered one of the tormentors to throw a fagot at him, which cut his face severely, caused him to cease singing, and to raise his hands to his face. Just as Dr. Story was remarking in jest that he had spoiled a good song, the pious martyr again chanted, spread his hands abroad in the flames, and through Christ Jesus resigned his soul into the hands of his Maker.

Mr. Packingham suffered at the same town on the twenty-eighth of the same month.

Mr. Newman, pewterer, was burnt at Saffron Waldon, in Essex, August 31, for the same cause, and Richard Hook about the same time perished at Chichester.

W. Coker, W. Hooper, H. Laurence, R. Colliar, R. Wright and W. Stere

These persons all of Kent, were examined at the same time with Mr. Bland and Shetterden, by Thornton, bishop of Dover, Dr. Harpsfield, and others. These six martyrs and witnesses of the truth were consigned to the flames in Canterbury, at the end of August, 1555.

Elizabeth Warne, widow of John Warne, upholsterer, martyr, was burnt at Stratford-le-bow, near London, at the end of August, 1555.

George Tankerfield, of London, cook, born at York, aged twenty-seven, in the reign of Edward VI had been a papist; but the cruelty of bloody Mary made him suspect the truth of those doctrines which were enforced by fire and torture. Tankerfield was imprisoned in Newgate about the end of February, 1555, and on

August 26, at St. Alban's, he braved the excruciating fire, and joy-fully died for the glory of his Redeemer.

Rev. Robert Smith was first in the service of Sir T. Smith, provost of Eton; and was afterward removed to Windsor, where he had a clerkship of ten pounds a year.

He was condemned, July 12, 1555, and suffered August 8, at Uxbridge. He doubted not but that God would give the spectators some token in support of his own cause; this actually happened; for, when he was nearly half burnt, and supposed to be dead, he suddenly rose up, moved the remaining parts of his arms and praised God; then, hanging over the fire, he sweetly slept in the Lord Jesus.

Mr. Stephen Harwood and Mr. Thomas Fust suffered about the same time with Smith and Tankerfield, with whom they were con-demned. Mr. William Hale also, of Thorp, in Essex, was sent to Barnet, where about the same time he joined the ever-blessed com-pany of martyrs.

George King, Thomas Leyes, and John Wade, falling sick in Lollard's Tower, were removed to different houses, and died. Their bodies were thrown out in the common fields as unworthy of burial, and lay until the faithful conveyed them away at night.

Mr. William Andrew of Horseley, Essex, was imprisoned in Newgate for heresy; but God chose to call him to himself by the severe treatment he endured in Newgate, and thus to mock the sanguinary expectations of his Catholic persecutors. His body was thrown into the open air, but his soul was received into the ever-lasting mansions of his heavenly Creator.

The Rev. Robert Samuel

This gentleman was minister of Bradford, Suffolk, where he in-dustriously taught the flock committed to his charge, while he was openly permitted to discharge his duty. He was first persecuted by Mr. Foster, of Copdock, near Ipswich, a severe and bigoted perse-cutor of the followers of Christ, according to the truth in the Gospel. Notwithstanding Mr. Samuel was ejected from his living, he continued to exhort and instruct privately; nor would he obey the order for putting away his wife, whom he had married in King Edward's reign; but kept her at Ipswich, where Foster, by warrant, surprised him by night with her. After being imprisoned in Ipswich jail, he was taken before Dr. Hopton, bishop of Nor-wich, and Dr. Dunnings, his chancellor, two of the most sanguinary among the bigots of those days. To intimidate the worthy pastor, he was in prison chained to a post in such a manner that the weight of his body was supported by the points of his toes: added to this his allowance of provision was reduced to a quantity so insufficient to sustain nature that he was almost ready to devour his own flesh.

From this dreadful extremity there was even a degree of mercy in ordering him to the fire. Mr. Samuel suffered August 31, 1555.

Bishop Ridley and Bishop Latimer

These reverend prelates suffered October 17, 1555, at Oxford, on the same day Wolsey and Pygot perished at Ely. Pillars of the Church and accomplished ornaments of human nature, they were the admiration of the realm, amiably conspicuous in their lives, and glorious in their deaths.

Dr. Ridley was born in Northumberland, was first taught grammar at Newcastle, and afterward removed to Cambridge, where his aptitude in education raised him gradually until he came to be the head of Pembroke College, where he received the title of Doctor of Divinity. Having returned from a trip to Paris, he was appointed chaplain by Henry VIII and bishop of Rochester, and was afterwards translated to the see of London in the time of Edward VI.

To his sermons the people resorted, swarming about him like bees, coveting the sweet flowers and wholesome juice of the fruitful doctrine, which he did not only preach, but showed the same by his life, as a glittering lanthorn to the eyes and senses of the blind, in such pure order that his very enemies could not reprove him in any one jot.

His tender treatment of Dr. Heath, who was a prisoner with him during one year, in Edward's reign, evidently proves that he had no Catholic cruelty in his disposition. In person he was erect and well proportioned; in temper forgiving; in self-mortification severe. His first duty in the morning was private prayer: he remained in his study until ten o'clock, and then attended the daily prayer used in his house. Dinner being done, he sat about an hour, conversing pleasantly, or playing at chess. His study next engaged his attention, unless business or visits occurred; about five o'clock prayers followed; and after he would recreate himself at chess for about an hour, then retire to his study until eleven o'clock, and pray on his knees as in the morning. In brief, he was a pattern of godliness and virtue, and such he endeavored to make men wherever he came.

His attentive kindness was displayed particularly to old Mrs. Bonner, mother of Dr. Bonner, the cruel bishop of London. Dr. Ridley, when at his manor at Fulham, always invited her to his house, placed her at the head of his table, and treated her like his own mother; he did the same by Bonner's sister and other relatives; but when Dr. Ridley was under persecution, Bonner pursued a conduct diametrically opposite, and would have sacrificed Dr. Ridley's sister and her husband, Mr. George Shipside, had not Providence delivered him by the means of Dr. Heath, bishop of Worcester.

Dr. Ridley was first in part converted by reading Bertram's book on the Sacrament, and by his conferences with archbishop Cranmer and Peter Martyr.

When Edward VI was removed from the throne, and the bloody Mary succeeded, Bishop Ridley was immediately marked as an object of slaughter. He was first sent to the Tower, and afterward, at Oxford, was consigned to the common prison of Bocardo, with archbishop Cranmer and Mr. Latimer. Being separated from them, he was placed in the house of one Irish, where he remained until the day of his martyrdom, from 1554, until October 16, 1555.

It will easily be supposed that the conversations of these chiefs of the martyrs were elaborate, learned, and instructive. Such indeed they were, and equally beneficial to all their spiritual comforts. Bishop Ridley's letters to various Christian brethren in bonds in all parts, and his disputations with the mitred enemies of Christ, alike proved the clearness of his head and the integrity of his heart. In a letter to Mr. Grindal, (afterward archbishop of Canterbury,) he mentions with affection those who had preceded him in dying for the faith, and those who were expected to suffer; he regrets that popery is re-established in its full abomination, which he attributes to the wrath of God, made manifest in return for the lukewarmness of the clergy and the people in justly appreciating the blessed light of the Reformation.

This old practiced soldier of Christ, Master Hugh Latimer, was the son of one Hugh Latimer, of Thurkesson in the county of Leicester, a husbandman, of a good and wealthy estimation; where also he was born and brought up until he was four years of age, or thereabout: at which time his parents, having him as then left for their only son, with six daughters, seeing his ready, prompt, and sharp wit, purposed to train him up in erudition, and knowledge of good literature; wherein he so profited in his youth at the common schools of his own country, that at the age of fourteen years, he was sent to the University of Cambridge; where he entered into the study of the school divinity of that day, and was from principle a zealous observer of the Romish superstitions of the time. In his oration when he commenced bachelor of divinity, he inveighed against the reformer Melancthon, and openly declaimed against good Mr. Stafford, divinity lecturer in Cambridge.

Mr. Thomas Bilney, moved by a brotherly pity towards Mr. Latimer, begged to wait upon him in his study, and to explain to him the groundwork of his (Mr. Bilney's) faith. This blessed interview effected his conversion: the persecutor of Christ became his zealous advocate, and before Dr. Stafford died he became reconciled to him.

Once converted, he became eager for the conversion of others, and commenced to be public preacher, and private instructor in the university. His sermons were so pointed against the absurdity of praying in the Latin tongue, and withholding the oracles of salvation from the people who were to be saved by belief in them, that he drew upon himself the pulpit animadversions of several of the resident friars and heads of houses, whom he subsequently silenced by his severe criticisms and eloquent arguments. This was at Christmas, 1529. At length Dr. West preached against Mr. Latimer at Barwell Abbey, and prohibited him from preaching again in the churches of the university, notwithstanding which, he continued during three years to advocate openly the cause of Christ, and even his enemies confessed the power of those talents he possessed. Mr. Bilney remained here some time with Mr. Latimer, and thus the place where they frequently walked together obtained the name of Heretics' Hill.

Mr. Latimer at this time traced out the innocence of a poor woman, accused by her husband of the murder of her child. Having preached before King Henry VIII at Windsor, he obtained the unfortunate mother's pardon. This, with many other benevolent acts, served only to excite the spleen of his adversaries. He was summoned before Cardinal Wolsey for heresy, but being a strenuous supporter of the king's supremacy, in opposition to the pope's, by favor of Lord Cromwell and Dr. Buts, (the king's physician,) he obtained the living of West Kingston, in Wiltshire. For his sermons here against purgatory, the immaculacy of the Virgin, and the worship of images, he was cited to appear before Warham, archbishop of Canterbury, and John, bishop of London. He was required to subscribe certain articles, expressive of his conformity to the accustomed usages; and there is reason to think, after repeated weekly examinations, that he did subscribe, as they did not seem to involve any important article of belief.

Guided by Providence, he escaped the subtle nets of his persecutors, and at length, through the powerful friends before mentioned, became bishop of Worcester, in which function he qualified or explained away most of the papal ceremonies he was for form's sake under the necessity of complying with. He continued in this active and dignified employment some years.

Beginning afresh to set forth his plow he labored in the Lord's harvest most fruitfully, discharging his talent as well in divers places of this realm, as before the king at the court. In the same place of the inward garden, which was before applied to lascivious and courtly pastimes, there he dispensed the fruitful Word of the glorious Gospel of Jesus Christ, preaching there before the king and his whole court, to the edification of many.

He remained a prisoner in the Tower until the coronation of Edward VI, when he was again called to the Lord's harvest in Stamford, and many other places: he also preached at London in the convocation house, and before the young king; indeed he lectured twice every Sunday, regardless of his great age (then above sixty-seven years,) and his weakness through a bruise received from the fall of a tree. Indefatigable in his private studies, he rose to them in winter and in summer at two o'clock in the morning.

By the strength of his own mind, or of some inward light from above, he had a prophetic view of what was to happen to the Church in Mary's reign, asserting that he was doomed to suffer for the truth, and that Winchester, then in the Tower, was preserved for that purpose. Soon after Queen Mary was proclaimed, a messenger was sent to summon Mr. Latimer to town, and there is reason to believe it was wished that he should make his escape.

Thus Master Latimer coming up to London, through Smithfield (where merrily he said that Smithfield had long groaned for him), was brought before the Council, where he patiently bore all the mocks and taunts given him by the scornful papists. He was cast into the Tower, where he, being assisted with the heavenly grace of Christ, sustained imprisonment a long time, notwithstanding the cruel and unmerciful handling of the lordly papists, which thought then their kingdom would never fall; he showed himself not only patient, but also cheerful in and above all that which they could or would work against him. Yea, such a valiant spirit the Lord gave him, that he was able not only to despise the terribleness of prisons and torments, but also to laugh to scorn the doings of his enemies.

Mr. Latimer, after remaining a long time in the Tower, was transported to Oxford, with Cranmer and Ridley, the disputations at which place have been already mentioned in a former part of this work. He remained imprisoned until October, and the principal objects of all his prayers were three—that he might stand faithful to the doctrine he had professed, that God would restore his Gospel to England once again, and preserve the Lady Elizabeth to be queen; all of which happened. When he stood at the stake without the Bocardo gate, Oxford, with Dr. Ridley, and fire was putting to the pile of fagots, he raised his eyes benignantly towards heaven, and said, "God is faithful, who will not suffer you to be tempted above that ye are able." His body was forcibly penetrated by the fire, and the blood flowed abundantly from the heart; as if to verify his constant desire that his heart's blood might be shed in defence of the Gospel. His polemical and friendly letters are lasting monuments of his integrity and talents. It has been before said, that public disputation took place in April, 1554, new examinations took place in October, 1555, previous to the degradation and condemnation of Cranmer, Ridley, and Latimer. We now draw to the conclusion of the lives of the two last.

Dr. Ridley, the night before execution, was very facetious, had himself shaved, and called his supper a marriage feast; he remarked upon seeing Mrs. Irish (the keeper's wife) weep, "Though my breakfast will be somewhat sharp, my supper will be more pleasant and sweet."

The place of death was on the north side of the town, opposite Baliol College. Dr. Ridley was dressed in a black gown furred, and Mr. Latimer had a long shroud on, hanging down to his feet. Dr. Ridley, as he passed Bocardo, looked up to see Dr. Cranmer, but the latter was then engaged in disputation with a friar. When they came to the stake, Mr. Ridley embraced Latimer fervently, and bid him: "Be of good heart, brother, for God will either assuage the fury of the flame, or else strengthen us to abide it." He then knelt by the stake, and after earnestly praying together, they had a short private conversation. Dr. Smith then preached a short sermon against the martyrs, who would have answered him, but were prevented by Dr. Marshal, the vice-chancellor. Dr. Ridley then took off his gown and tippet, and gave them to his brother-in-law, Mr. Shipside. He gave away also many trifles to his weeping friends, and the populace were anxious to get even a fragment of his garments. Mr. Latimer gave nothing, and from the poverty of his garb, was soon stripped to his shroud, and stood venerable and erect, fearless of death.

Dr. Ridley being unclothed to his shirt, the smith placed an iron chain about their waists, and Dr. Ridley bid him fasten it securely; his brother having tied a bag of gunpowder about his neck, gave some also to Mr. Latimer.

Dr. Ridley then requested of Lord Williams, of Fame, to advocate with the queen the cause of some poor men to whom he had, when bishop, granted leases, but which the present bishop refused to confirm. A lighted fagot was now laid at Dr. Ridley's feet, which caused Mr. Latimer to say: "Be of good cheer, Ridley; and play the man. We shall this day, by God's grace, light up such a candle in England, as I trust, will never be put out."

When Dr. Ridley saw the fire flaming up towards him, he cried with a wonderful loud voice, "Lord, Lord, receive my spirit." Master Latimer, crying as vehemently on the other side, "O Father of heaven, receive my soul!" received the flame as it were embracing of it. After that he had stroked his face with his hands, and as it were, bathed them a little in the fire, he soon died (as it appeareth) with very little pain or none.

Well! dead they are, and the reward of this world they have already. What reward remaineth for them in heaven, the day of the Lord's glory, when he cometh with His saints, shall declare.

In the following month died Stephen Gardiner, bishop of Winchester and lord chancellor of England. This papistical monster was born at Bury, in Suffolk, and partly educated at Cambridge. Ambitious, cruel, and bigoted, he served any cause; he first espoused the king's part in the affair of Anne Boleyn: upon the establishment of the Reformation he declared the supremacy of the pope an execrable tenet; and when Queen Mary came to the crown, he entered into all her papistical bigoted views, and became a second time bishop of Winchester. It is conjectured it was his intention to have moved the sacrifice of Lady Elizabeth, but when he arrived at this point, it pleased God to remove him.

It was on the afternoon of the day when those faithful soldiers of Christ, Ridley and Latimer, perished, that Gardiner sat down with a joyful heart to dinner. Scarcely had he taken a few mouthfuls, when he was seized with illness, and carried to his bed, where he lingered fifteen days in great torment, unable in any wise to evacuate, and burnt with a devouring fever, that terminated in death. Execrated by all good Christians, we pray the Father of mercies, that he may receive that mercy above he never imparted below.

Mr. John Philpot

This martyr was the son of a knight, born in Hampshire, and brought up at New College, Oxford, where for several years he studied the civil law, and became eminent in the Hebrew tongue. He was a scholar and a gentleman, zealous in religion, fearless in disposition, and a detester of flattery. After visiting Italy, he returned to England, affairs in King Edward's days wearing a more promising aspect. During this reign he continued to be archdeacon of Winchester under Dr. Poinet, who succeeded Gardiner. Upon the accession of Mary, a convocation was summoned, in which Mr. Philpot defended the Reformation against his ordinary, Gardiner, again made bishop of Winchester, and soon was conducted to Bonner and other commissioners for examination, October 2, 1555, after being eighteen months' imprisoned. Upon his demanding to see the commission, Dr. Story cruelly observed, "I will spend both my gown and my coat, but I will burn thee! Let him be in Lollard's tower, (a wretched prison,) for I will sweep the king's Bench and all other prisons of these heretics!"

Upon Mr. Philpot's second examination, it was intimated to him that Dr. Story had said that the lord chancellor had commanded that he should be made away with. It is easy to foretell the result of this inquiry. He was committed to Bonner's coal house, where he joined company with a zealous minister of Essex, who had been induced to sign a bill of recantation; but afterward, stung by his conscience, he asked the bishop to let him see the instrument again, when he tore it to pieces; which induced Bonner in a fury to strike him repeatedly, and tear away part of his beard. Mr. Philpot had a private interview with Bonner the same night, and was then remanded to his bed of straw like other prisoners, in the coal house. After seven examinations, Bonner ordered him to be set in the stocks, and on the following Sunday separated him from his fellow-prisoners as a sower of heresy, and ordered him up to a room near the battlements of St. Paul's, eight feet by thirteen, on the other side of Lollard's tower, and which could be overlooked by any one in the bishop's outer gallery. Here Mr. Philpot was searched, but happily he was successful in secreting some letters containing his examinations.

In the eleventh investigation before various bishops, and Mr. Morgan, of Oxford, the latter was so driven into a corner by the close pressure of Mr. Philpot's arguments, that he said to him, "Instead of the spirit of the Gospel which you boast to possess, I think it is the spirit of the buttery, which your fellows have had, who were drunk before their death, and went, I believe, drunken to it." To this unfounded and brutish remark, Mr. Philpot indignantly replied, "It appeareth by your communication that you are better acquainted with that spirit than the Spirit of God; wherefore I tell thee, thou painted wall and hypocrite, in the name of the living God, whose truth I have told thee, that God shall rain fire and brimstone upon such blasphemers as thou art!" He was then remanded by Bonner, with an order not to allow him his Bible nor candlelight.

On December 4, Mr. Philpot had his next hearing, and this was followed by two more, making in all, fourteen conferences, previous to the final examination in which he was condemned; such were the perseverance and anxiety of the Catholics, aided by the argumentative abilities of the most distinguished of the papal bishops, to bring him into the pale of their Church. Those examinations, which were very long and learned, were all written down by Mr. Philpot, and a stronger proof of the imbecility of the Catholic doctors, cannot, to an unbiased mind, be exhibited.

On December 16, in the consistory of St. Paul's Bishop Bonner, after laying some trifling accusations to his charge, such as secreting powder to make ink, writing some private letters, etc., proceeded to pass the awful sentence upon him, after he and the other bishops had urged him by every inducement to recant. He was afterward conducted to Newgate, where the avaricious Catholic keeper loaded him with heavy irons, which by the humanity of Mr. Macham were ordered to be taken off. On December 17, Mr. Philpot received intimation that he was to die next day, and the next morning about eight o'clock, he joyfully met the sheriffs, who were to attend him to the place of execution.

Upon entering Smithfield, the ground was so muddy that two officers offered to carry him to the stake, but he replied: "Would you make me a pope? I am content to finish my journey on foot." Arriving at the stake, he said, "Shall I disdain to suffer at the stake, when my Redeemer did not refuse to suffer the most vile death upon the cross for me?" He then meekly recited the One hundred and seventh and One hundred and eighth Psalms, and when he had finished his prayers, was bound to the post, and fire applied to the pile.

On December 18, 1555, perished this illustrious martyr, reverenced by man, and glorified in heaven!

John Lomas, Agnes Snoth, Anne Wright, Joan Sole, and Joan Catmer

These five martyrs suffered together, January 31, 1556. John Lomas was a young man of Tenterden. He was cited to appear at Canterbury, and was examined January 17. His answers being adverse to the idolatrous doctrine of the papacy, he was condemned on the following day, and suffered January 31.

Agnes Snoth, widow, of Smarden Parish, was several times summoned before the Catholic Pharisees, and rejecting absolution, indulgences, transubstantiation, and auricular confession, she was adjudged worthy to suffer death, and endured martyrdom, January 31, with Anne Wright and Joan Sole, who were placed in similar circumstances, and perished at the same time, with equal resignation. Joan Catmer, the last of this heavenly company, of the parish Hithe, was the wife of the martyr George Catmer.

Seldom in any country, for political controversy, have four women been led to execution, whose lives were irreproachable, and whom the pity of savages would have spared. We cannot but remark here that, when the Protestant power first gained the ascendency over the Catholic superstition, and some degree of force in the laws was necessary to enforce uniformity, whence some bigoted people suffered privation in their person or goods, we read of few burnings, savage cruelties, or poor women brought to the stake, but it is the nature of error to resort to force instead of argument, and to silence truth by taking away existence, of which the Redeemer himself is an instance.

The above five persons were burnt at two stakes in one fire, singing hosannahs to the glorified Savior, until the breath of life was extinct. Sir John Norton, who was present, wept bitterly at their unmerited sufferings.

Archbishop Cranmer

Dr. Thomas Cranmer was descended from an ancient family, and was born at the village of Arselacton, in the county of Northampton. After the usual school education he was sent to Cambridge, and was chosen fellow of Jesus College. Here he married a gentleman's daughter, by which he forfeited his fellowship, and became a reader in Buckingham College, placing his wife at the Dolphin Inn, the landlady of which was a relation of hers, whence arose the idle report that he was an ostler. His lady shortly after dying in childbed; to his credit he was re-chosen a fellow of the college before mentioned. In a few years after, he was promoted to be Divinity Lecturer, and appointed one of the examiners over those who were ripe to become Bachelors or Doctors in Divinity. It was his principle to judge of their qualifications by the knowledge they possessed of the Scriptures, rather than of the ancient fathers, and hence many popish priests were rejected, and others rendered much improved.

He was strongly solicited by Dr. Capon to be one of the fellows on the foundation of Cardinal Wolsey's college, Oxford, of which he hazarded the refusal. While he continued in Cambridge, the question of Henry VIII's divorce with Catharine was agitated. At that time, on account of the plague, Dr. Cranmer removed to the house of a Mr. Cressy, at Waltham Abbey, whose two sons were then educating under him. The affair of divorce, contrary to the king's approbation, had remained undecided above two or three years, from the intrigues of the canonists and civilians, and though the cardinals Campeius and Wolsey were commissioned from Rome to decide the question, they purposely protracted the sentence.

It happened that Dr. Gardiner (secretary) and Dr. Fox, defenders of the king in the above suit, came to the house of Mr. Cressy to lodge, while the king removed to Greenwich. At supper, a conversation ensued with Dr. Cranmer, who suggested that the question whether a man may marry his brother's wife or not, could be easily and speedily decided by the Word of God, and this as well in the English courts as in those of any foreign nation. The king, uneasy at the delay, sent for Dr. Gardiner and Dr. Fox to consult them, regretting that a new commission must be sent to Rome, and the suit be endlessly protracted. Upon relating to the king the conversation which had passed on the previous evening with Dr. Cranmer, his majesty sent for him, and opened the tenderness of conscience upon the near affinity of the queen. Dr. Cranmer advised that the matter should be referred to the most learned divines of Cambridge and Oxford, as he was unwilling to meddle in an affair of such weight; but the king enjoined him to deliver his sentiments in writing, and to repair for that purpose to the earl of Wiltshire's, who would accommodate him with books, and everything requisite for the occasion.

This Dr. Cranmer immediately did, and in his declaration not only quoted the authority of the Scriptures, of general councils, and the ancient writers, but maintained that the bishop of Rome had no authority whatever to dispense with the Word of God. The king asked him if he would stand by this bold declaration, to which replying in the affirmative, he was deputed ambassador to Rome, in conjunction with the earl of Wiltshire, Dr. Stokesley, Dr. Carne, Dr. Bennet, and others, previous to which, the marriage was discussed in most of the universities of Christendom and at home.

When the pope presented his toe to be kissed, as customary, the earl of Wiltshire and his party refused. Indeed, it is affirmed that a spaniel of the earl's attracted by the glitter of the pope's toe, made a snap at it, whence his holiness drew in his sacred foot, and kicked at the offender with the other.

Upon the pope demanding the cause of their embassy, the earl presented Dr. Cranmer's book, declaring that his learned friends had come to defend it. The pope treated the embassy honorably, and appointed a day for the discussion, which he delayed, as if afraid of the issue of the investigation. The earl returned, and Dr. Cranmer, by the king's desire, visited the emperor, and was successful in bringing him over to his opinion. Upon the doctor's return to England, Dr. Warham, archbishop of Canterbury, having quitted this transitory life, Dr. Cranmer was deservedly, and by Dr. Warham's desire, elevated to that eminent station.

In this function, it may be said that he followed closely the charge of St. Paul. Diligent in duty, he rose at five in the morning, and continued in study and prayer until nine: between then and dinner, he devoted to temporal affairs. After dinner, if any suitors wanted hearing, he would determine their business with such an affability that even the defaulters were scarcely displeased. Then he would play at chess for an hour, or see others play, and at five o'clock he heard the Common Prayer read, and from this until supper he took the recreation of walking. At supper his conversation was lively and entertaining; again he walked or amused himself until nine o'clock, and then entered his study.

He ranked high in favor with King Henry, and even had the purity and the interest of the English Church deeply at heart. His mild and forgiving disposition is recorded in the following instance. An ignorant priest, in the country, had called Cranmer an ostler, and spoken very derogatory of his learning. Lord Cromwell receiving information of it, the man was sent to the Fleet, and his case was told to the archbishop by a Mr. Chertsey, a grocer, and a relation of the priest's. His grace, having sent for the offender, reasoned with him, and solicited the priest to question him on any learned subject. This the man, overcome by the bishop's good nature, and knowing his own glaring incapacity, declined, and entreated his forgiveness, which was immediately granted, with a charge to employ his time better when he returned to his parish. Cromwell was much vexed at the lenity displayed, but the bishop was ever more ready to receive injury than to retaliate in any other manner than by good advice and good offices.

At the time that Cranmer was raised to be archbishop, he was king's chaplain, and archdeacon of Taunton; he was also constituted by the pope the penitentiary general of England. It was considered by the king that Cranmer would be obsequious; hence the latter married the king to Anne Boleyn, performed her coronation, stood godfather to Elizabeth, the first child, and divorced the king from Catharine. Though Cranmer received a confirmation of his dignity from the pope, he always protested against acknowledging any other authority than the king's, and he persisted in the same independent sentiments when before Mary's commissioners in 1555.

One of the first steps after the divorce was to prevent preaching throughout his diocese, but this narrow measure had rather a political view than a religious one, as there were many who inveighed against the king's conduct. In his new dignity Cranmer agitated the question of supremacy, and by his powerful and just arguments induced the parliament to "render to Cæsar the things that are Cæsar's." During Cranmer's residence in Germany, 1531, he became acquainted with Ossiander, at Nuremberg, and married his niece, but left her with him while on his return to England. After a season he sent for her privately, and she remained with him until the year 1539, when the Six Articles compelled him to return her to her friends for a time.

It should be remembered that Ossiander, having obtained the approbation of his friend Cranmer, published the laborious work of the Harmony of the Gospels in 1537. In 1534 the archbishop completed the dearest wish of his heart, the removal of every obstacle to the perfection of the Reformation, by the subscription of the nobles and bishops to the king's sole supremacy. Only Bishop Fisher and Sir Thomas More made objection; and their agreement not to oppose the succession Cranmer was willing to consider as sufficient, but the monarch would have no other than an entire concession.

Not long after, Gardiner, in a private interview with the king, spoke inimically of Cranmer, (whom he maliciously hated) for assuming the title of primate of all England, as derogatory to the supremacy of the king. This created much jealousy against Cranmer, and his translation of the Bible was strongly opposed by Stokesley, bishop of London. It is said, upon the demise of Queen Catharine, that her successor Anne Boleyn rejoiced—a lesson this to show how shallow is the human judgment! since her own execution took place in the spring of the following year, and the king, on the day following the beheading of this sacrificed lady, married the beautiful Jane Seymour, a maid of honor to the late queen. Cranmer was ever the friend of Anne Boleyn, but it was dangerous to oppose the will of the carnal tyrannical monarch.

In 1538, the Holy Scriptures were openly exposed to sale; and the places of worship overflowed everywhere to hear its holy doctrines expounded. Upon the king's passing into a law the famous Six Articles, which went nearly again to establish the essential tenets of the Romish creed, Cranmer shone forth with all the luster of a Christian patriot, in resisting the doctrines they contained, and in which he was supported by the bishops of Sarum, Worcester, Ely, and Rochester, the two former of whom resigned their bishoprics. The king, though now in opposition to Cranmer, still revered the sincerity that marked his conduct. The death of Lord Cromwell in the Tower, in 1540, the good friend of Cranmer, was a severe blow to the wavering Protestant cause, but even now Cranmer, when he saw the tide directly adverse to the truth, boldly waited on the king in person, and by his manly and heartfelt pleading, caused the Book of Articles to be passed on his side, to the great confusion of his enemies, who had contemplated his fall as inevitable.

Cranmer now lived in as secluded a manner as possible, until the rancor of Winchester preferred some articles against him, relative to the dangerous opinion he taught in his family, joined to other treasonable charges. These the king himself delivered to Cranmer, and believing firmly the fidelity and assertions of innocence of the accused prelate, he caused the matter to be deeply investigated, and Winchester and Dr. Lenden, with Thornton and Barber, of the bishop's household, were found by the papers to be the real conspirators. The mild, forgiving Cranmer would have interceded for all remission of punishment, had not Henry, pleased with the subsidy voted by parliament, let them be discharged. These nefarious men, however, again renewing their plots against Cranmer, fell victims to Henry's resentment, and Gardiner forever lost his confidence. Sir G. Gostwick soon after laid charges against the archbishop, which Henry quashed, and the primate was willing to forgive.

In 1544, the archbishop's palace at Canterbury was burnt, and his brother-in-law with others perished in it. These various afflictions may serve to reconcile us to a humble state; for of what happiness could this great and good man boast, since his life was constantly harassed either by political, religious, or natural crosses? Again the inveterate Gardiner laid high charges against the meek archbishop and would have sent him to the Tower; but the king was his friend, gave him his signet that he might defend him, and in the Council not only declared the bishop one of the best affected men in his realm, but sharply rebuked his accusers for their calumny.

A peace having been made, Henry, and the French king, Henry the Great, were unanimous to have the Mass abolished in their kingdom, and Cranmer set about this great work; but the death of the English monarch, in 1546, suspended the procedure, and King Edward his successor continued Cranmer in the same functions, upon whose coronation he delivered a charge that will ever honor his memory, for its purity, freedom, and truth. During this reign he prosecuted the glorious Reformation with unabated zeal, even in the year 1552, when he was seized with a severe ague, from which it pleased God to restore him that he might testify by his death the truth of that seed he had diligently sown.

The death of Edward, in 1553, exposed Cranmer to all the rage of his enemies. Though the archbishop was among those who supported Mary's accession, he was attainted at the meeting of parliament, and in November adjudged guilty of high treason at Guildhall, and degraded from his dignities. He sent a humble letter to Mary, explaining the cause of his signing the will in favor of Edward, and in 1554 he wrote to the Council, whom he pressed to obtain a pardon from the queen, by a letter delivered to Dr. Weston, but which the latter opened, and on seeing its contents, basely returned.

Treason was a charge quite inapplicable to Cranmer, who supported the queen's right; while others, who had favored Lady Jane were dismissed upon paying a small fine. A calumny was now spread against Cranmer that he complied with some of the popish ceremonies to ingratiate himself with the queen, which he dared publicly to disavow, and justified his articles of faith. The active part which the prelate had taken in the divorce of Mary's mother had ever rankled deeply in the heart of the queen, and revenge formed a prominent feature in the death of Cranmer.

We have in this work noticed the public disputations at Oxford, in which the talents of Cranmer, Ridley, and Latimer shone so conspicuously, and tended to their condemnation. The first sentence was illegal, inasmuch as the usurped power of the pope had not yet been re-established by law.

Being kept in prison until this was effected, a commission was despatched from Rome, appointing Dr. Brooks to sit as the representative of his holiness, and Drs. Story and Martin as those of the queen. Cranmer was willing to bow to the authority of Drs. Story and Martin, but against that of Dr. Brooks he protested. Such were the remarks and replies of Cranmer, after a long examination, that Dr. Brooks observed, "We come to examine you, and methinks you examine us."

Being sent back to confinement, he received a citation to appear at Rome within eighteen days, but this was impracticable, as he was imprisoned in England; and as he stated, even had he been at liberty, he was too poor to employ an advocate. Absurd as it must appear, Cranmer was condemned at Rome, and on February 14, 1556, a new commission was appointed, by which, Thirlby, bishop of Ely, and Bonner, of London, were deputed to sit in judgment at Christ-church, Oxford. By virtue of this instrument, Cranmer was gradually degraded, by putting mere rags on him to represent the dress of an archbishop; then stripping him of his attire, they took off his own gown, and put an old worn one upon him instead. This he bore unmoved, and his enemies, finding that severity only rendered him more determined, tried the opposite course, and placed him in the house of the dean of Christ-church, where he was treated with every indulgence.

This presented such a contrast to the three years' hard imprisonment he had received, that it threw him off his guard. His open, generous nature was more easily to be seduced by a liberal conduct than by threats and fetters. When Satan finds the Christian proof against one mode of attack, he tries another; and what form is so seductive as smiles, rewards, and power, after a long, painful imprisonment? Thus it was with Cranmer: his enemies promised him his former greatness if he would but recant, as well as the queen's favor, and this at the very time they knew that his death was determined in council. To soften the path to apostasy, the first paper brought for his signature was conceived in general terms; this once signed, five others were obtained as explanatory of the first, until finally he put his hand to the following detestable instrument:

"I, Thomas Cranmer, late archbishop of Canterbury, do renounce, abhor, and detest all manner of heresies and errors of Luther and Zuinglius, and all other teachings which are contrary to sound and true doctrine. And I believe most constantly in my heart, and with my mouth I confess one holy and Catholic Church visible, without which there is no salvation; and therefore I acknowledge the Bishop of Rome to be supreme head on earth, whom I acknowledge to be the highest bishop and pope, and Christ's vicar, unto whom all Christian people ought to be subject.

"And as concerning the sacraments, I believe and worship in the sacrament of the altar the body and blood of Christ, being contained most truly under the forms of bread and wine; the bread, through the mighty power of God being turned into the body of our Savior Jesus Christ, and the wine into his blood.

"And in the other six sacraments, also, (alike as in this) I believe and hold as the universal Church holdeth, and the Church of Rome judgeth and determineth.

"Furthermore, I believe that there is a place of purgatory, where souls departed be punished for a time, for whom the Church doth godlily and wholesomely pray, like as it doth honor saints and make prayers to them.

"Finally, in all things I profess, that I do not otherwise believe than the Catholic Church and the Church of Rome holdeth and teacheth. I am sorry that I ever held or thought otherwise. And I beseech Almighty God, that of His mercy He will vouchsafe to forgive me whatsoever I have offended against God or His Church, and also I desire and beseech all Christian people to pray for me.

"And all such as have been deceived either by mine example or doctrine, I require them by the blood of Jesus Christ that they will return to the unity of the Church, that we may be all of one mind, without schism or division.

"And to conclude, as I submit myself to the Catholic Church of Christ, and to the supreme head thereof, so I submit myself unto the most excellent majesties of Philip and Mary, king and queen of this realm of England, etc., and to all other their laws and ordinances, being ready always as a faithful subject ever to obey them. And God is my witness, that I have not done this for favor or fear of any person, but willingly and of mine own conscience, as to the instruction of others."

"Let him that standeth take heed lest he fall!" said the apostle, and here was a falling off indeed! The papists now triumphed in their turn: they had acquired all they wanted short of his life. His recantation was immediately printed and dispersed, that it might have its due effect upon the astonished Protestants. But God counter worked all the designs of the Catholics by the extent to which they carried the implacable persecution of their prey. Doubtless, the love of life induced Cranmer to sign the above declaration: yet death may be said to have been preferable to life to him who lay under the stings of a goaded conscience and the contempt of every Gospel Christian; this principle he strongly felt in all its force and anguish.

The queen's revenge was only to be satiated in Cranmer's blood, and therefore she wrote an order to Dr. Pole, to prepare a sermon to be preached March 21, directly before his martyrdom, at St. Mary's, Oxford. Dr. Pole visited him the day previous, and was induced to believe that he would publicly deliver his sentiments in confirmation of the articles to which he had subscribed. About nine in the morning of the day of sacrifice, the queen's commissioners, attended by the magistrates, conducted the amiable unfortunate to St. Mary's Church. His torn, dirty garb, the same in which they habited him upon his degradation, excited the commiseration of the people. In the church he found a low mean stage, erected opposite to the pulpit, on which being placed, he turned his face, and fervently prayed to God.

The church was crowded with persons of both persuasions, expecting to hear the justification of the late apostasy: the Catholics rejoicing, and the Protestants deeply wounded in spirit at the deceit of the human heart. Dr. Pole, in his sermon, represented Cranmer as having been guilty of the most atrocious crimes; encouraged the deluded sufferer not to fear death, not to doubt the support of God in his torments, nor that Masses would be said in all the churches of Oxford for the repose of his soul. The doctor then noticed his conversion, and which he ascribed to the evident working of Almighty power and in order that the people might be convinced of its reality, asked the prisoner to give them a sign. This Cranmer did, and begged the congregation to pray for him, for he had committed many and grievous sins; but, of all, there was one which awfully lay upon his mind, of which he would speak shortly.

During the sermon Cranmer wept bitter tears: lifting up his hands and eyes to heaven, and letting them fall, as if unworthy to live: his grief now found vent in words: before his confession he fell upon his knees, and, in the following words unveiled the deep contrition and agitation which harrowed up his soul.

"O Father of heaven! O Son of God, Redeemer of the world! O Holy Ghost, three persons all one God! have mercy on me, most wretched caitiff and miserable sinner. I have offended both against heaven and earth, more than my tongue can express. Whither then may I go, or whither may I flee? To heaven I may be ashamed to lift up mine eyes and in earth I find no place of refuge or succor. To Thee, therefore, O Lord, do I run; to Thee do I humble myself, saying, O Lord, my God, my sins be great, but yet have mercy upon me for Thy great mercy. The great mystery that God became man, was not wrought for little or few offences. Thou didst not give Thy Son, O Heavenly Father, unto death for small sins only, but for all the greatest sins of the world, so that the sinner return to Thee with his whole heart, as I do at present. Wherefore, have mercy on me, O God, whose property is always to have mercy, have mercy upon me, O Lord, for Thy great mercy. I crave nothing for my own merits, but for Thy name's sake, that it may be hallowed thereby, and for Thy dear Son, Jesus Christ's sake. And now therefore, O Father of Heaven, hallowed be Thy name," etc.

Then rising, he said he was desirous before his death to give them some pious exhortations by which God might be glorified and themselves edified. He then descanted upon the danger of a love for the world, the duty of obedience to their majesties, of love to one another and the necessity of the rich administering to the wants of the poor. He quoted the three verses of the fifth chapter of James, and then proceeded, "Let them that be rich ponder well these three sentences: for if they ever had occasion to show their charity, they have it now at this present, the poor people being so many, and victual so dear.

"And now forasmuch as I am come to the last end of my life, whereupon hangeth all my life past, and all my life to come, either to live with my master Christ for ever in joy, or else to be in pain for ever with the wicked in hell, and I see before mine eyes presently, either heaven ready to receive me, or else hell ready to swallow me up; I shall therefore declare unto you my very faith how I believe, without any color of dissimulation: for now is no time to dissemble, whatsoever I have said or written in times past.

"First, I believe in God the Father Almighty, Maker of heaven and earth, etc. And I believe every article of the Catholic faith, every word and sentence taught by our Savior Jesus Christ, His apostles and prophets, in the New and Old Testament.

"And now I come to the great thing which so much troubleth my conscience, more than any thing that ever I did or said in my whole life, and that is the setting abroad of a writing contrary to the truth, which now here I renounce and refuse, as things written with my hand contrary to the truth which I thought in my heart, and written for fear of death, and to save my life, if it might be; and that is, all such bills or papers which I have written or signed with my hand since my degradation, wherein I have written many things untrue. And forasmuch as my hand hath offended, writing contrary to my heart, therefore my hand shall first be punished; for when I come to the fire it shall first be burned.

"And as for the pope, I refuse him as Christ's enemy, and Antichrist, with all his false doctrine."

Upon the conclusion of this unexpected declaration, amazement and indignation were conspicuous in every part of the church. The Catholics were completely foiled, their object being frustrated, Cranmer, like Samson, having completed a greater ruin upon his enemies in the hour of death, than he did in his life.

Cranmer would have proceeded in the exposure of the popish doctrines, but the murmurs of the idolaters drowned his voice, and the preacher gave an order to "lead the heretic away!" The savage command was directly obeyed, and the lamb about to suffer was torn from his stand to the place of slaughter, insulted all the way by the revilings and taunts of the pestilent monks and friars.

With thoughts intent upon a far higher object than the empty threats of man, he reached the spot dyed with the blood of Ridley and Latimer. There he knelt for a short time in earnest devotion, and then arose, that he might undress and prepare for the fire. Two friars who had been parties in prevailing upon him to abjure, now endeavored to draw him off again from the truth, but he was steadfast and immovable in what he had just professed, and publicly taught. A chain was provided to bind him to the stake, and after it had tightly encircled him, fire was put to the fuel, and the flames began soon to ascend.

Then were the glorious sentiments of the martyr made manifest; then it was, that stretching out his right hand, he held it unshrinkingly in the fire until it was burnt to a cinder, even before his body was injured, frequently exclaiming, "This unworthy right hand."

His body did abide the burning with such steadfastness that he seemed to move no more than the stake to which he was bound; his eyes were lifted up to heaven, and he repeated "this unworthy right hand," as long as his voice would suffer him; and using often the words of Stephen, "Lord Jesus, receive my spirit," in the greatness of the flame, he gave up the ghost.

The Vision of Three Ladders

When Robert Samuel was brought forth to be burned, certain there were that heard him declare what strange things had happened unto him during the time of his imprisonment; to wit, that after he had famished or pined with hunger two or three days together, he then fell into a sleep, as it were one half in a slumber, at which time one clad all in white seemed to stand before him, who ministered comfort unto him by these words: "Samuel, Samuel, be of good cheer, and take a good heart unto thee: for after this day shalt thou never be either hungry or thirsty."

No less memorable it is, and worthy to be noted, concerning the three ladders which he told to divers he saw in his sleep, set up toward heaven; of the which there was one somewhat longer than the rest, but yet at length they became one, joining (as it were) all three together.

As this godly martyr was going to the fire, there came a certain maid to him, which took him about the neck, and kissed him, who, being marked by them that were present, was sought for the next day after, to be had to prison and burned, as the very party herself informed me: howbeit, as God of His goodness would have it, she escaped their fiery hands, keeping herself secret in the town a good while after.

But as this maid, called Rose Nottingham, was marvellously preserved by the providence of God, so there were other two honest women who did fall into the rage and fury of that time. The one was a brewer's wife, the other was a shoemaker's wife, but both together now espoused to a new husband, Christ.

With these two was this maid aforesaid very familiar and well acquainted, who, on a time giving counsel to the one of them, that she should convey herself away while she had time and space, had this answer at her hand again: "I know well," saith she, "that it is lawful enough to fly away; which remedy you may use, if you list. But my case standeth otherwise. I am tied to a husband, and have besides young children at home; therefore I am minded, for the love of Christ and His truth, to stand to the extremity of the matter."

And so the next day after Samuel suffered, these two godly wives, the one called Anne Potten, the other called Joan Trunchfield, the wife of Michael Trunchfield, shoemaker, of Ipswich, were apprehended, and had both into one prison together. As they were both by sex and nature somewhat tender, so were they at first less able to endure the straitness of the prison; and especially the brewer's wife was cast into marvellous great agonies and troubles of mind thereby. But Christ, beholding the weak infirmity of His servant, did not fail to help her when she was in this necessity; so at the length they both suffered after Samuel, in 1556, February 19. And these, no doubt, were those two ladders, which, being joined with the third, Samuel saw stretched up into heaven. This blessed Samuel, the servant of Christ, suffered the thirty-first of August, 1555.

The report goeth among some that were there present, and saw him burn, that his body in burning did shine in the eyes of them that stood by, as bright and white as new-tried silver.

When Agnes Bongeor saw herself separated from her prison-fellows, what piteous moan that good woman made, how bitterly she wept, what strange thoughts came into her mind, how naked and desolate she esteemed herself, and into what plunge of despair and care her poor soul was brought, it was piteous and wonderful to see; which all came because she went not with them to give her life in the defence of her Christ; for of all things in the world, life was least looked for at her hands.

For that morning in which she was kept back from burning, had she put on a smock, that she had prepared only for that purpose. And also having a child, a little young infant sucking on her, whom she kept with her tenderly all the time that she was in prison, against that day likewise did she send away to another nurse, and prepared herself presently to give herself for the testimony of the glorious Gospel of Jesus Christ. So little did she look for life, and so greatly did God's gifts work in her above nature, that death seemed a great deal better welcome than life. After which, she began a little to stay herself, and gave her whole exercise to reading and prayer, wherein she found no little comfort.

In a short time came a writ from London for the burning, which according to the effect thereof, was executed.

Hugh Laverick and John Aprice

Here we perceive that neither the impotence of age nor the affliction of blindness, could turn aside the murdering fangs of these Babylonish monsters. The first of these unfortunates was of the parish of Barking, aged sixty-eight, a painter and a cripple. The other was blind, dark indeed in his visual faculties, but intellectually illuminated with the radiance of the everlasting Gospel of truth. Inoffensive objects like these were informed against by some of the sons of bigotry, and dragged before the prelatical shark of London, where they underwent examination, and replied to the articles propounded to them, as other Christian martyrs had done before. On the ninth day of May, in the consistory of St. Paul's, they were entreated to recant, and upon refusal, were sent to Fulham, where Bonner, by way of a dessert after dinner, condemned them to the agonies of the fire. Being consigned to the secular officers, May 15, 1556, they were taken in a cart from Newgate to Stratford-le-Bow, where they were fastened to the stake. When Hugh Laverick was secured by the chain, having no further occasion for his crutch, he threw it away saying to his fellow-martyr, while consoling him, "Be of good cheer my brother; for my lord of London is our good physician; he will heal us both shortly—thee of thy blindness, and me of my lameness." They sank down in the fire, to rise to immortality!

The day after the above martyrdoms, Catharine Hut, of Bocking, widow: Joan Horns, spinster, of Billerica; Elizabeth Thackwel, spinster, of Great Burstead, suffered death in Smithfield.

Thomas Dowry. We have again to record an act of unpitying cruelty, exercised on this lad, whom Bishop Hooper, had confirmed in the Lord and the knowledge of his Word.

How long this poor sufferer remained in prison is uncertain. By the testimony of one John Paylor, register of Gloucester, we learn that when Dowry was brought before Dr. Williams, then chancellor of Gloucester, the usual articles were presented him for subscription. From these he dissented; and, upon the doctor's demanding of whom and where he had learned his heresies, the youth replied, "Indeed, Mr. Chancellor, I learned from you in that very pulpit. On such a day (naming the day) you said, in preaching upon the Sacrament, that it was to be exercised spiritually by faith, and not carnally and really, as taught by the papists." Dr. Williams then bid him recant, as he had done; but Dowry had not so learned his duty. "Though you," said he, "can so easily mock God, the world, and your own conscience, yet will I not do so."

Preservation of George Crow and His Testament

This poor man, of Malden, May 26, 1556, put to sea, to lade in Lent with fuller's earth, but the boat, being driven on land, filled with water, and everything was washed out of her; Crow, however, saved his Testament, and coveted nothing else. With Crow was a man and a boy, whose awful situation became every minute more alarming, as the boat was useless, and they were ten miles from land, expecting the tide should in a few hours set in upon them. After prayer to God, they got upon the mast, and hung there for the space of ten hours, when the poor boy, overcome by cold and exhaustion, fell off, and was drowned. The tide having abated, Crow proposed to take down the masts, and float upon them, which they did; and at ten o'clock at night they were borne away at the mercy of the waves. On Wednesday, in the night, Crow's companion died through the fatigue and hunger, and he was left alone, calling upon God for succor. At length he was picked up by a Captain Morse, bound to Antwerp, who had nearly steered away, taking him for some fisherman's buoy floating in the sea. As soon as Crow was got on board, he put his hand in his bosom, and drew out his Testament, which indeed was wet, but not otherwise injured. At Antwerp he was well received, and the money he had lost was more than made good to him.

Executions at Stratford-le-Bow

At this sacrifice, which we are about to detail, no less than thirteen were doomed to the fire.

Each one refusing to subscribe contrary to conscience, they were condemned, and the twenty-seventh of June, 1556, was appointed for their execution at Stratford-le-Bow. Their constancy and faith glorified their Redeemer, equally in life and in death.

Rev. Julius Palmer

This gentleman's life presents a singular instance of error and conversion. In the time of Edward, he was a rigid and obstinate papist, so adverse to godly and sincere preaching, that he was even despised by his own party; that this frame of mind should be changed, and he suffer persecution and death in Queen Mary's reign, are among those events of omnipotence at which we wonder and admire.

Mr. Palmer was born at Coventry, where his father had been mayor. Being afterward removed to Oxford, he became, under Mr. Harley, of Magdalen College, an elegant Latin and Greek scholar. He was fond of useful disputation, possessed of a lively wit, and a strong memory. Indefatigable in private study, he rose at four in the morning, and by this practice qualified himself to become reader in logic in Magralen College . The times of Edward, however, favoring the Reformation, Mr. Palmer became frequently punished for his contempt of prayer and orderly behavior, and was at length expelled the house.

He afterwards embraced the doctrines of the Reformation, which occasioned his arrest and final condemnation.

A certain nobleman offered him his life if he would recant. "If so," said he, "thou wilt dwell with me. And if thou wilt set thy mind to marriage, I will procure thee a wife and a farm, and help to stuff and fit thy farm for thee. How sayst thou?"

Palmer thanked him very courteously, but very modestly and reverently concluded that as he had already in two places renounced his living for Christ's sake, so he would with God's grace be ready to surrender and yield up his life also for the same, when God should send time.

When Sir Richard perceived that he would by no means relent: "Well, Palmer," saith he, "then I perceive one of us twain shall be damned: for we be of two faiths, and certain I am there is but one faith that leadeth to life and salvation."

Palmer: "O sir, I hope that we both shall be saved."

Sir Richard: "How may that be?"

Palmer: "Right well, sir. For as it hath pleased our merciful Savior, according to the Gospel's parable, to call me at the third hour of the day, even in my flowers, at the age of four and twenty years, even so I trust He hath called, and will call you, at the eleventh hour of this your old age, and give you everlasting life for your portion."

Sir Richard: "Sayest thou so? Well, Palmer, well, I would I might have thee but one month in my house: I doubt not but I would convert thee, or thou shouldst convert me."

Then said Master Winchcomb, "Take pity on thy golden years, and pleasant flowers of lusty youth, before it be too late."

Palmer: "Sir, I long for those springing flowers that shall never fade away."

He was tried on the fifteenth of July, 1556, together with one Thomas Askin, fellow prisoner. Askin and one John Guin had been sentenced the day before, and Mr. Palmer, on the fifteenth, was brought up for final judgment. Execution was ordered to follow the sentence, and at five o'clock in the same afternoon, at a place called the Sand-pits, these three martyrs were fastened to a stake. After devoutly praying together, they sung the Thirty-first Psalm.

When the fire was kindled, and it had seized their bodies, without an appearance of enduring pain, they continued to cry, "Lord Jesus, strengthen us! Lord Jesus receive our souls!" until animation was suspended and human suffering was past. It is remarkable, that, when their heads had fallen together in a mass as it were by the force of the flames, and the spectators thought Palmer as lifeless, his tongue and lips again moved, and were heard to pronounce the name of Jesus, to whom be glory and honor forever!

Joan Waste and Others

This poor, honest woman, blind from her birth, and unmarried, aged twenty-two, was of the parish of Allhallows, Derby. Her father was a barber, and also made ropes for a living: in which she assisted him, and also learned to knit several articles of apparel. Refusing to communicate with those who maintained doctrines contrary to those she had learned in the days of the pious Edward, she was called before Dr. Draicot, the chancellor of Bishop Blaine, and Peter Finch, official of Derby.

With sophistical arguments and threats they endeavored to confound the poor girl; but she proffered to yield to the bishop's doctrine, if he would answer for her at the Day of Judgment, (as pious Dr. Taylor had done in his sermons) that his belief of the real presence of the Sacrament was true. The bishop at first answered that he would; but Dr. Draicot reminding him that he might not in any way answer for a heretic, he withdrew his confirmation of his own tenets; and she replied that if their consciences would not permit them to answer at God's bar for that truth they wished her to subscribe to, she would answer no more questions. Sentence was then adjudged, and Dr. Draicot appointed to preach her condemned sermon, which took place August 1, 1556, the day of her martyrdom. His fulminating discourse being finished, the poor, sightless object was taken to a place called Windmill Pit, near the town, where she for a time held her brother by the hand, and then prepared herself for the fire, calling upon the pitying multitude to pray with her, and upon Christ to have mercy upon her, until the glorious light of the everlasting Sun of righteousness beamed upon her departed spirit.

In November, fifteen martyrs were imprisoned in Canterbury castle, of whom all were either burnt or famished. Among the latter were J. Clark, D. Chittenden, W. Foster of Stone, Alice Potkins, and J. Archer, of Cranbrooke, weaver. The two first of these had not received condemnation, but the others were sentenced to the fire. Foster, at his examination, observed upon the utility of carrying lighted candles about on Candlemas-day, that he might as well carry a pitchfork; and that a gibbet would have as good an effect as the cross.

We have now brought to a close the sanguinary proscriptions of the merciless Mary, in the year 1556, the number of which amounted to above EIGHTY-FOUR!

The beginning of the year 1557, was remarkable for the visit of Cardinal Pole to the University of Cambridge, which seemed to stand in need of much cleansing from heretical preachers and reformed doctrines. One object was also to play the popish farce of trying Martin Bucer and Paulus Phagius, who had been buried about three or four years; for which purpose the churches of St. Mary and St. Michael, where they lay, were interdicted as vile and unholy places, unfit to worship God in, until they were perfumed and washed with the pope's holy water, etc., etc. The trumpery act of citing these dead reformers to appear, not having had the least effect upon them, on January 26, sentence of condemnation was passed, part of which ran in this manner, and may serve as a specimen of proceedings of this nature: "We therefore pronounce the said Martin Bucer and Paulus Phagius excommunicated and anathematized, as well by the common law, as by letters of process; and that their memory be condemned, we also condemn their bodies and bones (which in that wicked time of schism, and other heresies flourishing in this kingdom, were rashly buried in holy ground) to be dug up, and cast far from the bodies and bones of the faithful, according to the holy canons, and we command that they and their writings, if any be there found, be publicly burnt; and we interdict all persons whatsoever of this university, town, or places adjacent, who shall read or conceal their heretical book, as well by the common law, as by our letters of process!"

After the sentence thus read, the bishop commanded their bodies to be dug out of their graves, and being degraded from holy orders, delivered them into the hands of the secular power; for it was not lawful for such innocent persons as they were, abhorring all bloodshed, and detesting all desire of murder, to put any man to death.

February 6, the bodies, enclosed as they were in chests, were carried into the midst of the market place at Cambridge, accompanied by a vast concourse of people. A great post was set fast in the ground, to which the chests were affixed with a large iron chain, and bound round their centers, in the same manner as if the dead bodies had been alive. When the fire began to ascend, and caught the coffins, a number of condemned books were also launched into the flames, and burnt. Justice, however, was done to the memories of these pious and learned men in Queen Elizabeth's reign, when Mr. Ackworth, orator of the university, and Mr. J. Pilkington, pronounced orations in honor of their memory, and in reprobation of their Catholic persecutors.

Cardinal Pole also inflicted his harmless rage upon the dead body of Peter Martyr's wife, who, by his command, was dug out of her grave, and buried on a distant dunghill, partly because her bones lay near St. Fridewide's relics, held once in great esteem in that college, and partly because he wished to purify Oxford of heretical remains as well as Cambridge. In the succeeding reign, however, her remains were restored to their former cemetery, and even intermingled with those of the Catholic saint, to the utter astonishment and mortification of the disciples of his holiness the pope.

Cardinal Pole published a list of fifty-four articles, containing instructions to the clergy of his diocese of Canterbury, some of which are too ludicrous and puerile to excite any other sentiment than laughter in these days.

Persecutions in the Diocese of Canterbury

In the month of February, the following persons were committed to prison: R. Coleman, of Waldon, laborer; Joan Winseley, of Horsley Magna, spinster; S. Glover, of Rayley; R. Clerk, of Much Holland, mariner; W. Munt, of Much Bentley, sawyer; Marg. Field, of Ramsey, spinster; R. Bongeor, currier; R. Jolley, mariner; Allen Simpson, Helen Ewire, C. Pepper, widow; Alice Walley (who recanted), W. Bongeor, glazier, all of Colchester; R. Atkin, of Halstead, weaver; R. Barcock, of Wilton, carpenter; R. George, of Westbarhonlt, laborer; R. Debnam of Debenham, weaver; C. Warren, of Cocksall, spinster; Agnes Whitlock, of Dover-court, spinster; Rose Allen, spinster; and T. Feresannes, minor; both of Colchester.

These persons were brought before Bonner, who would have immediately sent them to execution, but Cardinal Pole was for more merciful measures, and Bonner, in a letter of his to the cardinal, seems to be sensible that he had displeased him, for he has this expression: "I thought to have them all hither to Fulham, and to have given sentence against them; nevertheless, perceiving by my last doing that your grace was offended, I thought it my duty, before I proceeded further, to inform your grace." This circumstance verifies the account that the cardinal was a humane man; and though a zealous Catholic, we, as Protestants, are willing to render him that honor which his merciful character deserves. Some of the bitter persecutors denounced him to the pope as a favorer of heretics, and he was summoned to Rome, but Queen Mary, by particular entreaty, procured his stay. However, before his latter end, and a little before his last journey from Rome to England, he was strongly suspected of favoring the doctrine of Luther.

As in the last sacrifice four women did honor to the truth, so in the following *auto da fé* we have the like number of females and males, who suffered June 30, 1557, at Canterbury, and were J. Fishcock, F. White, N. Pardue, Barbary Final, widow, Bardbridge's widow, Wilson's wife, and Benden's wife.

Of this group we shall more particularly notice Alice Benden, wife of Edward Bender, of Staplehurst, Kent. She had been taken up in October, 1556, for non-attendance, and released upon a strong injunction to mind her conduct. Her husband was a bigoted Catholic, and publicly speaking of his wife's contumacy, she was conveyed to Canterbury Castle, where knowing, when she should be removed to the bishop's prison, she should be almost starved upon three farthings a day, she endeavored to prepare herself for this suffering by living upon twopence halfpenny per day.

On January 22, 1557, her husband wrote to the bishop that if his wife's brother, Roger Hall, were to be kept from consoling and relieving her, she might turn; on this account, she was moved to a prison called Monday's Hole. Her brother sought diligently for her, and at the end of five weeks providentially heard her voice in the dungeon, but could not otherwise relieve her, than by putting some money in a loaf, and sticking it on a long pole. Dreadful must have been the situation of this poor victim, lying on straw, between stone walls, without a change of apparel, or the meanest requisites of cleanliness, during a period of nine weeks!

On March 25 she was summoned before the bishop, who, with rewards, offered her liberty if she would go home and be comfortable; but Mrs. Benden had been inured to suffering, and, showing him her contracted limbs and emaciated appearance, refused to swerve from the truth. She was however removed from this black hole to the West Gate, whence, about the end of April, she was taken out to be condemned, and then committed to the castle prison until the nineteenth of June, the day of her burning. At the stake, she gave her handkerchief to one John Banks, as a memorial; and from her waist she drew a white lace, desiring him to give it to her brother, and tell him that it was the last band that had bound her, except the chain; and to her father she returned a shilling he had sent her.

The whole of these seven martyrs undressed themselves with alacrity, and, being prepared, knelt down, and prayed with an earnestness and Christian spirit that even the enemies of the cross were affected. After invocation made together, they were secured to the stake, and, being encompassed with the unsparing flames, they yielded their souls into the hands of the living Lord.

Matthew Plaise, weaver, a sincere and shrewd Christian, of Stone, Kent, was brought before Thomas, bishop of Dover, and other inquisitors, whom he ingeniously teased by his indirect answers, of which the following is a specimen.

Dr. Harpsfield. Christ called the bread His body; what dost thou say it is?

Plaise. I do believe it was that which He gave them.

Dr. H. What was that?

P. That which He brake.

Dr. H. What did He brake?

P. That which He took.

Dr. H. What did He take?

P. I say, what He gave them, that did they eat indeed.

Dr. H. Well, then, thou sayest it was but bread which the disciples did eat.

P. I say, what He gave them, that did they eat indeed.

A very long disputation followed, in which Plaise was desired to humble himself to the bishop; but this he refused. Whether this zealous person died in prison, was executed, or delivered, history does not mention.

Rev. John Hullier

Rev. John Hullier was brought up at Eton College, and in process of time became curate of Babram, three miles from Cambridge, and went afterward to Lynn; where, opposing the superstition of the papists, he was carried before Dr. Thirlby, bishop of Ely, and sent to Cambridge castle: here he lay for a time, and was then sent to Tolbooth prison, where, after three months, he was brought to St. Mary's Church, and condemned by Dr. Fuller. On Maunday Thursday he was brought to the stake: while undressing, he told the people to bear witness that he was about to suffer in a just cause, and exhorted them to believe that there was no other rock than Jesus Christ to build upon. A priest named Boyes, then desired the mayor to silence him. After praying, he went meekly to the stake, and being bound with a chain, and placed in a pitch barrel, fire was applied to the reeds and wood; but the wind drove the fire directly to his back, which caused him under the severe agony to pray the more fervently. His friends directed the executioner to fire the pile to windward of his face, which was immediately done.

A quantity of books were now thrown into the fire, one of which (the Communion Service) he caught, opened it, and joyfully continued to read it, until the fire and smoke deprived him of sight; then even, in earnest prayer, he pressed the book to his heart, thanking God for bestowing on him in his last moments this precious gift.

The day being hot, the fire burnt fiercely; and at a time when the spectators supposed he was no more, he suddenly exclaimed, "Lord Jesus, receive my spirit," and meekly resigned his life. He was burnt on Jesus Green, not far from Jesus College. He had gunpowder given him, but he was dead before it became ignited. This pious sufferer afforded a singular spectacle; for his flesh was so burnt from the bones, which continued erect, that he presented the idea of a skeleton figure chained to the stake. His remains were eagerly seized by the multitude, and venerated by all who admired his piety or detested inhuman bigotry.

Simon Miller and Elizabeth Cooper

In the following month of July, received the crown of martyrdom. Miller dwelt at Lynn, and came to Norwich, where, planting himself at the door of one of the churches, as the people came out, he requested to know of them where he could go to receive the Communion. For this a priest brought him before Dr. Dunning, who committed him to ward; but he was suffered to go home, and arrange his affairs; after which he returned to the bishop's house, and to his prison, where he remained until the thirteenth of July, the day of his burning.

Elizabeth Cooper, wife of a pewterer, of St. Andrews, Norwich, had recanted; but tortured for what she had done by the worm which dieth not, she shortly after voluntarily entered her parish church during the time of the popish service, and standing up, audibly proclaimed that she revoked her former recantation, and cautioned the people to avoid her unworthy example. She was taken from her own house by Mr. Sutton the sheriff, who very reluctantly complied with the letter of the law, as they had been servants and in friendship together. At the stake, the poor sufferer, feeling the fire, uttered the cry of "Oh!" upon which Mr. Miller, putting his hand behind him towards her, desired her to be of a good courage, "for (said he) good sister, we shall have a joyful and a sweet supper." Encouraged by this example and exhortation, she stood the fiery ordeal without flinching, and, with him, proved the power of faith over the flesh.

Executions at Colchester

It was before mentioned that twenty-two persons had been sent up from Colchester, who upon a slight submission, were afterward released. Of these, William Munt, of Much Bentley, husbandman, with Alice, his wife, and Rose Allin, her daughter, upon their return home, abstained from church, which induced the bigoted priest secretly to write to Bonner. For a short time they absconded, but returning again, March 7, one Edmund Tyrrel, (a relation of the Tyrrel who murdered King Edward V and his brother) with the officers, entered the house while Munt and his wife were in bed, and informed them that they must go to Colchester Castle. Mrs. Munt at that time being very ill, requested her daughter to get her some drink; leave being permitted, Rose took a candle and a mug; and in returning through the house was met by Tyrrel, who cautioned her to advise her parents to become good Catholics. Rose briefly informed him that they had the Holy Ghost for their adviser; and that she was ready to lay down her own life for the same cause. Turning to his company, he remarked that she was willing to burn; and one of them told him to prove her, and see what she would do by and by. The unfeeling wretch immediately executed this project; and, seizing the young woman by the wrist, he held the lighted candle under her hand, burning it crosswise on the back, until the tendons divided from the flesh, during which he loaded her with many opprobrious epithets. She endured his rage unmoved, and then, when he had ceased the torture, she asked him to begin at her feet or head, for he need not fear that his employer would one day repay him. After this she took the drink to her mother.

This cruel act of torture does not stand alone on record. Bonner had served a poor blind harper in nearly the same manner, who had steadily maintained a hope that if every joint of him were to be burnt, he should not fly from the faith. Bonner, upon this, privately made a signal to his men, to bring a burning coal, which they placed in the poor man's hand, and then by force held it closed, until it burnt into the flesh deeply.

George Eagles, tailor, was indicted for having prayed that 'God would turn Queen Mary's heart, or take her away'; the ostensible cause of his death was his religion, for treason could hardly be imagined in praying for the reformation of such an execrable soul as that of Mary. Being condemned for this crime, he was drawn to the place of execution upon a sledge, with two robbers, who were executed with him. After Eagles had mounted the ladder, and been turned off a short time, he was cut down before he was at all insensible; a bailiff, named William Swallow, then dragged him to the sledge, and with a common blunt cleaver, hacked off the head; in a manner equally clumsy and cruel, he opened his body and tore out the heart.

In all this suffering the poor martyr repined not, but to the last called upon his Savior. The fury of these bigots did not end here; the intestines were burnt, and the body was quartered, the four parts being sent to Colchester, Harwich, Chelmsford, and St. Rouse's. Chelmsford had the honor of retaining his head, which was affixed to a long pole in the market place. In time it was blown down, and lay several days in the street, until it was buried at night in the churchyard. God's judgment not long after fell upon Swallow, who in his old age became a beggar, and who was affected with a leprosy that made him obnoxious even to the animal creation; nor did Richard Potts, who troubled Eagles in his dying moments, escape the visiting hand of God.

Mrs. Joyce Lewes

This lady was the wife of Mr. T. Lewes, of Manchester. She had received the Romish religion as true, until the burning of that pious martyr, Mr. Saunders, at Coventry. Understanding that his death arose from a refusal to receive the Mass, she began to inquire into the ground of his refusal, and her conscience, as it began to be enlightened, became restless and alarmed. In this inquietude, she resorted to Mr. John Glover, who lived near, and requested that he would unfold those rich sources of Gospel knowledge he possessed, particularly upon the subject of transubstantiation. He easily succeeded in convincing her that the mummery of popery and the Mass were at variance with God's most holy Word, and honestly reproved her for following too much the vanities of a wicked world. It was to her indeed a word in season, for she soon became weary of her former sinful life and resolved to abandon the Mass and idolatrous worship. Though compelled by her husband's violence to go to church, her contempt of the holy water and other ceremonies was so manifest, that she was accused before the bishop for despising the sacramentals.

A citation, addressed to her, immediately followed, which was given to Mr. Lewes, who, in a fit of passion, held a dagger to the throat of the officer, and made him eat it, after which he caused him to drink it down, and then sent him away. But for this the bishop summoned Mr. Lewes before him as well as his wife; the former readily submitted, but the latter resolutely affirmed, that, in refusing holy water, she neither offended God, nor any part of his laws. She was sent home for a month, her husband being bound for her appearance, during which time Mr. Glover impressed upon her the necessity of doing what she did, not from self-vanity, but for the honor and glory of God.

Mr. Glover and others earnestly exhorted Lewes to forfeit the money he was bound in, rather than subject his wife to certain death; but he was deaf to the voice of humanity, and delivered her over to the bishop, who soon found sufficient cause to consign her to a loathsome prison, whence she was several times brought for examination. At the last time the bishop reasoned with her upon the fitness of her coming to Mass, and receiving as sacred the Sacrament and sacramentals of the Holy Ghost. "If these things were in the Word of God," said Mrs. Lewes, "I would with all my heart receive, believe, and esteem them." The bishop, with the most ignorant and impious effrontery, replied, "If thou wilt believe no more than what is warranted by Scriptures, thou art in a state of damnation!" Astonished at such a declaration, this worthy sufferer ably rejoined that his words were as impure as they were profane.

After condemnation, she lay a twelvemonth in prison, the sheriff not being willing to put her to death in his time, though he had been but just chosen. When her death warrant came from London, she sent for some friends, whom she consulted in what manner her death might be more glorious to the name of God, and injurious to the cause of God's enemies. Smilingly, she said: "As for death, I think but lightly of. When I know that I shall behold the amiable countenance of Christ my dear Savior, the ugly face of death does not much trouble me." The evening before she suffered, two priests were anxious to visit her, but she refused both their confession and absolution, when she could hold a better communication with the High Priest of souls. About three o'clock in the morning, Satan began to shoot his fiery darts, by putting into her mind to doubt whether she was chosen to eternal life, and Christ died for her. Her friends readily pointed out to her those consolatory passages of Scripture which comfort the fainting heart, and treat of the Redeemer who taketh away the sins of the world.

About eight o'clock the sheriff announced to her that she had but an hour to live; she was at first cast down, but this soon passed away, and she thanked God that her life was about to be devoted to His service. The sheriff granted permission for two friends to accompany her to the stake—an indulgence for which he was afterward severely handled. Mr. Reniger and Mr. Bernher led her to the place of execution; in going to which, from its distance, her great weakness, and the press of the people, she had nearly fainted. Three times she prayed fervently that God would deliver the land from popery and the idolatrous Mass; and the people for the most part, as well as the sheriff, said Amen.

When she had prayed, she took the cup, (which had been filled with water to refresh her,) and said, "I drink to all them that unfeignedly love the Gospel of Christ, and wish for the abolition of popery." Her friends, and a great many women of the place, drank with her, for which most of them afterward were enjoined penance.

When chained to the stake, her countenance was cheerful, and the roses of her cheeks were not abated. Her hands were extended towards heaven until the fire rendered them powerless, when her soul was received into the arms of the Creator. The duration of her agony was but short, as the under-sheriff, at the request of her friends, had prepared such excellent fuel that she was in a few minutes overwhelmed with smoke and flame. The case of this lady drew a tear of pity from everyone who had a heart not callous to humanity.

Executions at Islington

About the seventeenth of September, suffered at Islington the following four professors of Christ: Ralph Allerton, James Austoo, Margery Austoo, and Richard Roth.

James Austoo and his wife, of St. Allhallows, Barking, London, were sentenced for not believing in the presence. Richard Roth rejected the seven Sacraments, and was accused of comforting the heretics by the following letter written in his own blood, and intended to have been sent to his friends at Colchester:

"O dear Brethren and Sisters,

"How much reason have you to rejoice in God, that He hath given you such faith to overcome this bloodthirsty tyrant thus far! And no doubt He that hath begun that good work in you, will fulfil it unto the end. O dear hearts in Christ, what a crown of glory shall ye receive with Christ in the kingdom of God! O that it had been the good will of God that I had been ready to have gone with you; for I lie in my lord's Little-ease by day, and in the night I lie in the Coalhouse, apart from Ralph Allerton, or any other; and we look every day when we shall be condemned; for he said that I should be burned within ten days before Easter; but I lie still at the pool's brink, and every man goeth in before me; but we abide patiently the Lord's leisure, with many bonds, in fetters and stocks, by which we have received great joy of God. And now fare you well, dear brethren and sisters, in this world, but I trust to see you in the heavens face to face.

"O brother Munt, with your wife and my sister Rose, how blessed are you in the Lord, that God hath found you worthy to suffer for His sake! with all the rest of my dear brethren and sisters known and unknown. O be joyful even unto death. Fear it not, saith Christ, for I have overcome death. O dear heart, seeing that Jesus Christ will be our help, O tarry you the Lord's leisure. Be strong, let your hearts be of good comfort, and wait you still for the Lord. He is at hand. Yea, the angel of the Lord pitcheth his tent round about them that fear him, and delivereth them which way he seeth best. For our lives are in the Lord's hands; and they can do nothing unto us before God suffer them. Therefore give all thanks to God.

"O dear hearts, you shall be clothed in long white garments upon the mount of Sion, with the multitude of saints, and with Jesus Christ our Savior, who will never forsake us. O blessed virgins, ye have played the wise virgins' part, in that ye have taken oil in your lamps that ye may go in with the Bridegroom, when he cometh, into the everlasting joy with Him. But as for the foolish, they shall be shut out, because they made not themselves ready to suffer with Christ, neither go about to take up His cross. O dear hearts, how precious shall your death be in the sight of the Lord! for dear is the death of His saints. O fare you well, and pray. The grace of our Lord Jesus Christ be with you all. Amen, Amen. Pray, pray, pray!

"Written by me, with my own blood,
"RICHARD ROTH."

This letter, so justly denominating Bonner the "bloodthirsty tyrant," was not likely to excite his compassion. Roth accused him of bringing them to secret examination by night, because he was afraid of the people by day. Resisting every temptation to recant, he was condemned, and on September 17, 1557, these four martyrs perished at Islington, for the testimony of the Lamb, who was slain that they might be of the redeemed of God.

John Noyes, a shoemaker, of Laxfield, Suffolk, was taken to Eye, and at midnight, September 21, 1557, he was brought from Eye to Laxfield to be burned. On the following morning he was led to the stake, prepared for the horrid sacrifice. Mr. Noyes, on coming to the fatal spot, knelt down, prayed, and rehearsed the Fiftieth Psalm. When the chain enveloped him, he said, "Fear not them that kill the body, but fear him that can kill both body and soul, and cast it into everlasting fire!" As one Cadman placed a fagot against him, he blessed the hour in which he was born to die for the truth; and while trusting only upon the all-sufficient merits of the Redeemer, fire was set to the pile, and the blazing fagots in a short time stifled his last words, "Lord, have mercy on me! Christ, have mercy upon me!" The ashes of the body were buried in a pit, and with them one of his feet, whole to the ankle, with the stocking on.

Mrs. Cicely Ormes

This young martyr, aged twenty-two, was the wife of Mr. Edmund Ormes, worsted weaver of St. Lawrence, Norwich. At the death of Miller and Elizabeth Cooper, before mentioned, she had said that she would pledge them of the same cup they drank of. For these words she was brought to the chancellor, who would have discharged her upon promising to go to church, and to keep her belief to herself. As she would not consent to this, the chancellor urged that he had shown more lenity to her than any other person, and was unwilling to condemn her, because she was an ignorant foolish woman; to this she replied, (perhaps with more shrewdness than he expected,) that however great his desire might be to spare her sinful flesh, it could not equal her inclination to surrender it up in so great a quarrel. The chancellor then pronounced the fiery sentence, and September 23, 1557, she was brought to the stake, at eight o'clock in the morning.

After declaring her faith to the people, she laid her hand on the stake, and said, "Welcome, thou cross of Christ." Her hand was sooted in doing this, (for it was the same stake at which Miller and Cooper were burnt,) and she at first wiped it; but directly after again welcomed and embraced it as the "sweet cross of Christ." After the tormentors had kindled the fire, she said, "My soul doth magnify the Lord, and my spirit doth rejoice in God my Savior." Then crossing her hands upon her breast, and looking upwards with the utmost serenity, she stood the fiery furnace. Her hands continued gradually to rise until the sinews were dried, and then they fell. She uttered no sigh of pain, but yielded her life, an emblem of that celestial paradise in which is the presence of God, blessed forever.

It might be contended that this martyr voluntarily sought her own death, as the chancellor scarcely exacted any other penance of her than to keep her belief to herself; yet it should seem in this instance as if God had chosen her to be a shining light, for a twelvemonth before she was taken, she had recanted; but she was wretched until the chancellor was informed, by letter, that she repented of her recantation from the bottom of her heart. As if to compensate for her former apostasy, and to convince the Catholics that she meant no more to compromise for her personal security, she boldly refused his friendly offer of permitting her to temporize. Her courage in such a cause deserves commendation—the cause of Him who has said, "Whoever is ashamed of me on earth, of such will I be ashamed in heaven."

Rev. John Rough

This pious martyr was a Scotchman. At the age of seventeen, he entered himself as one of the order of Black Friars, at Stirling, in Scotland. He had been kept out of an inheritance by his friends, and he took this step in revenge for their conduct to him. After being there sixteen years, Lord Hamilton, earl of Arran, taking a liking to him, the archbishop of St. Andrew's induced the provincial of the house to dispense with his habit and order; and he thus became the earl's chaplain. He remained in this spiritual employment a year, and in that time God wrought in him a saving knowledge of the truth; for which reason the earl sent him to preach in the freedom of Ayr, where he remained four years; but finding danger there from the religious complexion of the times, and learning that there was much Gospel freedom in England, he travelled up to the duke of Somerset, then Lord Protector of England, who gave him a yearly salary of twenty pounds, and authorized him, to preach at Carlisle, Berwick, and Newcastle, where he married. He was afterward removed to a benefice at Hull, in which he remained until the death of Edward VI.

In consequence of the tide of persecution then setting in, he fled with his wife to Friesland, and at Nordon they followed the occupation of knitting hose, caps, etc., for subsistence. Impeded in his business by the want of yarn, he came over to England to procure a quantity, and on November 10, arrived in London, where he soon heard of a secret society of the faithful, to whom he joined himself, and was in a short time elected their minister, in which occupation he strengthened them in every good resolution.

On December 12, through the information of one Taylor, a member of the society, Mr. Rough, with Cuthbert Symson and others, was taken up in the Saracen's Head, Islington, where, under the pretext of coming to see a play, their religious exercises were holden. The queen's vice-chamberlain conducted Rough and Symson before the Council, in whose presence they were charged with meeting to celebrate the Communion. The Council wrote to Bonner and he lost no time in this affair of blood. In three days he had him up, and on the next (the twentieth) resolved to condemn him. The charges laid against him were, that he, being a priest, was married, and that he had rejected the service in the Latin tongue. Rough wanted not arguments to reply to these flimsy tenets. In short, he was degraded and condemned.

Mr. Rough, it should be noticed, when in the north, in Edward VI's reign, had saved Dr. Watson's life, who afterward sat with Bishop Bonner on the bench. This ungrateful prelate, in return for the kind act he had received, boldly accused Mr. Rough of being the most pernicious heretic in the country. The godly minister reproved him for his malicious spirit; he affirmed that, during the thirty years he had lived, he had never bowed the knee to Baal; and that twice at Rome he had seen the pope born about on men's shoulders with the false-named Sacrament carried before him, presenting a true picture of the very Antichrist; yet was more reverence shown to him than to the wafer, which they accounted to be their God. "Ah?" said Bonner, rising, and making towards him, as if he would have torn his garment, "Hast thou been at Rome, and seen our holy father the pope, and dost thou blaspheme him after this sort?" This said, he fell upon him, tore off a piece of his beard, and that the day might begin to his own satisfaction, he ordered the object of his rage to be burnt by half-past five the following morning.

Cuthbert Symson

Few professors of Christ possessed more activity and zeal than this excellent person. He not only labored to preserve his friends from the contagion of popery, but he labored to guard them against the terrors of persecution. He was deacon of the little congregation over which Mr. Rough presided as minister.

Mr. Symson has written an account of his own sufferings, which he cannot detail better than in his own words:

"On the thirteenth of December, 1557, I was committed by the Council to the Tower of London. On the following Thursday, I was called into the ward-room, before the constable of the Tower, and the recorder of London, Mr. Cholmly, who commanded me to inform them of the names of those who came to the English service. I answered that I would declare nothing; in consequence of my refusal, I was set upon a rack of iron, as I judge for the space of three hours!

"They then asked me if I would confess: I answered as before. After being unbound, I was carried back to my lodging. The Sunday after I was brought to the same place again, before the lieutenant and recorder of London, and they examined me. As I had answered before, so I answered now. Then the lieutenant swore by God I should tell; after which my two forefingers were bound together, and a small arrow placed between them, they drew it through so fast that the blood followed, and the arrow brake.

"After enduring the rack twice again, I was retaken to my lodging, and ten days after the lieutenant asked me if I would not now confess that which they had before asked of me. I answered, that I had already said as much as I would. Three weeks after I was sent to the priest, where I was greatly assaulted, and at whose hand I received the pope's curse, for bearing witness of the resurrection of Christ. And thus I commend you to God, and to the Word of His grace, with all those who unfeignedly call upon the name of Jesus; desiring God of His endless mercy, through the merits of His dear Son Jesus Christ, to bring us all to His everlasting Kingdom, Amen. I praise God for His great mercy shown upon us. Sing Hosanna to the Highest with me, Cuthbert Symson. God forgive my sins! I ask forgiveness of all the world, and I forgive all the world, and thus I leave the world, in the hope of a joyful resurrection!"

If this account be duly considered, what a picture of repeated tortures does it present! But even the cruelty of the narration is exceeded by the patient meekness with which it was endured. Here are no expressions of malice, no invocations even of God's retributive justice, not a complaint of suffering wrongfully! On the contrary, praise to God, forgiveness of sin, and a forgiving all the world, concludes this unaffected interesting narrative.

Bonner's admiration was excited by the steadfast coolness of this martyr. Speaking of Mr. Symson in the consistory, he said, "You see what a personable man he is, and then of his patience, I affirm, that, if he were not a heretic, he is a man of the greatest patience that ever came before me. Thrice in one day has he been racked in the Tower; in my house also he has felt sorrow, and yet never have I seen his patience broken."

The day before this pious deacon was to be condemned, while in the stocks in the bishop's coal-house, he had the vision of a glorified form, which much encouraged him. This he certainly attested to his wife, to Mr. Austen, and others, before his death.

With this ornament of the Christian Reformation were apprehended Mr. Hugh Foxe and John Devinish; the three were brought before Bonner, March 19, 1558, and the papistical articles tendered. They rejected them, and were all condemned. As they worshipped together in the same society, at Islington, so they suffered together in Smithfield, March 28; in whose death the God of Grace was glorified, and true believers confirmed!

Thomas Hudson, Thomas Carman, and William Seamen

Were condemned by a bigoted vicar of Aylesbury, named Berry. The spot of execution was called Lollard's Pit, without Bishopsgate, at Norwich. After joining together in humble petition to the throne of grace, they rose, went to the stake, and were encircled with their chains. To the great surprise of the spectators, Hudson slipped from under his chains, and came forward. A great opinion prevailed that he was about to recant; others thought that he wanted further time. In the meantime, his companions at the stake urged every promise and exhortation to support him. The hopes of the enemies of the cross, however, were disappointed: the good man, far from fearing the smallest personal terror at the approaching pangs of death, was only alarmed that his Savior's face seemed to be hidden from him. Falling upon his knees, his spirit wrestled with God, and God verified the words of His Son, "Ask, and it shall be given." The martyr rose in an ecstasy of joy, and exclaimed, "Now, I thank God, I am strong! and care not what man can do to me!" With an unruffled countenance he replaced himself under the chain, joined his fellow-sufferers, and with them suffered death, to the comfort of the godly, and the confusion of Antichrist.

Berry, unsatiated with this demoniacal act, summoned up two hundred persons in the town of Aylesham, whom he compelled to kneel to the cross at Pentecost, and inflicted other punishments. He struck a poor man for a trifling word, with a flail, which proved fatal to the unoffending object. He also gave a woman named Alice Oxes, so heavy a blow with his fist, as she met him entering the hall when he was in an ill-humor, that she died with the violence. This priest was rich, and possessed great authority; he was a reprobate, and, like the priesthood, he abstained from marriage, to enjoy the more a debauched and licentious life. The Sunday after the death of Queen Mary, he was revelling with one of his concubines, before vespers; he then went to church, administered baptism, and in his return to his lascivious pastime, he was smitten by the hand of God. Without a moment given for repentance, he fell to the ground, and a groan was the only articulation permitted him. In him we may behold the difference between the end of a martyr and a persecutor.

The Story of Roger Holland

In a retired close near a field, in Islington, a company of decent persons had assembled, to the number of forty. While they were religiously engaged in praying and expounding the Scripture, twenty-seven of them were carried before Sir Roger Cholmly. Some of the women made their escape, twenty-two were committed to Newgate, who continued in prison seven weeks. Previous to their examination, they were informed by the keeper, Alexander, that nothing more was requisite to procure their discharge, than to hear Mass. Easy as this condition may seem, these martyrs valued their purity of conscience more than loss of life or property; hence, thirteen were burnt, seven in Smithfield, and six at Brentford; two died in prison, and the other seven were providentially preserved. The names of the seven who suffered were, H. Pond, R. Estland, R. Southain, M. Ricarby, J. Floyd, J. Holiday, and Roger Holland. They were sent to Newgate, June 16, 1558, and executed on the twenty-seventh.

This Roger Holland, a merchant-tailor of London, was first an apprentice with one Master Kempton, at the Black Boy in Watling Street, giving himself to dancing, fencing, gaming, banqueting, and wanton company. He had received for his master certain money, to the sum of thirty pounds; and lost every groat at dice. Therefore he purposed to convey himself away beyond the seas, either into France or into Flanders.

With this resolution, he called early in the morning on a discreet servant in the house, named Elizabeth, who professed the Gospel, and lived a life that did honor to her profession. To her he revealed the loss his folly had occasioned, regretted that he had not followed her advice, and begged her to give his master a note of hand from him acknowledging the debt, which he would repay if ever it were in his power; he also entreated his disgraceful conduct might be kept secret, lest it would bring the gray hairs to his father with sorrow to a premature grave.

The maid, with a generosity and Christian principle rarely surpassed, conscious that his imprudence might be his ruin, brought him the thirty pounds, which was part of a sum of money recently left her by legacy. "Here," said she, "is the sum requisite: you shall take the money, and I will keep the note; but expressly on this condition, that you abandon all lewd and vicious company; that you neither swear nor talk immodestly, and game no more; for, should I learn that you do, I will immediately show this note to your master. I also require, that you shall promise me to attend the daily lecture at Allhallows, and the sermon at St. Paul's every Sunday; that you cast away all your books of popery, and in their place substitute the Testament and the Book of Service, and that you read the Scriptures with reverence and fear. calling upon God for his grace to direct you in his truth. Pray also fervently to God, to pardon your former offences, and not to remember the sins of your youth, and would you obtain his favor ever dread to break his laws or offend his majesty. So shall God have you in His keeping, and grant you your heart's desire." We must honor the memory of this excellent domestic, whose pious endeavors were equally directed to benefit the thoughtless youth in this life and that which is to come. God did not suffer the wish of this excellent domestic to be thrown upon a barren soil; within half a year after the licentious Holland became a zealous professor of the Gospel, and was an instrument of conversion to his father and others whom he visited in Lancashire, to their spiritual comfort and reformation from popery.

His father, pleased with his change of conduct, gave him forty pounds to commence business with in London.

Then Roger repaired to London again, and came to the maid that lent him the money to pay his master withal, and said unto her, "Elizabeth, here is thy money I borrowed of thee; and for the friendship, good will, and the good counsel I have received at thy hands, to recompense thee I am not able, otherwise than to make thee my wife." And soon after they were married, which was in the first year of Queen Mary.

After this he remained in the congregations of the faithful, until, the last year of Queen Mary, he, with the six others aforesaid, were taken.

And after Roger Holland there was none suffered in Smithfield for the testimony of the Gospel, God be thanked.

Flagellations by Bonner

When this Catholic hyena found that neither persuasions, threats, nor imprisonment, could produce any alteration in the mind of a youth named Thomas Hinshaw, he sent him to Fulham, and during the first night set him in the stocks, with no other allowance than bread and water. The following morning he came to see if this punishment had worked any change in his mind, and finding none, he sent Dr. Harpsfield, his archdeacon, to converse with him. The doctor was soon out of humor at his replies, called him peevish boy, and asked him if he thought he went about to damn his soul? "I am persuaded," said Thomas, "that you labor to promote the dark kingdom of the devil, not for the love of the truth." These words the doctor conveyed to the bishop, who, in a passion that almost prevented articulation, came to Thomas, and said, "Dost thou answer my archdeacon thus, thou naughty boy? But I'll soon handle thee well enough for it, be assured!" Two willow twigs were then brought him, and causing the unresisting youth to kneel against a long bench, in an arbor in his garden, he scourged him until he was compelled to cease for want of breath and fatigue. One of the rods was worn quite away.

Many other conflicts did Hinshaw undergo from the bishop; who, at length, to remove him effectually, procured false witnesses to lay articles against him, all of which the young man denied, and, in short, refused to answer any interrogatories administered to him. A fortnight after this, the young man was attacked by a burning ague, and at the request of his master, Mr. Pugson, of St. Paul's church-yard, he was removed, the bishop not doubting that he had given him his death in the natural way; he however remained ill above a year, and in the mean time Queen Mary died, by which act of providence he escaped Bonner's rage.

John Willes was another faithful person, on whom the scourging hand of Bonner fell. He was the brother of Richard Willes, before mentioned, burnt at Brentford. Hinshaw and Willes were confined in Bonner's coal house together, and afterward removed to Fulham, where he and Hinshaw remained during eight or ten days, in the stocks. Bonner's persecuting spirit betrayed itself in his treatment of Willes during his examinations, often striking him on the head with a stick, seizing him by the ears, and filliping him under the chin, saying he held down his head like a thief. This producing no signs of recantation, he took him into his orchard, and in a small arbor there he flogged him first with a willow rod, and then with birch, until he was exhausted. This cruel ferocity arose from the answer of the poor sufferer, who, upon being asked how long it was since he had crept to the cross, replied, 'Not since he had come to years of discretion, nor would he, though he should be torn to pieces by wild horses.' Bonner then bade him make the sign of the cross on his forehead, which he refused to do, and thus was led to the orchard.

One day, when in the stocks, Bonner asked him how he liked his lodging and fare. "Well enough," said Willes, "might I have a little straw to sit or lie upon." Just at this time came in Willes' wife, then largely pregnant, and entreated the bishop for her husband, boldly declaring that she would be delivered in the house, if he were not suffered to go with her. To get rid of the good wife's importunity, and the trouble of a lying-in woman in his palace, he bade Willes make the sign of the cross, and say, *In nomine Patris, et Filii, et Spiritus Sancti,* Amen. Willes omitted the sign, and repeated the words, "in the name of the Father, and of the Son, and of the Holy Ghost, Amen." Bonner would have the words repeated in Latin, to which Willes made no objection, knowing the meaning of the words. He was then permitted to go home with his wife, his kinsman Robert Rouze being charged to bring him to St. Paul's the next day, whither he himself went, and subscribing to a Latin instrument of little importance, was liberated.   This is the last of the twenty-two taken at Islington.

Rev. Richard Yeoman

This devout aged person was curate to Dr. Taylor, at Hadley, and eminently qualified for his sacred function. Dr. Taylor left him the curacy at his departure, but no sooner had Mr. Newall gotten the benefice, than he removed Mr. Yeoman, and substituted a Romish priest. After this he wandered from place to place, exhorting all men to stand faithfully to God's Word, earnestly to give themselves unto prayer, with patience to bear the cross now laid upon them for their trial, with boldness to confess the truth before their adversaries, and with an undoubted hope to wait for the crown and reward of eternal felicity. But when he perceived his adversaries lay wait for him, he went into Kent, and with a little packet of laces, pins, points, etc., he travelled from village to village, selling such things, and in this manner subsisted himself, his wife, and children.

At last Justice Moile, of Kent, took Mr. Yeoman, and set him in the stocks a day and a night; but, having no evident matter to charge him with, he let him go again. Coming secretly again to Hadley, he tarried with his poor wife, who kept him privately, in a chamber of the town house, commonly called the Guildhall, more than a year. During this time the good old father abode in a chamber locked up all the day, spending his time in devout prayer, in reading the Scriptures, and in carding the wool which his wife spun. His wife also begged bread for herself and her children, by which precarious means they supported themselves. Thus the saints of God sustained hunger and misery, while the prophets of Baal lived in festivity, and were costily pampered at Jezebel's table.

Information being at length given to Newall, that Yeoman was secreted by his wife, he came, attended by the constables, and broke into the room where the object of his search lay in bed with his wife. He reproached the poor woman with being a whore, and would have indecently pulled the clothes off, but Yeoman resisted both this act of violence and the attack upon his wife's character, adding that he defied the pope and popery. He was then taken out, and set in stocks until day.

In the cage also with him was an old man, named John Dale, who had sat there three or four days, for exhorting the people during the time service was performing by Newall and his curate. His words were, "O miserable and blind guides, will ye ever be blind leaders of the blind? Will ye never amend? Will ye never see the truth of God's Word? Will neither God's threats nor promises enter into your hearts? Will the blood of the martyrs nothing mollify your stony stomachs? O obdurate, hard-hearted, perverse, and crooked generation! to whom nothing can do good."

These words he spake in fervency of spirit against the superstitious religion of Rome; wherefore Newall caused him forthwith to be attached, and set in the stocks in a cage, where he was kept until Sir Henry Doile, a justice, came to Hadley.

When Yeoman was taken, the parson called earnestly upon Sir Henry Doile to send them both to prison. Sir Henry Doile as earnestly entreated the parson to consider the age of the men, and their mean condition; they were neither persons of note nor preachers; wherefore he proposed to let them be punished a day or two and to dismiss them, at least John Dale, who was no priest, and therefore, as he had so long sat in the cage, he thought it punishment enough for this time. When the parson heard this, he was exceedingly mad, and in a great rage called them pestilent heretics, unfit to live in the commonwealth of Christians.

Sir Henry, fearing to appear too merciful, Yeoman and Dale were pinioned, bound like thieves with their legs under the horses' bellies, and carried to Bury jail, where they were laid in irons; and because they continually rebuked popery, they were carried into the lowest dungeon, where John Dale, through the jail-sickness and evil-keeping, died soon after: his body was thrown out, and buried in the fields. He was a man of sixty-six years of age, a weaver by occupation, well learned in the holy Scriptures, steadfast in his confession of the true doctrines of Christ as set forth in King Edward's time; for which he joyfully suffered prison and chains, and from this worldly dungeon he departed in Christ to eternal glory, and the blessed paradise of everlasting felicity.

After Dale's death, Yeoman was removed to Norwich prison, where, after strait and evil keeping, he was examined upon his faith and religion, and required to submit himself to his holy father the pope. "I defy him, (quoth he), and all his detestable abomination: I will in no wise have to do with him." The chief articles objected to him, were his marriage and the Mass sacrifice. Finding he continued steadfast in the truth, he was condemned, degraded, and not only burnt, but most cruelly tormented in the fire. Thus he ended this poor and miserable life, and entered into that blessed bosom of Abraham, enjoying with Lazarus that rest which God has prepared for His elect.

Thomas Benbridge

Mr. Benbridge was a single gentleman, in the diocese of Winchester. He might have lived a gentleman's life, in the wealthy possessions of this world; but he chose rather to enter through the strait gate of persecution to the heavenly possession of life in the Lord's Kingdom, than to enjoy present pleasure with disquietude of conscience. Manfully standing against the papists for the defence of the sincere doctrine of Christ's Gospel, he was apprehended as an adversary to the Romish religion, and led for examination before the bishop of Winchester, where he underwent several conflicts for the truth against the bishop and his colleague; for which he was condemned, and some time after brought to the place of martyrdom by Sir Richard Pecksal, sheriff.

When standing at the stake he began to untie his points, and to prepare himself; then he gave his gown to the keeper, by way of fee. His jerkin was trimmed with gold lace, which he gave to Sir Richard Pecksal, the high sheriff. His cap of velvet he took from his head, and threw away. Then, lifting his mind to the Lord, he engaged in prayer.

When fastened to the stake, Dr. Seaton begged him to recant, and he should have his pardon; but when he saw that nothing availed, he told the people not to pray for him unless he would recant, no more than they would pray for a dog.

Mr. Benbridge, standing at the stake with his hands together in such a manner as the priest holds his hands in his *Memento,* Dr. Seaton came to him again, and exhorted him to recant, to whom he said, "Away, Babylon, away!" One that stood by said, "Sir, cut his tongue out"; another, a temporal man, railed at him worse than Dr. Seaton had done.

When they saw he would not yield, they bade the tormentors to light the pile, before he was in any way covered with fagots. The fire first took away a piece of his beard, at which he did not shrink. Then it came on the other side and took his legs, and the nether stockings of his hose being leather, they made the fire pierce the sharper, so that the intolerable heat made him exclaim, "I recant!" and suddenly he thrust the fire from him. Two or three of his friends being by, wished to save him; they stepped to the fire to help remove it, for which kindness they were sent to jail. The sheriff also of his own authority took him from the stake, and remitted him to prison, for which he was sent to the Fleet, and lay there sometime. Before, however, he was taken from the stake, Dr. Seaton wrote articles for him to subscribe to. To these Mr. Benbridge made so many objections that Dr. Seaton ordered them to set fire again to the pile. Then with much pain and grief of heart he subscribed to them upon a man's back.

This done, his gown was given him again, and he was led to prison. While there, he wrote a letter to Dr. Seaton, recanting those words he had spoken at the stake, and the articles which he had subscribed, for he was grieved that he had ever signed them. The same day se'night he was again brought to the stake, where the vile tormentors rather broiled than burnt him. The Lord give his enemies repentance!

Mrs. Prest

From the number condemned in this fanatical reign, it is almost impossible to obtain the name of every martyr, or to embellish the history of all with anecdotes and exemplifications of Christian conduct. Thanks be to Providence, our cruel task begins to draw towards a conclusion, with the end of the reign of papal terror and bloodshed. Monarchs, who sit upon thrones possessed by hereditary right, should, of all others, consider that the laws of nature are the laws of God, and hence that the first law of nature is the preservation of their subjects. Maxims of persecutions, of torture, and of death, they should leave to those who have effected sovereignty by fraud or by sword; but where, except among a few miscreant emperors of Rome, and the Roman pontiffs, shall we find one whose memory is so "damned to everlasting fame" as that of Queen Mary? Nations bewail the hour which separates them forever from a beloved governor, but, with respect to that of Mary, it was the most blessed time of her whole reign. Heaven has ordained three great scourges for national sins—plague, pestilence, and famine. It was the will of God in Mary's reign to bring a fourth upon this kingdom, under the form of papistical persecution. It was sharp, but glorious; the fire which consumed the martyrs has undermined the popedom; and the Catholic states, at present the most bigoted and unenlightened, are those which are sunk lowest in the scale of moral dignity and political consequence. May they remain so, until the pure light of the Gospel shall dissipate the darkness of fanaticism and superstition! But to return.

Mrs. Prest for some time lived about Cornwall, where she had a husband and children, whose bigotry compelled her to frequent the abominations of the Church of Rome. Resolving to act as her conscience dictated, she quitted them, and made a living by spinning. After some time, returning home, she was accused by her neighbors, and brought to Exeter, to be examined before Dr. Troubleville, and his chancellor Blackston. As this martyr was accounted of inferior intellect, we shall put her in competition with the bishop, and let the reader judge which had the most of that knowledge conducive to everlasting life. The bishop bringing the question to issue, respecting the bread and wine being flesh and blood, Mrs. Prest said, "I will demand of you whether you can deny your creed, which says, that Christ doth perpetually sit at the right hand of His Father, both body and soul, until He come again; or whether He be there in heaven our Advocate, and to make prayer for us unto God His Father? If He be so, He is not here on earth in a piece of bread. If He be not here, and if He do not dwell in temples made with hands, but in heaven, what! shall we seek Him here? If He did not offer His body once for all, why make you a new offering? If with one offering

He made all perfect, why do you with a false offering make all imperfect? If He be to be worshipped in spirit and in truth, why do you worship a piece of bread? If He be eaten and drunken in faith and truth, if His flesh be not profitable to be among us, why do you say you make His flesh and blood, and say it is profitable for body and soul? Alas! I am a poor woman, but rather than to do as you do, I would live no longer. I have said, Sir."

Bishop. I promise you, you are a jolly Protestant. I pray you in what school have you been brought up?

Mrs. Prest. I have upon the Sundays visited the sermons, and there have I learned such things as are so fixed in my breast, that death shall not separate them.

B. O foolish woman, who will waste his breath upon thee, or such as thou art? But how chanceth it that thou wentest away from thy husband? If thou wert an honest woman, thou wouldst not have left thy husband and children, and run about the country like a fugitive.

Mrs. P. Sir, I labored for my living; and as my Master Christ counselleth me, when I was persecuted in one city, I fled into another.

B. Who persecuted thee?

Mrs. P. My husband and my children. For when I would have them to leave idolatry, and to worship God in heaven, he would not hear me, but he with his children rebuked me, and troubled me. I fled not for whoredom, nor for theft, but because I would be no partaker with him and his of that foul idol the Mass; and wheresoever I was, as oft as I could, upon Sundays and holydays. I made excuses not to go to the popish Church.

B. Belike then you are a good housewife, to fly from your husband and the Church.

Mrs. P. My housewifery is but small; but God gave me grace to go to the true Church.

B. The true Church, what dost thou mean?

Mrs. P. Not your popish Church, full of idols and abominations, but where two or three are gathered together in the name of God, to that Church will I go as long as I live.

B. Belike then you have a church of your own. Well, let this mad woman be put down to prison until we send for her husband.

Mrs. P. No, I have but one husband, who is here already in this city, and in prison with me, from whom I will never depart.

Some persons present endeavoring to convince the bishop she was not in her right senses, she was permitted to depart. The keeper of the bishop's prisons took her into his house, where she either spun worked as a servant, or walked about the city, discoursing upon the Sacrament of the altar. Her husband was sent for to take her home, but this she refused while the cause of religion could be served. She was too active to be idle, and her conversation, simple as they affected to think her, excited the attention of several Catholic priests and friars. They teased her with questions, until she answered them angrily, and this excited a laugh at her warmth.

"Nay," said she, "you have more need to weep than to laugh, and to be sorry that ever you were born, to be the chaplains of that whore of Babylon. I defy him and all his falsehood; and get you away from me, you do but trouble my conscience. You would have me follow your doings; I will first lose my life. I pray you depart."

"Why, thou foolish woman," said they, "we come to thee for thy profit and soul's health." To which she replied, "What profit ariseth by you, that teach nothing but lies for truth? how save you souls, when you preach nothing but lies, and destroy souls?"

"How provest thou that?" said they.

"Do you not destroy your souls, when you teach the people to worship idols, stocks, and stones, the works of men's hands? and to worship a false God of your own making of a piece of bread, and teach that the pope is God's vicar, and hath power to forgive sins? and that there is a purgatory, when God's Son hath by His passion purged all? and say you make God and sacrifice Him, when Christ's body was a sacrifice once for all? Do you not teach the people to number their sins in your ears, and say they will be damned if they confess not all; when God's Word saith, Who can number his sins? Do you not promise them trentals and dirges and Masses for souls, and sell your prayers for money, and make them buy pardons, and trust to such foolish inventions of your imaginations? Do you not altogether act against God? Do you not teach us to pray upon beads, and to pray unto saints, and say they can pray for us? Do you not make holy water and holy bread to fray devils? Do you not do a thousand more abominations? And yet you say, you come for my profit, and to save my soul. No, no, one hath saved me. Farewell, you with your salvation."

During the liberty granted her by the bishop, before-mentioned, she went into St. Peter's Church, and there found a skilful Dutchman, who was affixing new noses to certain fine images which had been disfigured in King Edward's time; to whom she said, "What a madman art thou, to make them new noses, which within a few days shall all lose their heads?" The Dutchman accused her and laid it hard to her charge. And she said unto him, "Thou art accursed, and so are thy images." He called her a whore. "Nay," said she, "thy images are whores, and thou art a whore-hunter; for doth not God say, 'You go a whoring after strange gods, figures of your own making? and thou art one of them.'" After this she was ordered to be confined, and had no more liberty.

During the time of her imprisonment, many visited her, some sent by the bishop, and some of their own will; among these was one Daniel, a great preacher of the Gospel, in the days of King Edward.

about Cornwall and Devonshire, but who, through the grievous persecution he had sustained, had fallen off. Earnestly did she exhort him to repent with Peter, and to be more constant in his profession.

Mrs. Walter Rauley and Mr. William and John Kede, persons of great respectability, bore ample testimony of her godly conversation, declaring, that unless God were with her, it were impossible she could have so ably defended the cause of Christ. Indeed, to sum up the character of this poor woman, she united the serpent and the dove, abounding in the highest wisdom joined to the greatest simplicity. She endured imprisonment, threatenings, taunts, and the vilest epithets, but nothing could induce her to swerve; her heart was fixed; she had cast anchor; nor could all the wounds of persecution remove her from the rock on which her hopes of felicity were built.

Such was her memory, that, without learning, she could tell in what chapter any text of Scripture was contained: on account of this singular property, one Gregory Basset, a rank papist, said she was deranged, and talked as a parrot, wild without meaning. At length, having tried every manner without effect to make her nominally a Catholic, they condemned her. After this, one exhorted her to leave her opinions, and go home to her family, as she was poor and illiterate. "True, (said she) though I am not learned, I am content to be a witness of Christ's death, and I pray you make no longer delay with me; for my heart is fixed, and I will never say otherwise, nor turn to your superstitious doing."

To the disgrace of Mr. Blackston, treasurer of the church, he would often send for this poor martyr from prison, to make sport for him and a woman whom he kept; putting religious questions to her, and turning her answers into ridicule. This done, he sent her back to her wretched dungeon, while he battened upon the good things of this world.

There was perhaps something simply ludicrous in the form of Mrs. Prest, as she was of a very short stature, thick set, and about fifty-four years of age; but her countenance was cheerful and lively, as if prepared for the day of her marriage with the Lamb. To mock at her form was an indirect accusation of her Creator, who framed her after the fashion He liked best, and gave her a mind that far excelled the transient endowments of perishable flesh. When she was offered money, she rejected it, "because (said she) I am going to a city where money bears no mastery, and while I am here God has promised to feed me."

When sentence was read, condemning her to the flames, she lifted up her voice and praised God, adding, "This day have I found that which I have long sought." When they tempted her to recant, "That will I not, (said she) God forbid that I should lose the life eternal, for this carnal and short life. I will never turn from my heavenly husband to my earthly husband; from the fellowship of angels to mortal children; and if my husband and children be faithful, then am I theirs. God is my father, God is my mother, God is my sister, my brother, my kinsman; God is my friend, most faithful."

Being delivered to the sheriff, she was led by the officer to the place of execution, without the walls of Exeter, called Sothenhey, where again the superstitious priests assaulted her. While they were tying her to the stake, she continued earnestly to exclaim "God be merciful to me, a sinner!" Patiently enduring the devouring conflagration, she was consumed to ashes, and thus ended a life which in unshaken fidelity to the cause of Christ, was not surpassed by that of any preceding martyr.

Richard Sharpe, Thomas Banion, and Thomas Hale

Mr. Sharpe, weaver, of Bristol, was brought the ninth day of March, 1556, before Dr. Dalby, chancellor of the city of Bristol, and after examination concerning the Sacrament of the altar, was persuaded to recant; and on the twenty-ninth, he was enjoined to make his recantation in the parish church. But, scarcely had he publicly avowed his backsliding, before he felt in his conscience such a tormenting fiend, that he was unable to work at his occupation; hence, shortly after, one Sunday, he came into the parish church, called Temple, and after high Mass, stood up in the choir door, and said with a loud voice, "Neighbors, bear me record that yonder idol (pointing to the altar) is the greatest and most abominable that ever was; and I am sorry that ever I denied my Lord God!" Notwithstanding the constables were ordered to apprehend him, he was suffered to go out of the church; but at night he was apprehended and carried to Newgate. Shortly after, before the chancellor, denying the Sacrament of the altar to be the body and blood of Christ, he was condemned to be burned by Mr. Dalby. He was burnt the seventh of May, 1558, and died godly, patiently, and constantly, confessing the Protestant articles of faith.

With him suffered Thomas Hale, shoemaker, of Bristol, who was condemned by Chancellor Dalby. These martyrs were bound back to back.

Thomas Banion, a weaver, was burnt on August 27, of the same year, and died for the sake of the evangelical cause of his Savior.

J. Corneford, of Wortham; C. Browne, of Maidstone; J. Herst, of Ashford; Alice Snoth, and Catharine Knight, an Aged Woman

With pleasure we have to record that these five martyrs were the last who suffered in the reign of Mary for the sake of the Protestant cause; but the malice of the papists was conspicuous in hastening their martyrdom, which might have been delayed until the event of the queen's illness was decided. It is reported that the archdeacon of Canterbury, judging that the sudden death of the queen would suspend the execution, travelled post from London, to have the satisfaction of adding another page to the black list of papistical sacrifices.

The articles against them were, as usual, the Sacramental elements and the idolatry of bending to images. They quoted St. John's words, "Beware of images!" and respecting the real presence, they urged according to St. Paul, "the things which are seen are temporal." When sentence was about to be read against them, and excommunication to take place in the regular form, John Corneford, illuminated by the Holy Spirit, awfully turned the latter proceeding against themselves, and in a solemn impressive manner, recriminated their excommunication in the following words: "In the name of our Lord Jesus Christ, the Son of the most mighty God, and by the power of His Holy Spirit, and the authority of His holy Catholic and apostolic Church, we do here give into the hands of Satan to be destroyed, the bodies of all those blasphemers and heretics that maintain any error against His most holy Word, or do condemn His most holy truth for heresy, to the maintenance of any false church or foreign religion, so that by this Thy just judgment, O most mighty God, against Thy adversaries, Thy true religion may be known to Thy great glory and our comfort and to the edifying of all our nation. Good Lord, so be it. Amen."

This sentence was openly pronounced and registered, and, as if Providence had awarded that it should not be delivered in vain, within six days after, Queen Mary died, detested by all good men and accursed of God!

Though acquainted with these circumstances, the archdeacon's implacability exceeded that of his great exemplary, Bonner, who, though he had several persons at that time under his fiery grasp, did not urge their deaths hastily, by which delay he certainly afforded them an opportunity of escape. At the queen's decease, many were in bonds: some just taken, some examined, and others condemned. The writs indeed were issued for several burnings, but by the death of the three instigators of Protestant murder—the chancellor, the bishop, and the queen, who fell nearly together, the condemned sheep were liberated, and lived many years to praise God for their happy deliverance.

These five martyrs, when at the stake, earnestly prayed that their blood might be the last shed, nor did they pray in vain. They died gloriously, and perfected the number God had selected to bear witness of the truth in this dreadful reign, whose names are recorded in the Book of Life; though last, not least among the saints made meet for immortality through the redeeming blood of the Lamb!

Catharine Finlay, alias Knight, was first converted by her son's expounding the Scriptures to her, which wrought in her a perfect work that terminated in martyrdom. Alice Snoth at the stake sent for her grandmother and godfather, and rehearsed to them the articles of her faith, and the Commandments of God, thereby convincing the world that she knew her duty. She died calling upon the spectators to bear witness that she was a Christian woman, and suffered joyfully for the testimony of Christ's Gospel.

William Fetty Scourged to Death

Among the numberless enormities committed by the merciless and unfeeling Bonner, the murder of this innocent and unoffending child may be ranged as the most horrid. His father, John Fetty, of the parish of Clerkenwell, by trade a tailor, and only twenty-four years of age, had made blessed election; he was fixed secure in eternal hope, and depended on Him who so builds His Church that the gates of hell shall not prevail against it. But alas! the very wife of his bosom, whose heart was hardened against the truth, and whose mind was influenced by the teachers of false doctrine, became his accuser. Brokenbery, a creature of the pope, and parson of the parish, received the information of this wedded Delilah, in consequence of which the poor man was apprehended. But here the awful judgment of an ever-righteous God, who is "of purer eyes than to behold evil," fell upon this stone-hearted and perfidious woman; for no sooner was the injured husband captured by her wicked contriving, than she also was suddenly seized with madness, and exhibited an awful and awakening instance of God's power to punish the evil-doer. This dreadful circumstance had some effect upon the hearts of the ungodly hunters who had eagerly grasped their prey; but, in a relenting moment, they suffered him to remain with his unworthy wife, to return her good for evil, and to comfort two children, who, on his being sent to prison, would have been left without a protector, or have become a burden to the parish. As bad men act from little motives, we may place the indulgence shown him to the latter account.

We have noticed in the former part of our narratives of the martyrs, some whose affection would have led them even to sacrifice their own lives, to preserve their husbands; but here, agreeable to Scripture language, a mother proves, indeed, a monster in nature! Neither conjugal nor maternal affection could impress the heart of this disgraceful woman.

Although our afflicted Christian had experienced so much cruelty and falsehood from the woman who was bound to him by every tie both human and divine, yet, with a mild and forbearing spirit, he overlooked her misdeeds, during her calamity endeavoring all he could to procure relief for her malady, and soothing her by every possible expression of tenderness: thus she became in a few weeks nearly restored to her senses. But, alas! she returned again to her sin, "as a dog returneth to his vomit." Malice against the saints of the Most High was seated in her heart too firmly to be removed; and as her strength returned, her inclination to work wickedness returned with it. Her heart was hardened by the prince of darkness; and to her may be applied these afflicting and soul-harrowing words, "Can the Ethiopian change his skin, or the leopard his spots? then may ye also do good, that are accustomed to do evil." Weighing this text duly with another, "I will have mercy on whom I will have mercy," how shall we presume to refine away the sovereignty of God by arraigning Jehovah at the bar of human reason, which, in religious matters, is too often opposed by infinite wisdom? "Broad is the way, that leadeth to destruction, and many there be which go in thereat. Narrow is the way, which leadeth unto life, and few there be that find it." The ways of heaven are indeed inscrutable, and it is our bounden duty to walk ever dependent on God, looking up to Him with humble confidence, and hope in His goodness, and ever confess His justice; and where we "cannot unravel, there learn to trust." This wretched woman, pursuing the horrid dictates of a heart hardened and depraved, was scarcely confirmed in her recovery, when, stifling the dictates of honor, gratitude, and every natural affection, she again accused her husband, who was once more apprehended, and taken before Sir John Mordant, knight, and one of Queen Mary's commissioners.

Upon examination, his judge finding him fixed in opinions which militated against those nursed by superstition and maintained by cruelty, he was sentenced to confinement and torture in Lollard's Tower. Here he was put into the painful stocks, and had a dish of water set by him, with a stone put into it, to what purpose God knoweth, except it were to show that he should look for little other subsistence: which is credible enough, if we consider their like practices upon divers before mentioned in this history; as, among others, upon Richard Smith, who died through their cruel imprisonment touching whom, when a godly woman came to Dr. Story to have leave she might bury him, he asked her if he had any straw or blood in his mouth; but what he means thereby, I leave to the judgment of the wise.

On the first day of the third week of our martyr's sufferings, an object presented itself to his view, which made him indeed feel his tortures with all their force, and to execrate, with bitterness only short of cursing, the author of his misery. To mark and punish the proceedings of his tormentors, remained with the Most High, who noteth even the fall of a sparrow, and in whose sacred Word it is written, "Vengeance is mine; I will repay." This object was his own son, a child of the tender age of eight years. For fifteen days, had its hapless father been suspended by his tormentor by the right arm and left leg, and sometimes by both, shifting his

positions for the purpose of giving him strength to bear and to
lengthen the date of his sufferings. When the unoffending innocent, desirous of seeing and speaking to its parent, applied to
Bonner for permission to do so, the poor child being asked by the
bishop's chaplain the purport of his errand, he replied he wished
to see his father. "Who is thy father?" said the chaplain. "John
Fetty," returned the boy, at the same time pointing to the place
where he was confined. The interrogating miscreant on this said,
"Why, thy father is a heretic!" The little champion again rejoined,
with energy sufficient to raise admiration in any breast, except that
of this unprincipled and unfeeling wretch—this miscreant, eager
to execute the behests of a remorseless queen—"My father is no
heretic: for you have Balaam's mark."

Irritated by reproach so aptly applied, the indignant and mortified
priest concealed his resentment for a moment, and took the undaunted boy into the house, where having him secure, he presented
him to others, whose baseness and cruelty being equal to his own,
they stripped him to the skin, and applied their scourges to so
violent a degree, that, fainting beneath the stripes inflicted on his
tender frame, and covered with the blood that flowed from them,
the victim of their ungodly wrath was ready to expire under his
heavy and unmerited punishment.

In this bleeding and helpless state was the suffering infant, covered only with his shirt, taken to his father by one of the actors
in the horrid tragedy, who, while he exhibited the heart-rending
spectacle, made use of the vilest taunts, and exulted in what he had
done. The dutiful child, as if recovering strength at the sight of his
father, on his knees implored his blessing. "Alas! Will," said the
afflicted parent, in trembling amazement, "who hath done this to
thee!" The artless innocent related the circumstances that led to
the merciless correction which had been so basely inflicted on him;
but when he repeated the reproof bestowed on the chaplain, and
which was prompted by an undaunted spirit, he was torn from
his weeping parent, and conveyed again to the house, where he
remained a close prisoner.

Bonner, somewhat fearful that what had been done could not
be justified even among the bloodhounds of his own voracious
pack, concluded in his dark and wicked mind, to release John Fetty,
for a time at least, from the severities he was enduring in the
glorious cause of everlasting truth! whose bright rewards are fixed
beyond the boundaries of time, within the confines of eternity;
where the arrow of the wicked cannot wound, even "where there
shall be no more sorrowing for the blessed, who, in the mansion
of eternal bliss shall glorify the Lamb forever and ever." He
was accordingly by order of Bonner, (how disgraceful to all dignity,
to say bishop!) liberated from the painful bonds, and led from

Lollard's Tower, to the chamber of that ungodly and infamous butcher, where he found the bishop bathing himself before a great fire; and at his first entering the chamber, Fetty said, "God be here and peace!" "God be here and peace, (said Bonner,) that is neither God speed nor good morrow!" "If ye kick against this peace, (said Fetty,) then this is not the place that I seek for."

A chaplain of the bishop, standing by, turned the poor man about, and thinking to abash him, said, in mocking wise, "What have we here—a player!" While Fetty was thus standing in the bishop's chamber, he espied, hanging about the bishop's bed, a pair of great black beads, whereupon he said, "My Lord, I think the hangman is not far off: for the halter (pointing to the beads) is here already!" At which words the bishop was in a marvellous rage. Then he immediately after espied also, standing in the bishop's chamber, in the window, a little crucifix. Then he asked the bishop what it was, and he answered, that it was Christ. "Was He handled as cruelly as He is here pictured!" said Fetty. "Yea, that He was," said the bishop. "And even so cruelly will you handle such as come before you; for you are unto God's people as Caiaphas was unto Christ!" The bishop, being in a great fury, said, "Thou art a vile heretic, and I will burn thee, or else I will spend all I have, unto my gown." "Nay, my Lord, (said Fetty) you were better to give it to some poor body, that he may pray for you." Bonner, notwithstanding his passion, which was raised to the utmost by the calm and pointed remarks of this observing Christian, thought it most prudent to dismiss the father, on account of the nearly murdered child. His coward soul trembled for the consequences which might ensue; fear is inseparable from little minds; and this dastardly pampered priest experienced its effects so far as to induce him to assume the appearance of that he was an utter stranger to, namely, MERCY.

The father, on being dismissed, by the tyrant Bonner, went home with a heavy heart, with his dying child, who did not survive many days the cruelties which had been inflicted on him.

How contrary to the will of our great King and Prophet, who mildly taught His followers, was the conduct of this sanguinary and false teacher, this vile apostate from his God to Satan! But the archfiend had taken entire possession of his heart, and guided every action of the sinner he had hardened; who, given up to terrible destruction, was running the race of the wicked, marking his footsteps with the blood of the saints, as if eager to arrive at the goal of eternal death.

Deliverance of Dr. Sands

This eminent prelate, vice-chancellor of Cambridge, at the request of the duke of Northumberland, when he came down to Cambridge in support of Lady Jane Grey's claim to the throne, undertook at a few hours' notice, to preach before the duke and the university. The text he took was such as presented itself in opening the Bible, and a more appropriate one he could not have chosen, namely, the three last verses of Joshua. As God gave him the text, so He gave him also such order and utterance that it excited the most lively emotions in his numerous auditors. The sermon was about to be sent to London to be printed, when news arrived that the duke had returned and Queen Mary was proclaimed.

The duke was immediately arrested, and Dr. Sands was compelled by the university to give up his office. He was arrested by the queen's order, and when Mr. Mildmay wondered that so learned a man could wilfully incur danger, and speak against so good a princess as Mary, the doctor replied, "If I would do as Mr. Mildmay has done, I need not fear bonds. He came down armed against Queen Mary; before a traitor—now a great friend. I cannot with one mouth blow hot and cold in this manner." A general plunder of Dr. Sands' property ensued, and he was brought to London upon a wretched horse. Various insults he met on the way from the bigoted Catholics, and as he passed through Bishopsgate-street, a stone struck him to the ground. He was the first prisoner that entered the Tower, in that day, on a religious account; his man was admitted with his Bible, but his shirts and other articles were taken from him.

On Mary's coronation day the doors of the dungeon were so laxly guarded that it was easy to escape. A Mr. Mitchell, like a true friend, came to him, afforded him his own clothes as a disguise, and was willing to abide the consequence of being found in his place. This was a rare friendship: but he refused the offer; saying, "I know no cause why I should be in prison. To do thus were to make myself guilty. I will expect God's good will, yet do I think myself much obliged to you"; and so Mr. Mitchell departed.

With Doctor Sands was imprisoned Mr. Bradford; they were kept close in prison twenty-nine weeks. John Fowler, their keeper, was a perverse papist, yet, by often persuading him, at length he began to favor the Gospel, and was so persuaded in the true religion, that on a Sunday, when they had Mass in the chapel, Dr. Sands administered the Communion to Bradford and to Fowler. Thus Fowler was their son begotten in bonds. To make room for Wyat and his accomplices, Dr. Sands and nine other preachers were sent to the Marshalsea.

The keeper of the Marshalsea appointed to every preacher a man to lead him in the street; he caused them to go on before, and he and Dr. Sands followed conversing together. By this time popery began to be unsavory. After they had passed the bridge, the keeper said to Dr. Sands: "I perceive the vain people would set you forward to the fire. You are as vain as they, if you, being a young man, will stand in your own conceit, and prefer your own judgment before that of so many worthy prelates, ancient, learned, and grave men as be in this realm. If you do so, you shall find me a severe keeper, and one that utterly dislikes your religion." Dr. Sands answered, "I know my years to be young, and my learning but small; it is enough to know Christ crucified, and he hath learned nothing who seeth not the great blasphemy that is in popery. I will yield unto God, and not unto man; I have read in the Scriptures of many godly and courteous keepers: may God make you one! if not, I trust He will give me strength and patience to bear your hard usage." Then said the keeper, "Are you resolved to stand to your religion?" "Yes," quoth the doctor, "by God's grace!" "Truly," said the keeper, "I love you the better for it; I did but tempt you: what favor I can show you, you shall be assured of; and I shall think myself happy if I might die at the stake with you."

He was as good as his word, for he trusted the doctor to walk in the fields alone, where he met with Mr. Bradford, who was also a prisoner in the King's Bench, and had found the same favor from his keeper. At his request, he put Mr. Saunders in along with him, to be his bedfellow, and the Communion was administered to a great number of communicants.

When Wyat with his army came to Southwark, he offered to liberate all the imprisoned Protestants, but Dr. Sands and the rest of the preachers refused to accept freedom on such terms.

After Dr. Sands had been nine weeks prisoner in the Marshalsea, by the mediation of Sir Thomas Holcroft, knight marshal, he was set at liberty. Though Mr. Holcroft had the queen's warrant, the bishop commanded him not to set Dr. Sands at liberty, until he had taken sureties of two gentlemen with him, each one bound in £500, that Dr. Sands should not depart out of the realm without license. Mr. Holcroft immediately after met with two gentlemen of the north, friends and cousins to Dr. Sands, who offered to be bound for him.

After dinner, the same day, Sir Thomas Holcroft sent for Dr. Sands to his lodgings at Westminster, to communicate to him all he had done. Dr. Sands answered: "I give God thanks, who hath moved your heart to mind me so well, that I think myself most bound unto you. God shall requite you, nor shall I ever be found unthankful. But as you have dealt friendly with me, I will also deal plainly with you. I came a freeman into prison; I will not go forth a bondman. As I cannot benefit my friends, so will I not hurt them. And if I be set at liberty, I will not tarry six days in this realm, if I may get out. If therefore I may not get free forth, send me to the Marshalsea again, and there you shall be sure of me."

This answer Mr. Holcroft much disapproved of; but like a true friend he replied: "Seeing you cannot be altered, I will change my purpose, and yield unto you. Come of it what will, I will set you at liberty; and seeing you have a mind to go over sea, get you gone as quick as you can. One thing I require of you, that, while you are there, you write nothing to me hither, for this may undo me."

Dr. Sands having taken an affectionate farewell of him and his other friends in bonds, departed. He went by Winchester house, and there took boat, and came to a friend's house in London, called William Banks, and tarried there one night. The next night he went to another friend's house, and there he heard that strict search was making for him, by Gardiner's express order.

Dr. Sands now conveyed himself by night to one Mr. Berty's house, a stranger who was in the Marshalsea prison with him a while; he was a good Protestant and dwelt in Mark-lane. There he was six days, and then removed to one of his acquaintances in Cornhill; he caused his man Quinton to provide two geldings for him, resolved on the morrow to ride into Essex, to Mr. Sands, his father-in-law, where his wife was, which, after a narrow escape, he effected. He had not been there two hours, before Mr. Sands was told that two of the guards would that night apprehend Dr. Sands.

That night Dr. Sands was guided to an honest farmer's near the sea, where he tarried two days and two nights in a chamber without company. After that he removed to one James Mower's, a shipmaster, who dwelt at Milton-Shore, where he waited for a wind to Flanders. While he was there, James Mower brought to him forty or fifty mariners, to whom he gave an exhortation; they liked him so well that they promised to die rather than he should be apprehended.

The sixth of May, Sunday, the wind served. In taking leave of his hostess, who had been married eight years without having a child, he gave her a fine handkerchief and an old royal of gold, and said, "Be of good comfort; before that one whole year be past, God shall give you a child, a boy." This came to pass, for, that day twelvemonth, wanting one day, God gave her a son.

Scarcely had he arrived at Antwerp, when he learned that King Philip had sent to apprehend him. He next flew to Augsburg, in Cleveland, where Dr. Sands tarried fourteen days, and then travelled towards Strassburg, where, after he had lived one year, his wife came to him. He was sick of a flux nine months, and had a child which died of the plague. His amiable wife at length fell into a consumption, and died in his arms. When his wife was dead, he went to Zurich, and there was in Peter Martyr's house for the space of five weeks.

As they sat at dinner one day, word was suddenly brought that Queen Mary was dead, and Dr. Sands was sent for by his friends at Strassburg, where he preached. Mr. Grindal and he came over to England, and arrived in London the same day that Queen Elizabeth was crowned. This faithful servant of Christ, under Queen Elizabeth, rose to the highest distinction in the Church, being successively bishop of Worcester, bishop of London, and archbishop of York.

Queen Mary's Treatment of Her Sister, the Princess Elizabeth

The preservation of Princess Elizabeth may be reckoned a remarkable instance of the watchful eye which Christ had over His Church. The bigotry of Mary regarded not the ties of consanguinity, of natural affection, of national succession. Her mind, physically morose, was under the dominion of men who possessed not the milk of human kindness, and whose principles were sanctioned and enjoined by the idolatrous tenets of the Romish pontiff. Could they have foreseen the short date of Mary's reign, they would have imbrued their hands in the Protestant blood of Elizabeth, and, as a *sine qua non* of the queen's salvation, have compelled her to bequeath the kingdom to some Catholic prince. The contest might have been attended with the horrors incidental to a religious civil war, and calamities might have been felt in England similar to those under Henry the Great in France, whom Queen Elizabeth assisted in opposing his priest-ridden Catholic subjects. As if Providence had the perpetual establishment of the Protestant faith in view, the difference of the duration of the two reigns is worthy of notice. Mary might have reigned many years in the course of nature, but the course of grace willed it otherwise. Five years and four months was the time of persecution alloted to this weak, disgraceful reign, while that of Elizabeth reckoned a number of years among the highest of those who have sat on the English throne, almost nine times that of her merciless sister!

Before Mary attained the crown, she treated Elizabeth with a sisterly kindness, but from that period her conduct was altered, and the most imperious distance substituted. Though Elizabeth had no concern in the rebellion of Sir Thomas Wyat, yet she was apprehended, and treated as a culprit in that commotion. The manner too of her arrest was similar to the mind that dictated it: the three cabinet members, whom she deputed to see the arrest executed, rudely entered the chamber at ten o'clock at night, and, though she was extremely ill, they could scarcely be induced to let her remain until the following morning. Her enfeebled state permitted her to be moved only by short stages in a journey of such length to London; but the princess, though afflicted in person, had a consolation in mind which her sister never could purchase: the people, through whom she passed on her way pitied her, and put up their prayers for her preservation.

Arrived at court, she was made a close prisoner for a fortnight, without knowing who was her accuser, or seeing anyone who could console or advise her. The charge, however, was at length unmasked by Gardiner, who, with nineteen of the Council, accused her of abetting Wyat's conspiracy, which she religiously affirmed to be false.

Failing in this, they placed against her the transactions of Sir Peter Carew in the west, in which they were as unsuccessful as in the former. The queen now signified that it was her pleasure she should be committed to the Tower, a step which overwhelmed the princess with the greatest alarm and uneasiness. In vain she hoped the queen's majesty would not commit her to such a place; but there was no lenity to be expected; her attendants were limited, and a hundred northern soldiers appointed to guard her day and night.

On Palm Sunday she was conducted to the Tower. When she came to the palace garden, she cast her eyes towards the windows, eagerly anxious to meet those of the queen, but she was disappointed. A strict order was given in London that every one should go to church, and carry palms, that she might be conveyed without clamor or commiseration to her prison.

At the time of passing under London Bridge the fall of the tide made it very dangerous, and the barge some time stuck fast against the starlings. To mortify her the more, she was landed at Traitors' Stairs. As it rained fast, and she was obliged to step in the water to land, she hesitated; but this excited no complaisance in the lord in waiting. When she set her foot on the steps, she exclaimed, "Here lands as true a subject, being prisoner, as ever landed at these stairs; and before Thee, O God, I speak it, having no friend but Thee alone!"

A large number of the wardens and servants of the Tower were arranged in order between whom the princess had to pass. Upon inquiring the use of this parade, she was informed it was customary to do so. "If," said she, "it is on account of me, I beseech you that they may be dismissed." On this the poor men knelt down, and prayed that God would preserve her grace, for which they were the next day turned out of their employments. The tragic scene must have been deeply interesting, to see an amiable and irreproachable princess sent like a lamb to languish in expectation of cruelty and death; against whom there was no other charge than her superiority in Christian virtues and acquired endowments. Her attendants openly wept as she proceeded with a dignified step to the frowning battlements of her destination. "Alas!" said Elizabeth, "what do you mean? I took you to comfort, not to dismay me; for my truth is such that no one shall have cause to weep for me."

The next step of her enemies was to procure evidence by means which, in the present day, are accounted detestable. Many poor prisoners were racked, to extract, if possible, any matters of accusation which might affect her life, and thereby gratify Gardiner's sanguinary disposition. He himself came to examine her, respecting her removal from her house at Ashbridge to Dunnington castle a long while before. The princess had quite forgotten this trivial circumstance, and Lord Arundel, after the investigation, kneeling down, apologized for having troubled her in such a frivolous matter. "You sift me narrowly," replied the princess, "but of this I am assured, that God has appointed a limit to your proceedings; and so God forgive you all."

Her own gentlemen, who ought to have been her purveyors, and served her provision, were compelled to give place to the common soldiers, at the command of the constable of the Tower, who was in every respect a servile tool of Gardiner; her grace's friends, however, procured an order of Council which regulated this petty tyranny more to her satisfaction.

After having been a whole month in close confinement, she sent for the lord chamberlain and Lord Chandois, to whom she represented the ill state of her health from a want of proper air and exercise. Application being made to the Council, Elizabeth was with some difficulty admitted to walk in the queen's lodgings, and afterwards in the garden, at which time the prisoners on that side were attended by their keepers, and not suffered to look down upon her. Their jealousy was excited by a child of four years, who daily brought flowers to the princess. The child was threatened with a whipping, and the father ordered to keep him from the princess's chambers.

On the fifth of May the constable was discharged from his office, and Sir Henry Benifield appointed in his room, accompanied by a hundred ruffian-looking soldiers in blue. This measure created considerable alarm in the mind of the princess, who imagined it was preparatory to her undergoing the same fate as Lady Jane Grey, upon the same block. Assured that this project was not in agitation, she entertained an idea that the new keeper of the Tower was commissioned to make away with her privately, as his equivocal character was in conformity with the ferocious inclination of those by whom he was appointed.

A report now obtained that her Grace was to be taken away by the new constable and his soldiers, which in the sequel proved to be true. An order of Council was made for her removal to the manor Woodstock, which took place on Trinity Sunday, May 13, under the authority of Sir Henry Benifield and Lord Tame. The ostensible cause of her removal was to make room for other prisoners. Richmond was the first place they stopped at, and here the princess slept, not however without much alarm at first, as her own servants were superseded by the soldiers, who were placed as guards at her chamber door. Upon representation, Lord Tame overruled this indecent stretch of power, and granted her perfect safety while under his custody.

In passing through Windsor, she saw several of her poor dejected servants waiting to see her. "Go to them," said she, to one of her attendants, "and say these words from me, *tanquim ovis,* that is, like a sheep to the slaughter."

The next night her Grace lodged at the house of a Mr. Dormer, in her way to which the people manifested such tokens of loyal affection that Sir Henry was indignant, and bestowed on them very liberally the names of rebels and traitors. In some villages they rang the bells for joy, imagining the princess's arrival among them was from a very different cause; but this harmless demonstration of gladness was sufficient with the persecuting Benifield to order his soldiers to seize and set these humble persons in the stocks.

The day following, her Grace arrived at Lord Tame's house, where she stayed all night, and was most nobly entertained. This excited Sir Henry's indignation, and made him caution Lord Tame to look well to his proceedings; but the humanity of Lord Tame was not to be frightened, and he returned a suitable reply. At another time, this official prodigal, to show his consequence and disregard of good manners, went up into a chamber, where was appointed for her Grace a chair, two cushions, and a foot carpet, wherein he presumptuously sat and called his man to pull off his boots. As soon as it was known to the ladies and gentlemen they laughed him to scorn. When supper was done, he called to his lordship, and directed that all gentlemen and ladies should withdraw home, marvelling much that he would permit such a large company, considering the great charge he had committed to him. "Sir Henry," said his lordship, "content yourself; all shall be avoided, your men and all." "Nay, but my soldiers," replied Sir Henry, "shall watch all night." Lord Tame answered, "There is no need." "Well," said he, "need or need not, they shall so do."

The next day her Grace took her journey from thence to Woodstock, where she was enclosed, as before in the Tower of London, the soldiers keeping guard within and without the walls, every day, to the number of sixty; and in the night, without the walls were forty during all the time of her imprisonment.

At length she was permitted to walk in the gardens, but under the most severe restrictions, Sir Henry keeping the keys himself, and placing her always under many bolts and locks, whence she was induced to call him her jailer, at which he felt offended, and begged her to substitute the word officer. After much earnest entreaty to the Council, she obtained permission to write to the queen; but the jailer who brought her pen, ink, and paper stood by her while she wrote, and, when she left off, he carried the things away until they were wanted again. He also insisted upon carrying it himself to the queen, but Elizabeth would not suffer him to be the bearer, and it was presented by one of her gentlemen.

After the letter, Doctors Owen and Wendy went to the princess, as the state of her health rendered medical assistance necessary.

They stayed with her five or six days, in which time she grew much better; they then returned to the queen, and spoke flatteringly of the princess' submission and humility, at which the queen seemed moved; but the bishops wanted a concession that she had offended her majesty. Elizabeth spurned this indirect mode of acknowledging herself guilty. "If I have offended," said she, "and am guilty, I crave no mercy but the law, which I am certain I should have had ere this, if anything could have been proved against me. I wish I were as clear from the peril of my enemies; then should I not be thus bolted and locked up within walls and doors."

Much question arose at this time respecting the propriety of uniting the princess to some foreigner, that she might quit the realm with a suitable portion. One of the Council had the brutality to urge the necessity of beheading her, if the king (Philip) meant to keep the realm in peace; but the Spaniards, detesting such a base thought, replied, "God forbid that our king and master should consent to such an infamous proceeding!" Stimulated by a noble principle, the Spaniards from this time repeatedly urged to the king that it would do him the highest honor to liberate the Lady Elizabeth, nor was the king impervious to their solicitation. He took her out of prison, and shortly after she was sent for to Hampton court. It may be remarked in this place, that the fallacy of human reasoning is shown in every moment. The barbarian who suggested the policy of beheading Elizabeth little contemplated the change of condition which his speech would bring about. In her journey from Woodstock, Benifield treated her with the same severity as before; removing her on a stormy day, and not suffering her old servant, who had come to Colnbrook, where she slept, to speak to her.

She remained a fortnight strictly guarded and watched, before anyone dared to speak with her; at length the vile Gardiner with three more of the Council, came with great submission. Elizabeth saluted them, remarked that she had been for a long time kept in solitary confinement, and begged they would intercede with the king and queen to deliver her from prison. Gardiner's visit was to draw from the princess a confession of her guilt; but she was guarded against his subtlety, adding, that, rather than admit she had done wrong, she would lie in prison all the rest of her life. The next day Gardiner came again, and kneeling down, declared that the queen was astonished she should persist in affirming that she was blameless—whence it would be inferred that the queen had unjustly imprisoned her grace. Gardiner further informed her that the queen had declared that she must tell another tale, before she could be set at liberty. "Then," replied the high-minded Elizabeth, "I had rather be in prison with honesty and truth, than have my liberty, and be suspected by her majesty. What I have said, I will stand to; nor will I ever speak falsehood!" The bishop and his friends then departed, leaving her locked up as before.

Seven days after the queen sent for Elizabeth at ten o'clock at night; two years had elapsed since they had seen each other. It created terror in the mind of the princess, who, at setting out, desired her gentlemen and ladies to pray for her, as her return to them again was uncertain.

Being conducted to the queen's bedchamber, upon entering it the princess knelt down, and having begged of God to preserve her majesty, she humbly assured her that her majesty had not a more loyal subject in the realm, whatever reports might be circulated to the contrary. With a haughty ungraciousness, the imperious queen replied: "You will not confess your offence, but stand stoutly to your truth. I pray God it may so fall out."

"If it do not," said Elizabeth, "I request neither favor nor pardon at your majesty's hands." "Well," said the queen, "you stiffly still persevere in your truth. Besides, you will not confess that you have not been wrongfully punished."

"I must not say so, if it please your majesty, to you."

"Why, then," said the queen, "belike you will to others."

"No, if it please you majesty: I have borne the burden, and must bear it. I humbly beseech your majesty to have a good opinion of me and to think me to be your subject, not only from the beginning hitherto, but for ever, as long as life lasteth." They departed without any heartfelt satisfaction on either side; nor can we think the conduct of Elizabeth displayed that independence and fortitude which accompanies perfect innocence. Elizabeth's admitting that she would not say, neither to the queen nor to others, that she had been unjustly punished, was in direct contradiction to what she had told Gardiner, and must have arisen from some motive at this time inexplicable. King Philip is supposed to have been secretly concealed during the interview, and to have been friendly to the princess.

In seven days from the time of her return to imprisonment, her severe jailer and his men were discharged, and she was set at liberty, under the constraint of being always attended and watched by some of the queen's Council. Four of her gentlemen were sent to the Tower without any other charge against them than being zealous servants of their mistress. This event was soon after followed by the happy news of Gardiner's death, for which all good and merciful men glorified God, inasmuch as it had taken the chief tiger from the den, and rendered the life of the Protestant successor of Mary more secure.

This miscreant, while the princess was in the Tower, sent a secret writ, signed by a few of the Council, for her private execution, and, had Mr. Bridges, lieutenant of the Tower, been as little scrupulous of dark assassination as this pious prelate was, she must have perished. The warrant not having the queen's signature, Mr. Bridges hastened to her majesty to give her information of it, and to know her mind. This was a plot of Winchester's, who, to convict her of treasonable practices, caused several prisoners to be racked; particularly Mr. Edmund Tremaine and Smithwicke were offered considerable bribes to accuse the guiltless princess.

Her life was several times in danger. While at Woodstock, fire was apparently put between the boards and ceiling under which she lay. It was also reported strongly that one Paul Penny, the keeper of Woodstock, a notorious ruffian, was appointed to assassinate her, but, however this might be, God counteracted in this point the nefarious designs of the enemies of the Reformation. James Basset was another appointed to perform the same deed: he was a peculiar favorite of Gardiner, and had come within a mile of Woodstock, intending to speak with Benifield on the subject. The goodness of God however so ordered it that while Basset was travelling to Woodstock, Benifield, by an order of Council, was going to London: in consequence of which, he left a positive order with his brother, that no man should be admitted to the princess during his absence, not even with a note from the queen; his brother met the murderer, but the latter's intention was frustrated, as no admission could be obtained.

When Elizabeth quitted Woodstock, she left the following lines written with her diamond on the window:

> Much suspected by me,
> Nothing proved can be. Quoth Elizabeth, prisoner.

With the life of Winchester ceased the extreme danger of the princess, as many of her other secret enemies soon after followed him, and, last of all, her cruel sister, who outlived Gardiner but three years.

The death of Mary was ascribed to several causes. The Council endeavored to console her in her last moments, imagining it was the absence of her husband that lay heavy at her heart, but though his treatment had some weight, the loss of Calais, the last fortress possessed by the English in France, was the true source of her sorrow. "Open my heart," said Mary, "when I am dead, and you shall find Calais written there." Religion caused her no alarm; the priests had lulled to rest every misgiving of conscience, which might have obtruded, on account of the accusing spirits of the murdered martyrs. Not the blood she had spilled, but the loss of a town excited her emotions in dying, and this last stroke seemed to be awarded, that her fanatical persecution might be paralleled by her political imbecility.

We earnestly pray that the annals of no country, Catholic or pagan, may ever be stained with such a repetition of human sacrifices to papal power, and that the detestation in which the character of Mary is holden, may be a beacon to succeeding monarchs to avoid the rocks of fanaticism!

Gods Punishment upon Some of the Persecutors of His People in Mary's Reign

After that arch-persecutor, Gardiner, was dead, others followed, of whom Dr. Morgan, bishop of St. David's, who succeeded Bishop Farrar, is to be noticed. Not long after he was installed in his bishopric, he was stricken by the visitation of God; his food passed through the throat, but rose again with great violence. In this manner, almost literally starved to death, he terminated his existence.

Bishop Thornton, suffragan of Dover, was an indefatigable persecutor of the true Church. One day after he had exercised his cruel tyranny upon a number of pious persons at Canterbury, he came from the chapter-house to Borne, where as he stood on a Sunday looking at his men playing at bowls, he fell down in a fit of the palsy, and did not long survive.

After the latter, succeeded another bishop or suffragan, ordained by Gardiner, who not long after he had been raised to the see of Dover, fell down a pair of stairs in the cardinal's chamber at Greenwich, and broke his neck. He had just received the cardinal's blessing—he could receive nothing worse.

John Cooper, of Watsam, Suffolk, suffered by perjury; he was from private pique persecuted by one Fenning, who suborned two others to swear that they heard Cooper say, 'If God did not take away Queen Mary, the devil would.' Cooper denied all such words, but Cooper was a Protestant and a heretic, and therefore he was hung, drawn and quartered, his property confiscated, and his wife and nine children reduced to beggary. The following harvest, however, Grimwood of Hitcham, one of the witnesses before mentioned, was visited for his villainy: while at work, stacking up corn, his bowels suddenly burst out, and before relief could be obtained, he died. Thus was deliberate perjury rewarded by sudden death!

In the case of the martyr Mr. Bradford, the severity of Mr. Sheriff Woodroffe has been noticed—he rejoiced at the death of the saints, and at Mr. Rogers' execution, he broke the carman's head, because he stopped the cart to let the martyr's children take a last farewell of him. Scarcely had Mr. Woodroffe's sheriffalty expired a week, when he was struck with a paralytic affection, and languished a few days in the most pitiable and helpless condition, presenting a striking contrast to his former activity in the cause of blood.

Ralph Lardyn, who betrayed the martyr George Eagles, is believed to have been afterward arraigned and hanged in consequence of accusing himself. At the bar, he denounced himself in these words: "This has most justly fallen upon me, for betraying the innocent blood of that just and good man George Eagles, who was here condemned in the time of Queen Mary by my procurement, when I sold his blood for a little money."

As James Abbes was going to execution, and exhorting the pitying bystanders to adhere steadfastly to the truth, and like him to seal the cause of Christ with their blood, a servant of the sheriff's interrupted him, and blasphemously called his religion heresy, and the good man a lunatic. Scarcely however had the flames reached the martyr, before the fearful stroke of God fell upon the hardened wretch, in the presence of him he had so cruelly ridiculed. The man was suddenly seized with lunacy, cast off his clothes and shoes before the people, (as Abbes had done just before, to distribute among some poor persons,) at the same time exclaiming, "Thus did James Abbes, the true servant of God, who is saved but I am damned." Repeating this often, the sheriff had him secured, and made him put his clothes on, but no sooner was he alone, than he tore them off, and exclaimed as before. Being tied in a cart, he was conveyed to his master's house, and in about half a year he died; just before which a priest came to attend him, with the crucifix, etc., but the wretched man bade him take away such trumpery, and said that he and other priests had been the cause of his damnation, but that Abbes was saved.

One Clark, an avowed enemy of the Protestants in King Edward's reign, hung himself in the Tower of London.

Froling, a priest of much celebrity, fell down in the street and died on the spot.

Dale, an indefatigable informer, was consumed by vermin, and died a miserable spectacle.

Alexander, the severe keeper of Newgate, died miserably, swelling to a prodigious size, and became so inwardly putrid, that none could come near him. This cruel minister of the law would go to Bonner, Story, and others, requesting them to rid his prison, he was so much pestered with heretics! The son of this keeper, in three years after his father's death, dissipated his great property, and died suddenly in Newgate market. "The sins of the father," says the decalogue, "shall be visited on the children." John Peter, son-in-law of Alexander, a horrid blasphemer and persecutor, died wretchedly. When he affirmed anything, he would say, "If it be not true, I pray I may rot ere I die." This awful state visited him in all its loathsomeness.

Sir Radph Ellerker was eagerly desirous to see the heart taken out of Adam Damlip, who was wrongfully put to death. Shortly after Sir Ralph was slain by the French, who mangled him dreadfully, cut off his limbs, and tore his heart out.

When Gardiner heard of the miserable end of Judge Hales, he called the profession of the Gospel a doctrine of desperation; but he forgot that the judge's despondency arose after he had consented to the papistry. But with more reason may this be said of the Catholic tenets, if we consider the miserable end of Dr. Pendleton, Gardiner, and most of the leading persecutors. Gardiner, upon his death bed, was reminded by a bishop of Peter denying his master, "Ah," said Gardiner, "I have denied with Peter, but never repented with Peter."

After the accession of Elizabeth, most of the Catholic prelates were imprisoned in the Tower or the Fleet; Bonner was put into the Marshalsea.

Of the revilers of God's Word, we detail, among many others, the following occurrence. One William Maldon, living at Greenwich in servitude, was instructing himself profitably in reading an English primer one winter's evening. A serving man, named John Powell, sat by, and ridiculed all that Maldon said, who cautioned him not to make a jest of the Word of God. Powell nevertheless continued, until Maldon came to certain English Prayers, and read aloud, "Lord, have mercy upon us, Christ have mercy upon us," etc. Suddenly the reviler started, and exclaimed, "Lord, have mercy upon us!" He was struck with the utmost terror of mind, said the evil spirit could not abide that Christ should have any mercy upon him, and sunk into madness. He was remitted to Bedlam, and became an awful warning that God will not always be insulted with impunity.

Henry Smith, a student in the law, had a pious Protestant father, of Camden, in Gloucestershire, by whom he was virtuously educated. While studying law in the middle temple, he was induced to profess Catholicism, and, going to Louvain, in France, he returned with pardons, crucifixes, and a great freight of popish toys. Not content with these things, he openly reviled the Gospel religion he had been brought up in; but conscience one night reproached him so dreadfully, that in a fit of despair he hung himself in his garters. He was buried in a lane, without the Christian service being read over him.

Dr. Story, whose name has been so often mentioned in the preceding pages, was reserved to be cut off by public execution, a practice in which he had taken great delight when in power. He is supposed to have had a hand in most of the conflagrations in Mary's time, and was even ingenious in his invention of new modes of inflicting torture. When Elizabeth came to the throne, he was committed to prison, but unaccountably effected his escape to the continent, to carry fire and sword there among the Protestant brethren. From the duke of Alva, at Antwerp, he received a special commission to search all ships for contraband goods, and particularly for English heretical books.

Dr. Story gloried in a commission that was ordered by Providence to be his ruin, and to preserve the faithful from his sanguinary cruelty. It was contrived that one Parker, a merchant, should sail to Antwerp and information should be given to Dr. Story that he had a quantity of heretical books on board. The latter no sooner heard this, than he hastened to the vessel, sought everywhere above, and then went under the hatches, which were fastened down upon him. A prosperous gale brought the ship to England, and this traitorous, persecuting rebel was committed to prison, where he remained a considerable time, obstinately objecting to recant his Antichristian spirit, or admit of Queen Elizabeth's supremacy. He alleged, though by birth and education an Englishman, that he was a sworn subject of the king of Spain, in whose service the famous duke of Alva was. The doctor being condemned, was laid upon a hurdle, and drawn from the Tower to Tyburn, where after being suspended about half an hour, he was cut down, stripped, and the executioner displayed the heart of a traitor.

Thus ended the existence of this Nimrod of England.

CHAPTER XVII

Rise and Progress of the Protestant Religion in Ireland; with an Account of the Barbarous Massacre of 1641

THE gloom of popery had overshadowed Ireland from its first establishment there until the reign of Henry VIII when the rays of the Gospel began to dispel the darkness, and afford that light which until then had been unknown in that island. The abject ignorance in which the people were held, with the absurd and superstitious notions they entertained, were sufficiently evident to many; and the artifices of their priests were so conspicuous, that several persons of distinction, who had hitherto been strenuous papists, would willingly have endeavored to shake off the yoke, and embrace the Protestant religion; but the natural ferocity of the people, and their strong attachment to the ridiculous doctrines which they had been taught, made the attempt dangerous. It was, however, at length undertaken, though attended with the most horrid and disastrous consequences.

The introduction of the Protestant religion into Ireland may be principally attributed to George Browne, an Englishman, who was consecrated archbishop of Dublin on the nineteenth of March, 1535. He had formerly been an Augustine friar, and was promoted to the mitre on account of his merit.

After having enjoyed his dignity about five years, he, at the time that Henry VIII was suppressing the religious houses in England, caused all the relics and images to be removed out of the two cathedrals in Dublin, and the other churches in his diocese; in the place of which he caused to be put up the Lord's Prayer, the Creed, and the Ten Commandments.

A short time after this he received a letter from Thomas Cromwell, lord-privy seal, informing him that Henry VIII having thrown off the papal supremacy in England, was determined to do the like in Ireland; and that he thereupon had appointed him (Archbishop Browne) one of the commissioners for seeing this order put in execution. The archbishop answered that he had employed his utmost endeavors at the hazard of his life, to cause the Irish nobility and gentry to acknowledge Henry as their supreme head, in matters both spiritual and temporal; but had met with a most violent opposition, especially from George, archbishop of Armagh; that this prelate had, in a speech to his clergy, laid a curse on all those who should own his highness' supremacy: adding, that their isle, called in the Chronicles *Insula Sacra,* or the Holy Island, belonged to none but the bishop of Rome, and that the king's progenitors had received it from the pope. He observed likewise, that the archbishop and clergy of Armagh had each despatched a courier to Rome; and that it would be necessary for a parliament to be called in Ireland, to pass an act of supremacy, the people not regarding the king's commission without the sanction of the legislative assembly. He concluded with observing, that the popes had kept the people in the most profound ignorance; that the clergy were exceedingly illiterate; that the common people were more zealous in their blindness than the saints and martyrs had been in the defence of truth at the beginning of hte Gospel; and that it was to be feared that Shan O'Neal, a chieftain of great power in the northern part of the island, was decidedly opposed to the king's commission.

In pursuance of this advice, the following year a parliament was summoned to meet at Dublin, by order of Leonard Grey, at that time lord-lieutenant. At this assembly Archbishop Browne made a speech, in which he set forth that the bishops of Rome used, anciently, to acknowledge emperors, kings, and princes, to be supreme in their own dominions; and, therefore, that he himself would vote King Henry VIII as supreme in all matters, both ecclesiastical and temporal. He concluded with saying that whosoever should refuse to vote for this act, was not a true subject of the king. This speech greatly startled the other bishops and lords; but at length, after violent debates, the king's supremacy was allowed.

Two years after this, the archbishop wrote a second letter to Lord Cromwell, complaining of the clergy, and hinting at the machinations which the pope was then carrying on against the advocates of the Gospel. This letter is dated from Dublin, in April, 1538; and among other matters, the archbishop says, "A bird may be taught to speak with as much sense as many of the clergy do in this country. These, though not scholars, yet are crafty to cozen the poor common people and to dissuade them from following his highness orders. The country folk here much hate your lordship, and despitefully call you, in their Irish tongue, the Blacksmith's Son. As a friend, I desire your lordship to look well to your noble person. Rome hath a great kindness for the duke of Norfolk, and great favors for this nation, purposely to oppose his highness."

A short time after this, the pope sent over to Ireland (directed to the archbishop of Armagh and his clergy) a bull of excommunication against all who had, or should own the king's supremacy within the Irish nation; denouncing a curse on all of them, and theirs, who should not, within forty days, acknowledge to their confessors, that they had done amiss in so doing.

Archbishop Browne gave notice of this in a letter dated, Dublin, May, 1538. Part of the form of confession, or vow, sent over to these Irish papists, ran as follows: "I do further declare him or her, father or mother, brother or sister, son or daughter, husband or wife, uncle or aunt, nephew or niece, kinsman or kinswoman, master or mistress, and all others, nearest or dearest relations, friend or acquaintance whatsoever, accursed, that either do or shall hold, for the time to come, any ecclesiastical or civil power above the authority of the Mother Church; or that do or shall obey, for the time to come, any of her, the Mother of Churches' opposers or enemies, or contrary to the same, of which I have here sworn unto: so God, the Blessed Virgin, St. Peter, St. Paul, and the Holy Evangelists, help me," etc. is an exact agreement with the doctrines promulgated by the Councils of Lateran and Constance, which expressly declare that no favor should be shown to heretics, nor faith kept with them; that they ought to be excommunicated and condemned, and their estates confiscated, and that princes are obliged, by a solemn oath, to root them out of their respective dominions.

How abominable a church must that be, which thus dares to trample upon all authority! How besotted the people who regard the injunctions of such a church!

In the archbishop's last-mentioned letter, dated May, 1538, he says: "His highness' viceroy of this nation is of little or no power with the old natives. Now both English and Irish begin to oppose your lordship's orders, and to lay aside their national quarrels, which I fear will (if anything will) cause a foreigner to invade this nation."

Not long after this, Archbishop Browne seized one Thady O'Brian, a Franciscan friar, who had in his possession a paper sent from Rome, dated May, 1538, and directed to O'Neal. In this letter were the following words: "His Holiness, Paul, now pope, and the council of the fathers, have lately found, in Rome, a prophecy of one St. Lacerianus, an Irish bishop of Cashel, in which he saith that the

Mother Church of Rome falleth, when, in Ireland, the Catholic faith is overcome. Therefore, for the glory of the Mother Church, the honor of St. Peter, and your own secureness, suppress heresy, and his holiness' enemies."

This Thady O'Brian, after further examination and search made, was pilloried, and kept close prisoner until the king's orders arrived in what manner he should be further disposed of. But order coming over from England that he was to be hanged, he laid violent hands on himself in the castle of Dublin. His body was afterwards carried to Gallows-green, where, after being hanged up for some time, it was interred.

After the accession of Edward VI to the throne of England, an order was directed to Sir Anthony Leger, the lord-deputy of Ireland, commanding that the liturgy in English be forthwith set up in Ireland, there to be observed within the several bishoprics, cathedrals, and parish churches; and it was first read in Christ-church, Dublin, on Easter day, 1551, before the said Sir Anthony, Archbishop Browne, and others. Part of the royal order for this purpose was as follows: "Whereas, our gracious father, King Henry VIII taking into consideration the bondage and heavy yoke that his true and faithful subjects sustained, under the jurisdiction of the bishop of Rome; how several fabulous stories and lying wonders misled our subjects; dispensing with the sins of our nations, by their indulgences and pardons, for gain; purposely to cherish all evil vices, as robberies, rebellions, thefts, whoredoms, blasphemy, idolatry, etc., our gracious father hereupon dissolved all priories, monasteries, abbeys, and other pretended religious houses; as being but nurseries for vice or luxury, more than for sacred learning," etc.

On the day after the Common Prayer was first used in Christchurch, Dublin, the following wicked scheme was projected by the papists:

In the church was left a marble image of Christ, holding a reed in his hand, with a crown of thorns on his head. Whilst the English service (the Common Prayer) was being read before the lord-lieutenant, the archbishop of Dublin, the privy-council, the lord-mayor, and a great congregation, blood was seen to run through the crevices of the crown of thorns, and trickle down the face of the image. On this, some of the contrivers of the imposture cried aloud, "See how our Savior's image sweats blood! But it must necessarily do this, since heresy is come into the church." Immediately many of the lower order of people, indeed the *vulgar of all ranks,* were terrified at the sight of so *miraculous* and *undeniable* an evidence of the divine displeasure; they hastened from the church, convinced that the doctrines of Protestantism emanated from an infernal source, and that salvation was only to be found in the bosom of their own *infallible* Church.

This incident, however ludicrous it may appear to the enlightened reader, had great influence over the minds of the ignorant Irish, and answered the ends of the impudent impostors who contrived it, so far as to check the progress of the reformed religion in Ireland very materially; many persons could not resist the conviction that there were many errors and corruptions in the Romish Church, but they were awed into silence by this pretended manifestation of Divine wrath, which was magnified beyond measure by the bigoted and interested priesthood.

We have very few particulars as to the state of religion in Ireland during the remaining portion of the reign of Edward VI and the greater part of that of Mary. Towards the conclusion of the barbarous sway of that relentless bigot, she attempted to extend her inhuman persecutions to this island; but her diabolical intentions were happily frustrated in the following providential manner, the particulars of which are related by historians of good authority.

Mary had appointed Dr. Pole (an agent of the bloodthirsty Bonner) one of the commissioners for carrying her barbarous intentions into effect. He having arrived at Chester with his commission, the mayor of that city, being a papist, waited upon him; when the doctor taking out of his cloak bag a leathern case, said to him, "Here is a commission that shall lash the heretics of Ireland." The good woman of the house being a Protestant, and having a brother in Dublin, named John Edmunds, was greatly troubled at what she heard. But watching her opportunity, whilst the mayor was taking his leave, and the doctor politely accompanying him downstairs, she opened the box, took out the commission, and in its stead laid a sheet of paper, with a pack of cards, and the *knave of clubs* at top. The doctor, not suspecting the trick that had been played him, put up the box, and arrived with it in Dublin, in September, 1558.

Anxious to accomplish the intentions of his *"pious"* mistress, he immediately waited upon Lord Fitz-Walter, at that time viceroy, and presented the box to him; which being opened, nothing was found in it but a pack of cards. This startling all the persons present, his lordship said, "We must procure another commission; and in the meantime let us shuffle the cards."

Dr. Pole, however, would have directly returned to England to get another commission; but waiting for a favorable wind, news arrived that Queen Mary was dead, and by this means the Protestants escaped a most cruel persecution. The above relation as we before observed, is confirmed by historians of the greatest credit, who add, that Queen Elizabeth settled a pension of forty pounds per annum upon the above mentioned Elizabeth Edmunds, for having thus saved the lives of her Protestant subjects.

During the reigns of Elizabeth and James I, Ireland was almost constantly agitated by rebellions and insurrections, which, although not always taking their rise from the difference of religious opinions, between the English and Irish, were aggravated and rendered more bitter and irreconcilable from that cause. The popish priests artfully exaggerated the faults of the English government, and continually urged to their ignorant and prejudiced hearers the lawfulness of killing the Protestants, assuring them that all Catholics who were slain in the prosecution of so *pious* an enterprise, would be immediately received into everlasting felicity. The naturally ungovernable dispositions of the Irish, acted upon by these designing men, drove them into continual acts of barbarous and unjustifiable violence; and it must be confessed that the unsettled and arbitrary nature of the authority exercised by the English governors, was but little calculated to gain their affections. The Spaniards, too, by landing forces in the south, and giving every encouragement to the discontented natives to join their standard, kept the island in a continual state of turbulence and warfare. In 1601, they disembarked a body of four thousand men at Kinsale, and commenced what they called *"the Holy War for the preservation of the faith in Ireland;"* they were assisted by great numbers of the Irish, but were at length totally defeated by the deputy, Lord Mountjoy, and his officers.

This closed the transactions of Elizabeth's reign with respect to Ireland; an interval of apparent tranquillity followed, but the popish priesthood, ever restless and designing, sought to undermine by secret machinations that government and that faith which they durst no longer openly attack. The pacific reign of James afforded them the opportunity of increasing their strength and maturing their schemes, and under his successor, Charles I, their numbers were greatly increased by titular Romish archbishops, bishops, deans, vicars-general, abbots, priests, and friars; for which reason, in 1629, the public exercise of the popish rites and ceremonies was forbidden.

But notwithstanding this, soon afterwards, the Romish clergy erected a new popish university in the city of Dublin. They also proceeded to build monasteries and nunneries in various parts of the kingdom; in which places these very Romish clergy, and the chiefs of the Irish, held frequent meetings; and from thence, used to pass to and fro, to France, Spain, Flanders, Lorraine, and Rome; where the detestable plot of 1641 was hatching by the family of the O'Neals and their followers.

A short time before the horrid conspiracy broke out, which we are now going to relate, the papists in Ireland had presented a remonstrance to the lords-justice of that kingdom, demanding the free exercise of their religion, and a repeal of all laws to the contrary; to which both houses of parliament in England solemnly answered that they would never grant any toleration to the popish religion in that kingdom.

This further irritated the papists to put in execution the diabolical plot concerted for the destruction of the Protestants; and it failed not of the success wished for by its malicious and rancorous projectors.

The design of this horrid conspiracy was that a general insurrection should take place at the same time throughout the kingdom, and that all the Protestants, without exception, should be murdered. The day fixed for this horrid massacre, was the twenty-third of October, 1641, the feast of Ignatius Loyola, founder of the Jesuits; and the chief conspirators in the principal parts of the kingdom made the necessary preparations for the intended conflict.

In order that this detested scheme might the more infallibly succeed, the most distinguished artifices were practiced by the papists; and their behavior in their visits to the Protestants, at this time, was with more seeming kindness than they had hitherto shown, which was done the more completely to effect the inhuman and treacherous designs then meditating against them.

The execution of this savage conspiracy was delayed until the approach of winter, that sending troops from England might be attended with greater difficulty. Cardinal Richelieu, the French minister, had promised the conspirators a considerable supply of men and money; and many Irish officers had given the strongest assurances that they would heartily concur with their Catholic brethren, as soon as the insurrection took place.

The day preceding that appointed for carrying this horrid design into execution was now arrived, when, happily for the metropolis of the kingdom, the conspiracy was discovered by one Owen O'Connelly, an Irishman, for which most signal service the English Parliament voted him £500 and a pension of £200 during his life.

So very seasonably was this plot discovered, even but a few hours before the city and castle of Dublin were to have been surprised, that the lords-justice had but just time to put themselves, and the city, in a proper posture of defence. Lord M'Guire, who was the principal leader here, with his accomplices, was seized the same evening in the city; and in their lodgings were found swords, hatchets, pole-axes, hammers, and such other instruments of death as had been prepared for the destruction and extirpation of the Protestants in that part of the kingdom.

Thus was the metropolis happily preserved; but the bloody part of the intended tragedy was past prevention. The conspirators were in arms all over the kingdom early in the morning of the day appointed, and every Protestant who fell in their way was immediately murdered. No age, no sex, no condition, was spared. The wife weeping for her butchered husband, and embracing her helpless children, was pierced with them, and perished by the same stroke. The old, the young, the vigorous, and the infirm, underwent the same fate, and were blended in one common ruin. In vain did flight save from the first assault, destruction was everywhere let loose, and met the hunted victims at every turn. In vain was recourse had to relations, to companions, to friends; all connections were dissolved; and death was dealt by that hand from which protection was implored and expected. Without provocation, without opposition, the astonished English, living in profound peace, and, as they thought, full security, were massacred by their nearest neighbors, with whom they had long maintained a continued intercourse of kindness and good offices. Nay, even death was the slightest punishment inflicted by these monsters in human form; all the tortures which wanton cruelty could invent, all the lingering pains of body, the anguish of mind, the agonies of despair, could not satiate revenge excited without injury, and cruelly derived from no just cause whatever. Depraved nature, even perverted religion, though encouraged by the utmost license, cannot reach to a greater pitch of ferocity than appeared in these merciless barbarians. Even the weaker sex themselves, naturally tender to their own sufferings, and compassionate to those of others, have emulated their robust companions in the practice of every cruelty. The very children, taught by example and encouraged by the exhortation of their parents, dealt their feeble blows on the dead carcasses of the defenceless children of the English.

Nor was the avarice of the Irish sufficient to produce the least restraint on their cruelty. Such was their frenzy, that the cattle they had seized, and by rapine had made their own, were, because they bore the name of English, wantonly slaughtered, or, when covered with wounds, turned loose into the woods, there to perish by slow and lingering torments.

The commodious habitations of the planters were laid in ashes, or levelled with the ground. And where the wretched owners had shut themselves up in the houses, and were preparing for defence, they perished in the flames together with their wives and children.

Such is the general description of this unparalleled massacre; but it now remains, from the nature of our work, that we proceed to particulars.

The bigoted and merciless papists had no sooner begun to imbrue their hands in blood than they repeated the horrid tragedy day after day, and the Protestants in all parts of the kingdom fell victims to their fury by deaths of the most unheard-of cruelty.

The ignorant Irish were more strongly instigated to execute the infernal business by the Jesuits, priests, and friars, who, when the day for the execution of the plot was agreed on, recommended in their prayers, diligence in the great design, which they said would greatly tend to the prosperity of the kingdom, and to the advancement of the Catholic cause. They everywhere declared to the common people, that the Protestants were heretics, and ought not to be suffered to live any longer among them; adding that it was no more sin to kill an Englishman than to kill a dog; and that the relieving or protecting them was a crime of the most unpardonable nature.

The papists having besieged the town and castle of Longford, and the inhabitants of the latter, who were Protestants, surrendering on condition of being allowed quarter, the besiegers, the instant the townspeople appeared, attacked them in a most unmerciful manner, their priest, as a signal for the rest to fall on, first ripping open the belly of the English Protestant minister; after which his followers murdered all the rest, some of whom they hanged, others were stabbed or shot, and great numbers knocked on the head with axes provided for the purpose.

The garrison at Sligo was treated in like manner by O'Connor Slygah; who, upon the Protestants quitting their holds, promised them quarter, and to convey them safe over the Curlew mountains, to Roscommon. But he first imprisoned them in a most loathsome jail, allowing them only grains for their food. Afterward, when some papists were merry over their cups, who were come to congratulate their wicked brethren for their victory over these unhappy creatures, those Protestants who survived were brought forth by the White-friars, and were either killed, or precipitated over the bridge into a swift river, where they were soon destroyed. It is added, that this wicked company of White-friars went, some time after, in solemn procession, with holy water in their hands, to sprinkle the river; on pretence of cleansing and purifying it from the stains and pollution of the blood and dead bodies of the heretics, as they called the unfortunate Protestants who were inhumanly slaughtered at this very time.

At Kilmore, Dr. Bedell, bishop of that see, had charitably settled and supported a great number of distressed Protestants, who had fled from their habitations to escape the diabolical cruelties committed by the papists. But they did not long enjoy the consolation of living together; the good prelate was forcibly dragged from his episcopal residence, which was immediately occupied by Dr. Swiney, the popish titular bishop of Kilmore, who said Mass in the church the Sunday following, and then seized on all the goods and effects belonging to the persecuted bishop.

Soon after this, the papists forced Dr. Bedell, his two sons, and the rest of his family, with some of the chief of the Protestants whom he had protected, into a ruinous castle, called Lochwater, situated in a lake near the sea. Here he remained with his companions some weeks, all of them daily expecting to be put to death. The greatest part of them were stripped naked, by which means, as the season was cold, (it being in the month of December) and the building in which they were confined open at the top, they suffered the most severe hardships. They continued in this situation until the seventh of January, when they were all released. The bishop was courteously received into the house of Dennis O'Sheridan, one of his clergy, whom he had made a convert to the Church of England; but he did not long survive this kindness. During his residence here, he spent the whole of his time in religious exercises, the better to fit and prepare himself and his sorrowful companions for their great change, as nothing but certain death was perpetually before their eyes. He was at this time in the seventy-first year of his age, and being afflicted with a violent ague caught in his late cold and desolate habitation on the lake, it soon threw him into a fever of the most dangerous nature. Finding his dissolution at hand, he received it with joy, like one of the primitive martyrs just hastening to his crown of glory. After having addressed his little flock, and exhorted them to patience, in the most pathetic manner, as they saw their own last day approaching, after having solemnly blessed his people, his family, and his children, he finished the course of his ministry and life together, on the seventh day of February 1642.

His friends and relations applied to the intruding bishop for leave to bury him, which was with difficulty obtained; he, at first telling them that the churchyard was holy ground, and should be no longer defiled with heretics: however, leave was at last granted, and though the church funeral service was not used at the solemnity, (for fear of the Irish papists) yet some of the better sort, who had the highest veneration for him while living, attended his remains to the grave. At his interment they discharged a volley of shot, crying out, *Requiescat in pace ultimus Anglorum,* that is, "May the last of the English rest in peace." Adding, that as he was one of the best so he should be the last English bishop found among them. His learning was very extensive; and he would have given the world a greater proof of it, had he printed all he wrote. Scarce any of his writings were saved; the papists having destroyed most of his papers and his library. He had gathered a vast heap of critical expositions of Scripture, all which with a great trunk full of his manuscripts, fell into the hands of the Irish. Happily his great Hebrew manuscript was preserved, and is now in the library of Emanuel College, Oxford.

In the barony of Terawley, the papists, at the instigation of the friars, compelled above forty English Protestants, some of whom were women and children, to the hard fate of either falling by the sword, or of drowning in the sea. These choosing the latter, were accordingly forced, by the naked weapons of their inexorable persecutors, into the deep, where, with their children in their arms, they first waded up to their chins, and afterwards sunk down and perished together.

In the castle of Lisgool upwards of one hundred and fifty men, women, and children, were all burnt together; and at the castle of

Moneah not less than one hundred were all put to the sword. Great numbers were also murdered at the castle of Tullah, which was delivered up to M'Guire on condition of having fair quarter; but no sooner had that base villain got possession of the place than he ordered his followers to murder the people, which was immediately done with the greatest cruelty.

Many others were put to deaths of the most horrid nature, and such as could have been invented only by demons instead of men. Some of them were laid with the center of their backs on the axle-tree of a carriage, with their legs resting on the ground on one side, and their arms and head on the other. In this position, one of the savages scourged the wretched object on the thighs, legs, etc., while another set on furious dogs, who tore to pieces the arms and upper parts of the body; and in this dreadful manner were they deprived of their existence. Great numbers were fastened to horses' tails, and the beasts being set on full gallop by their riders, the wretched victims were dragged along until they expired. Others were hung on lofty gibbets, and a fire being kindled under them, they finished their lives, partly by hanging, and partly by suffocation.

Nor did the more tender sex escape the least particle of cruelty that could be projected by their merciless and furious persecutors. Many women, of all ages, were put to deaths of the most cruel nature. Some, in particular, were fastened with their backs to strong posts, and being stripped to their waists, the inhuman monsters cut off their right breasts with shears, which, of course, put them to the most excruciating torments; and in this position they were left, until, from the loss of blood, they expired.

Such was the savage ferocity of these barbarians, that even unborn infants were dragged from the womb to become victims to their rage. Many unhappy mothers were hung naked in the branches of trees, and their bodies being cut open, the innocent offsprings were taken from them, and thrown to dogs and swine. And to increase the horrid scene, they would oblige the husband to be a spectator before suffering himself.

At the town of Issenskeath they hanged above a hundred Scottish Protestants, showing them no more mercy than they did to the English. M'Guire, going to the castle of that town, desired to speak with the governor, when being admitted, he immediately burnt the records of the county, which were kept there. He then demanded £1000 of the governor, which, having received, he immediately compelled him to hear Mass, and to swear that he would continue to do so. And to complete his horrid barbarities, he ordered the wife and children of the governor to be hanged before his face; besides massacring at least one hundred of the inhabitants. Upwards of one thousand men, women, and children, were driven, in different companies, to Portadown bridge, which was broken in the middle, and there compelled to throw themselves into the water, and such as attempted to reach the shore were knocked on the head.

In the same part of the country, at least four thousand persons were drowned in different places. The inhuman papists, after first stripping them, drove them like beasts to the spot fixed on for their destruction; and if any, through fatigue, or natural infirmities, were slack in their pace, they pricked them with their swords and pikes; and to strike terror on the multitude, they murdered some by the way. Many of these poor wretches, when thrown into the water, endeavored to save themselves by swimming to the shore but their merciless persecutors prevented their endeavors taking effect, by shooting them in the water.

In one place one hundred and forty English, after being driven for many miles stark naked, and in the most severe weather, were all murdered on the same spot, some being hanged, others burnt, some shot, and many of them buried alive; and so cruel were their tormentors that they would not suffer them to pray before they robbed them of their miserable existence.

Other companies they took under pretence of safe conduct, who, from that consideration, proceeded cheerfully on their journey; but when the treacherous papists had got them to a convenient spot, they butchered them all in the most cruel manner.

One hundred and fifteen men, women, and children, were conducted, by order of Sir Phelim O'Neal, to Portadown bridge, where they were all forced into the river, and drowned. One woman, named Campbell, finding no probability of escaping, suddenly clasped one of the chief of the papists in her arms, and held him so fast that they were both drowned together.

In Killyman they massacred forty-eight families, among whom twenty-two were burnt together in one house. The rest were either hanged, shot, or drowned.

In Kilmore, the inhabitants, which consisted of about two hundred families, all fell victims to their rage. Some of them sat in the stocks until they confessed where their money was; after which they put them to death. The whole county was one common scene of butchery, and many thousands perished, in a short time, by sword, famine, fire, water, and others the most cruel deaths, that rage and malice could invent.

These bloody villains showed so much favor to some as to despatch them immediately; but they would by no means suffer them to pray. Others they imprisoned in filthy dungeons, putting heavy bolts on their legs, and keeping them there until they were starved to death.

At Casel they put all the Protestants into a loathsome dungeon, where they kept them together, for several weeks, in the greatest misery. At length they were released, when some of them were barbarously mangled, and left on the highways to perish at leisure;

others were hanged, and some were buried in the ground upright, with their heads above the earth, and the papists, to increase their misery, treating them with derision during their sufferings. In the county of Antrim they murdered nine hundred and fifty-four Protestants in one morning; and afterwards about twelve hundred more in that county.

At a town called Lisnegary, they forced twenty-four Protestants into a house, and then setting fire to it, burned them together, counterfeiting their outcries in derision to the others.

Among other acts of cruelty they took two children belonging to an Englishwoman, and dashed out their brains before her face; after which they threw the mother into a river, and she was drowned. They served many other children in the like manner, to the great affliction of their parents, and the disgrace of human nature.

In Kilkenny all the Protestants, without exception, were put to death; and some of them in so cruel a manner, as, perhaps, was never before thought of.

They beat an Englishwoman with such savage barbarity, that she had scarce a whole bone left; after which they threw her into a ditch; but not satisfied with this, they took her child, a girl about six years of age, and after ripping up its belly, threw it to its mother, there to languish until it perished. They forced one man to go to Mass, after which they ripped open his body, and in that manner left him. They sawed another asunder, cut the throat of his wife, and after having dashed out the brains of their child, an infant, threw it to the swine, who greedily devoured it.

After committing these, and several other horrid cruelties, they took the heads of seven Protestants, and among them that of a pious minister, all of which they fixed up at the market cross. They put a gag into the minister's mouth, then slit his cheeks to his ears, and laying a leaf of a Bible before it, bid him preach, for his mouth was wide enough. They did several other things by way of derision, and expressed the greatest satisfaction at having thus murdered and exposed the unhappy Protestants.

It is impossible to conceive the pleasure these monsters took in exercising their cruelty, and to increase the misery of those who fell into their hands, when they butchered them they would say, "Your soul to the devil." One of these miscreants would come into a house with his hands imbued in blood, and boast that it was English blood, and that his sword had pricked the white skins of the Protestants, even to the hilt. When any one of them had killed a Protestant, others would come and receive a gratification in cutting and mangling the body; after which they left it exposed to be devoured by dogs; and when they had slain a number of them they would boast, that the devil was beholden to them for sending so many souls to hell. But it is no wonder they should thus treat the innocent Christians, when they hesitated not to commit blasphemy against God and His most holy Word.

In one place they burnt two Protestant Bibles, and then said they had burnt hell-fire. In the church at Powerscourt they burnt the pulpit, pews, chests, and Bibles belonging to it. They took other Bibles, and after wetting them with dirty water, dashed them in the faces of the Protestants, saying, "We know you love a good lesson; here is an excellent one for you; come to-morrow, and you shall have as good a sermon as this."

Some of the Protestants they dragged by the hair of their heads into the church, where they stripped and whipped them in the most cruel manner, telling them, at the same time, that if they came to-morrow, they should hear the like sermon.

In Munster they put to death several ministers in the most shocking manner. One, in particular, they stripped stark naked, and driving him before them, pricked him with swords and darts until he fell down, and expired.

In some places they plucked out the eyes, and cut off the hands of the Protestants, and in that manner turned them into the fields, there to wander out their miserable existence. They obliged many young men to force their aged parents to a river, where they were drowned; wives to assist in hanging their husbands; and mothers to cut the throats of their children.

In one place they compelled a young man to kill his father, and then immediately hanged him. In another they forced a woman to kill her husband, then obliged the son to kill her, and afterward shot him through the head.

At a place called Glaslow, a popish priest, with some others, prevailed on forty Protestants to be reconciled to the Church of Rome. They had no sooner done this than they told them they were in good faith, and that they would prevent their falling from it, and turning heretics, by sending them out of the world, which they did by immediately cutting their throats.

In the county of Tipperary upwards of thirty Protestants, men, women, and children, fell into the hands of the papists, who, after stripping them naked, murdered them with stones, pole-axes, swords, and other weapons.

In the county of Mayo about sixty Protestants, fifteen of whom were ministers, were, upon covenant, to be safely conducted to Galway, by one Edmund Burke and his soldiers; but that inhuman monster by the way drew his sword, as an intimation of his design to the rest, who immediately followed his example, and murdered the whole, some of whom they stabbed, others were run through the body with pikes, and several were drowned.

In Queen's County great numbers of Protestants were put to the most shocking deaths. Fifty or sixty were placed together in one house, which being set on fire, they all perished in the flames. Many were stripped naked, and being fastened to horses by ropes placed round their middles, were dragged through bogs until they expired. Some were hung by the feet to tenterhooks driven into poles; and in that wretched posture left until they perished. Others were fastened to the trunk of a tree, with a branch at top. Over this branch hung one arm, which principally supported the weight of the body; and one of the legs was turned up, and fastened to the trunk, while the other hung straight. In this dreadful and uneasy posture did they remain as long as life would permit, pleasing spectacles to their bloodthirsty persecutors.

At Clownes seventeen men were buried alive; and an Englishman, his wife, five children, and a servant maid, were all hanged together, and afterward thrown into a ditch. They hung many by the arms to branches of trees, with a weight to their feet; and others by the middle, in which posture they left them until they expired. Several were hanged on windmills, and before they were half dead, the barbarians cut them in pieces with their swords. Others, both men, women, and children, they cut and hacked in various parts of their bodies, and left them wallowing in their blood to perish where they fell. One poor woman they hanged on a gibbet, with her child, an infant about a twelve-month old, the latter of whom was hanged by the neck with the hair of its mother's head, and in that manner finished its short but miserable existence.

In the county of Tyrone no less than three hundred Protestants were drowned in one day; and many others were hanged, burned, and otherwise put to death. Dr. Maxwell, rector of Tyrone, lived at this time near Armagh, and suffered greatly from these merciless savages. This person, in his examination, taken upon oath before the king's commissioners, declared that the Irish papists owned to him, that they, at several times, had destroyed, in one place, 12,000 Protestants, whom they inhumanly slaughtered at Glynwood, in their flight from the county of Armagh.

As the river Bann was not fordable, and the bridge broken down, the Irish forced thither at different times, a great number of unarmed, defenceless Protestants, and with pikes and swords violently thrust about one thousand into the river, where they miserably perished.

Nor did the cathedral of Armagh escape the fury of those barbarians, it being maliciously set on fire by their leaders, and burnt to the ground. And to extirpate, if possible, the very race of those unhappy Protestants, who lived in or near Armagh, the Irish first burnt all their houses, and then gathered together many hundreds of those innocent people, young and old, on pretence of allowing them a guard and safe conduct to Colerain, when they treacherously fell on them by the way, and inhumanly murdered them.

The like horrid barbarities with those we have particularized, were practiced on the wretched Protestants in almost all parts of the kingdom; and, when an estimate was afterward made of the number who were sacrificed to gratify diabolical souls of the papists, it amounted to one hundred and fifty thousand. But it now remains that we proceed to the particulars that followed.

These desperate wretches, flushed and grown insolent with success, (though by methods attended with such excessive barbarities as perhaps not to be equalled) soon got possession of the castle of Newry, where the king's stores and ammunition were lodged; and, with as little difficulty, made themselves masters of Dundalk. They afterward took the town of Ardee, where they murdered all the Protestants, and then proceeded to Drogheda. The garrison of Drogheda was in no condition to sustain a siege, notwithstanding which, as often as the Irish renewed their attacks they were vigorously repulsed by a very unequal number of the king's forces, and a few faithful Protestant citizens under Sir Henry Tichborne, the governor, assisted by the Lord Viscount Moore. The siege of Drogheda began on the thirtieth of November, 1641, and held until the fourth of March, 1642, when Sir Phelim O'Neal, and the Irish miscreants under him were forced to retire.

In the meantime ten thousand troops were sent from Scotland to the remaining Protestants in Ireland, which being properly divided in the most capital parts of the kingdom, happily eclipsed the power of the Irish savages; and the Protestants for a time lived in tranquillity.

In the reign of King James II they were again interrupted, for in a parliament held at Dublin in the year 1689, great numbers of the Protestant nobility, clergy, and gentry of Ireland, were attainted of high treason. The government of the kingdom was, at that time, invested in the earl of Tyrconnel, a bigoted papist, and an inveterate enemy to the Protestants. By his orders they were again persecuted in various parts of the kingdom. The revenues of the city of Dublin were seized, and most of the churches converted into prisons. And had it not been for the resolution and uncommon bravery of the garrisons in the city of Londonderry, and the town of Inniskillin, there had not one place remained for refuge to the distressed Protestants in the whole kingdom; but all must have been given up to King James, and to the furious popish party that governed him.

The remarkable siege of Londonderry was opened on the eighteenth of April, 1689, by twenty thousand papists, the flower of the Irish army. The city was not properly circumstanced to sustain a siege, the defenders consisting of a body of raw undisciplined Protestants, who had fled thither for shelter, and half a regiment of Lord Mountjoy's disciplined soldiers, with the principal part of the inhabitants, making in all only seven thousand three hundred and sixty-one fighting men.

The besieged hoped, at first, that their stores of corn and other necessaries, would be sufficient; but by the continuance of the siege their wants increased; and these became at last so heavy that for a considerable time before the siege was raised a pint of coarse barley, a small quantity of greens, a few spoonfuls of starch, with a very moderate proportion of horse flesh, were reckoned a week's provision for a soldier. And they were, at length, reduced to such extremities that they ate dogs, cats, and mice.

Their miseries increasing with the siege, many, through mere hunger and want, pined and languished away, or fell dead in the streets. And it is remarkable, that when their long-expected succors arrived from England, they were upon the point of being reduced to this alternative, either to preserve their existence by eating each other, or attempting to fight their way through the Irish, which must have infallibly produced their destruction.

These succors were most happily brought by the ship *Mountjoy* of Derry, and the *Phœnix* of Colerain, at which time they had only nine lean horses left with a pint of meal to each man. By hunger, and the fatigues of war, their seven thousand three hundred and sixty-one fighting men were reduced to four thousand three hundred, one fourth part of whom were rendered unserviceable.

As the calamities of the besieged were great, so likewise were the terrors and sufferings of their Protestant friends and relations; all of whom (even women and children) were forcibly driven from the country thirty miles round, and inhumanly reduced to the sad necessity of continuing some days and nights without food or covering, before the walls of the town; and were thus exposed to the continual fire both of the Irish army from without and the shot of their friends from within.

But the succors from England happily arriving put an end to their affliction; and the siege was raised on the thirty-first of July, having been continued upwards of three months.

The day before the siege of Londonderry was raised, the Inniskillers engaged a body of six thousand Irish Roman Catholics, at Newton, Butler, or Crown-Castle, of whom near five thousand were slain. This, with the defeat at Londonderry, dispirited the papists, and they gave up all farther attempts to persecute the Protestants.

The year following, viz. 1690, the Irish took up arms in favor of the abdicated prince, King James II but they were totally defeated by his successor King William the Third. That monarch, before he left the country, reduced them to a state of subjection, in which they have ever since continued.

But notwithstanding all this, the Protestant interest at present stands upon a much stronger basis than it did a century ago. The

Irish, who formerly led an unsettled and roving life, in the woods, bogs, and mountains, and lived on the depredation of their neighbors, they who, in the morning seized the prey, and at night divided the spoil, have, for many years past, become quiet and civilized. They taste the sweets of English society, and the advantages of civil government. They trade in our cities, and are employed in our manufactories. They are received also into English families; and treated with great humanity by the Protestants.

CHAPTER XVIII

The Rise, Progress, Persecutions, and Sufferings of the Quakers

In treating of these people in a historical manner, we are obliged to have recourse to much tenderness. That they differ from the generality of Protestants in some of the capital points of religion cannot be denied, and yet, as Protestant dissenters they are included under the description of the toleration act. It is not our business to inquire whether people of similar sentiments had any existence in the primitive ages of Christianity: perhaps, in some respects, they had not, but we are to write of them not as what they were, but what they now are. That they have been treated by several writers in a very contemptuous manner is certain; that they did not deserve such treatment, is equally certain.

The appellation *Quakers,* was bestowed upon them as a term of reproach, in consequence of their apparent convulsions which they labored under when they delivered their discourses, because they imagined they were the effect of divine inspiration.

It is not our business, at present, to inquire whether the sentiments of these people are agreeable to the Gospel, but this much is certain, that the first leader of them, as a separate body, was a man of obscure birth, who had his first existence in Leicestershire, about the year 1624. In speaking of this man we shall deliver our own sentiments in a historical manner, and joining these to what have been said by the Friends themselves, we shall endeavor to furnish out a complete narrative.

George Fox was descended of honest and respected parents, who brought him up in the national religion: but from a child he appeared religious, still, solid, and observing, beyond his years, and uncommonly knowing in divine things. He was brought up to husbandry, and other country business, and was particularly inclined to the solitary occupation of a shepherd; an employment, that very well suited his mind in several respects, both for its innocency and solitude; and was a just emblem of his after ministry and service. In the year 1646, he entirely forsook the national Church, in whose tenets he had been brought up, as before observed; and in 1647, he travelled into Derbyshire and Nottinghamshire, without any set purpose of visiting particular places, but in a solitary manner he walked through several towns and villages, which way soever his mind turned. "He fasted much," said Sewell, "and walked often in retired places, with no other companion than his Bible." "He visited the most retired and religious people in those parts," says Penn, "and some there were, short of few, if any, in this nation, who waited for the consolation of Israel night and day; as Zacharias, Anna, and Simeon, did of old time. To these he was sent, and these he sought out in the neighboring counties, and among them he sojourned until his more ample ministry came upon him. At this time he taught, and was an example of silence, endeavoring to bring them from self-performances; testifying of, and turning them to the light of Christ within them, and encouraging them to wait in patience, and to feel the power of it to stir in their hearts, that their knowledge and worship of God might stand in the power of an endless life, which was to be found in the light, as it was obeyed in the manifestation of it in man: for in the Word was life, and that life is the light of men. Life in the Word, light in men; and life in men too, as the light is obeyed; the children of the light living by the life of the Word, by which the Word begets them again to God, which is the generation and new birth, without which there is no coming into the Kingdom of God, and to which whoever comes is greater than John: that is, than John's dispensation, which was not that of the Kingdom, but the consummation of the legal, and forerunning of the Gospel times, the time of the Kingdom. Accordingly several meetings were gathering in those parts; and thus his time was employed for some years."

In the year 1652, "he had a visitation of the great work of God in the earth, and of the way that he was to go forth, in a public ministry, to begin it." He directed his course northward, "and in every place where he came, if not before he came to it, he had his particular exercise and service shown to him, so that the Lord was his leader indeed." He made great numbers of converts to his opinions, and many pious and good men joined him in his ministry. These were drawn forth especially to visit the public assemblies to reprove, reform, and exhort them; sometimes in markets, fairs, streets, and by the highway-side, "calling people to repentance, and to return to the Lord, with their hearts as well as their mouths; directing them to the light of Christ within them, to see, examine, and to consider their ways by, and to eschew the evil, and to do the good and acceptable will of God."

They were not without opposition in the work they imagined themselves called to, being often set in the stocks, stoned, beaten, whipped and imprisoned, though honest men of good report, that had left wives, children, houses, and lands, to visit them with a living call to repentance. But these coercive methods rather forwarded than abated their zeal, and in those parts they brought over many proselytes, and amongst them several magistrates, and others of the better sort. They apprehended the Lord had forbidden them to pull off their hats to anyone, high or low, and required them to speak to the people, without distinction, in the language of thou and thee. They scrupled bidding people good-morrow, or good-night, nor might they bend the knee to anyone, even in supreme authority. Both men and women went in a plain and simple dress, different from the fashion of the times. They neither gave nor accepted any titles of respect or honor, nor would they call any man master on earth. Several texts of Scripture they quoted in defence of these singularities; such as, "Swear not at all." "How can ye believe, which receive honor one of another, and seek not the honor that cometh from God only?" etc., etc. They placed the basis of religion in an inward light, and an extraordinary impulse of the Holy Spirit.

In 1654, their first separate meeting in London was held in the house of Robert Dring, in Watling-street, for by that time they spread themselves into all parts of the kingdom, and had in many places set up meetings or assemblies, particularly in Lancashire, and the adjacent parts, but they were still exposed to great persecutions and trials of every kind. One of them in a letter to the protector, Oliver Cromwell, represents, though there are no penal laws in force obliging men to comply with the established religion, yet the Quakers are exposed upon other accounts; they are fined and imprisoned for refusing to take an oath; for not paying their tithes; for disturbing the public assemblies, and meeting in the streets, and places of public resort; some of them have been whipped for vagabonds, and for their plain speeches to the magistrate.

Under favor of the then toleration, they opened their meetings at the Bull and Mouth, in Aldersgate-street, where women, as well as men, were moved to speak. Their zeal transported them to some extravagancies, which laid them still more open to the lash of their enemies, who exercised various severities upon them throughout the next reign. Upon the suppression of Venner's mad insurrection, the government, having published a proclamation, forbidding the Anabaptists, Quakers, and Fifth Monarchy Men, to assemble or meet together under pretence of worshipping God, except it be in some parochial church, chapel, or in private houses, by consent of the persons there inhabiting, all meetings in other places being declared to be unlawful and riotous, etc., etc., the Quakers thought it expedient to address the king thereon, which they did in the following words:

"*O King Charles!*

"Our desire is, that thou mayest live forever in the fear of God, and thy council. We beseech thee and thy council, to read these following lines in tender bowels, and compassion for our souls, and for your good.

"And this consider, we are about four hundred imprisoned, in and about this city, of men and women from their families, besides, in the county jails, about ten hundred; we desire that our meetings may not be broken up, but that all may come to a fair trial, that our innocency may be cleared up.

"London, 16th day, eleventh month, 1660."

On the twenty-eighth of the same month, they published the declaration referred to in their address, entitled: "A declaration from the harmless and innocent people of God, called Quakers, against all sedition, plotters, and fighters in the world, for removing the ground of jealousy and suspicion, from both magistrates and people in the kingdom, concerning wars and fightings." It was presented to the king the twenty-first day of the eleventh month, 1660, and he promised them upon his royal word, that they should not suffer for their opinions as long as they lived peaceably; but his promises were very little regarded afterward.

In 1661 they assumed courage to petition the House of Lords for a toleration of their religion, and for a dispensation from taking the oaths, which they held unlawful, not from any disaffection to the government, or a belief that they were less obliged by an affirmation, but from a persuasion that all oaths were unlawful; and that swearing upon the most solemn occasions was forbidden in the New Testament. Their petition was rejected, and instead of granting them relief, an act was passed against them, the preamble to which set forth, "That whereas several persons have taken up an opinion that an oath, even before a magistrate, is unlawful, and contrary to the Word of God: and whereas, under pretence of religious worship, the said persons do assemble in great numbers in several parts of the kingdom, separating themselves from the rest of his majesty's subjects, and the public congregations and usual places of divine worship; be it therefore enacted, that if any such persons, after the twenty-fourth of March, 1661-2, shall refuse to take an oath when lawfully tendered, or persuade others to do it, or maintain in writing or otherwise, the unlawfulness of taking an oath; or if they shall assemble for religious worship, to the number of five or more, of the age of fifteen, they shall for the first offence forfeit five pounds; for the second, ten pounds; and for the third shall abjure the realm, or be transported to the plantations: and the justices of peace at their open sessions may hear and finally determine in the affair."

This act had a most dreadful effect upon the Quakers, though it was well known and notorious that these conscientious persons were far from sedition or disaffection to the government. George Fox, in his address to the king, acquaints him that three thousand and sixty-eight of their friends had been imprisoned since his majesty's restoration; that their meetings were daily broken up by men with clubs and arms, and their friends thrown into the water, and trampled under foot until the blood gushed out, which gave rise to their meeting in the open streets. A relation was printed, signed by twelve witnesses, which says that more than four thousand two hundred Quakers were imprisoned; and of them five hundred were in and about London, and the suburbs; several of whom were dead in the jails.

However, they ever gloried in their sufferings, which increased every day; so that in 1665, and the intermediate years, they were harassed without example. As they persisted resolutely to assemble, openly, at the Bull and Mouth, before mentioned, the soldiers, and other officers, dragged them from thence to prison, until Newgate was filled with them, and multitudes died of close confinement, in that and other jails.

Six hundred of them, says an account published at that time, were in prison, merely for religion's sake, of whom several were banished to the plantations. In short, the Quakers gave such full employment to the informers, that they had less leisure to attend the meetings of other dissenters.

Yet, under all these calamities, they behaved with patience and modesty towards the government, and upon occasion of the Ryehouse plot in 1682, thought proper to declare their innocence of that sham plot, in an address to the king, wherein "appealing to the Searcher of all hearts," they say, "their principles do not allow them to take up defensive arms, much less to avenge themselves for the injuries they received from others: that they continually pray for the king's safety and preservation; and therefore take this occasion humbly to beseech his majesty to compassionate their suffering friends, with whom the jails are so filled, that they want air, to the apparent hazard of their lives, and to the endangering an infection in divers places. Besides, many houses, shops, barns, and fields are ransacked, and the goods, corn, and cattle swept away, to the discouraging trade and husbandry, and impoverishing great numbers of quiet and industrious people; and this, for no other cause, but for the exercise of a tender conscience in the worship of Almighty God, who is sovereign Lord and King of men's consciences."

On the accession of James II they addressed that monarch honestly and plainly, telling him: "We are come to testify our sorrow for the death of our good friend Charles, and our joy for thy being made our governor. We are told thou art not of the persuasion of the Church of England, no more than we; therefore we hope thou wilt grant us the same liberty which thou allowest thyself, which doing, we wish thee all manner of happiness."

When James, by his dispensing power, granted liberty to the dissenters, they began to enjoy some rest from their troubles; and indeed it was high time, for they were swelled to an enormous amount. They, the year before this, to them one of glad release, in a petition to James for a cessation of their sufferings, set forth, "that of late above one thousand five hundred of their friends, both men and women, and that now there remain one thousand three hundred and eighty-three; of which two hundred are women, many under sentence of præmunire; and more than three hundred near it, for refusing the oath of allegiance, because they could not swear. Three hundred and fifty have died in prison since the year 1680; in London, the jail of Newgate has been crowded, within these two years sometimes with near twenty in a room, whereby several have been suffocated, and others, who have been taken out sick, have died of malignant fevers within a few days. Great violences, outrageous distresses, and woful havoc and spoil, have been made upon people's goods and estates, by a company of idle, extravagant, and merciless informers, by persecutions on the conventicle-act, and others, also on *qui tam* writs, and on other processes, for twenty pounds a month, and two thirds of their estates seized for the king. Some had not a bed to rest on, others had no cattle to till the ground, nor corn for feed or bread, nor tools to work with; the said informers and bailiffs in some places breaking into houses, and making great waste and spoil, under pretence of serving the king and the Church. Our religious assemblies have been charged at common law with being rioters and disturbers of the public peace, whereby great numbers have been confined in prison without regard to age, and many confined to holes and dungeons. The seizing for £20 a month has amounted to many thousands, and several who have employed some hundreds of poor people in manufactures, are disabled to do so any more, by reason of long imprisonment. They spare neither widow nor fatherless, nor have they so much as a bed to lie on. The informers are both witnesses and prosecutors, to the ruin of great numbers of sober families; and justices of the peace have been threatened with the forfeiture of one hundred pounds, if they do not issue out warrants upon their informations." With this petition they presented a list of their friends in prison, in the several counties, amounting to four hundred and sixty.

During the reign of King James II these people were, through the intercession of their friend Mr. Penn, treated with greater indulgence than ever they had been before. They were now become extremely numerous in many parts of the country, and the settlement of Pennsylvania taking place soon after, many of them went over to America. There they enjoyed the blessings of a peaceful government, and cultivated the arts of honest industry.

As the whole colony was the property of Mr. Penn, so he invited people of all denominations to come and settle with him. A universal liberty of conscience took place; and in this new colony the natural rights of mankind were, for the first time, established.

These Friends are, in the present age, a very harmless, inoffensive body of people; but of that we shall take more notice hereafter. By their wise regulations, they not only do honor to themselves, but they are of vast service to the community.

It may be necessary here to observe, that as the Friends, commonly called Quakers, will not take an oath in a court of justice, so their affirmation is permitted in all civil affairs; but they cannot prosecute a criminal, because, in the English courts of justice, all evidence must be upon oath.

An Account of the Persecutions of Friends, Commonly Called Quakers, in the United States

About the middle of the seventeenth century, much persecution and suffering were inflicted on a sect of Protestant dissenters, commonly called Quakers: a people which arose at that time in England some of whom sealed their testimony with their blood.

For an account of the above people, see Sewell's, or Gough's history of them.

The principal points upon which their conscientious nonconformity rendered them obnoxious to the penalties of the law, were,

1. The Christian resolution of assembling publicly for the worship of God, in a manner most agreeable to their consciences.

2. Their refusal to pay tithes, which they esteemed a Jewish ceremony, abrogated by the coming of Christ.

3. Their testimony against wars and fighting, the practice of which they judged inconsistent with the command of Christ: "Love your enemies," Matt. 5:44.

4. Their constant obedience to the command of Christ: "Swear not at all," Matt. 5:34.

5. Their refusal to pay rates or assessments for building and repairing houses for a worship which they did not approve.

6. Their use of the proper and Scriptural language, "thou," and "thee," to a single person: and their disuse of the custom of uncovering their heads, or pulling off their hats, by way of homage to man.

7. The necessity many found themselves under, of publishing what they believed to be the doctrine of truth; and sometimes even in the places appointed for the public national worship.

Their conscientious noncompliance in the preceding particulars, exposed them to much persecution and suffering, which consisted in prosecutions, fines, cruel beatings, whippings, and other corporal punishments; imprisonment, banishment, and even death.

To relate a particular account of their persecutions and sufferings, would extend beyond the limits of this work: we shall therefore refer, for that information, to the histories already mentioned, and more particularly to Besse's Collection of their sufferings; and shall confine our account here mostly to those who sacrificed their lives, and evinced, by their disposition of mind, constancy, patience, and faithful perseverance, that they were influenced by a sense of religious duty.

Numerous and repeated were the persecutions against them; and sometimes for transgressions or offences which the law did not contemplate or embrace.

Many of the fines and penalties exacted of them, were not only unreasonable and exorbitant, but as they could not consistently pay them, were sometimes distrained to several times the value of the demand; whereby many poor families were greatly distressed, and obliged to depend on the assistance of their friends.

Numbers were not only cruelly beaten and whipped in a public manner, like criminals, but some were branded and others had their ears cut off.

Great numbers were long confined in loathsome prisons; in which some ended their days in consequence thereof.

Many were sentenced to banishment; and a considerable number were transported. Some were banished on pain of death; and four were actually executed by the hands of the hangman, as we shall here relate, after inserting copies of some of the laws of the country where they suffered.

"At a General Court Held at Boston, the Fourteenth of October, 1656

"Whereas, there is a cursed sect of heretics, lately risen up in the world, which are commonly called Quakers, who take upon them to be immediately sent from God, and infallibly assisted by the Spirit, to speak and write blasphemous opinions, despising government, and the order of God, in the Church and commonwealth, speaking evil of dignities, reproaching and reviling magistrates and ministers, seeking to turn the people from the faith, and gain proselytes to their pernicious ways: this court taking into consideration the premises, and to prevent the like mischief, as by their means is wrought in our land, doth hereby order, and by authority of this court, be it ordered and enacted, that what master or commander of any ship, bark, pink, or ketch, shall henceforth bring into any harbor, creek, or cove, within this jurisdiction, any Quaker or Quakers, or other blasphemous heretics, shall pay, or cause to be paid, the fine of one hundred pounds to the treasurer of the country, except it appear he want true knowledge or information of their being such; and, in that case, he hath liberty to clear himself by his oath, when sufficient proof to the contrary is wanting: and, for default of good payment, or good security for it, shall be cast into prison, and there to continue until the said sum be satisfied to the treasurer as foresaid.

"And the commander of any ketch, ship, or vessel, being legally convicted, shall give in sufficient security to the governor, or any one or more of the magistrates, who have power to determine the same, to carry them back to the place whence he brought them; and, on his refusal so to do, the governor, or one or more of the magistrates, are hereby empowered to issue out his or their warrants to commit such master or commander to prison, there to continue, until he give in sufficient security to the content of the governor, or any of the magistrates, as aforesaid.

"And it is hereby further ordered and enacted, that what Quaker soever shall arrive in this country from foreign parts, or shall come into this jurisdiction from any parts adjacent, shall be forthwith committed to the House of Correction; and, at their entrance, to be severely whipped, and by the master thereof be kept constantly to work, and none suffered to converse or speak with them, during the time of their imprisonment, which shall be no longer than necessity requires.

"And it is ordered, if any person shall knowingly import into any harbor of this jurisdiction, any Quakers' books or writings, concerning their devilish opinions, shall pay for such book or writing, being legally proved against him or them the sum of five pounds; and whosoever shall disperse or conceal any such book or writing, and it be found with him or her, or in his or her house and shall not immediately deliver the same to the next magistrate, shall forfeit or pay five pounds, for the dispersing or concealing of any such book or writing.

"And it is hereby further enacted, that if any persons within this colony shall take upon them to defend the heretical opinions of the Quakers, or any of their books or papers, shall be fined for the first time forty shillings; if they shall persist in the same, and shall again defend it the second time, four pounds; if notwithstanding they again defend and maintain the said Quakers' heretical opinions, they shall be committed to the House of Correction until there be convenient passage to send them out of the land, being sentenced by the court of Assistants to banishment.

"Lastly, it is hereby ordered, that what person or persons soever, shall revile the persons of the magistrates or ministers, as is usual with the Quakers, such person or persons shall be severely whipped or pay the sum of five pounds.

"This is a true copy of the court's order, as attests
"EDWARD RAWSON, SEC."

"At a General Court Held at Boston, the Fourteenth of October, 1657

"As an addition to the late order, in reference to the coming or bringing of any of the cursed sect of the Quakers into this jurisdiction, it is ordered that whosoever shall from henceforth bring, or cause to be brought, directly, or indirectly, any known Quaker or Quakers, or other blasphemous heretics, into this jurisdiction, every such person shall forfeit the sum of one hundred pounds to the country, and shall by warrant from any magistrate be committed to prison, there to remain until the penalty be satisfied and paid; and if any person or persons within this jurisdiction, shall henceforth entertain and conceal any such Quaker or Quakers, or other blasphemous heretics, knowing them so to be, every such person shall forfeit to the country forty shillings for every hour's entertainment and concealment of any Quaker or Quaker, etc., as aforesaid, and shall be committed to prison as aforesaid, until the forfeiture be fully satisfied and paid.

"And it is further ordered, that if any Quaker or Quakers shall presume, after they have once suffered what the law requires, to come into this jurisdiction, every such male Quaker shall, for the first offence, have one of his ears cut off, and be kept at work in the House of Correction, until he can be sent away at his own charge; and for the second offence, shall have his other ear cut off; and every woman Quaker, that has suffered the law here, that shall presume to come into this jurisdiction, shall be severely whipped, and kept at the House of Correction at work, until she be sent away at her own charge, and so also for her coming again, she shall be alike used as aforesaid.

"And for every Quaker, he or she, that shall a third time herein again offend, they shall have their tongues bored through with a hot iron, and be kept at the House of Correction close to work, until they be sent away at their own charge.

"And it is further ordered, that all and every Quaker arising from among ourselves, shall be dealt with, and suffer the like punishment as the law provides against foreign Quakers.

"EDWARD RAWSON, Sec."

"An Act Made at a General Court, Held at Boston, the Twentieth of October, 1658

"Whereas, there is a pernicious sect, commonly called Quakers, lately risen, who by word and writing have published and maintained many dangerous and horrid tenets, and do take upon them to change and alter the received laudable customs of our nation, in giving civil respects to equals, or reverence to superiors; whose actions tend to undermine the civil government, and also to destroy the order of the churches, by denying all established forms of worship, and by withdrawing from orderly Church fellowship, allowed and approved by all orthodox professors of truth, and instead thereof, and in opposition thereunto, frequently meeting by themselves, insinuating themselves into the minds of the simple, or such as are at least affected to the order and government of church and commonwealth, whereby divers of our inhabitants have been infected, notwithstanding all former laws, made upon the experience of their arrogant and bold obtrusions, to disseminate their principles amongst us, prohibiting their coming into this jurisdiction, they have not been deferred from their impious attempts to undermine our peace, and hazard our ruin.

"For prevention thereof, this court doth order and enact, that any person or persons, of the cursed sect of the Quakers, who is not an inhabitant of, but is found within this jurisdiction, shall be apprehended without warrant, where no magistrate is at hand, by any constable, commissioner, or selectman, and conveyed from constable to constable, to the next magistrate, who shall commit the said person to close prison, there to remain (without bail) until the next court of Assistants, where they shall have legal trial.

"And being convicted to be of the sect of the Quakers, shall be sentenced to banishment, on pain of death. And that every inhabitant of this jurisdiction, being convicted to be of the aforesaid sect, either by taking up, publishing, or defending the horrid opinions of the Quakers, or the stirring up mutiny, sedition, or rebellion against the government, or by taking up their abusive and destructive practices, viz. denying civil respect to equals and superiors, and withdrawing from the Church assemblies; and instead thereof, frequenting meetings of their own, in opposition to our Church order; adhering to, or approving of any known Quaker, and the tenets and practices of Quakers, that are opposite to the orthodox received opinions of the godly; and endeavoring to disaffect others to civil government and Church order, or condemning the practice and proceedings of this court against the Quakers, manifesting thereby their complying with those, whose design is to overthrow the order established in Church and state: every such person, upon conviction before the said court of Assistants, in manner aforesaid, shall be committed to close prison for one month, and then, unless they choose voluntarily to depart this jurisdiction, shall give bond for their good behavior and appear at the next court, continuing obstinate, and refusing to retract and reform the aforesaid opinions, they shall be sentenced to banishment, upon pain of death. And any one magistrate, upon information given him of any such person, shall cause him to be apprehended, and shall commit any such person to prison, according to his discretion, until he come to trial as aforesaid."

It appears there were also laws passed in both of the then colonies of New Plymouth and New Haven, and in the Dutch settlement at New Amsterdam, now New York, prohibiting the people called Quakers, from coming into those places, under severe penalties; in consequence of which, some underwent considerable suffering.

The two first who were executed were William Robinson, merchant, of London, and Marmaduke Stevenson, a countryman, of Yorkshire. These coming to Boston, in the beginning of September, were sent for by the court of Assistants, and there sentenced to banishment, on pain of death. This sentence was passed also on Mary Dyar, mentioned hereafter, and Nicholas Davis, who were both at Boston. But William Robinson, being looked upon as a teacher, was also condemned to be whipped severely; and the constable was commanded to get an able man to do it. Then Robinson was brought into the street, and there stripped; and having his hands put through the holes of the carriage of a great gun, where the jailer held him, the executioner gave him twenty stripes, with a threefold cord whip, Then he and the other prisoners were shortly after released, and banished, as appears from the following warrant:

"You are required by these, presently to set at liberty William Robinson, Marmaduke Stevenson, Mary Dyar, and Nicholas Davis, who, by an order of the court and council, had been imprisoned, because it appeared by their own confession, words, and actions, that they are Quakers: wherefore, a sentence was pronounced against them, to depart this jurisdiction, on pain of death; and that they must answer it at their peril, if they or any of them, after the fourteenth of this present month, September, are found within this jurisdiction, or any part thereof.

"EDWARD RAWSON."

"Boston, September 12, 1659."

Though Mary Dyar and Nicholas Davis left that jurisdiction for that time, yet Robinson and Stevenson, though they departed the town of Boston, could not yet resolve (not being free in mind) to depart that jurisdiction, though their lives were at stake. And so they went to Salem, and some places thereabouts, to visit and build up their friends in the faith. But it was not long before they were taken and put again into prison at Boston, and chains locked to their legs. In the next month, Mary Dyar returned also. And as she stood before the prison, speaking with one Christopher Holden, who was come thither to inquire for a ship bound for England, whither he intended to go, she was also taken into custody.

Thus, they had now three persons, who, according to their law, had forfeited their lives. And, on the twentieth of October, these three were brought into court, where John Endicot and others were assembled. And being called to the bar, Endicot commanded the keeper to pull off their hats; and then said, that they had made several laws to keep the Quakers from amongst them, and neither whipping, nor imprisoning, nor cutting off ears, nor banishment upon pain of death, would keep them from amongst them. And further, he said, that he or they desired not the death of any of them. Yet, notwithstanding, his following words, without more ado were, "Give ear, and hearken to your sentence of death." Sentence of death was also passed upon Marmaduke Stevenson, Mary Dyar, and William Edrid. Several others were imprisoned, whipped, and fined.

We have no disposition to justify the Pilgrims for these proceedings, but we think, considering the circumstances of the age in which they lived, their conduct admits of much palliation.

The fathers of New England, endured incredible hardships in providing for themselves a home in the wilderness; and to protect themselves in the undisturbed enjoyment of rights, which they had purchased at so dear a rate, they sometimes adopted measures, which, if tried by the more enlightened and liberal views of the present day, must at once be pronounced altogether unjustifiable. But shall they be condemned without mercy for not acting up to principles which were unacknowledged and unknown throughout the whole of Christendom? Shall they alone be held responsible for opinions and conduct which had become sacred by antiquity, and which were common to Christians of all other denominations? Every government then in existence assumed to itself the right to legislate in matters of religion; and to restrain heresy by penal statutes. This right was claimed by rulers, admitted by subjects, and is sanctioned by the names of Lord Bacon and Montesquieu, and many others equally famed for their talents and learning. It is unjust then, to 'press upon one poor persecuted sect, the sins of all Christendom.' The fault of our fathers was the fault of the age; and though this cannot justify, it certainly furnishes an extenuation of their conduct. As well might you condemn them for not understanding and acting up to the principles of religious toleration. At the same time, it is but just to say, that imperfect as were their views of the rights of conscience, they were nevertheless far in advance of the age to which they belonged; and it is to them more than to any other class of men on earth, the world is indebted for the more rational views that now prevail on the subject of civil and religious liberty.

CHAPTER XIX

An Account of the Life and Persecutions of John Bunyan

THIS great Puritan was born the same year that the Pilgrim Fathers landed at Plymouth. His home was Elstow, near Bedford, in England. His father was a tinker and he was brought up to the same trade. He was a lively, likeable boy with a serious and almost morbid side to his nature. All during his young manhood he was repenting for the vices of his youth and yet he had never been either a drunkard or immoral. The particular acts that troubled his conscience were dancing, ringing the church bells, and playing tipcat. It was while playing the latter game one day that "a voice did suddenly dart from Heaven into my soul, which said, 'Wilt thou leave thy sins and go to Heaven, or have thy sins and go to Hell?'" At about this time he overheard three or four poor women in Bedford talking, as they sat at the door in the sun. "Their talk was about the new birth, the work of God in the hearts. They were far above my reach."

In his youth he was a member of the parliamentary army for a year. The death of his comrade close beside him deepened his tendency to serious thoughts, and there were times when he seemed almost insane in his zeal and penitence. He was at one time quite assured that he had sinned the unpardonable sin against the Holy Ghost. While he was still a young man he married a good woman who bought him a library of pious books which he read with assiduity, thus confirming his earnestness and increasing his love of religious controversies.

His conscience was still further awakened through the persecution of the religious body of Baptists to whom he had joined himself. Before he was thirty years old he had become a leading Baptist preacher.

Then came his turn for persecution. He was arrested for preaching without license. "Before I went down to the justice, I begged of God that His will be done; for I was not without hopes that my imprisonment might be an awakening to the saints in the country. Only in that matter did I commit the thing to God. And verily at my return I did meet my God sweetly in the prison."

His hardships were genuine, on account of the wretched condition of the prisons of those days. To this confinement was added the personal grief of being parted from his young and second wife and four small children, and particularly, his little blind daughter. While he was in jail he was solaced by the two books which he had brought with him, the Bible and Fox's "Book of Martyrs."

Although he wrote some of his early books during this long imprisonment, it was not until his second and shorter one, three years after the first, that he composed his immortal "Pilgrim's Progress," which was published three years later. In an earlier tract he had thought briefly of the similarity between human life and a pilgrimage, and he now worked this theme out in fascinating detail, using the rural scenery of England for his background, the splendid city of London for his Vanity Fair, and the saints and villains of his own personal acquaintance for the finely drawn characters of his allegory.

The "Pilgrim's Progress" is truly the rehearsal of Bunyan's own spiritual experiences. He himself had been the 'man cloathed in Rags, with his Face from his own House, a Book in his hand, and a great Burden upon his Back.' After he had realized that Christ was his Righteousness, and that this did not depend on "the good frame of his Heart"—or, as we should say, on his feelings—"now did the Chains fall off my legs indeed." His had been Doubting Castle and Sloughs of Despond, with much of the Valley of Humiliation and the Shadow of Death. But, above all, it is a book of Victory. Once when he was leaving the doors of the courthouse where he himself had been defeated, he wrote: "As I was going forth of the doors, I had much ado to bear saying to them, that I carried the peace of God along with me." In his vision was ever the Celestial City, with all its bells ringing. He had fought Apollyon constantly, and often wounded, shamed and fallen, yet in the end "more than conqueror through Him that loved us."

His book was at first received with much criticism from his Puritan friends, who saw in it only an addition to the worldly literature of his day, but there was not much then for Puritans to read, and it was not long before it was devoutly laid beside their Bibles and perused with gladness and with profit. It was perhaps two centuries later before literary critics began to realize that this story, so full of human reality and interest and so marvelously modeled upon the English of the King James translation of the Bible, is one of the glories of English literature. In his later years he wrote several other allegories, of which of one of them, "The Holy War," it has been said that, "If the 'Pilgrim's Progress' had never been written it would be regarded as the finest allegory in the language."

During the later years of his life, Bunyan remained in Bedford as a venerated local pastor and preacher. He was also a favorite speaker in the non-conformist pulpits of London. He became so national a leader and teacher that he was frequently called "Bishop Bunyan."

In his helpful and unselfish personal life he was apostolic. His last illness was due to exposure upon a journey in which he was endeavoring to reconcile a father with his son. His end came on the third of August, 1688. He was buried in Bunhill Fields, a church yard in London.

There is no doubt but that the "Pilgrim's Progress" has been more helpful than any other book but the Bible. It was timely, for they were still burning martyrs in Vanity Fair while he was writing. It is enduring, for while it tells little of living the Christian life in the family and community, it does interpret that life so far as it is an expression of the solitary soul, in homely language. Bunyan indeed "showed how to build a princely throne on humble truth." He has been his own Greatheart, dauntless guide to pilgrims, to many.

CHAPTER XX

An Account of the Life of John Wesley

JOHN WESLEY was born on the seventeenth of June, 1703, in Epworth rectory, England, the fifteenth of nineteen children of Charles and Suzanna Wesley. The father of Wesley was a preacher, and Wesley's mother was a remarkable woman in wisdom and intelligence. She was a woman of deep piety and brought her little ones into close contact with the Bible stories, telling them from the tiles about the nursery fireplace. She also used to dress the children in their best on the days when they were to have the privilege of learning their alphabet as an introduction to the reading of the Holy Scriptures.

Young Wesley was a gay and manly youth, fond of games and particularly of dancing. At Oxford he was a leader, and during the latter part of his course there, was one of the founders of the "Holy Club," an organization of serious-minded students. His religious nature deepened through study and experience, but it was not until several years after he left the university and came under the influence of Luther's writings that he felt that he had entered into the full riches of the Gospel.

He and his brother Charles were sent by the Society for the Propagation of the Gospel to Georgia, where both of them developed their powers as preachers.

Upon their passage they fell into the company of several Moravian brethren, members of the association recently renewed by the labors of Count Zinzendorf. It was noted by John Wesley in his diary that, in a great tempest, when the English people on board lost all self-possession, these Germans impressed him by their composure and entire resignation to God. He also marked their humility under shameful treatment.

It was on his return to England that he entered in__ those deeper experiences and developed those marvelous powers as a popular preacher which made him a national leader. He was associated at this time also with George Whitefield, the tradition of whose marvelous eloquence has never died.

What he accomplished borders upon the incredible. Upon entering his eighty-fifth year he thanked God that he was still almost as vigorous as ever. He ascribed it, under God, to the fact that he had always slept soundly, had risen for sixty years at four o'clock in the morning, and for fifty years had preached every morning at five. Seldom in all his life did he feel any pain, care, or anxiety. He preached twice each day, and often thrice or four times. It has been estimated that he traveled every year forty-five hundred English miles, mostly upon horseback.

The successes won by Methodist preaching had to be gained through a long series of years, and amid the most bitter persecutions. In nearly every part of England it was met at the first by the mob with stonings and peltings, with attempts at wounding and slaying. Only at times was there any interference on the part of the civil power. The two Wesleys faced all these dangers with amazing courage, and with a calmness equally astonishing. What was more irritating was the heaping up of slander and abuse by the writers of the day. These books are now all forgotten.

Wesley had been in his youth a high churchman and was always deeply devoted to the Established Communion. When he found it necessary to ordain preachers, the separation of his followers from the established body became inevitable. The name "Methodist" soon attached to them, because of the particular organizing power of their leader and the ingenious methods that he applied.

The Wesley fellowship, which after his death grew into the great Methodist Church, was characterized by an almost military perfection of organization.

The entire management of his ever-growing denomination rested upon Wesley himself. The annual conference, established in 1744, acquired a governing power only after the death of Wesley. Charles Wesley rendered the society a service incalculably great by his hymns. They introduced a new era in the hymnology of the English Church. John Wesley apportioned his days to his work in leading the Church, to studying (for he was an incessant reader), to traveling, and to preaching.

Wesley was untiring in his efforts to disseminate useful knowledge throughout his denomination. He planned for the mental culture of his traveling preachers and local exhorters, and for schools of instruction for the future teachers of the Church. He himself prepared books for popular use upon universal history, church history, and natural history. In this Wesley was an apostle of the modern union of mental culture with Christian living. He published also the best matured of his sermons and various theological works. These, both by their depth and their penetration of thought, and by their purity and precision of style, excite our admiration.

John Wesley was of but ordinary stature, and yet of noble presence. His features were very handsome even in old age. He had an open brow, an eagle nose, a clear eye, and a fresh complexion. His manners were fine, and in choice company with Christian people he enjoyed relaxation. Persistent, laborious love for men's souls, steadfastness, and tranquillity of spirit were his most prominent traits of character. Even in doctrinal controversies he exhibited the greatest calmness. He was kind and very liberal. His industry has been named already. In the last fifty-two years of his life, it is estimated that he preached more than forty thousand sermons.

Wesley brought sinners to repentance throughout three kingdoms and over two hemispheres. He was the bishop of such a diocese as neither the Eastern nor the Western Church ever witnessed before. What is there in the circle of Christian effort—foreign missions, home missions, Christian tracts and literature, field preaching, circuit preaching, Bible readings, or aught else—which was not attempted by John Wesley, which was not grasped by his mighty mind through the aid of his Divine Leader?

To him it was granted to arouse the English Church, when it had lost sight of Christ the Redeemer to a renewed Christian life. By preaching the justifying and renewing of the soul through belief upon Christ, he lifted many thousands of the humbler classes of the English people from their exceeding ignorance and evil habits, and made them earnest, faithful Christians. His untiring effort made itself felt not in England alone, but in America and in continental Europe. Not only the germs of almost all the existing zeal in England on behalf of Christian truth and life are due to Methodism, but the activity stirred up in other portions of Protestant Europe we must trace indirectly, at least, to Wesley.

He died in 1791 after a long life of tireless labor and unselfish service. His fervent spirit and hearty brotherhood still survives in the body that cherishes his name.

CHAPTER XXI

Persecutions of the French Protestants in the South of France, During the Years 1814 and 1820

THE persecution in this Protestant part of France continued with very little intermission from the revocation of the edict of Nantes, by Louis XIV until a very short period previous to the commencement of the late French Revolution. In the year 1785, M. Rebaut St. Etienne and the celebrated M. de la Fayette were among the first persons who interested themselves with the court of Louis XVI in removing the scourge of persecution from this injured people, the inhabitants of the south of France.

Such was the opposition on the part of the Catholics and the courtiers, that it was not until the end of the year 1790, that the Protestants were freed from their alarms. Previously to this, the Catholics at Nismes in particular, had taken up arms; Nismes then presented a frightful spectacle; armed men ran through the city, fired from the corners of the streets, and attacked all they met with swords and forks.

A man named Astuc was wounded and thrown into the aqueduct; Baudon fell under the repeated strokes of bayonets and sabers, and his body was also thrown into the water; Boucher, a young man only seventeen years of age, was shot as he was looking out of his window; three electors wounded, one dangerously; another elector wounded, only escaped death by repeatedly declaring he was a Catholic; a third received four saber wounds, and was taken home dreadfully mangled. The citizens that fled were arrested by the Catholics upon the roads, and obliged to give proofs of their religion before their lives were granted. M. and Madame Vogue were at their country house, which the zealots broke open, where they massacred both, and destroyed their dwelling. M. Blacher, a Protestant seventy years of age, was cut to pieces with a sickle; young Pyerre, carrying some food to his brother, was asked, "Catholic or Protestant?" "Protestant," being the reply, a monster fired at the lad, and he fell. One of the murderer's companions said, "You might as well have killed a lamb." "I have sworn," replied he, "to kill four Protestants for my share, and this will count for one." However, as these atrocities provoked the troops to unite in defence of the people, a terrible vengeance was retaliated upon the Catholic party that had used arms, which with other circumstances, especially the toleration exercised by Napoleon Bonaparte, kept them down completely until the year 1814, when the unexpected return of the ancient government rallied them all once more round the old banners.

The Arrival of King Louis XVIII at Paris

This was known at Nismes on the thirteenth of April, 1814. In a quarter of an hour, the white cockade was seen in every direction, the white flag floated on the public buildings, on the splendid monuments of antiquity, and even on the tower of Mange, beyond the city walls. The Protestants, whose commerce had suffered materially during the war, were among the first to unite in the general joy, and to send in their adhesion to the senate, and the legislative body; and several of the Protestant departments sent addresses to the throne, but unfortunately, M. Froment was again at Nismes at the moment, when many bigots being ready to join him, the blindness and fury of the sixteenth century rapidly succeeded the intelligence and philanthropy of the nineteenth. A line of distinction was instantly traced between men of different religious opinions; the spirit of the old Catholic Church was again to regulate each person's share of esteem and safety.

The difference of religion was now to govern everything else; and even Catholic domestics who had served Protestants with zeal and affection began to neglect their duties, or to perform them ungraciously, and with reluctance. At the fêtes and spectacles that were given at the public expense, the absence of the Protestants was charged on them as a proof of their disloyalty; and in the midst of the cries of *Vive le Roi!* the discordant sounds of *A bas le Maire,* down with the mayor, were heard. M. Castletan was a Protestant; he appeared in public with the prefect M. Ruland, a Catholic, when potatoes were thrown at him, and the people declared that he ought to resign his office. The bigots of Nismes, even succeeded in procuring an address to be presented to the king, stating that there ought to be in France but one God, one king, and one faith. In this they were imitated by the Catholics of several towns.

The History of the Silver Child

About this time, M. Baron, counsellor of the Cour Royale of Nismes, formed the plan of dedicating to God a silver child, if the Duchess d'Angouleme would give a prince to France. This project was converted into a public religious vow, which was the subject of conversation both in public and private, whilst persons, whose imaginations were inflamed by these proceedings, ran about the streets crying *Vivent les Bourbons,* or "the Bourbons forever." In consequence of this superstitious frenzy, it is said that at Alais women were advised and instigated to poison their Protestant husbands, and at length it was found convenient to accuse them of political crimes. They could no longer appear in public without insults and injuries. When the mobs met with Protestants, they seized them, and danced round them with barbarous joy, and amidst repeated cries of *Vive le Roi,* they sang verses, the burden of which was, "We will wash our hands in Protestant blood, and make black puddings of the blood of Calvin's children."

The citizens who came to the promenades for air and refreshment from the close and dirty streets were chased with shouts of *Vive le Roi,* as if those shouts were to justify every excess. If Protestants referred to the charter, they were directly assured it would be of no use to them, and that they had only been managed to be more effectually destroyed. Persons of rank were heard to say in the public streets, "All the Huguenots must be killed; this time their children must be killed, that none of the accursed race may remain."

Still, it is true, they were not murdered, but cruelly treated; Protestant children could no longer mix in the sports of Catholics, and were not even permitted to appear without their parents. At dark their families shut themselves up in their apartments; but even then stones were thrown against their windows. When they arose in the morning it was not uncommon to find gibbets drawn on their doors or walls; and in the streets the Catholics held cords already soaped before their eyes, and pointed out the instruments by which they hoped and designed to exterminate them. Small gallows or models were handed about, and a man who lived opposite to one of the pastors, exhibited one of these models in his window, and made signs sufficiently intelligible when the minister passed. A figure represent-ing a Protestant preacher was also hung up on a public crossway, and the most atrocious songs were sung under his window.

Towards the conclusion of the carnival, a plan had even been formed to make a caricature of the four ministers of the place, and burn them in effigy; but this was prevented by the mayor of Nismes, a Protestant. A dreadful song presented to the prefect, in the country dialect, with a false translation, was printed by his approval, and had a great run before he saw the extent of the error into which he had been betrayed. The sixty-third regiment of the line was publicly censured and insulted, for having, according to order, protected Protestants. In fact, the Protestants seemed to be as sheep destined for the slaughter.

The Catholic Arms at Beaucaire

In May, 1815, a federative association, similar to that of Lyons, Grenoble, Paris, Avignon, and Montpelier, was desired by many persons at Nismes; but this federation terminated here after an ephemeral and illusory existence of fourteen days. In the meanwhile a large party of Catholic zealots were in arms at Beaucaire, and who soon pushed their patroles so near the walls of Nismes, "so as to alarm the inhabitants." These Catholics applied to the English off Marseilles for assistance, and obtained the grant of one thousand muskets, ten thousand cartouches, etc. General Gilly, however, was soon sent against these partizans, who prevented them from coming to extremes by granting them an armistice; and yet when Louis XVIII had returned to Paris, after the expiration of Napoleon's reign of a hundred days, and peace and party spirit seemed to have been subdued, even at Nismes, bands from Beaucaire joined Trestaillon in this city, to glut the vengeance they had so long premeditated. General Gilly had left the department several days: the troops of the line left behind had taken the white cockade, and waited further orders, whilst the new commissioners had only to proclaim the cessation of hostilities and the complete establishment of the king's authority. In vain, no commissioners appeared, no despatches arrived to calm and regulate the public mind; but towards evening the advanced guard of the banditti, to the amount of several hundreds, entered the city, undesired but unopposed.

As they marched without order or discipline, covered with clothes or rags of all colors, decorated with cockades, not *white,* but *white* and *green,* armed with muskets, sabers, forks, pistols and reaping hooks, intoxicated with wine, and stained with the blood of the Protestants whom they had murdered on their route, they presented a most hideous and appalling spectacle. In the open place in the front of the barracks, this banditti was joined by the city armed mob, headed by Jaques Dupont, commonly called Trestaillon. To save the effusion of blood, this garrison of about five hundred men consented to capitulate, and marched out sad and defenceless; but when about fifty had passed, the rabble commenced a tremendous fire on their confiding and unprotected victims; nearly all were killed or wounded, and but very few could re-enter the yard before the garrison gates were again closed. These were again forced in an instant, and all were massacred who could not climb over roofs, or leap into the adjoining gardens. In a word, death met them in every place and in every shape, and this Catholic massacre rivalled in cruelty and surpassed in treachery the crimes of the September assassins of Paris, and the Jacobinical butcheries of Lyons and Avignon. It was marked not only by the fervor of the Revolution but by the subtlety of the league, and will long remain a blot upon the history of the second restoration.

Massacre and Pillage at Nismes

Nismes now exhibited a most awful scene of outrage and carnage, though many of the Protestants had fled to the Convennes and the Gardonenque. The country houses of Messrs. Rey, Guiret, and several others, had been pillaged, and the inhabitants treated with wanton barbarity. Two parties had glutted their savage appetites on the farm of Madame Frat: the first, after eating, drinking, and breaking the furniture, and stealing what they thought proper, took leave by announcing the arrival of their comrades, 'compared with whom,' they said, 'they should be thought merciful.' Three men and an old woman were left on the premises: at the sight of the second company two of the men fled. "Are you a Catholic?" said the banditti to the old woman. "Yes." "Repeat, then, your *Pater* and *Ave.*" Being terrified, she hesitated, and was instantly knocked down with a musket. On recovering her senses, she stole out of the house, but met Ladet, the old *valet de ferme,* bringing in a salad which the depredators had ordered him to cut. In vain she endeavored to persuade him to fly. "Are you a Protestant?" they exclaimed; "I am." A musket being discharged at him, he fell wounded, but not dead. To consummate their work, the monsters lighted a fire with straw and boards, threw their living victim into the flames, and suffered him to expire in the most dreadful agonies. They then ate their salad, omelet, etc. The next day, some laborers, seeing the house open and deserted, entered, and discovered the half consumed body of Ladet. The prefect of the Gard, M. Darbaud Jouques, attempting to palliate the crimes of the Catholics, had the audacity to assert that Ladet was a Catholic; but this was publicly contradicted by two of the pastors at Nismes.

Another party committed a dreadful murder at St. Cezaire, upon Imbert la Plume, the husband of Suzon Chivas. He was met on returning from work in the fields. The chief promised him his life, but insisted that he must be conducted to the prison at Nismes. Seeing, however, that the party was determined to kill him, he resumed his natural character, and being a powerful and courageous man advanced and exclaimed, "You are brigands—fire!" Four of them fired, and he fell, but he was not dead; and while living they mutilated his body; and then passing a cord round it, drew it along, attached to a cannon of which they had possession. It was not until after eight days that his relatives were apprised of his death. Five individuals of the family of Chivas, all husbands and fathers, were massacred in the course of a few days.

The merciless treatment of the women, in this persecution at Nismes, was such as would have disgraced any savages ever heard of. The widows Rivet and Bernard were forced to sacrifice enormous sums; and the house of Mrs. Lecointe was ravaged, and her goods destroyed. Mrs. F. Didier had her dwelling sacked and nearly demolished to the foundation. A party of these bigots visited the widow Perrin, who lived on a little farm at the windmills; having committed every species of devastation, they attacked even the sanctuary of the dead, which contained the relics of her family. They dragged the coffins out, and scattered the contents over the adjacent grounds. In vain this outraged widow collected the bones of her ancestors and replaced them: they were again dug up; and, after several useless efforts, they were reluctantly left spread over the surface of the fields.

Royal Decree in Favor of the Persecuted

At length the decree of Louis XVIII which annulled all the extraordinary powers conferred either by the king, the princes, or subordinate agents, was received at Nismes, and the laws were now to be administered by the regular organs, and a new prefect arrived to carry them into effect; but in spite of proclamations, the work of destruction, stopped for a moment, was not abandoned, but soon renewed with fresh vigor and effect. On the thirtieth of July, Jacques Combe, the father of a family, was killed by some of the national guards of Rusau, and the crime was so public, that the commander of the party restored to the family the pocketbook and papers of the deceased. On the following day tumultuous crowds roamed about the city and suburbs, threatening the wretched peasants; and on the first of August they butchered them without opposition.

About noon on the same day, six armed men, headed by Truphemy, the butcher, surrounded the house of Monot, a carpenter; two of the party, who were smiths, had been at work in the house the day before, and had seen a Protestant who had taken refuge there, M. Bourillon, who had been a lieutenant in the army, and had retired on a pension. He was a man of an excellent character, peaceable and harmless, and had never served the emperor Napoleon. Truphemy not knowing him, he was pointed out partaking of a frugal breakfast with the family. Truphemy ordered him to go along with him, adding, "Your friend, Saussine, is already in the other world." Truphemy placed him in the middle of his troop, and artfully ordered him to cry *Vive l'Empereur* he refused, adding, he had never served the emperor. In vain did the women and children of the house intercede for his life, and praise his amiable and virtuous qualities. He was marched to the Esplanade and shot, first by Truphemy and then by the others. Several persons, attracted by the firing approached, but were threatened with a similar fate.

After some time the wretches departed, shouting *Vive le Roi.* Some women met them, and one of them appearing affected, said, "I have killed seven to-day, for my share, and if you say a word, you shall be the eighth." Pierre Courbet, a stocking weaver, was torn from his loom by an armed band, and shot at his own door. His eldest daughter was knocked down with the butt end of a musket; and a poignard was held at the breast of his wife while the mob plundered her apartments. Paul Heraut, a silk weaver, was literally cut in pieces, in the presence of a large crowd, and amidst the unavailing cries and tears of his wife and four young children. The murderers only abandoned the corpse to return to Heraut's house and secure everything valuable. The number of murders on this day could not be ascertained. One person saw six bodies at the *Cours Neuf,* and nine were carried to the hospital.

If murder some time after, became less frequent for a few days, pillage and forced contributions were actively enforced. M. Salle d'Hombro, at several visits was robbed of seven thousand francs; and on one occasion, when he pleaded the sacrifices he had made. "Look," said a bandit, pointing to his pipe, "this will set fire to your house; and this," brandishing his sword, "will finish you." No reply could be made to these arguments. M. Feline, a silk manufacturer, was robbed of thirty-two thousand francs in gold, three thousand francs in silver, and several bales of silk.

The small shopkeepers were continually exposed to visits and demands of provisions, drapery, or whatever they sold; and the same hands that set fire to the houses of the rich, and tore up the vines of the cultivator, broke the looms of the weaver, and stole the tools of the artisan. Desolation reigned in the sanctuary and in the city. The armed bands, instead of being reduced, were increased; the fugitives, instead of returning, received constant accessions, and their friends who sheltered them were deemed rebellious. Those Protestants who remained were deprived of all their civil and religious rights, and even the advocates and huissiers entered into a resolution to exclude all of "the pretended reformed religion" from their bodies. Those who were employed in selling tobacco were deprived of their licenses. The Protestant deacons who had the charge of the poor were all scattered. Of five pastors only two remained; one of these was obliged to change his residence, and could only venture to administer the consolations of religion, or perform the functions of his ministry under cover of the night.

Not content with these modes of torment, calumnious and inflammatory publications charged the Protestants with raising the proscribed standard in the communes, and invoking the fallen Napoleon; and, of course, as unworthy the protection of the laws and the favor of the monarch.

Hundreds after this were dragged to prison without even so much as a *written order;* and though an official newspaper, bearing the title of the *Journal du Gard,* was set up for five months, while it was influenced by the prefect, the mayor, and other functionaries, the word "charter" was never once used in it. One of the first numbers, on the contrary, represented the suffering Protestants, as "Crocodiles, only weeping from rage and regret that they had no more victims to devour; as persons who had surpassed Danton, Marat, and Robespierre, in doing mischief; and as having prostituted their daughters to the garrison to gain it over to Napoleon." An extract from this article, stamped with the crown and the arms of the Bourbons, was hawked about the streets, and the vender was adorned with the medal of the police.

Petition of the Protestant Refugees

To these reproaches it is proper to oppose the petition which the Protestant refugees in Paris presented to Louis XVIII in behalf of their brethren at Nismes.

"We lay at your feet, sire, our acute sufferings. In your name our fellow citizens are slaughtered, and their property laid waste. Misled peasants, in pretended obedience to your orders, had assembled at the command of a commissioner appointed by your august nephew. Although ready to attack us, they were received with the assurances of peace. On the fifteenth of July, 1815, we learned your majesty's entrance into Paris, and the white flag immediately waved on our edifices. The public tranquillity had not been disturbed, when armed peasants introduced themselves. The garrison capitulated, but were assailed on their departure, and almost totally massacred. Our national guard was disarmed, the city filled with strangers, and the houses of the principal inhabitants, professing the reformed religion, were attacked and plundered. We subjoin the list. Terror has driven from our city the most respectable inhabitants.

"Your majesty has been deceived if there has not been placed before you the picture of the horrors which make a desert of your good city of Nismes. Arrests and proscriptions are continually taking place, and difference of *religious* opinions is the real and only cause. The calumniated Protestants are the defenders of the throne. Your nephew has beheld our children under his banners; our fortunes have been placed in his hands. Attacked without reason, the Protestants have not, even by a just resistance, afforded their enemies the fatal pretext for calumny. Save us, sire! extinguish the brand of civil war; a single act of your will would restore to political existence a city interesting for its population and its manufactures. Demand an account of their conduct from the chiefs who have brought our misfortunes upon us. We place before your eyes all the documents that have reached us. Fear paralyzes the hearts, and stifles the complaints of our fellow citizens. Placed in a more secure situation, we venture to raise our voice in their behalf," etc., etc.

Monstrous Outrage Upon Females

At Nismes it is well known that the women wash their clothes either at the fountains or on the banks of streams. There is a large basin near the fountain, where numbers of women may be seen every day, kneeling at the edge of the water, and beating the clothes with heavy pieces of wood in the shape of battledores. This spot became the scene of the most shameful and indecent practices. The Catholic rabble turned the women's petticoats over their heads, and so fastened them as to continue their exposure, and their subjection to a newly invented species of chastisement; for nails being placed in the wood of the *battoirs* in the form of *fleur-de-lis,* they beat them until the blood streamed from their bodies, and their cries rent the air. Often was death demanded as a commutation of this ignominious punishment, but refused with a malignant joy. To carry their outrage to the highest possible degree, several who were in a state of pregnancy were assailed in this manner. The scandalous nature of these outrages prevented many of the sufferers from making them public, and, especially, from relating the most aggravating circumstances. "I have seen," says M. Duran, "a Catholic advocat, accompanying the assassins of the fauxbourg Bourgade, arm a *battoir* with sharp nails in the form of *fleur-de-lis;* I have seen them raise the garments of females, and apply, with heavy blows, to the bleeding body this *battoir* or battledore, to which they gave a name which my pen refuses to record. The cries of the sufferers—the streams of blood—the murmurs of indignation which were suppressed by fear—nothing could move them. The surgeons who attended on those women who are dead, can attest, by the marks of their wounds, the agonies which they must have endured, which, however horrible, is most strictly true."

Nevertheless, during the progress of these horrors and obscenities, so disgraceful to France and the Catholic religion, the agents of government had a powerful force under their command, and by honestly employing it they might have restored tranquillity. Murder and robbery, however, continued, and were winked at, by the Catholic magistrates, with very few exceptions; the administrative authorities, it is true, used words in their proclamations, etc., but never had recourse to actions to stop the enormities of the persecutors, who boldly declared that, on the twenty-fourth, the anniversary of St. Bartholomew, they intended to make a general massacre. The members of the Reformed Church were filled with terror, and, instead of taking part in the election of deputies, were occupied as well as they could in providing for their own personal safety.

Outrages Committed in the Villages, etc.

We now quit Nismes to take a view of the conduct of the persecutors in the surrounding country. After the re-establishment of the royal government, the local authorities were distinguished for their zeal and forwardness in supporting their employers, and, under pretence of rebellion, concealment of arms, nonpayment of contributions, etc., troops, national guards, and armed mobs, were permitted to plunder, arrest, and murder peaceable citizens, not merely with impunity, but with encouragement and approbation. At the village of Milhaud, near Nismes, the inhabitants were frequently forced to pay large sums to avoid being pillaged. This, however, would not avail at Madame Teulon's: On Sunday, the sixteenth of July, her house and grounds were ravaged; the valuable furniture removed or destroyed, the hay and wood burnt, and the corpse of a child, buried in the garden, taken up and dragged round a fire made by the populace. It was with great difficulty that M. Teulon escaped with his life.

M. Picherol, another Protestant, had deposited some of his effects with a Catholic neighbor; this house was attacked, and though all the property of the latter was respected, that of his friend was seized and destroyed. At the same village, one of a party doubting whether M. Hermet, a tailor, was the man they wanted, asked, "Is he a Protestant?" this he acknowledged. "Good," said they, and he was instantly murdered. In the canton of Vauvert, where there was a consistory church, eighty thousand francs were extorted.

In the communes of Beauvoisin and Generac similar excesses were committed by a handful of licentious men, under the eye of the Catholic mayor, and to the cries of *Vive le Roi!* St. Gilles was the scene of the most unblushing villainy. The Protestants, the most wealthy of the inhabitants, were disarmed, whilst their houses were pillaged.

The mayor was appealed to; but he laughed and walked away. This officer had, at his disposal, a national guard of several hundred men, organized by his own orders. It would be wearisome to read the lists of the crimes that occurred during many months. At Clavisson the mayor prohibited the Protestants the practice of singing the Psalms commonly used in the temple, that, as he said, the Catholics might not be offended or disturbed.

At Sommieres, about ten miles from Nismes, the Catholics made a splendid procession through the town, which continued until evening and was succeeded by the plunder of the Protestants. On the arrival of foreign troops at Sommieres, the pretended search for arms was resumed; those who did not possess muskets were even compelled to buy them on purpose to surrender them up, and soldiers were quartered on them at six francs per day until they produced the articles in demand. The Protestant church which had been closed, was converted into barracks for the Austrians. After divine service had been suspended for six months at Nismes, the church, called the Temple by the Protestants, was re-opened, and public worship performed on the morning of the twenty-fourth of December. On examining the belfry, it was discovered that some persons had carried off the clapper of the bell. As the hour of service approached, a number of men, women, and children collected at the house of M. Ribot, the pastor, and threatened to prevent the worship. At the appointed time, when he proceeded towards the church, he was surrounded; the most savage shouts were raised against him; some of the women seized him by the collar; but nothing could disturb his firmness, or excite his impatience; he entered the house of prayer, and ascended the pulpit. Stones were thrown in and fell among the worshippers; still the congregation remained calm and attentive, and the service was concluded amidst noise, threats, and outrage.

On retiring many would have been killed but for the chasseurs of the garrison, who honorably and zealously protected them. From the captain of these chasseurs, M. Ribot soon after received the following letter.

January 2, 1816.

"I deeply lament the prejudices of the Catholics against the *Protestants,* who they pretend do not love the king. Continue to act as you have hitherto done, and time and your conduct will convince the Catholics to the contrary: should any tumult occur similar to that of Saturday last inform me. I preserve my reports of these acts, and if the agitators prove incorrigible, and forget what they owe to the best of kings and the *charter,* I will do my duty and inform the government of their proceedings. Adieu, my dear sir; assure the consistory of my esteem, and of the sense I entertain of the moderation with which they have met the provocations of the evil-disposed at Sommieres. I have the honor to salute you with respect.

SUVAL DE LAINE."

Another letter to this worthy pastor from the Marquis de Mont-lord, was received on the sixth of January, to encourage him to unite with all good men who believe in God to obtain the punishment of the assassins, brigands, and disturbers of public tranquillity, and to read the instructions he had received from the government to this effect publicly. Notwithstanding this, on the twentieth of January, 1816, when the service in commemoration of the death of Louis XVI was celebrated, a procession being formed, the National Guards fired at the white flag suspended from the windows of the Protestants, and concluded the day by plundering their houses.

In the commune of Angargues, matters were still worse; and in that of Fontanes, from the entry of the king in 1815, the Catholics broke all terms with the Protestants; by day they insulted them, and in the night broke open their doors, or marked them with chalk to be plundered or burnt. St. Mamert was repeatedly visited by these robberies; and at Montmiral, as lately as the sixteenth of June, 1816, the Protestants were attacked, beaten, and imprisoned, for daring to celebrate the return of a king who had sworn to preserve religious liberty and to maintain the charter.

Further Account of the Proceedings of the Catholics at Nismes

The excesses perpetrated in the country it seems did not by any means divert the attention of the persecutors from Nismes. October, 1815, commenced without any improvement in the principles or measures of the government, and this was followed by corresponding presumption on the part of the people. Several houses in the Quartier St. Charles were sacked, and their wrecks burnt in the streets amidst songs, dances, and shouts of *Vive le Roi!* The mayor appeared, but the merry multitude pretended not to know him, and when he ventured to remonstrate, they told him, 'his presence was unnecessary, and that he might retire.' During the sixteenth of October, every preparation seemed to announce a night of carnage; orders for assembling and signals for attack were circulated with regularity and confidence; Trestaillon reviewed his satellites, and urged them on to the perpetration of crimes, holding with one of those wretches the following dialogue:

Satellite. "If all the Protestants, without one exception, are to be killed, I will cheerfully join; but as you have so often deceived me, unless they are all to go I will not stir."

Trestaillon. "Come along, then, for this time not a single man shall escape."

This horrid purpose would have been executed had it not been for

General La Garde, the commandant of the department. It was not until ten o'clock at night that he perceived the danger; he now felt that not a moment could be lost. Crowds were advancing through the suburbs, and the streets were filling with ruffians, uttering the most horrid imprecations. The generale sounded at eleven o'clock, and added to the confusion that was now spreading through the city. A few troops rallied round the Count La Garde, who was wrung with distress at the sight of the evil which had arrived at such a pitch. Of this M. Durand, a Catholic advocate, gave the following account:

"It was near midnight, my wife had just fallen asleep; I was writing by her side, when we were disturbed by a distant noise; drums seemed crossing the town in every direction. What could all this mean! To quiet her alarm, I said it probably announced the arrival or departure of some troops of the garrison. But firing and shouts were immediately audible; and on opening my window I distinguished horrible imprecations mingled with cries of *Vive le Roi!* I roused an officer who lodged in the house, and M. Chancel, Director of the Public Works. We went out together, and gained the Boulevarde. The moon shone bright, and almost every object was nearly as distinct as day; a furious crowd was pressing on vowing extermination, and the greater part half naked, armed with knives, muskets, sticks, and sabers. In answer to my inquiries I was told the massacre was general, that many had been already killed in the suburbs. M. Chancel retired to put on his uniform as captain of the *Pompiers;* the officers retired to the barracks, and anxious for my wife I returned home. By the noise I was convinced that persons followed. I crept along in the shadow of the wall, opened my door, entered, and closed it, leaving a small aperture through which I could watch the movements of the party whose arms shone in the moonlight. In a few moments some armed men appeared conducting a prisoner to the very spot where I was concealed. They stopped, I shut my door gently, and mounted on an alder tree planted against the garden wall. What a scene! a man on his knees imploring mercy from wretches who mocked his agony, and loaded him with abuse. 'In the name of my wife and children,' he said, 'spare me! What have I done? Why would you murder me for nothing?' I was on the point of crying out and menacing the murderers with vengeance. I had not long to deliberate, the discharge of several fusils terminated my suspense; the unhappy supplicant, struck in the loins and the head, fell to rise no more. The backs of the assassins were towards the tree; they retired immediately, reloading their pieces. I descended and approached the dying man, uttering some deep and dismal groans. Some national guards arrived at the moment, and I again retired and shut the door. 'I see,' said one, 'a dead man.' 'He sings still,' said another. 'It will be better,' said a third, 'to finish him and put him out of his misery.' Five or six muskets were fired instantly, and the groans ceased. On the following day crowds came to inspect and insult the deceased. A day after a massacre was always observed as a sort of fête, and every occupation was left to go and gaze upon the victims." This was Louis Lichare, the father of four children; and four years after the event, M. Durand verified this account by his oath upon the trial of one of the murderers.

Attack Upon the Protestant Churches

Some time before the death of General La Garde, the duke d'Angouleme had visited Nismes, and other cities in the south, and at the former place honored the members of the Protestant consistory with an interview, promising them protection, and encouraging them to re-open their temple so long shut up. They have two churches at Nismes, and it was agreed that the small one should be preferred on this occasion, and that the ringing of the bell should be omitted, General La Garde declared that he would answer with his head for the safety of his congregation. The Protestants privately informed each other that worship was once more to be celebrated at ten o'clock, and they began to assemble silently and cautiously. It was agreed that M. Juillerat Chasseur should perform the service, though such was his conviction of danger that he entreated his wife, and some of his flock, to remain with their families. The temple being opened only as a matter of form, and in compliance with the orders of the duke d'Angouleme, this pastor wished to be the only victim. On his way to the place he passed numerous groups who regarded him with ferocious looks. "This is the time," said some, "to give them the last blow." "Yes," added others, "and neither women nor children must be spared." One wretch, raising his voice above the rest, exclaimed, "Ah, I will go and get my musket, and ten for my share." Through these ominous sounds M. Juillerat pursued his course, but when he gained the temple the sexton had not the courage to open the door, and he was obliged to do it himself. As the worshippers arrived they found strange persons in possession of the adjacent streets, and upon the steps of the church, vowing their worship should not be performed, and crying, "Down with the Protestants! kill them! kill them!" At ten o'clock the church being nearly filled, M. J. Chasseur commenced the prayers; a calm that succeeded was of short duration. On a sudden the minister was interrupted by a violent noise, and a number of persons entered, uttering the most dreadful cries, mingled with *Vive le Roi!* but the gendarmes succeeded in excluding these fanatics, and closing the doors. The noise and tumult without now redoubled, and the blows of the populace trying to break open the doors, caused the house to resound with shrieks and groans. The voice of the pastors who endeavored to console their flock, was inaudible; they attempted in vain to sing the Forty-second Psalm.

Three quarters of an hour rolled heavily away. "I placed myself," said Madame Juillerat, "at the bottom of the pulpit, with my daughter in my arms; my husband at length joined and sustained me; I remembered that it was the anniversary of my marriage. After six years of happiness, I said, I am about to die with my husband and my daughter; we shall be slain at the altar of our God, the victims of a sacred duty, and heaven will open to receive us and our unhappy brethren. I blessed the Redeemer, and without cursing our murderers, I awaited their approach."

M. Oliver, son of a pastor, an officer in the royal troops of the line, attempted to leave the church, but the friendly sentinels at the door advised him to remain besieged with the rest. The national guards refused to act, and the fanatical crowd took every advantage of the absence of General La Garde, and of their increasing numbers. At length the sound of martial music was heard, and voices from without called to the besieged, "Open, open and save yourselves!" Their first impression was a fear of treachery, but they were soon assured that a detachment returning from Mass was drawn up in front of the church to favor the retreat of the Protestants. The door was opened, and many of them escaped among the ranks of the soldiers, who had driven the mob before them; but this street, as well as others through which the fugitives had to pass, was soon filled again. The venerable pastor, Olivier Desmond, between seventy and eighty years of age, was surrounded by murderers; they put their fists in his face, and cried, "Kill the chief of brigands." He was preserved by the firmness of some officers, among whom was his own son; they made a bulwark round him with their bodies, and amidst their naked sabers conducted him to his house. M. Juillerat, who had assisted at divine service with his wife at his side and his child in his arms, was pursued and assailed with stones, his mother received a blow on the head, and her life was some time in danger. One woman was shamefully whipped, and several wounded and dragged along the streets; the number of Protestants more or less ill treated on this occasion amounted to between seventy and eighty.

Murder of General La Garde

At length a check was put to these excesses by the report of the murder of Count La Garde, who, receiving an account of this tumult, mounted his horse, and entered one of the streets, to disperse a crowd. A villain seized his bridle; another presented the muzzle of a pistol close to his body, and exclaimed, "Wretch, you make me retire!" He immediately fired. The murderer was Louis Boissin, a sergeant in the national guard; but, though known to everyone, no person endeavored to arrest him, and he effected his escape. As soon as the general found himself wounded, he gave orders to the gendarmerie to protect the Protestants, and set off on a gallop to his hotel; but fainted immediately on his arrival. On recovering, he prevented the surgeon from searching his wound until he had written a letter to the government, that, in case of his death, it might be known from what quarter the blow came, and that none might dare to accuse the Protestants of this crime.

The probable death of this general produced a small degree of relaxation on the part of their enemies, and some calm; but the mass of the people had been indulged in licentiousness too long to be restrained even by the murder of the representative of their king. In the evening they again repaired to the temple, and with hatchets broke open the door; the dismal noise of their blows carried terror into the bosom of the Protestant families sitting in their houses in tears. The contents of the poor box, and the clothes prepared for distribution, were stolen; the minister's robes rent in pieces; the books torn up or carried away; the closets were ransacked, but the rooms which contained the archives of the church, and the synods, were providentially secured; and had it not been for the numerous patrols on foot, the whole would have become the prey of the flames, and the edifice itself a heap of ruins. In the meanwhile, the fanatics openly ascribed the murder of the general to his own self-devotion, and said, 'that it was the will of God.' Three thousand francs were offered for the apprehension of Boissin; but it was well known that the Protestants dared not arrest him, and that the fanatics would not. During these transactions, the system of forced conversions to Catholicism was making regular and fearful progress.

Interference of the British Government

To the credit of England, the report of these cruel persecutions carried on against our Protestant brethren in France, produced such a sensation on the part of the government as determined them to interfere; and now the persecutors of the Protestants made this spontaneous act of humanity and religion the pretext for charging the sufferers with a treasonable correspondence with England; but in this state of their proceedings, to their great dismay, a letter appeared, sent some time before to England by the duke of Wellington, stating that 'much information existed on the events of the south.'

The ministers of the three denominations in London, anxious not to be misled, requested one of their brethren to visit the scenes of persecution, and examine with impartiality the nature and extent of the evils they were desirous to relieve. Rev. Clement Perot undertook this difficult task, and fulfilled their wishes with a zeal, prudence, and devotedness, above all praise. His return furnished abundant and incontestible proof of a shameful persecution, materials for an appeal to the British Parliament, and a printed report which was circulated through the continent, and which first conveyed correct information to the inhabitants of France.

Foreign interference was now found eminently useful; and the declarations of tolerance which it elicited from the French government, as well as the more cautious march of the Catholic persecutors, operated as decisive and involuntary acknowledgments of the importance of that interference, which some persons at first censured and despised, put through the stern voice of public opinion in England and elsewhere produced a resultant suspension of massacre and pillage, the murderers and plunderers were still left unpunished, and even caressed and rewarded for their crimes; and whilst Protestants in France suffered the most cruel and degrading pains and penalties for alleged trifling crimes, Catholics, covered with blood, and guilty of numerous and horrid murders, were acquitted.

Perhaps the virtuous indignation expressed by some of the more enlightened Catholics against these abominable proceedings, had no small share in restraining them. Many innocent Protestants had been condemned to the galleys and otherwise punished for supposed crimes, upon the oaths of wretches the most unprincipled and abandoned. M. Madier de Montgau, judge of the *cour royale* of Nismes, and president of the *cour d'assizes* of the Gard and Vaucluse, upon one occasion felt himself compelled to break up the court, rather than take the deposition of that notorious and sanguinary monster, Truphemy: "In a hall," says he, "of the Palace of Justice, opposite that in which I sat, several unfortunate persons persecuted by the faction were upon trial, every deposition tending to their crimination was applauded with the cries of *Vive le Roi!* Three times the explosion of this atrocious joy became so terrible that it was necessary to send for reinforcements from the barracks, and two hundred soldiers were often unable to restrain the people. On a sudden the shouts and cries of *Vive le Roi!* redoubled: a man arrived, caressed, applauded, borne in triumph—it was the horrible Truphemy; he approached the tribunal—he came to depose against the prisoners—he was admitted as a witness—he raised his hand to take the oath! Seized with horror at the sight, I rushed from my seat, and entered the hall of council; my colleagues followed me; in vain they persuaded me to resume my seat; 'No!' exclaimed I, 'I will not consent to see that wretch admitted to give evidence in a court of justice in the city which he has filled with murders; in the palace, on the steps of which he has murdered the unfortunate Bourillon. I cannot admit that he should kill his victims by his testimonies no more than by his poignards. He an accuser! he a witness! No, never will I consent to see this monster rise, in the presence of magistrates, to take a sacrilegious oath, his hand still reeking with blood.' These words were repeated out of doors; the witness trembled; the factious also trembled; the factious who guided the tongue of Truphemy as they had directed his arm, who dictated calumny after they had taught him murder. These words penetrated the dungeons of the condemned, and inspired hope; they gave another courageous advocate the resolution to espouse the cause of the persecuted; he carried the prayers of innocence and misery to the foot of the throne; there he asked if the evidence of a Truphemy was not sufficient to annul a sentence. The king granted a full and free pardon."

Ultimate Resolution of the Protestants at Nismes

With respect to the conduct of the Protestants, these highly outraged citizens, pushed to extremities by their persecutors, felt at length that they had only to choose the manner in which they were to perish. They unanimously determined that they would die fighting in their own defence. This firm attitude apprised their butchers that they could no longer murder with impunity. Everything was immediately changed. Those, who for four years had filled others with terror, now felt it in their turn. They trembled at the force which men, so long resigned, found in despair, and their alarm was heightened when they heard that the inhabitants of the Cevennes, persuaded of the danger of their brethren, were marching to their assistance. But, without waiting for these reinforcements, the Protestants appeared at night in the same order and armed in the same manner as their enemies. The others paraded the Boulevards, with their usual noise and fury, but the Protestants remained silent and firm in the posts they had chosen. Three days these dangerous and ominous meetings continued; but the effusion of blood was prevented by the efforts of some worthy citizens distinguished by their rank and fortune. By sharing the dangers of the Protestant population, they obtained the pardon of an enemy who now trembled while he menaced.

CHAPTER XXII

The Beginnings of American Foreign Missions

SAMUEL J. MILLS, when a student in Williams College, gathered about him a group of fellow students, all feeling the burden of the great heathen world. One day in 1806 four of them, overtaken by a thunderstorm, took refuge in the shelter of a haystack. They passed the time in prayer for the salvation of the world, and resolved, if opportunity offered, to go themselves as missionaries. This "haystack prayer meeting" has become historic.

These young men went later to Andover Theological Seminary, where Adoniram Judson joined them. Four of these sent a petition to the Massachusetts Congregational Association at Bradford, June 29, 1810, offering themselves as missionaries and asking whether they might expect support from a society in this country, or whether they must apply to a British society. In response to this appeal the American Board of Commissioners for Foreign Missions was formed.

When a charter for the Board was applied for, an unbelieving soul objected upon the floor of the legislature, alleging in opposition to the petition that the country contained so limited a supply of Christianity that none could be spared for export, but was aptly reminded by another, who was blessed with a more optimistic make, that this was a commodity such that the more of it was sent abroad the more remained at home. There was much perplexity concerning plans and finances, so Judson was dispatched to England to confer with the London Society as to the feasibility of the two organizations coöperating in sending and sustaining the candidates, but this scheme came to nothing. At last sufficient money was raised, and in February, 1812, the first missionaries of the American Board sailed for the Orient. Mr. Judson was accompanied by his wife, having married Ann Hasseltine shortly before sailing.

On the long voyage out, in some way Mr. and Mrs. Judson and Mr. Rice were led to revise their convictions with reference to the proper mode of baptism, reached the conclusion that only immersion was valid, and were rebaptized by Carey soon after their arrival in Calcutta. This step necessarily sundered their connection with the body which had sent them forth, and left them wholly destitute of support. Mr. Rice returned to America to report this condition of affairs to the Baptist brethren. They looked upon the situation as the result of an act of Providence, and eagerly planned to accept the responsibility thrust upon them. Accordingly the Baptist Missionary Union was formed. So Mr. Judson was the occasion of the organization of two great missionary societies.

The Persecution of Doctor Judson

After laboring for some time in Hindustan Dr. and Mrs. Judson finally established themselves at Rangoon in the Burman Empire, in 1813. In 1824 war broke out between the British East India Company and the emperor of Burma. Dr. and Mrs. Judson and Dr. Price, who were at Ava, the capital of the Burman Empire, when the war commenced, were immediately arrested and confined for several months. The account of the sufferings of the missionaries was written by Mrs. Judson, and is given in her own words.

"*Rangoon, May 26,* 1826.

"My beloved Brother,

"I commence this letter with the intention of giving you the particulars of our captivity and sufferings at Ava. How long my patience will allow my reviewing scenes of disgust and horror, the conclusion of this letter will determine. I had kept a journal of everything that had transpired from our arrival at Ava, but destroyed it at the commencement of our difficulties.

"The first certain intelligence we received of the declaration of war by the Burmese, was on our arrival at Tsenpyoo-kywon, about a hundred miles this side of Ava, where part of the troops, under the command of the celebrated Bandoola, had encamped. As we proceeded on our journey, we met Bandoola himself, with the remainder of his troops, gaily equipped, seated on his golden barge, and surrounded by a fleet of gold war boats, one of which was instantly despatched the other side of the river to hail us, and make all necessary inquiries. We were allowed to proceed quietly on, when he had informed the messenger that we were Americans, *not English,* and were going to Ava in obedience to the command of his Majesty.

"On our arrival at the capital, we found that Dr. Price was out of favor at court, and that suspicion rested on most of the foreigners then at Ava. Your brother visited at the palace two or three times, but found the king's manner toward him very different from what it formerly had been; and the queen, who had hitherto expressed wishes for my speedy arrival, now made no inquiries after me, nor intimated a wish to see me. Consequently, I made no effort to visit at the palace, though almost daily invited to visit some of the branches of the royal family, who were living in their own houses, out of the palace enclosure. Under these circumstances, we thought our most prudent course lay in prosecuting our original intention of building a house, and commencing missionary operations as occasion offered, thus endeavoring to convince the government that we had really nothing to do with the present war.

"In two or three weeks after our arrival, the king, queen, all the members of the royal family, and most of the officers of government, returned to Amarapora, in order to come and take possession of the new palace in the customary style.

"I dare not attempt a description of that splendid day, when majesty with all its attendant glory entered the gates of the golden city, and amid the acclamations of millions, I may say, took possession of the palace. The saupwars of the provinces bordering on China, all the viceroys and high officers of the kingdom were assembled on the occasion, dressed in their robes of state, and ornamented with the insignia of their office. The white elephant, richly adorned with gold and jewels, was one of the most beautiful objects in the procession. The king and queen alone were unadorned, dressed in the simple garb of the country; they, hand in hand, entered the garden in which we had taken our seats, and where a banquet was prepared for their refreshment. All the riches and glory of the empire were on this day exhibited to view. The number and immense size of the elephants, the numerous horses, and great variety of vehicles of all descriptions, far surpassed anything I have ever seen or imagined. Soon after his majesty had taken possession of the new palace, an order was issued that no foreigner should be allowed to enter, excepting Lansago. We were a little alarmed at this, but concluded it was from political motives, and would not, perhaps, essentially affect us.

"For several weeks nothing took place to alarm us, and we went on with our school. Mr. J. preached every Sabbath, all the materials for building a brick house were procured, and the masons had made considerable progress in raising the building.

"On the twenty-third of May, 1824, just as we had concluded worship at the Doctor's house, the other side of the river, a messenger came to inform us that Rangoon was taken by the English. The intelligence produced a shock, in which was a mixture of fear and joy. Mr. Gouger, a young merchant residing at Ava, was then with us, and had much more reason to fear than the rest of us. We all, however, immediately returned to our house, and began to consider what was to be done. Mr. G. went to Prince Thar-yar-wa-dee, the king's most influential brother, who informed him he need not give himself any uneasiness, as he had mentioned the subject to his majesty, who had replied, that 'the few foreigners residing at Ava had nothing to do with the war, and should not be molested.'

"The government were now all in motion. An army of ten or twelve thousand men, under the command of the Kyee-woon-gyee, were sent off in three or four days, and were to be joined by the Sakyer-woon-gyee, who had previously been appointed viceroy of Rangoon, and who was on his way thither, when the news of its attack reached him. No doubt was entertained of the defeat of the English; the only fear of the king was that the foreigners hearing of the advance of the Burmese troops, would be so alarmed as to flee on board their ships and depart, before there would be time to secure them as slaves. 'Bring for me,' said a wild young buck of the palace, 'six kala pyoo, (white strangers,) to row my boat;' and 'to me,' said the lady of Woon-gyee, 'send four white strangers to manage the affairs of my house, as I understand they are trusty servants.' The war boats, in high glee, passed our house, the soldiers singing and dancing, and exhibiting gestures of the most joyful kind. Poor fellows! said we, you will probably never dance again. And so it proved, for few if any ever saw again their native home.

"At length Mr. Judson and Dr. Price were summoned to a court of examination, where strict inquiry was made relative to all they knew. The great point seemed to be whether they had been in the habit of making communications to foreigners, of the state of the country, etc. They answered that they had always written to their friends in America, but had no correspondence with English officers, or the Bengal government. After their examination, they were not put in confinement as the Englishmen had been, but were allowed to return to their houses. In examining the accounts of Mr. G. it was found that Mr. J. and Dr. Price had taken money of him to a considerable amount. Ignorant, as were the Burmese, of our mode of receiving money, by orders on Bengal, this circumstance, to their suspicious minds, was a sufficient evidence that the missionaries were in the pay of the English, and very probably spies. It was thus represented to the king, who, in an angry tone, ordered the immediate arrest of the 'two teachers.'

"On the eighth of June, just as we were preparing for dinner, in rushed an officer, holding a black book, with a dozen Burmans, accompanied by *one,* whom, from his spotted face, we knew to be an executioner, and a 'son of the prison.' 'Where is the teacher?' was the first inquiry. Mr. Judson presented himself. 'You are called by the king,' said the officer; a form of speech always used when about to arrest a criminal. The spotted man instantly seized Mr. Judson, threw him on the floor, and produced the small cord, the instrument of torture. I caught hold of his arm; 'Stay, (said I,) I will give you money.' 'Take her too,' said the officer; 'she also is a foreigner.' Mr. Judson, with an imploring look, begged they would let me remain until further orders. The scene was now shocking beyond description.

"The whole neighborhood had collected—the masons at work on the brick house threw down their tools, and ran—the little Burman children were screaming and crying—the Bengalee servants stood in amazement at the indignities offered their master—and the hardened executioner, with a hellish joy, drew tight the cords, bound Mr. Judson fast, and dragged him off, I knew not whither. In vain I begged and entreated the spotted face to take the silver, and loosen the ropes, but he spurned my offers, and immediately departed. I gave the money, however, to Moung Ing to follow after, to make some further attempt to mitigate the torture of Mr. Judson; but instead of succeeding, when a few rods from the house, the unfeeling wretches again threw their prisoner on the ground, and drew the cords still tighter, so as almost to prevent respiration.

"The officer and his gang proceeded on to the courthouse, where the governor of the city and the officers were collected, one of whom read the order of the king, to commit Mr. Judson to the death prison, into which he was soon hurled, the door closed—and Moung Ing saw no more. What a night was now before me! I retired into my room, and endeavored to obtain consolation from committing my case to God, and imploring fortitude and strength to suffer whatever awaited me. But the consolation of retirement was not long allowed me, for the magistrate of the place had come into the veranda, and continually called me to come out, and submit to his examination. But previously to going out, I destroyed all my letters, journals, and writings of every kind, lest they should disclose the fact that we had correspondents in England, and had minuted down every occurrence since our arrival in the country. When this work of destruction was finished, I went out and submitted to the examination of the magistrate, who inquired very minutely of everything I knew; then ordered the gates of the compound to be shut, no person be allowed to go in or out, placed a guard of ten ruffians, to whom he gave a strict charge to keep me safe, and departed.

"It was now dark. I retired to an inner room with my four little Burman girls, and barred the doors. The guard instantly ordered me to unbar the doors and come out, or they would break the house down. I obstinately refused to obey, and endeavored to intimidate them by threatening to complain of their conduct to higher authorities on the morrow. Finding me resolved in disregarding their orders, they took the two Bengalee servants, and confined them in the stocks in a very painful position. I could not endure this; but called the head man to the window, and promised to make them all a present in the morning, if they would release the servants. After much debate, and many severe threatenings, they consented, but seemed resolved to annoy me as much as possible. My unprotected, desolate state, my entire uncertainty of the fate of Mr. Judson, and the dreadful carousings and almost diabolical language of the guard, all conspired to make it by far the most distressing night I had ever passed. You may well imagine, my dear brother, that sleep was a stranger to my eyes, and peace and composure to my mind.

"The next morning, I sent Moung Ing to ascertain the situation of your brother, and give him food, if still living. He soon returned, with the intelligence that Mr. Judson, and all the white foreigners, were confined in the *death prison,* with three pairs of iron fetters each, and fastened to a long pole, to prevent their moving! The point of my anguish now was that I was a prisoner myself, and could make no efforts for the release of the missionaries. I begged and entreated the magistrate to allow me to go to some member of government to state my case; but he said he did not dare to consent, for fear I should make my escape. I next wrote a note to one of the king's sisters, with whom I had been intimate, requesting her to use her influence for the release of the teachers. The note was returned with this message—She 'did not understand it'—which was a polite refusal to interfere; though I afterwards ascertained that she had an anxious desire to assist us, but dared not on account of the queen. The day dragged heavily away, and another dreadful night was before me. I endeavored to soften the feelings of the guard by giving them tea and cigars for the night; so that they allowed me to remain inside of my room, without threatening as they did the night before. But the idea of your brother being stretched on the bare floor in irons and confinement, haunted my mind like a spectre, and prevented my obtaining any quiet sleep, though nature was almost exhausted.

"On the third day, I sent a message to the governor of the city, who has the entire direction of prison affairs, to allow me to visit him with a present. This had the desired effect; and he immediately sent orders to the guards, to permit my going into town. The governor received me pleasantly, and asked me what I wanted. I stated to him the situation of the foreigners, and particularly that of the teachers, who were Americans, and had nothing to do with the war. He told me it was not in his power to release them from prison or irons, but that he could make their situation more comfortable; there was his head officer, with whom I must consult, relative to the means. The officer, who proved to be one of the city writers, and whose countenance at the first glance presented the most perfect assemblage of all the evil passions attached to human nature, took me aside, and endeavored to convince me, that myself, as well as the prisoners, was entirely at his disposal—that our future comfort must depend on my liberality in regard to presents—and that these must be made in a private way and unknown to any officer in the government! 'What must I do,' said I 'to obtain a mitigation of the present sufferings of the two teachers?' 'Pay to me,' said he, 'two hundred tickals, (about a hundred dollars,) two pieces of fine cloth, and two pieces of handkerchiefs.' I had taken money with me in the morning, our house being two miles from the prison—I could not easily return. This I offered to the writer, and begged he would not insist on the other articles, as they were not in my possession. He hesitated for some time, but fearing to lose the sight of so much money, he concluded to take it, promising to relieve the teachers from their most painful situation.

"I then procured an order from the governor, for my admittance into prison; but the sensations, produced by meeting your brother in that *wretched, horrid* situation—and the affecting scene which ensued, I will not attempt to describe. Mr. Judson crawled to the door of the prison—for I was never allowed to enter—gave me some directions relative to his release; but before we could make any arrangement, I was ordered to depart, by those iron-hearted jailers, who could not endure to see us enjoy the poor consolation of meeting in that miserable place. In vain I pleaded the order of the governor for my admittance; they again, harshly repeated, 'Depart, or we will pull you out.' The same evening, the missionaries, together with the other foreigners, who had paid an equal sum, were taken out of the common prison, and confined in an open shed in the prison inclosure. Here I was allowed to send them food, and mats to sleep on; but was not permitted to enter again for several days.

"My next object was to get a petition presented to the queen; but no person being admitted into the palace, who was in disgrace with his majesty, I sought to present it through the medium of her brother's wife. I had visited her in better days, and received particular marks of her favor. But now times were altered: Mr. Judson was in prison, and I in distress, which was a sufficient reason for giving me a cold reception. I took a present of considerable value. She was lolling on her carpet as I entered, with her attendants around her. I waited not for the usual question to a suppliant, 'What do you want?' but in a bold, earnest, yet respectful manner, stated our distresses and our wrongs, and begged her assistance. She partly raised her head, opened the present I had brought, and coolly replied, 'Your case is not singular; all the foreigners are treated alike.' 'But it is singular,' said I, 'the teachers are Americans; they are ministers of religion, have nothing to do with war or politics, and came to Ava in obedience to the king's command. They have never done any thing to deserve such treatment; and is it right they should be treated thus?' 'The king does as he pleases,' said she; 'I am not the king, what can I do?' 'You can state their case to the queen, and obtain their release,' replied I. 'Place yourself in my situation—were you in America, your husband, innocent of crime, thrown into prison, in irons, and you a solitary, unprotected female—what would you do?' With a slight degree of feeling, she said, 'I will present your petition, come again to-morrow.' I returned to the house, with considerable hope, that the speedy release of the missionaries was at hand. But the next day Mr. Gouger's property, to the amount of fifty thousand dollars, was taken and carried to the palace. The officers, on their return, politely informed me, they should *visit our house* on the morrow. I felt obliged for this information, and accordingly made preparations to receive them, by secreting as many little articles as possible; together with considerable silver, as I knew, if the war should be protracted, we should be in a state of starvation without it. But my mind was in a dreadful state of agitation, lest it should be discovered, and cause my being thrown into prison. And had it been possible to procure money from any other quarter, I should not have ventured on such a step.

"The following morning, the royal treasurer, Prince Tharyawa-dees, Chief Woon, and Koung-tone Myoo-tsa, who was in future our steady friend, attended by forty or fifty followers, came to take possession of all we had. I treated them civilly, gave them chairs to sit on, tea and sweetmeats for their refreshment; and justice obliges me to say that they conducted the business of confiscation with more regard to my feelings than I should have thought it possible for Burmese officers to exhibit. The three officers, with one of the royal secretaries, alone entered the house; their attendants were ordered to remain outside. They saw I was deeply affected, and apologized for what they were about to do, by saying that it was painful for them to take possession of property not their own, but they were compelled thus to do by order of the king.

" 'Where is your silver, gold, and jewels?' said the royal treasurer. 'I have no gold or jewels; but here is the key of a trunk which contains the silver—do with it as you please.' The trunk was produced, and the silver weighed. 'This money,' said I, 'was collected in America, by the disciples of Christ, and sent here for the purpose of building a kyoung, (the name of a priest's dwelling) and for our support while teaching the religion of Christ. Is it suitable that you should take it?' (The Burmans are averse to taking what is offered in a religious point of view, which was the cause of my making the inquiry.) 'We will state this circumstance to the king,' said one of them, 'and perhaps he will restore it. But this is all the silver you have?' I could not tell a falsehood: 'The house is in your possession,' I replied, 'search for yourselves.' 'Have you not deposited silver with some person of your acquaintance?' 'My acquaintances are all in prison, with whom should I deposit silver?'

"They next ordered my trunk and drawers to be examined. The secretary only was allowed to accompany me in this search. Everything nice or curious, which met his view, was presented to the officers, for their decision, whether it should be taken or retained. I begged they would not take our wearing apparel, as it would be disgraceful to take clothes partly worn into the possession of his majesty, and to us they were of unspeakable value. They assented, and took a list only, and did the same with the books, medicines, etc. My little work table and rocking chair, presents from my beloved brother, I rescued from their grasp, partly by artifice, and partly through their ignorance. They left also many articles, which were of inestimable value, during our long imprisonment.

"As soon as they had finished their search and departed, I hastened to the queen's brother, to hear what had been the fate of my petition; when, alas! all my hopes were dashed, by his wife's coolly saying, 'I stated your case to the queen; but her majesty replied, *The teachers will not die: let them remain as they are.* My expectations had been so much excited that this sentence was like a thunderbolt to my feelings. For the truth at one glance assured me that if the queen refused assistance, who would dare to intercede for me? With a heavy heart I departed, and on my way home, attempted to enter the prison gate, to communicate the sad tidings to your brother, but was harshly refused admittance; and for the ten days following notwithstanding my daily efforts, I was not allowed to enter. We attempted to communicate by writing, and after being successful for a few days, it was discovered; the poor fellow who carried the communications was beaten and put in the stocks; and the circumstance cost me about ten dollars, besides two or three days of agony, for fear of the consequences.

"The officers who had taken possession of our property, presented it to his majesty, saying, 'Judson is a true teacher; we found nothing in his house, but what belongs to priests. In addition to this money, there are an immense number of books, medicines, trunks of wearing apparel, of which we have only taken a list. Shall we take them, or let them remain?' 'Let them remain,' said the king, 'and put this property by itself, for it shall be restored to him again, if he is found innocent.' This was an allusion to the idea of his being a spy.

"For two or three months following, I was subject to continual harassments, partly through my ignorance of police management and partly through the insatiable desire of every petty officer to enrich himself through our misfortunes.

"You, my dear brother, who know my strong attachment to my friends, and how much pleasure I have hitherto experienced from retrospect, can judge from the above circumstances, how intense were my sufferings. But the point, the acme of my distresses, consisted in the awful uncertainty of our final fate. My prevailing opinion was that my husband would suffer violent death; and that I should, of course, become a slave, and languish out a miserable though short existence, in the tyrannic hands of some unfeeling monster. But the consolations of religion, in these trying circumstances, were neither 'few nor small.' It taught me to look beyond this world, to that rest, that peaceful, happy rest, where Jesus reigns, and oppression never enters.

"Some months after your brother's imprisonment, I was permitted to make a little bamboo room in the prison inclosures, where he could be much by himself, and where I was sometimes allowed to spend two or three hours. It so happened that the two months he occupied this place, was the coldest part of the year, when he would have suffered much in the open shed he had previously occupied. After the birth of your little niece, I was unable to visit the prison and the governor as before, and found I had lost considerable influence, previously gained; for he was not so forward to hear my petitions when any difficulty occurred, as he formerly had been. When Maria was nearly two months old, her father one morning sent me word that he and all the white prisoners were put into the inner prison, in five pairs of fetters each, that his little room had been torn down, and his mat, pillow, etc. been taken by the jailers. This was to me a dreadful shock, as I thought at once it was only a prelude to greater evils.

"The situation of the prisoners was now distressing beyond description. It was at the commencement of the hot season. There were above a hundred prisoners shut up in one room, without a breath of air excepting from the cracks in the boards. I sometimes obtained permission to go to the door for five minutes, when my heart sickened at the wretchedness exhibited. The white prisoners, from incessant perspiration and loss of appetite, looked more like the dead than the living. I made daily applications to the governor, offering him money, which he refused; but all that I gained was permission for the foreigners to eat their food outside, and this continued but a short time.

"After continuing in the inner prison for more than a month, your brother was taken with a fever. I felt assured he would not live long, unless removed from that noisome place. To effect this, and in order to be near the prison, I removed from our house and put up a small bamboo room in the governor's inclosure, which was nearly opposite the prison gate. Here I incessantly begged the governor to give me an order to take Mr. J. out of the large prison, and place him in a more comfortable situation; and the old man, being worn out with my entreaties at length gave me the order in an official form; and also gave orders to the head jailer, to allow me to go in and out, all times of the day, to administer medicines. I now felt happy, indeed, and had Mr. J. instantly removed into a little bamboo hovel, so low, that neither of us could stand upright—but a palace in comparison with the place he had left.

Removal of the Prisoners to Oung-pen-la—Mrs. Judson Follows Them

"Notwithstanding the order the governor had given for my admittance into prison, it was with the greatest difficulty that I could persuade the under jailer to open the gate. I used to carry Mr. J's food myself, for the sake of getting in, and would then remain an hour or two, unless driven out. We had been in this comfortable situation but two or three days, when one morning, having carried in Mr. Judson's breakfast, which, in consequence of fever, he was unable to take, I remained longer than usual, when the governor in great haste sent for me. I promised him to return as soon as I had ascertained the governor's will, he being much alarmed at this unusual message. I was very agreeably disappointed, when the governor informed, that he only wished to consult me about his watch, and seemed unusually pleasant and conversable. I found afterwards, that his only object was, to detain me until the dreadful scene, about to take place in the prison, was over. For when I left him to go to my room, one of the servants came running, and with a ghastly countenance informed me, that all the white prisoners were carried away.

"I would not believe the report, but instantly went back to the governor, who said he had just heard of it, but did not wish to tell me. I hastily ran into the street, hoping to get a glimpse of them before they were out of sight, but in this was disappointed. I ran first into one street, then another, inquiring of all I met, but none would answer me. At length an old woman told me the white prisoners had gone towards the little river; for they were to be carried to Amarapora. I then ran to the banks of the little river, about half a mile, but saw them not, and concluded the old woman had deceived me. Some of the friends of the foreigners went to the place of execution, but found them not. I then returned to the governor to try to discover the cause of their removal, and the probability of their future fate. The old man assured me that he was ignorant of the intention of government to remove the foreigners until that morning. That since I went out, he had learned that the prisoners had been sent to Amarapora; but for what purpose, he knew not. 'I will send off a man immediately,' said he, 'to see what is to be done with them. You can do nothing more for your husband,' continued he, *Take care of yourself*.

"Never before had I suffered so much from fear in traversing the streets of Ava. The last words of the governor, 'Take care of yourself,' made me suspect there was some design with which I was unacquainted. I saw, also, he was afraid to have me go into the streets, and advised me to wait until dark, when he would send me in a cart, and a man to open the gates. I took two or three trunks of the most valuable articles, together with the medicine chest, to deposit in the house of the governor; and after committing the house and premises to our faithful Moung Ing and a Bengalee servant, who continued with us, (though we were unable to pay his wages,) I took leave, as I then thought probable, of our house in Ava forever.

"The day was dreadfully hot; but we obtained a covered boat, in which we were tolerably comfortable, until within two miles of the government house. I then procured a cart; but the violent motion, together with the dreadful heat and dust, made me almost distracted. But what was my disappointment on my arriving at the courthouse, to find that the prisoners had been sent on two hours before, and that I must go in that uncomfortable mode four miles further with little Maria in my arms, whom I held all the way from Ava. The cart man refused to go any further; and after waiting an hour in the burning sun, I procured another, and set off for that never to be forgotten place, Oung-pen-la. I obtained a guide from the governor and was conducted directly to the prison-yard.

"But what a scene of wretchedness was presented to my view! The prison was an old shattered building, without a roof; the fence was entirely destroyed; eight or ten Burmese were on the top of the building, trying to make something like a shelter with the leaves; while under a little low protection outside of the prison sat the foreigners, chained together two and two, almost dead with suffering and fatigue. The first words of your brother were: 'Why have you come? I hoped you would not follow, for you cannot live here.'

"It was now dark. I had no refreshment for the suffering prisoners, or for myself, as I had expected to procure all that was necessary at the market in Amarapora, and I had no shelter for the night. I asked one of the jailers if I might put up a little bamboo house near the prisoners; he said 'No, it was not customary.' I then begged he would procure me a shelter for the night, when on the morrow I could find some place to live in. He took me to his house, in which there were only two small rooms—one in which he and his family lived—the other, which was then half full of grain, he offered to me; and in that little filthy place, I spent the next six months of wretchedness. I procured some half boiled water, instead of my tea, and, worn out with fatigue, laid myself down on a mat spread over the paddy, and endeavored to obtain a little refreshment from sleep. The next morning your brother gave me the following account of the brutal treatment he had received on being taken out of prison.

"As soon as I had gone out at the call of the governor, one of the jailers rushed into Mr. J's little room—roughly seized him by the arm—pulled him out—stripped of all his clothes, excepting shirt and pantaloons—took his shoes, hat, and all his bedding—tore off his chains—tied a rope round his waist, dragged him to the courthouse, where the other prisoners had previously been taken. They were then tied two and two, and delivered into the hands of the Lamine Woon, who went on before them on horseback, while his slaves drove the prisoners, one of the slaves holding the rope which connected two of them together. It was in May, one of the hottest months in the year, and eleven o'clock in the day, so that the sun was intolerable indeed.

"They had proceeded only half a mile, when your brother's feet became blistered, and so great was his agony, even at this early period, that as they were crossing the little river, he longed to throw himself into the water to be free from misery. But the sin attached to such an act alone prevented. They had then eight miles to walk. The sand and gravel were like burning coals to the feet of the prisoners, which soon became perfectly destitute of skin; and in this wretched state they were goaded on by their unfeeling drivers. Mr. J's debilitated state, in consequence of the fever, and having taken no food that morning, rendered him less capable of bearing such hardships than the other prisoners.

"When about halfway on their journey, as they stopped for water, your brother begged the Lamine Woon to allow him to ride his horse a mile or two, as he could proceed no farther in that dreadful state. But a scornful, malignant look was all the reply that was made. He then requested Captain Laird, who was tied with him, and who was a strong, healthy man, to allow him to take hold of his shoulder, as he was fast sinking. This the kind-hearted man granted for a mile or two, but then found the additional burden insupportable. Just at that period, Mr. Gouger's Bengalee servant came up to them, and seeing the distresses of your brother, took off his headdress, which was made of cloth, tore it in two, gave half to his master, and half to Mr. Judson, which he instantly wrapped round his wounded feet, as they were not allowed to rest even for a moment. The servant then offered his shoulder to Mr. J. and was almost carried by him the remainder of the way.

"The Lamine Woon, seeing the distressing state of the prisoners, and that one of their number was dead, concluded they should go no farther that night, otherwise they would have been driven on until they reached Oung-pen-la the same day. An old shed was appointed for their abode during the night, but without even a mat or pillow, or anything to cover them. The curiosity of the Lamine Woon's wife, induced her to make a visit to the prisoners, whose wretchedness considerably excited her compassion, and she ordered some fruit, sugar, and tamarinds, for their refreshment; and the next morning rice was prepared for them, and as poor as it was, it was refreshing to the prisoners, who had been almost destitute of food the day before. Carts were also provided for their conveyance, as none of them were able to walk. All this time the foreigners were entirely ignorant of what was to become of them; and when they arrived at Oung-pen-la, and saw the dilapidated state of the prison, they immediately, all as one, concluded that they were there to be burned, agreeably to the report which had previously been in circulation at Ava. They all endeavored to prepare themselves for the awful scene anticipated, and it was not until they saw preparations making for repairing the prison that they had the least doubt that a cruel lingering death awaited them. My arrival was an hour or two after this.

"The next morning I arose and endeavored to find something like food. But there was no market, and nothing to be procured. One of Dr. Price's friends, however, brought some cold rice and vegetable curry, from Amarapora, which, together with a cup of tea from Mr. Lansago, answered for the breakfast of the prisoners; and for dinner, we made a curry of dried salt fish, which a servant of Mr. Gouger had brought. All the money I could command in the world I had brought with me, secreted about my person; so you may judge what our prospects were, in case the war should continue long. But our heavenly Father was better to us than our fears; for notwithstanding the constant extortions of the jailers, during the whole six months we were at Oung-pen-la, and the frequent straits to which we were brought, we never really suffered for the want of money, though frequently for want of provisions, which were not procurable.

"Here at this place my personal bodily sufferings commenced. While your brother was confined in the city prison, I had been allowed to remain in our house, in which I had many conveniences left, and my health continued good beyond all expectations. But now I had not a single article of convenience—not even a chair or seat of any kind, excepting a bamboo floor. The very morning after my arrival, Mary Hasseltine was taken with the smallpox, the natural way. She, though very young, was the only assistant I had in taking care of little Maria. But she now required all the time I could spare from Mr. Judson whose fever still continued in prison, and whose feet were so dreadfully mangled that for several days he was unable to move.

"I knew not what to do, for I could procure no assistance from the neighborhood, or medicine for the sufferers, but was all day long going backwards and forwards from the house to the prison, with little Maria in my arms. Sometimes I was greatly relieved by leaving her, for an hour, when asleep, by the side of her father, while I returned to the house to look after Mary, whose fever ran so high as to produce delirium. She was so completely covered with the smallpox that there was no distinction in the pustules. As she was in the same little room with myself, I knew Maria would take it; I therefore inoculated her from another child, before Mary's had arrived at such a state to be infectious. At the same time, I inoculated Abby, and the jailer's children, who all had it so lightly as hardly to interrupt their play. But the inoculation in the arm of my poor little Maria did not take—she caught it of Mary, and had it the natural way. She was then only three months and a half old, and had been a most healthy child; but it was above three months before she perfectly recovered from the effects of this dreadful disorder.

"You will recollect I never had the smallpox, but was vaccinated previously to leaving America. In consequence of being for so long a time constantly exposed, I had nearly a hundred pustules formed, though no previous symptoms of fever, etc. The jailer's children having had the smallpox so lightly, in consequence of inoculation, my fame was spread all over the village, and every child, young and old, who had not previously had it, was brought for inoculation. And although I knew nothing about the disorder, or the mode of treating it, I inoculated them all with a needle, and told them to take care of their diet—all the instructions I could give them. Mr. Judson's health was gradually restored, and he found himself much more comfortably situated than when in the city prison.

"The prisoners were at first chained two and two; but as soon as the jailers could obtain chains sufficient, they were separated, and each prisoner had but one pair. The prison was repaired, a new fence made, and a large airy shed erected in front of the prison, where the prisoners were allowed to remain during the day, though locked up in the little close prison at night. All the children recovered from the smallpox; but my watchings and fatigue, together with my miserable food, and more miserable lodgings, brought on one of the diseases of the country, which is almost always fatal to foreigners.

"My constitution seemed destroyed, and in a few days I became so weak as to be hardly able to walk to Mr. Judson's prison. In this debilitated state, I set off in a cart for Ava, to procure medicines, and some suitable food, leaving the cook to supply my place. I reached the house in safety, and for two or three days the disorder seemed at a stand; after which it attacked me violently, that I had no hopes of recovery left—and my anxiety now was, to return to Oung-pen-la to die near the prison. It was with the greatest difficulty that I obtained the medicine chest from the governor, and then had no one to administer medicine. I however got at the laudanum, and by taking two drops at a time for several hours, it so far checked the disorder as to enable me to get on board a boat, though so weak that I could not stand, and again set off for Oung-pen-la. The last four miles were in that painful conveyance, the cart, and in the midst of the rainy season, when the mud almost buries the oxen. You may form some idea of a Burmese cart, when I tell you their wheels are not constructed like ours, but are simply round thick planks with a hole in the middle, through which a pole that supports the body is thrust.

"I just reached Oung-pen-la when my strength seemed entirely exhausted. The good native cook came out to help me into the house but so altered and emaciated was my appearance that the poor fellow burst into tears at the first sight. I crawled on the mat in the little room, to which I was confined for more than two months, and never perfectly recovered, until I came to the English camp. At this period when I was unable to take care of myself, or look after Mr. Judson we must both have died, had it not been for the faithful and affectionate care of our Bengalee cook. A common Bengalee cook will do nothing but the simple business of cooking; but he seemed to forget his caste, and almost his own wants, in his efforts to serve us. He would provide, cook, and carry your brother's food, and then return and take care of me. I have frequently known him not to taste of food until near night, in consequence of having to go so far for wood and water, and in order to have Mr. Judson's dinner ready at the usual hour. He never complained, never asked for his wages, and never for a moment hesitated to go anywhere, or to perform any act we required. I take great pleasure in speaking of the faithful conduct of this servant, who is still with us, and I trust has been well rewarded for his services.

"Our dear little Maria was the greatest sufferer at this time, my illness depriving her of her usual nourishment, and neither a nurse nor a drop of milk could be procured in the village. By making presents to the jailers, I obtained leave for Mr. Judson to come out of prison, and take the emaciated creature around the village, to beg a little nourishment from those mothers who had young children. Her cries in the night were heartrending, when it was impossible to supply her wants. I now began to think the very afflictions of Job had come upon me. When in health, I could bear the various trials and vicissitudes through which I was called to pass. But to be confined with sickness, and unable to assist those who were so dear to me, when in distress, was almost too much for me to bear; and had it not been for the consolations of religion, and an assured conviction that every additional trial was ordered by infinite love and mercy, I must have sunk under my accumulated sufferings. Sometimes our jailers seemed a little softened at our distress, and for several days together allowed Mr. Judson to come to the house, which was to me an unspeakable consolation. Then again they would be as iron-hearted in their demands as though we were free from sufferings, and in affluent circumstances. The annoyance, the extortions, and oppressions, to which we were subject, during our six months residence in Oungpen-la, are beyond enumeration or description.

"The time at length arrived for our release from that detested place, the Oung-pen-la prison. A messenger from our friend, the governor of the north gate of the palace, who was formerly Koungtone, Myoo-tsa, informed us that an order had been given, the evening before, in the palace, for Mr. Judson's release. On the same evening an official order arrived; and with a joyful heart I set about preparing for our departure early the following morning. But an unexpected obstacle occurred, which made us fear that *I* should still be retained as a prisoner. The avaricious jailers, unwilling to lose their prey, insisted that as my name was not included in the order,

I should not go. In vain I urged that I was not sent there as a prisoner, and that they had no authority over me—they still determined I should not go, and forbade the villagers from letting me a cart. Mr. Judson was then taken out of prison, and brought to the jailer's house, where, by promises and threatenings, he finally gained their consent, on condition that we would leave the remaining part of our provisions we had recently received from Ava.

It was noon before we were allowed to depart. When we reached Amarapora, Mr. Judson was obliged to follow the guidance of the jailer, who conducted him to the governor of the city. Having made all necessary inquiries, the governor appointed another guard, which conveyed Mr. Judson to the courthouse in Ava, to which place he arrived some time in the night. I took my own course, procured a boat, and reached our house before dark.

"My first object the next morning was to go in search of your brother, and I had the mortification to meet him again in prison, though not the death prison. I went immediately to my old friend the governor of the city, who was now raised to the rank of a Woongyee. He informed me that Mr. Judson was to be sent to the Burmese camp, to act as translator and interpreter; and that he was put in confinement for a short time only, until his affairs were settled. Early the following morning I went to this officer again, who told me that Mr. Judson had that moment received twenty tickals from government, with orders to go immediately on board a boat for Maloun, and that he had given him permission to stop a few moments at the house, it being on his way. I hastened back to the house, where Mr. Judson soon arrived; but was allowed to remain only a short time, while I could prepare food and clothing for future use. He was crowded into a little boat, where he had not room sufficient to lie down, and where his exposure to the cold, damp nights threw him into a violent fever, which had nearly ended all his sufferings. He arrived at Maloun on the third day, where, ill as he was, he was obliged to enter immediately on the work of translating. He remained at Maloun six weeks, suffering as much as he had at any time in prison, excepting that he was not in irons, nor exposed to the insults of those cruel jailers.

"For the first fortnight after his departure, my anxiety was less than it had been at any time previous, since the commencement of our difficulties. I knew the Burmese officers at the camp would feel the value of Mr. Judson's services too much to allow their using any measures threatening his life. I thought his situation, also, would be much more comfortable than it really was—hence my anxiety was less. But my health, which had never been restored, since that violent attack at Oung-pen-la, now daily declined, until I was seized with the spotted fever, with all its attendant horrors. I knew the nature of the fever from its commencement; and from the shattered state of my constitution, together with the want of medical attendants, I concluded it must be fatal. The day I was taken, a Burmese nurse came and offered her services for Maria. This circumstance filled me with gratitude and confidence in God; for though I had so long and so constantly made efforts to obtain a person of this description, I had never been able; when at the very time I most needed one, and without any exertion, a voluntary offer was made.

"My fever raged violently and without any intermission. I began to think of settling my worldly affairs, and of committing my dear little Maria to the care of the Portuguese woman, when I lost my reason, and was insensible to all around me. At this dreadful period Dr. Price was released from prison; and hearing of my illness, obtained permission to come and see me. He has since told me that my situation was the most distressing he had ever witnessed, and that he did not then think I should survive many hours. My hair was shaved, my head and feet covered with blisters, and Dr. Price ordered the Bengalee servant who took care of me to endeavor to persuade me to take a little nourishment, which I had obstinately refused for several days. One of the first things I recollect was, seeing this faithful servant standing by me, trying to induce me to take a little wine and water. I was in fact so far gone that the Burmese neighbors who had come in to see me expire, said, 'She is dead; and if the king of angels should come in, he could not recover her.'

"The fever, I afterwards understood, had run seventeen days when the blisters were applied. I now began to recover slowly; but it was more than a month after this before I had strength to stand. While in this weak, debilitated state, the servant who had followed your brother to the Burmese camp came in and informed me that his master had arrived, and was conducted to the courthouse in town. I sent off a Burman to watch the movements of government, and to ascertain, if possible, in what way Mr. Judson was to be disposed of. He soon returned with the sad intelligence that he saw Mr. Judson go out of the palace yard, accompanied by two or three Burmans, who conducted him to one of the prisons; and that it was reported in town, that he was to be sent back to the Oung-pen-la prison. I was too weak to bear ill tidings of any kind; but a shock as dreadful as this almost annihilated me. For some time, I could hardly breathe; but at last gained sufficient composure to dispatch Moung Ing to our friend, the governor of the north gate, and begged him to make *one more effort* for the release of Mr. Judson, and prevent his being sent back to the country prison, where I knew he must suffer much, as I could not follow. Moung Ing then went in search of Mr. Judson; and it was nearly dark when he found him in the interior of an obscure prison. I had sent food early in the afternoon, but being unable to find him, the bearer had returned with it, which added another pang to my distresses, as I feared he was already sent to Oung-pen-la.

"If I ever felt the value and efficacy of prayer, I did at this time. I could not rise from my couch; I could make no efforts to secure my husband; I could only plead with that great and powerful Being who has said, 'Call upon Me in the day of trouble, and I *will hear,* and thou shalt glorify Me;' and who made me at this time feel so powerfully this promise that I became quite composed, feeling assured that my prayers would be answered.

"When Mr. Judson was sent from Maloun to Ava, it was within five minutes' notice, and without his knowledge of the cause. On his way up the river he accidentally saw the communication made to government respecting him, which was simply this: 'We have no further use for Yoodathan, we therefore return him to the golden city.' On arriving at the courthouse, there happened to be no one present who was acquainted with Mr. J. The presiding officer inquired from what place he had been sent to Maloun. He was answered from Oung-pen-la. 'Let him then,' said the officer, 'be returned thither'—when he was delivered to a guard and conducted to the place above-mentioned, there to remain until he could be conveyed to Oung-pen-la. In the meantime the governor of the north gate presented a petition to the high court of the empire, offered himself as Mr. Judson's security, obtained his release, and took him to his house, where he treated him with every possible kindness, and to which I was removed as soon as returning health would allow.

"It was on a cool, moonlight evening, in the month of March, that with hearts filled with gratitude to God, and overflowing with joy at our prospects, we passed down the Irrawaddy, surrounded by six or eight golden boats, and accompanied by all we had on earth.

"We now, for the first time, for more than a year and a half, felt that we were free, and no longer subject to the oppressive yoke of the Burmese. And with what sensations of delight, on the next morning, did I behold the masts of the steamboat, the sure presage of being within the bounds of civilized life. As soon as our boat reached the shore, Brigadier A. and another officer came on board, congratulated us on our arrival, and invited us on board the steamboat, where I passed the remainder of the day; while your brother went on to meet the general, who, with a detachment of the army, had encamped at Yandaboo, a few miles farther down the river. Mr. Judson returned in the evening, with an invitation from Sir Archibald, to come immediately to his quarters, where I was the next morning introduced, and received with the greatest kindness by the general, who had a tent pitched for us near his own—took us to his own table, and treated us with the kindness of a father, rather than as strangers of another country.

"For several days, this single idea wholly occupied my mind, that we were out of the power of the Burmese government, and once more under the protection of the English. Our feelings continually dictated expressions like these: *What shall we render to the Lord for all His benefits towards us.*

"The treaty of peace was soon concluded, signed by both parties, and a termination of hostilities publicly declared. We left Yandaboo, after a fortnight's residence, and safely reached the mission house in Rangoon, after an absence of two years and three months."

Through all this suffering the precious manuscript of the Burmese New Testament was guarded. It was put into a bag and made into a hard pillow for Dr. Judson's prison. Yet he was forced to be apparently careless about it, lest the Burmans should think it contained something valuable and take it away. But with the assistance of a faithful Burmese convert, the manuscript, representing so many long days of labor, was kept in safety.

At the close of this long and melancholy narrative, we may appropriately introduce the following tribute to the benevolence and talents of Mrs. Judson, written by one of the English prisoners, who were confined at Ava with Mr. Judson. It was published in a Calcutta paper after the conclusion of the war:

"Mrs. Judson was the author of those eloquent and forcible appeals to the government which prepared them by degrees for submission to terms of peace, never expected by any, who knew the hauteur and inflexible pride of the Burman court.

"And while on this subject, the overflowings of grateful feelings, on behalf of myself and fellow prisoners, compel me to add a tribute of public thanks to that amiable and humane female, who, though living at a distance of two miles from our prison, without any means of conveyance, and very feeble in health, forgot her own comfort and infirmity, and almost every day visited us, sought out and administered to our wants, and contributed in every way to alleviate our misery.

"While we were left by the government destitute of food, she, with unwearied perseverance, by some means or another, obtained for us a constant supply.

"When the tattered state of our clothes evinced the extremity of our distress, she was ever ready to replenish our scanty wardrobe.

"When the unfeeling avarice of our keepers confined us inside, or made our feet fast in the stocks, she, like a ministering angel, never ceased her applications to the government, until she was authorized to communicate to us the grateful news of our enlargement, or of a respite from our galling oppressions.

"Besides all this, it was unquestionably owing, in a chief degree, to the repeated eloquence, and forcible appeals of Mrs. Judson, that the untutored Burman was finally made willing to secure the welfare and happiness of his country, by a sincere peace."

Missionary Beginnings

1800.   Carey's first convert baptized.
1804.   British and Foreign Bible Society organized.
1805.   Henry Martyn sails for India.
1807.   Robert Morrison sails for China.
1808.   Haystack meeting held near Williams College.
1810.   American Board organized.
1811.   Wesleyans found Sierra Leone Mission.
1812.   First American Board missionaries sail.
1816.   American Bible Society organized.
1816.   Robert Moffat sails for South Africa.
1818.   London Missionary Society enters Madagascar.
1819.   Methodist Missionary Society organized.
1819.   American Board opens Sandwich Islands Mission.
1819.   Judson baptizes first Burmese convert.

Epilogue to the Original Edition

And now to conclude, good Christian readers, this present tractation, not for the lack of matter, but to shorten rather the matter for largeness of the volume. In the meantime the grace of the Lord Jesus Christ work with thee, gentle reader, in all thy studious readings. And when thou hast faith, so employ thyself to read, that by reading thou mayest learn daily to know that which may profit thy soul, may teach thee experience, may arm thee with patience, and instruct thee in all spiritual knowledge more and more, to thy perfect comfort and salvation in Christ Jesus, our Lord, to whom be glory *in secula seculorum*. Amen.